The Iri... ...by W. R. S. Stott,
origina... ...*London News*. (NLI)

WE BLED TOGETHER

MICHAEL COLLINS, THE SQUAD AND THE DUBLIN BRIGADE

Tiomnaithe dóibh siúd a thug a mbeatha ar son saoirse na hÉireann.

Dedicated to those who gave their lives for Irish freedom.

WE BLED TOGETHER

MICHAEL COLLINS, THE SQUAD AND THE DUBLIN BRIGADE

DOMINIC PRICE

The Collins Press

First published in 2017 by
The Collins Press
West Link Park
Doughcloyne
Wilton
Cork
T12 N5EF
Ireland

A CIP record for this book is available from the British Library.

ISBN 978-1-84889-331-3

Typesetting by Carrigboy Typesetting Services
Typeset in Garamond

Printed in Malta by Gutenberg Press Limited

Contents

Acknowledgements

My thanks are due to the following for their help and expertise in the course of my research: the staff at Ballyroan Library, South Dublin County Council; Eoin Brennan; Niamh Brennan; Dr John Bourne, Western Front Association; Celio Burke; Damien Burke, Irish Jesuit Archives; Lisa Carley; Neil G. Cobbett, National Archives, Kew, UK; Síle Coleman, Local Studies, South Dublin County Council Libraries; Marianne Cosgrave, Mercy Congregational Archives; Raychel Coyle, Phoenix Park OPW; Eithne Daly; Richard Davies, Regimental Museum of the Royal Welsh; Noelle Dowling, Dublin Diocesan Archives; Máiréad Foley, Archives of the Roman Catholic Archdiocese of Perth, Highgate, Western Australia; Hugh Forrester, PSNI Museum; Declan Furey; Paddy Furlong; Liz Gillis; David Hanley; Michael Hanley, Dublin Diocesan Archives; Séamus Haughey, Oireachtas Library and Research Centre; Patricia Healy, Kenmare; Tim Horgan, County Kerry; Gráinne Hughes; the staff at the Imperial War Museum, Lambeth, London; Karen Johnson, Archivist, Christian Brothers Province Centre; Commandant Padraic Kennedy; Dr Clair Kilgarriff; Commandant Stephen MacEoin, Officer in Charge, Military Archives, and civilian archivist staff Hugh Beckett, Lisa Dolan and Noelle Grothier; Gráinne McCaffrey, Provincial's Office, Irish Province of the Dominican Order; Niall McCarville; Dr John McCullen, Chief Park Superintendent, Phoenix Park (retired); Finn McCumhaill; Brian McGee, Cork City & County Archivist; Senator Michael McDowell; Berni Metcalfe, National Library of Ireland; Peter Molloy; Stephen Moriarty, Cahersiveen; Terry Moylan, Archivist, Na Píobairí Uilleann; Éamon and Terry Newell; Elan Owen, Llyfrgell Genedlaethol Cymru/National Library of Wales; Maureen O'Connor-O'Sullivan, Cahersiveen Library; Patrick O'Connor-Scarteen, Kenmare; Éamon Ó Cuív TD; Dr Rory O'Hanlon; the staff at the Oireachtas Library & Research Service; Cormac K. H. O'Malley; Christine Pullen, Curator, Royal Green Jackets (Rifles) Museum, Winchester UK; Siobhán Ryan, Heritage Officer, Sligo County Council; Sandra Shallow-Brennan; Pat Shannon; Laurence Spring, Surrey History Centre; Dave Swift, Claíomh –

Irish Living History and Military Heritage, The British Library, London; the staff at the library, NUI Maynooth; the staff at the The National Archives, Kew, London; the staff at the The National Archives of Ireland; Aoife Torpey, Kilmainham Gaol; UCD Archives; Michael Walsh, Cahersiveen; Ian Whyte.

I am also indebted to Brendan Kelly, John Nolan and Aidan O'Toole, former members of staff at Drimnagh Castle CBS, for sharing their knowledge of Dublin in the Rare Auld Times.

I wish also to thank The Collins Press for all their hard work, advice and belief in this project.

My heartfelt thanks to Dominic, Pauline and David Price for their generosity and time for engaging in so much discussion and debate.

I especially pay tribute to my wife Catherine, to whom I am deeply grateful. Her love, support and encouragement were an inspiration on the long trek through the research, study and writing of this history. I also thank my children, Heather, Emma and Shane, for their love, patience and understanding. This history could not have been written without them.

Timeline of events

11 April 1912	Third Home Rule Bill introduced to House of Commons
31 January 1913	UVF founded
24/25 April 1913	Larne gunrunning
26 July 1913	Howth gunrunning
August 1913–January 1914	Dublin workers are locked out of places of employment for being members of the ITGWU trade union
23 November 1913	Irish Citizen Army founded
25 November 1913	Irish Volunteers founded
4 August 1914	Outbreak of the First World War
15 September 1914	Home Rule suspended until after the war
20 September 1914	John Redmond speech at Woodenbridge County results in split in the Irish Volunteer movement
24–29 April 1916	Easter Rising takes place
3–12 May 1916	Fifteen leaders of the Rising executed
3 August 1916	Roger Casement executed
1917	Republican prisoners released from Frongoch under terms of a general amnesty
October 1917	De Valera elected President of Sinn Féin
November 1917	De Valera elected President of the Irish Volunteer movement
11 July 1917	Death of DI Mills, the first policeman killed in Dublin since the Easter Rising
January 1918	*An t-Óglach*, the Irish Volunteer paper, is reintroduced
April 1918	Conscription crisis begins
May 1918	Lord French appointed as Lord Lieutenant of Ireland
June 1918	Dick McKee elected Commandant of the Dublin Brigade
11 November 1918	Armistice signed which ends the First World War
28 December 1918	General election leading to Sinn Féin victory and the collapse of Irish Parliamentary Party
21 January 1919	Dáil Éireann meets for the first time; ambush by Irish Volunteers at Soloheadbeg in Tipperary beginning the War of Independence
January 1919	Seán T. O'Ceallaigh dispatched by the Dáil to the Versailles Peace Conference

3 February 1919	De Valera escapes from Lincoln Gaol
20–21 March 1919	Dublin Brigade raid on the RAF aerodrome at Collinstown, County Dublin
April 1919	Michael Collins and Seán Nunan gain access to G Division secret files room at DMP Station on Brunswick Street
June 1919	Éamon de Valera departs for the US
July 1919	First 'Special Duties' Unit of the Dublin Brigade formed under the command of 2nd Battalion QM, Michael McDonnell
30 July 1919	'Special Duties' Unit carry out first assassination: DS Patrick Smyth
20 August 1919	Irish Volunteers swear allegiance to Dáil Éireann and are now known as the IRA
September 1919	Second 'Special Duties' Unit of the Dublin Brigade formed under the command of O/C B Company 2nd Battalion Paddy O'Daly
December 1919	Lily Mernin, a typist at Dublin Castle, becomes an intelligence agent for the IRA
19 December 1919	Assassination attempt on Lord French and the death of IRA Lieutenant Martin Savage
March 1920	Black and Tans become active members of the RIC throughout Ireland
20 March 1920	Tomás MacCurtain murdered by members of the RIC
May 1920	The 'Special Duties' Units of the Dublin Brigade are amalgamated to form the assassination unit known as the Squad
9 August 1920	Restoration of Order in Ireland Act introduced by British government
September 1920	Auxiliary Division RIC becomes active
20 September 1920	Balbriggan sacked by RIC Black and Tans
11–12 October 1920	Seán Treacy and Dan Breen gun battle with British intelligence officers in Drumcondra
25 October 1920	Terence MacSwiney, Lord Mayor of Cork, dies on hunger strike
14 October 1920	Seán Treacy killed on Talbot Street, Dublin
1 November 1920	Kevin Barry hanged at Mountjoy Gaol
21 November 1920	Bloody Sunday: British agents assassinated in Dublin and in response Auxiliaries attack the crowd at a Gaelic football match at Croke Park
24 November 1920	IRA ambush Auxiliaries at Kilmichael, West Cork, killing 17 cadets
11–12 December 1920	Cork sacked by the Auxiliaries
December 1920	Hundreds of republicans arrested in British government response to IRA operation on Bloody Sunday
13 May 1920	Sinn Féin victorious in general election

25 May 1921	Custom House burned in an attack by the Dublin Brigade
22 June 1921	King George V opens the Northern Ireland parliament
11 July 1921	Truce agreed between IRA and British Crown forces
14–21 July 1921	De Valera and Lloyd George meet for private talks in London
October 1921	Negotiations between Irish and British political representatives begin in Downing Street
6 December 1921	Anglo-Irish Treaty signed
7 January 1922	Dáil approves the Treaty by a vote of 64 to 57. The vote causes a split in Sinn Féin into a pro-Treaty camp led by Arthur Griffith and Michael Collins and an anti-Treaty camp led by Éamon de Valera
9 January 1922	Arthur Griffith elected President of Dáil Éireann after de Valera's resignation
February 1922	Dublin Guards officially formed at Beggars Bush barracks
14 April 1922	Split in the IRA as anti-Treaty forces seize the Four Courts
28 June 1922	Civil War begins as Provisional Government troops attack anti-Treaty IRA HQ at the Four Courts
24 July 1922	Free State troop landings in Mayo
2 August 1922	Free State troop landings in Kerry
8 August 1922	Free State troop landings in Cork
12 August 1922	Arthur Griffith dies of a brain haemorrhage
22 August 1922	Michael Collins killed in a republican ambush at Beal na Bláth, County Cork
9 September 1922	W. T. Cosgrave becomes President of the Executive Council of the Irish Free State
25 October 1922	Constitution of the Free State approved by Dáil Éireann
15 November 1922	Four republicans executed by the Free State. These republicans are the first of 77 official executions
5 December 1922	Irish Free State constitution receives royal assent
January 1923	Major-General Paddy O'Daly becomes O/C Kerry Command
6 March 1923	IRA trap mine explosion at Knocknagoshel kills five National Army troops
7 March 1923	National Army executes eight republican prisoners by mine explosion at Ballyseedy, County Kerry
7 March 1923	National Army executes five republican prisoners by mine explosion at Countess Bridge, Killarney, County Kerry
12 March 1923	National Army executes five republican prisoners by mine explosion at Bahaghs, Cahersiveen, County Kerry
10 April 1923	Liam Lynch, Chief of Staff of the IRA, mortally wounded by National Army troops on the Knockmealdown Mountains, County Tipperary
24 May 1923	Civil War comes to an end as Frank Aiken, new IRA Chief of staff, issues ceasefire order

16 May 1926   Fianna Fáil founded

10 July 1927   Kevin O'Higgins, Minister for External Affairs in the Cumann
                     na nGaedheal government, is assassinated

11 December 1931   Statute of Westminster receives royal assent, granting Common-
                     wealth countries legal freedom to implement their own laws
                     independently of Britain

1 July 1937   Bunreacht na hÉireann, new Irish Constitution replacing the
                     Irish Free State Constitution, is enacted

July–October 1938   Handover of the Treaty Ports of Spike Island, Berehaven and
                     Lough Swilly

1939–1946   'The Emergency' declared in Éire to chart the country's neutral
                     course through the years of the Second World War

18 April 1949   Ireland officially becomes a republic

1947–1957   Bureau of Military History in operation to collect eyewitness
                     accounts, contemporary documents and photographs of the
                     Irish revolutionary period

Abbreviations

ADRIC	Auxiliary Division Royal Irish Constabulary
ASU	Active Service Unit
Bde	Brigade
BMH	Bureau of Military History
Bn	Battalion
CID	Criminal Investigations Department
Coy	Company
DMP	Dublin Metropolitan Police
GAA	Gaelic Athletic Association
GHQ	General Headquarters
GOC	General Officer Commanding
GPO	General Post Office
IO	Intelligence Officer
IRA	Irish Republican Army
IRB	Irish Republican Brotherhood
ITGWU	Irish Transport and General Workers' Union
NCO	Non-commissioned Officer (e.g. sergeant, corporal)
O/C	Officer Commanding
PRO	Public Record Office
QM	Quartermaster
RAF	Royal Air Force
RAMC	Royal Army Medical Corps
RDC	Rural District Council
RE	Royal Engineers
RGA	Royal Garrison Artillery
RIC	Royal Irish Constabulary
SMLE	Short Magazine Lee-Enfield rifle
TD	Teachta Dála

Introduction

On 31 December 1924 Bill Stapleton, a colonel in the National Army, sat down to write a letter to Minister for Defence Peter Hughes TD. Stapleton had been accused of disloyalty to the Irish Free State and was to be dismissed from the Army. As he wrote he pleaded his innocence of the charge. A veteran of the Dublin Brigade in 1916, Stapleton had been imprisoned after the Rising and upon his release had rejoined his old unit, B Company of the 2nd Battalion. During the War of Independence he became a member of an elite unit called the Squad and served with the Dublin Brigade of the IRA in a major operation to wipe out the British military intelligence network in Dublin on 21 November 1920. This day was known ever afterwards as Bloody Sunday. Stapleton was dismissed from the Army and denied a pension. Being branded as a traitor hurt him very deeply. In his appeals to the Irish Free State government he referred to his former comrades, pointing out all they had done together to achieve Irish freedom. Stapleton had 'fought and bled with these men' right through the Irish revolutionary period of 1916 to 1923. How had it come to this? Those who had been at the very centre of the war against the British empire, which resulted in Irish independence and had saved the Irish Free State in a vicious civil war, were now condemned as traitors.

Throughout this book, there is particular emphasis on the experiences of IRA and Cumann na mBan Volunteers, British soldiers, politicians, civilians and British and American observers who witnessed the conflict. The resort to war came only after efforts by Dáil Éireann to achieve recognition for an independent Irish republic at the Versailles Peace Conference in 1919 failed. As the violence progressed, those who took part were changed utterly by their experiences. The nature of the active service undertaken by the Squad and the Dublin Brigade in the War of Independence led some of these soldiers to commit terrible atrocities in the Civil War that followed.

When the years of conflict were at an end, those who survived faced their greatest task – living with themselves in the peace. Some veterans could not cope with the memories and, haunted by ghosts and voices, suffered psychological breakdown. Others became leaders determined to create a more peaceful and prosperous future for all. A small few dedicated the rest of their lives to healing the living souls of their comrades, shattered by their experiences in war. Most looked to work, faith and a pension to grant them and their families peace and security.

'Dublin was, and is, the heart and soul of the whole conspiracy.' Thus wrote a senior British army officer in describing the role of the city in the Irish War of Independence. As time passes, myth, often dressed as dark humour, is accepted as history. Such a representation of the past presents the heroes and the villains in plain sight for all to see. It serves a purpose in that the struggles of the past are seen to be worth the sacrifice and the loss. Such history also shields a society from the terror and bloodshed enacted, often on its behalf. The story of the Squad and the Dublin Brigade during the Irish revolutionary period is both inspiring and shocking. It reveals the very best and also the very worst that human beings are capable of. In the capital city of Ireland, the heart of British rule in Ireland for 700 years, a brigade of revolutionaries embarked on the road to freedom. This is their story.

1

'A Few Hundred Rounds under God's Blue Sky'

The Lessons of 1916

On Monday 1 May 1916, Michael Lynch was tired and hungry. For over twenty-four hours he had had little to eat or drink and hardly any sleep. Around him were hundreds of other prisoners all sitting in the cramped conditions of the floor of the gymnasium of Richmond British Army Barracks, Inchicore, on the outskirts of Dublin.[1] Thus the surviving revolutionary troops of the Easter Rising – the Irish Volunteers, Irish Citizen Army, Hibernian Rifles and Cumann na mBan – awaited their fate.[2] The Rising had begun over a week earlier on Easter Monday, 24 April. A combined force of 1,656 Irish men and women had declared an Irish republic and had occupied a number of strategic buildings throughout the city. In doing so they believed they could put an end to over 700 years of British rule in Ireland. The Rising had been planned by the leadership of a secret revolutionary group, the Irish Republican Brotherhood (IRB). The IRB had succeeded in infiltrating and eventually controlling the Irish Volunteers. The IRB leadership, headed by Thomas Clarke and Pádraig Pearse, also managed to win support for the Rising from socialist James Connolly, who led the Irish Citizen Army. The British army's Dublin garrison was the 13th Infantry Brigade. They numbered 2,500. As the Rising progressed, additional troops arrived from Britain and other parts of Ireland to increase their numbers to 5,500 as they attempted to oust the Irish from their well-defended positions.[3] The fighting was intense and saw much of the centre of the city destroyed. Ernie O'Malley, who was a medical student at the time and would later become a fierce revolutionary, met up with a pal and did some sniping at British troops. From the outskirts of north Dublin they could see the city sky glowing red in the darkness: 'The fire had spread; it seemed as if the whole centre of the city was in flames. Sparks shot up and the fire jumped high as the wind increased. The noise of machine-guns and rifles was continuous; there did not seem to be any pause.'[4]

By Friday 28 April, the headquarters of the Irish revolutionaries at the General Post Office (GPO) in Sackville Street (now O'Connell Street) was engulfed in flames after days of shelling by British artillery. Commandant Pearse, who just days earlier had proclaimed the Irish republic outside this same building, now ordered it to be evacuated. The Irish attempted to reach the Williams and Woods factory on Great Britain Street (now Parnell Street) via Moore Street.[5] Taking shelter in shops and houses while attempting to force their way through British lines, the leaders of the Irish revolutionaries held a Council of War. Given the destruction of the city and the suffering endured by the civilian population it was decided to surrender to prevent further loss of life. Nurse Elizabeth O'Farrell accompanied the senior Irish officer, Commandant Pádraig Pearse, under a flag of truce to speak with the British commander, General Lowe. The result was an unconditional surrender. Nurse O'Farrell delivered Commandant Pearse's order to surrender to the various revolutionary garrisons throughout the city. The revolutionaries were reluctant to capitulate as they had yet to be defeated and their strongholds taken by British troops. On the orders of their senior officers, however, they laid down their arms. As the revolutionaries were marched to Richmond Barracks by their British captors, angry Dublin slum dwellers emerged to heap abuse upon them.[6] Many of the prisoners, like Michael Lynch, were bitterly disappointed, their dream of an Irish Republic reduced to ashes along with the GPO. 'The grand adventure', as Ernie O'Malley called it, seemed to be over.[7] The human spirit, however, is not so easily extinguished and the dream of the Republic lived on in the hearts of the prisoners.

Michael Lynch looked around the crowd in the gymnasium. He recognised one man just in front of him. Edging himself across the floor, he moved alongside and tapped the man on the arm. It was Major John MacBride, who had spent the Rising under the command of Commandant Tomás MacDonagh in occupation of Jacob's biscuit factory. MacBride was also a former officer commanding (O/C) of the Irish Transvaal Brigade, a group of Irishmen who had fought for the Boer Republics against the British in the South African Boer War 1899–1902.[8] This made MacBride a marked man as far as the British were concerned. Lynch shook hands warmly with the major, who had been a friend of his father. MacBride then offered Lynch some sound advice based on his experience of the Rising:

> 'Listen Michael', he said. 'All my life I have waited for the week that has just gone by. I spent it shut up like a rat in a trap in Jacob's factory, and I never fired a shot. I wanted McDonagh to get out several times, but he would not. However, it does not matter – it's all over now.' 'You don't mean to say ...?' I asked. 'Yes,' he replied. 'They have wanted me for many years and they have got me now. I am for it, but you, Michael, will live to fight again and, when next you fight, don't let anyone shut you up like a rat in a trap. Get a rifle, a few hundred rounds of ammunition, and get out under God's blue sky. And shoot until they get you, but never let them lock you up.' I felt heartbroken, and we talked along about the various things that had happened, but all the time he kept referring to being shut up in a building like a rat in a trap.[9]

As MacBride and Lynch were speaking, the door of the gymnasium opened and the detectives of G Division of the Dublin Metropolitan Police (DMP) entered. They knew the Irish revolutionary leaders by sight, having had them under surveillance for years. Scanning the prisoners, the detectives identified the Irish leaders easily and ordered them outside. MacBride was picked out by Detective Hoey. Major John MacBride shook hands with Michael Lynch and walked out, head held high. It was the last Lynch ever saw of MacBride, who was executed by firing squad four days later on 5 May 1916.[10] He was one of sixteen of the revolutionaries executed. Ninety had been sentenced to death. In the immediate aftermath of the Rising, the national newspapers called for retribution against the leaders of the insurrection. On 5 May, *The Irish Times* argued for 'a just firm hand in Dublin Castle' and 'no further tolerance of aggressive disloyalty in Ireland'. In that same paper Edward Carson, leader of the Unionist and pro-British movement in Ireland, was surprisingly measured when he was reported as saying 'this is no occasion for vengeance'. The following day, *The Irish Times* was forced to defend itself against claims that its editorials were little more than 'blood thirsty incitements to the Government':

> We said and we repeat, that the surgeon's knife of the State must not be stayed until the whole malignant growth has been removed ... We have called for the severest punishment of the leaders and responsible

agents of the insurrection; but we have insisted that there shall be no campaign of mere vengeance. We desire for the ignorant dupes of the real agitators such punishment only as will give them cause and opportunity for reflection, and will make them rejoice at some future day that the State has saved them from themselves.[11]

The *Irish Independent* editorial of 4 May called the Rising 'criminal madness' and declared that the men who had organised and led it had 'a heavy moral and legal responsibility from which they cannot hope to escape'. The editor echoed the words of a great number of people in Ireland in calling the Rising 'a miserable fiasco, leaving behind its trail of woe and horror'. Even an account of the marriage of Joseph Plunkett to Grace Gifford in Kilmainham Gaol chapel just hours before his death, which could not fail to move even the hardest of hearts, the *Irish Independent* dismissed as 'a pathetic incident'[12] and suggested that the only way for Irishmen to wipe away the stain of what had happened in Easter Week was 'a rush to the colours'.[13] But there would be no such 'rush to the colours' of the British empire. Events were to take a very unexpected turn and would be directed by the British commander in Dublin, General Sir John Maxwell.

In spite of all the vitriol forthcoming from elected officials and both the provincial and national press, the public mood changed very quickly. The executions ordered by General Maxwell were swift. Beginning on 3 May, notices were pinned to the gate at Kilmainham Gaol each morning announcing who had been shot earlier that day. The announcements continued until 12 May when Seán MacDiarmada and James Connolly were executed, the last to be shot. Roger Casement was executed by hanging at Pentonville Prison in England on 3 August that year. Accounts of the final days and hours of the executed leaders soon reached the public through families and priests who ministered to the condemned men in their prison cells. The dignity and sincerity with which they held themselves during their courts martial won great respect, even among their foes. The anger aroused by the executions was further compounded by the shooting of pacifist Francis Sheehy Skeffington at Portobello Barracks and the murder of sixteen innocent civilians in North King Street by British troops. In particular, the execution of James Connolly, shot while tied to a chair (he had been shot during the Rising and was unable to stand), changed villains into martyrs.[14] The burial of the executed revolutionaries in a grave of quicklime to ensure their very bones were obliterated only added to the sense of loss on the part of the majority of Irish people. John Dillon, Irish Parliamentary Party MP, summed up the general feeling of anger in Ireland when he rounded on Prime Minister Herbert Asquith in the House of Commons in a passionate address:

> You are letting loose a river of blood, and, make no mistake about it, between two races who, after three hundred years of hatred and strife, we had nearly succeeded in bringing together ... we are held up to odium as traitors by those men who made this rebellion, and our lives have been in danger a hundred times during the last thirty years because we have endeavoured to reconcile the two things, and now you are washing out our whole life work in a sea of blood.[15]

As the debates raged in Westminster, Irish Volunteer Michael Lynch was now a prisoner and would not be free under 'God's blue sky' for some time. Lynch was one of over 3,000 men and 77 women arrested after the Rising.[16] Sinn Féin, the political party founded in 1905 by Arthur Griffith, had been blamed for the Rising despite having had nothing to do with it. As a result, hundreds of Sinn Féin members were arrested in a general sweep of those thought to be a threat to British rule. In all, 2,519 men were deported to various prisons in England; 123 of the men sent to England were sentenced to terms of penal servitude at Lewes, Dartmoor, Portland and Aylesbury prisons. Others were sent to Knutsford, Stafford, Wakefield and Wandsworth jails.[17] A select group of prisoners, including Arthur Griffith, were interned at Reading Gaol. Five women, including Winifred Carney and Helena Molony, were interned at Aylesbury prison.[18] The majority of the prisoners eventually ended up in Frongoch, a former German prisoner-of-war camp in north Wales.

The experience of prison was difficult. Joseph Peppard, later an intelligence officer in the Fingal Brigade in north County Dublin, described the experience of a 'dry bath' in Lewes:

> We had a weekly bath and occasionally what was called a dry bath. The dry bath meant that at irregular intervals, sometimes weekly, you were taken to the bath house and stripped naked. Your clothes were thoroughly searched and even your mouth, ears and the most private parts of your body were also thoroughly examined. What they suspected we might be concealing I don't know. The whole

affair was very degrading. When you got back to your cell after this ordeal you usually found your belongings had been ripped up during an examination also.[19]

By the end of July 1916 large numbers of prisoners were released, leaving 600 in Frongoch and the rest still spread across the more secure prisons in England. The concentration of dedicated revolutionaries in one place was to lead to a reassessment of Irish revolutionary methods and the realisation of exactly what it would take for Ireland to win her independence, a realisation that saw the evolution of a twin political and military strategy.

After the release of Easter Rising veterans from prison in 1916 and 1917, the Royal Irish Constabulary (RIC) had tracked and noted the movements and speeches of as many as they could. On return, the Irish Volunteers had sought to reorganise themselves under the leadership of Thomas Ashe. Commandant Ashe had led a successful ambush on the RIC at Ashbourne during the Easter Rising. His leadership did not last long as he was rearrested and imprisoned at Mountjoy Gaol, Dublin, in August 1917. Ashe and his fellow republicans demanded to be treated as prisoners of war rather than common criminals. When this was denied to them, they went on hunger strike. Ashe died on 25 September 1917 from injuries sustained while being force-fed on the orders of the prison authorities. After the death of Ashe, both Sinn Féin and the Irish Volunteers were completely reorganised. Two men were destined to assume the leadership of different strands of the Irish independence movement at this time. Their influence would shape and direct the course of events on both a political and military level in the years ahead. One of them was the surviving commandant of the Easter Rising, Éamon de Valera; the other, a junior officer in the Irish Volunteers stationed in the GPO during Easter Week, was Michael Collins.

Éamon de Valera was born in the United States to an Irish mother and Spanish father in 1882. At the early age of three he was sent back to Ireland to be raised by his relatives in Bruree, County Limerick. This young American-Irish man was to rise to become a leading light in the Irish political scene. As is often the case with political giants, de Valera would also invoke great controversy. A mathematics teacher prior to his entry to military and political life, de Valera also showed a keen interest in the Irish language and Irish culture. He joined the Gaelic League in 1908 and soon fell in love with his teacher, Sinéad Flanagan. The couple married in 1910.[20]

Éamon de Valera, President of Dáil Éireann. Photograph taken during de Valera's tour of the USA 1919–1920. (Keogh Collection, Courtesy National Library of Ireland)

De Valera joined the Irish Volunteers in 1913, becoming Commandant of the 3rd Battalion of the Dublin Brigade. It was this battalion that held Boland's Mill during the Rising. Outposts from de Valera's battalion at Clanwilliam House and Northumberland Road inflicted heavy casualties on British troops during the action of Easter Week. De Valera escaped the sentence of execution handed down to other leaders of the Rising and was instead sent to prison in England along with the other captured Irish Volunteers. He quickly established himself as a personality of considerable ability and influence. As the sole surviving commandant of the Rising he assumed a mythical persona. His height of 6 ft (1.82m) gave him a physical presence that quite literally towered above others. He was released from prison in June 1917 under a general amnesty for all those imprisoned after the Rising. Within a month de Valera had been selected as the Sinn Féin candidate for the East Clare by-election.

The vacancy for this seat had been created by the death of the sitting MP William Redmond at the battle of Messines Ridge in France on 7

June 1917. William was the brother of John Redmond, leader of the Irish Parliamentary Party. The British government hoped this election would create conditions conducive to agreement on the Irish question by holding a national convention for a Home Rule settlement in Ireland, but it was already too late. The majority of Irish people had given up belief in Home Rule and would give their verdict in East Clare. Attracting the support of the Catholic Bishop of Killaloe was crucial in de Valera winning the support of moderate former Home Rulers. Campaigning in his Irish Volunteer uniform, he defeated the Irish Parliamentary Party candidate, Patrick Lynch KC, by 5,010 votes to 2,035 on 11 July 1917.[21] The *Irish Independent* described the effect of the announcement of a win for de Valera as a bombshell. While a de Valera victory was expected, it was the scale of his win, by 2,975 votes, which 'was received with amazement throughout the country'.[22] This was the third win for Sinn Féin and the third successive defeat for the Irish Parliamentary Party within a few months, with Count Plunkett having been victorious in North Roscommon and J. P. McGuinness in South Longford. De Valera delivered his victory speech from the steps of the courthouse in Ennis; in his speech he said his victory was a victory for Ireland which would be celebrated across the world: 'This election would always be history. This victory would show to the world that if Irishmen had only a ghost of a chance they would fight for the independence of Ireland. It was a victory for the independence of Ireland and for an Irish Republic.'[23]

In an analysis of the East Clare election result, the *Irish Independent* lacerated the Irish Parliamentary Party, accusing it of being weak, blundering and inefficient and for mutilating the country through partition. The *Irish Independent* argued that five out of every six electors voted for de Valera in disgust at the 'cringing and crawling of the Irish Party, and especially the blundering tactics of the leaders'.[24] In a shocking display of how quickly a newspaper of the day had demonstrated a complete volte-face in its editorial stance after the Easter Rising, the *Irish Independent* sat in judgement on the Irish Parliamentary Party: 'The people seemed to say, "We are sick of the Party, who have been simply humbugging the country, and we will have nobody who supports this wretched crowd of politicians".'[25]

De Valera's election victory produced a shockwave of enormous proportions. The series of Sinn Féin electoral victories were no flash in the pan. The country could feel it and the leaders of Sinn Féin and the Irish Volunteers were determined to be ready to direct events when the time came. '*Bí Ullamh*' or 'Be Prepared', the Boy Scout motto, was the order of the day and the new generation of Irish political and military leaders wasted no time in reorganising their respective movements. The first show of strength was the funeral of Thomas Ashe in Dublin on 30 September 1917. Michael Collins organised a turnout of 9,000 Irish Volunteers from all parts of Ireland to bury their deceased O/C with full military honours.[26]

At the Sinn Féin Ard Fheis (annual convention) on 25 October 1917, de Valera was elected president of the party. In the interests of party unity, Arthur Griffith, the founder and former leader, stepped aside to allow de Valera to assume the leadership. Griffith was then elected joint vice-president along with Fr Michael O'Flanagan. Griffith openly referred to de Valera as a 'statesman and soldier',[27] believing he was the one man with the ability to unite various forms of Irish nationalism in realising the goal of Irish independence.[28] Michael Collins was among twenty-four delegates appointed to a Sinn Féin executive. On 19 November the Irish Volunteers held its third convention at Croke Park, Dublin. Éamon de Valera was elected president while Cathal Brugha was elected chief of staff. A Volunteer Executive was assembled with representatives from each of the four provinces. A committee of 'resident members' was appointed alongside the provincial representatives. The 'resident members' were: Rory O'Connor, Michael Staines, Cathal Brugha, Éamon de Valera, Eamon Duggan (Chairman), William M. O'Reilly (Deputy Chairman), Diarmuid O'Hegarty, Michael Collins and Richard Mulcahy.[29] The IRB gained significant influence over the Volunteers through the appointment of Michael Collins as Director of Organisation, Diarmuid Lynch as Director of Communications and Seán McGarry as General Secretary.[30]

As a result of the reorganisation of Sinn Féin and the Irish Volunteers, there now existed for the first time in modern history a unified Irish popular movement which found expression through a political party and a military organisation. Both political and military structures would now cooperate more and more to bring about Irish independence. Before this strategy could be put into operation, a new recruiting drive was required for both Sinn Féin and the Irish Volunteers. During the First World War, Ireland had seen an increase in employment opportunities for young Irish men and women who would otherwise have emigrated. There was also the additional attraction that by remaining in Ireland, young men would avoid conscription into the armies of the British empire or American military.[31]

Peadar Clancy, Vice-Commandant and Director of Munitions, Dublin Brigade IRA. Photograph taken after the surrender in 1916, when he was aged twenty-seven. (Courtesy Kilmainham Gaol, OPW)

In October 1917 de Valera returned to County Clare on a victory tour to thank the people of Clare for electing him as MP. The tour was also a recruiting drive to establish new Sinn Féin clubs and to recruit for the Irish Volunteers. With de Valera was Peadar Clancy, from Cranny, County Clare. Together, they made a powerful impact on popular opinion. At this point in time, Clancy was seen as the next MP for West Clare and was introduced as such by Fr Griffin, chairman of the Ennistymon Sinn Féin Club, at a number of rallies.[32] After leaving school, Clancy had worked in a drapery business in Kildysart on the Shannon Estuary. After working briefly in Limerick as a milliner, he moved to Dublin, where he continued to work at his chosen trade. When the Irish Volunteers were founded in November 1913, Clancy joined C Company, 1st Battalion of the Dublin Brigade. He was elected lieutenant almost immediately. Pat McCrea, a Volunteer with the 2nd Battalion who would later become a member of a group of assassins assembled by Michael Collins, described Clancy as 'restless and full of life'.[33] Clancy was also courageous and demonstrated his ability to bring the fight to the enemy many times. During the Rising, Clancy was in charge of a barricade at Church Street Bridge alongside the Four Courts. Initially he had twelve men in his command but this was increased to twenty-two from the GPO garrison on the Tuesday.[34] During the week British snipers installed themselves in a building on the quay opposite the Four Courts. Clancy, ordering his men to direct their fire on the sniper positions in Bridgefoot Street, grabbed some tins of petrol and calmly walked across the Liffey Bridge to the snipers' nest. Clancy smashed the windows, drenched the building with petrol and set it alight. He returned safely to his own lines. The following day he captured two high-profile prisoners, Lord Dunsany and Colonel Lindsay, who had attempted to drive through Clancy's position. Dunsany was hit in the face by a ricochet fired by Clancy, who later apologised for wounding him. Lord Dunsany later referred to his captors as 'gentlemen'.[35] After the Rising, Clancy was court-martialled and sentenced to death. The sentence was commuted to ten years' penal servitude. While hundreds of Irish Volunteers were released at Christmas 1916, Clancy was not one of them. His liberty finally came in June 1917 along with others who had been considered to be a serious threat.[36] Upon release Clancy threw himself behind the reorganisation of the Irish Volunteers in Dublin and in his own native Clare.

In the space of just six days, de Valera and Clancy addressed an estimated 2,140 in the main towns of the district including Ennis, Ennistymon, Milltown Malbay, Ballyvaughan, Ballinacally, Factory Cross, Ruane, Inagh and Corofin.[37] The RIC, who were on hand to keep a close eye on the proceedings, viewed the speeches as 'disloyal and seditious'.[38] The tone of the addresses made by de Valera and his colleagues left no one in any doubt that 1916 had been prelude for what was to come. De Valera encouraged the men to join the Volunteers, to arm themselves and to drill. Speaking in Ennistymon he encouraged Irishmen to pursue what might be described as a less-than-parliamentary approach: '... one rifle would have more effect in asserting their rights than 1,000 men speaking ... the people who thought they would get anything from England by begging were dreamers'.[39]

Initially, the local RIC officers were not sure how to deal with de Valera, the senior Irish political and military figure. When de Valera and Clancy had departed, District Inspector O'Brien for Ennistymon wrote an interesting observation at the conclusion of his report: 'There is another side to all this, and it is should we take any notice whatever of him [de Valera]. I notice that latterly he is not as violent in his talk.'[40]

The uncertainty as to the intentions of the Irish Volunteers were soon dispelled at Corofin when de Valera delivered a more forthright address: 'If we cannot get what we are out for by peaceful methods we can get it by physical force. We will do our best to arm you. Get all the arms you can, any kind of arms – shot guns – you know what a useful weapon a double barrel shot gun is at night.'[41]

De Valera's colleagues echoed his sentiments. During the course of his many speeches, Peadar Clancy declared he would rather die once, twice or a hundred times over than ever wear khaki – a reference to the expected attempt by the British government to introduce conscription to Ireland. Clancy was also blunter in his references to the members of the RIC, describing them as 'murderers' for their recent killing of a Volunteer at Ballybunion in County Kerry.[42]

During the course of his speeches in Clare, de Valera also drew attention to food shortages being experienced in Ireland due to exports of crops and livestock to Britain. He believed the Volunteers should be used to stop this by force if necessary. Referring to food exports from Ireland to Britain exposed a raw nerve in the psyche of the Irish population. In 1847, at the time of the worst of the Great Famine, a record wheat harvest was exported from Ireland while the potato crop failed due to blight. As a result of the failure of the potato crop hundreds of thousands starved to death in the year known as 'Black 47'.[43] The memory of the Great Famine was a major source of bitterness and resentment among the Irish in Ireland and abroad towards the British for many generations. By 1918 RIC County Inspectors' reports still contained yearly references to the health of the potato harvest as a crop failure would lead to civic unrest. There were also references to prevailing high prices in agricultural produce caused by the First World War.[44] De Valera, tapping into that memory and the contemporary reality of hunger, was also making the claim that Ireland was a separate entity and not subservient to Britain. For the Sinn Féin movement, Ireland's resources and produce belonged to Ireland and not to a colonial power. In Dublin, the Irish Volunteers were to make the case for Irish food to remain in Ireland in dramatic fashion at the end of February 1918. Bill Stapleton of B Company, 2nd Battalion, Dublin Brigade was mobilised with his company. Diarmuid Lynch, Director of

Communications, had ordered them to seize a consignment of pigs en route to Britain. The pigs were intercepted near Dorset Street and taken to the Dublin Corporation Yard nearby. Two of the Volunteers, who were butchers by trade, then began to slaughter the pigs. Up to 100 policemen were prevented from gaining entry and were forced to wait outside while the slaughtering continued. The noise of the pigs carried a good distance and attracted a large crowd.[45] Women arrived with jugs of tea and slices of bread for the Volunteers. Charlie Dalton, a young Volunteer at the time and a future member of Michael Collins' intelligence unit, later wrote: 'I drank the tea with great satisfaction, recalling the time when I had seen the very same refreshments handed to the British Tommies in my neighbourhood during the Rising. The tide had turned. It was we who were now the heroes of the people.'[46]

The slaughter went on from early morning till evening when the carcases were brought to Donnelly's Bacon Curing in Meath Street and then distributed throughout the city with all relevant parties in the chain being paid. The whole operation was a great morale boost for the population as they could now buy bacon in the shops and ease the pangs of hunger. Due to the war it had previously been in very short supply. Bill Stapleton arrived home from the operation to his mother at half two in the morning. He was splattered with blood and gave his mother quite a fright.[47] The events in Dublin were an example of the growing challenge posed by a resurgent Sinn Féin and Irish Volunteer movement.

In spite of the positive impression Peadar Clancy made on tour with de Valera in West Clare in October 1917, he was not destined to become its MP, or Teachta Dála (TD) as Sinn Féin would rename parliamentary representatives at the next general election. Clancy's future would be determined by events beginning to unfold in County Longford. Those events concerned a rising star of both the Irish Volunteers and Sinn Féin: Michael Collins.

While de Valera toured West Clare, Michael Collins was also touring a number of counties including west Cork, Roscommon, Leitrim and Armagh. Collins had also campaigned extensively during a number of by-elections in 1917 and 1918. With him, on occasion, were Thomas Ashe, O/C of the Irish Volunteers, Arthur Griffith, vice-president of Sinn Féin, and Gearóid O'Sullivan, future member of GHQ of the IRA. Collins arrived in Granard, County Longford on 20 October 1917 for the Columb Cille Aeridheacht (festival). He stayed at the Greville Arms, a hotel run by three sisters, to one of whom Collins would later become engaged: Kitty Kiernan.

Michael Collins was from Woodfield near Clonakilty. After leaving school he worked in London for a number of years before returning to Ireland to take part in the Easter Rising. A staff officer to Joseph Mary Plunkett, one of the senior officers who planned the Rising, Collins served in the GPO and surrounding area during Easter Week. After the surrender of the Volunteers, Collins was imprisoned first in Stafford prison and then in Frongoch, along with hundreds of fellow Irish Volunteers. Michael Collins was a true leader and inspired utter devotion from those who followed him. Once settled in Frongoch, Collins and others began to reorganise the IRB. In the aftermath of the Rising, all of the leaders of the IRB had been sentenced to death and executed by firing squad at Kilmainham Gaol. Collins was a very determined individual and applied great energy and powers of concentration to anything he undertook. He had little time for those who were not as committed as he was. Frank Thornton, who came with the Liverpool Company of the Irish Volunteers to Dublin to take part in the Easter Rising, got to know Collins very well over the next few years and offered the following insight into the character of this 'bright star':

> Michael Collins was a man with a determination to make a complete success of everything he put his hands to. He had a marvellous memory ... never to my knowledge was anything left unattended to the next day. He was full of the exuberance of life and full of vitality. He had no time for half measures and expected from those who were under him the same amount of enthusiasm and constructive energy that he himself was putting into the job.[48]

Collins was also a hard taskmaster. Michael Noyk said his motto could be described as similar to a Spartan mother to her son: 'Come back with your shield or on it.'[49] Collins was not liked by everyone. Gearoid Ua h-Uallacháin (Garry Holohan), O/C of Na Fianna Éireann of the Dublin Brigade 1919–22, got to know Collins while imprisoned in Frongoch. Ua h-Ullacháin said that Collins held IRB meetings in the camp but only invited certain people. Ua h-Uallacháin later wrote: 'I must say I never liked him. I always considered him a rude, bouncing bully, but a very competent worker and very popular.'[50]

Michael Collins in London 1922. It was in civilian clothes such as this that Michael Collins managed to move without detection through the streets of Dublin during the War of Independence. (Courtesy of the National Library of Ireland)

Upon his release in December 1916, Michael Collins was given the records of the IRB by Kathleen Clarke, widow of executed IRB leader Tom Clarke. Collins also became secretary to the National Aid and

Volunteer Dependents' Fund Association. Operating from 10 Exchequer Street, Collins was under constant surveillance by the detectives of G Division of the DMP.[51] From the moment of his arrival back in Ireland, his activities were of serious concern for the RIC. They considered him to belong 'to a family of dangerous extremists'.[52] RIC reports from west Cork and Granard in Longford, areas where he spent a good deal of time, said Collins was well known to them. They observed his movements assiduously, noted his speeches and carefully identified his associates. G Division detectives issued the following description of Collins in August 1917: '... 28 years, 5ft. 10 ins. high, well built, square shoulders, dark brown hair, round face, clean shaven, pale complexion, wears grey tweed suit and brown trilby hat.'[53]

In a speech Collins gave at Legga, County Longford, he warned those present not to take part in raids for useless old shotguns or swords and condemned the lawlessness associated with cattle drives. These drives involved local people taking over landed estates. They were frustrated by the lack of movement on the sale of big estates and the use of any available land by non-resident ranchers to supply beef to the British war market. Collins concluded by urging the Irish Volunteers to raid for arms that would be of some use to them and also to defend their arms to the death. Collins boldly stated that 'it would take five soldiers to take one man and 50,000 with fixed bayonets to enforce it [conscription] in Ireland'.[54] He called on those present to stand together and remember Thomas Ashe. After the speeches were over, Collins carried out the marching and drilling of eighty-eight young men up and down the public road.[55]

The local district inspector of the RIC, Charles Collins, offered a keen assessment of the potential threat offered by Michael Collins: 'He appears to be a very dangerous criminal, is a member of the Sinn Féin Council and boasts about the part he took in capturing the G.P.O. He has paid frequent visits to this District, and his activities, if not speedily restrained, will lead to serious mischief.'[56]

Collins' tireless campaigning to raise a new Irish Volunteer movement bore impressive results. By the autumn of 1917 he reported to the Irish Volunteer convention that there were now 1,200 companies when compared to 390 in existence at the end of 1916.[57] It was as a direct result of his activities at Legga that Michael Collins was arrested in Dublin on 3 April 1918 by detectives while outside his Bachelor's Walk office.[58] Collins was brought before Resident Magistrate Jephson at Longford town. Collins declared the proceedings to be 'a farce'. Mr Jephson RM set bail at £40 with two sureties of £20. Collins responded, 'I do not enter into bail with blackguards and tyrants!', describing the RM's setting of bail as 'Nonsense!' This defiant behaviour resulted in him being sent to Sligo Gaol to await trial on the dual charges of incitement to raid for arms and for illegal drilling.[59] Before departing for gaol, Collins was permitted to have breakfast, provided by Cumann na mBan at a nearby house. Afterwards, he was led to the RIC Barracks and then to the railway station. The RIC guard in charge of Collins were accompanied by a large procession of cheering, flag-waving Sinn Féin supporters on their way to the railway station. Collins, under guard, was seen safely aboard the train for Sligo. The railway platform was very crowded as a large group of Irish Parliamentary Party supporters had also turned up to heap abuse on the Sinn Féiners. There were repeated cheers for Mr Collins. A rousing chorus of 'The Soldier's Song' broke out as the train pulled slowly out of the station.[60] Collins may not have realised it but he was on his way to war. In the following four years, this Irish Volunteer would transform for ever the history of Ireland and its relationship with its colonial ruler of 700 years. Michael Collins would spend three weeks in Sligo Gaol in April 1917. With Collins in prison, a change in tactics was decided upon and his bail was ordered to be paid to secure his liberty. He was released on 22 April to await trial at the changed venue of Derry.[61] He, of course, had no intention of turning up for a court appearance. Now freed, Michael Collins was on the run and was determined not to be detained at 'His Majesty's pleasure' again. On his return to Dublin, Collins managed to secure the release of another Irish Volunteer who had also refused to pay bail. This young man was Tom Cullen. Originally from County Wicklow, Cullen would work to form part of Michael Collins' intelligence operations.[62] Collins' escape from a certain prison sentence marked a major shift in Irish Volunteer policy. Key members of the Irish Volunteers now went underground and took a less prominent role in political activities.

Under de Valera's leadership, Sinn Féin, in conjunction with the Irish Volunteers, set about strengthening their position. Sinn Féin were seeking to prepare for the coming general election, which would follow the end of the First World War. A strong performance in those elections would strengthen their call for international recognition for Irish independence at the Peace Conference which would conclude hostilities and reconstruct Europe at the war's end. De Valera, speaking at a rally of 7,000 enthusiastic supporters in Kilkenny city, said that if Ireland's claim to independence was not recognised at the coming conference in Versailles, the Irish people would make the government of this country impossible for the English.[63] Yet the events which were to put in motion the final moves towards Irish independence did not occur at home but hundreds of miles away on the Western Front in the final months of the First World War.

At 4.40 a.m. on the morning of 21 March 1918, General Ludendorff, the German commander on the Western Front, gave the order for Operation Michael to commence, unleashing a hurricane bombardment of over a million high-explosive and gas shells upon the British army in the Somme Valley. The shelling was followed by wave upon wave of elite German shock troops or stormtroopers who easily mopped up the survivors before breaking through to the rear and pushing on to Paris. This was the beginning of what the Germans would call the *Kaiserschlacht*,[64] the Emperor's Battle, which they hoped would bring them final victory in a war that had been at an impasse since its beginning in 1914. The Russian Revolution of 1917 and the abdication of Tsar Nicholas II had resulted in the withdrawal of Russia from the war against Germany. Britain and France greatly missed their Russian ally as it meant German divisions on the Eastern Front were now free to join their comrades on the Western Front. German commanders were hoping for a quick victory before the United States army could be brought into action after their declaration of war on Germany on 6 April 1917. The British suffered greatly in the battle, suffering 20,000 dead and over 36,000 wounded.[65] The fighting continued until early August when the Germans were finally halted at the Second Battle of the Marne by the combined armies of France, Britain and the arrival of the American Expeditionary Force.[66] The consequences of this battle in France were to lead to a British initiative in Ireland that would create a movement for national unity and ultimately lead to a war for independence.

By the spring of 1918 the British empire had been at war with Germany and its allies for nearly four years. The First World War had introduced the names of Ypres, Gallipoli, the Somme and Passchendaele to the annals of history. These battlefields witnessed the killing or maiming of hundreds of thousands of soldiers. There was still no final victory in sight and the British, despite calling on its colonies for aid, were now desperately short of recruits to fill the gaps on the Western Front. Most of the British divisions numbered between 12,000 and 19,000.[67] The American 1ˢᵗ Division, to

British envy, consisted of over 27,000 men.[68] British Prime Minister Lloyd George decided that to meet the shortfall in numbers of troops he would require the introduction of conscription in Ireland.[69] Lloyd George was a formidable political opponent and Ireland would come to know him only too well in the years ahead. As the Military Service Bill for Ireland was debated in the House of Commons, Lloyd George asked as the war was one for small nationalities, why should the Irish not fight for such nationalities, and Catholic ones at that? He reminded John Redmond MP, leader of the Irish Home Rule Party, of a speech Redmond had delivered at the Mansion House in Dublin. In the course of this speech Redmond referred to a meeting with Cardinal Mercier of Belgium, stating: 'I took the liberty of promising him then that Ireland would bring her arms and her strength to avenge Louvain and to uphold the integrity and independence of Belgium – aye, yes, Belgium, Poland, Alsace-Lorraine, France ...'[70]

For Lloyd George and for Britain, the situation was grave. Men from England, Wales and Scotland were playing their part in keeping the German army from taking Paris. Although thousands of Irishmen had already given their lives for the British empire in the First World War, for the Prime Minister it was 'both necessary and expedient' that Irishmen play their part in preventing defeat at the hands of Germany and its allies.[71] Conscription had been introduced to England, Scotland and Wales in January 1916 under the terms of the Military Service Act.[72] The Home Rule MPs surprisingly rejected his pleas, warning that he would have a new battlefront in Ireland. The Home Rule MPs viewed the passing of the Military Service Bill as a 'declaration of war against Ireland'.[73] Despite Irish opposition the Bill was passed, by 301 votes to 103, and became law on 16 April 1918. All of the Home Rule MPs voted against the measure.[74] The effect of the introduction of conscription to Ireland was to unify the up-to-now divided strands of nationalist and republican opinion. The person who emerged to lead this political phase and strategy was Éamon de Valera.

On 18 April 1918, a conference chaired by the Lord Mayor of Dublin, Laurence O'Neill, met at the Mansion House. Its brief was to formulate and coordinate a strategy to defeat the introduction of conscription for Ireland. In attendance were Irish Parliamentary Party MPs John Dillon and Joseph Devlin, Labour Party members William O'Brien (Dublin), Michael Egan and Thomas Johnson, William O'Brien (Cork) of the 'All for Ireland League' and Timothy M. Healy. Also present were Sinn Féin representatives Éamon de Valera and Arthur Griffith. The conference decided to issue a pledge to be taken in every parish across the country the following Sunday: 'Denying the right of the British Government to enforce compulsory service in this country, we pledge ourselves solemnly to one another to resist Conscription by the most effective means at our disposal.'[75]

They issued a declaration that saw Ireland as a separate and distinct nation and argued that the British attempt to enforce conscription on the country was a violation of the rights of small nations to self-determination.[76] De Valera appealed to the Irish bishops, who were concluding their annual meeting at Maynooth, for their support. After consideration of de Valera's appeal, they decided to support the anti-conscription movement,[77] issuing a statement in which conscription was condemned as 'an oppressive and inhuman law which the Irish people have a right to resist by every means that are consonant with the law of God'.[78] Lloyd George's 'necessity and expediency' in enforcing conscription in Ireland rather than face losing the First World War had unexpectedly forged a united Irish political movement. It was quite an achievement for Lloyd George and one which was totally unnecessary, given the prospect of imminent reinforcements and war material from the United States. The leadership and energy provided by Sinn Féin placed them in a strong position in the intense political atmosphere preceding the general election of December 1918. Despite having lost three by-elections in a row, Sinn Féin were confident that the coming election would bring substantial gains at the expense of the Irish Parliamentary Party.

On Sunday 21 April 1918, the anti-conscription pledge was signed outside all Catholic churches in Ireland. This was followed by a general strike on 23 April. All shops and factories were closed, no trams or trains ran and no newspapers rolled off the presses.[79] Belfast was the only Irish city in which work continued as usual.

The Viceroy, the King's representative to Ireland, Lord Wimborne, was replaced by Field-Marshal Lord French, who intended to push through conscription with force if necessary. On 12 April 1918, Joseph Dowling was found by the RIC on an island off the west coast of Ireland. Dowling was a member of Roger Casement's Irish Brigade and had been dropped ashore by a German U-boat.[80] Dowling's capture gave the British the excuse they needed to arrest the leading members of Sinn Féin and as many senior officers of the Irish Volunteers as possible. The head of the British administration in Ireland, Lord French, claimed they had uncovered a German plot. On 17 May, the RIC, accompanied by British troops, rounded up seventy-three prominent Sinn Féin men and women. A considerable number of them were also Irish Volunteer officers. Éamon de Valera, Arthur Griffith, Count Plunkett, William Cosgrave, Countess Markievicz, Maud Gonne MacBride and Kathleen Clarke were jailed. Joseph Dowling was imprisoned for six years.[81] Due to the 'German plot' many Irish Volunteer commanders now languished in jail once again. In March 1918, the Irish Volunteers decided to establish a new GHQ. Richard Mulcahy, an IRB member and 1916 veteran, was appointed chief of staff. Mulcahy had fought alongside Thomas Ashe in the Ashbourne fight during 1916. He was a strong supporter of Michael Collins and a good organiser. Collins now became adjutant general as well as remaining Director of Organisation.

Collins and Mulcahy anticipated that opposing conscription could lead to an outbreak of military action. Therefore, to organise and prepare the Irish Volunteers for a new type of war, they began to print a bimonthly paper entitled *An t-Óglach*. The content of the paper would leave their command structures in no doubt of what was required by their troops should fighting break out with the British.

What was proposed in 1918 was stark. *An t-Óglach* presented the facts in an article entitled 'Ruthless Warfare':

> It would be desirable for instance, to eliminate all talk and thought of passive resistance ... our active military resistance is the only thing that will tell and any plans, theories or doubts to distract the minds of the people from the policy of fierce and ruthless fighting ought to be ruthlessly discouraged ... If England decides on this atrocity, then we, on our part, must decide that in our resistance shall acknowledge no limit and scruple.[82]

An t-Óglach went further and identified as a target anyone who knowingly and willingly facilitated conscription, saying he would be 'dealt with' as if he were an enemy soldier. Examples given included doctors who might treat wounded enemy soldiers or drivers who transported the police. Their fate was spelled out: 'We must recognise, that anyone, civilian or soldier, who assists directly or by connivance in this crime against us, merits no more consideration than a wild beast and should be killed without mercy or hesitation as opportunity offers ... those who assist the enemy will be shot.'[83] Anyone, from the King's representative to Ireland, the Lord Lieutenant, to a hotel porter, was considered a legitimate target.[84] GHQ also warned that it would not be wise for anyone to display 'undue zeal in the service of England in Ireland, or in opposition to the Irish Republic'.[85]

It was not just bellicose articles that were printed in *An t-Óglach* but also detailed instructions on the military organisation and operations. Articles addressed topics such as engineering, sabotage, guerrilla warfare and the administration of companies and battalions. Details for proposed military operations included railway demolition, railway demolition without explosives, scouting and tracking, hedge fighting for small units, and mapping.[86] Many of the articles on guerrilla warfare were written by Ginger O'Connell, a staff officer at Irish Volunteers GHQ.[87] There were also articles that indicated the brutal nature of conflict itself: one article, 'Firearms As Clubs', explained that the butt of a rifle or shotgun made a 'formidable weapon in hand-to-hand conflict'. Readers were introduced to the use of a weapon to incapacitate an enemy with a variety of blows to the face, the head, the pit of the stomach or knees.[88] *An t-Óglach* was, unsurprisingly, proscribed as a paper of an illegal organisation.

The nature of its content made *An t-Óglach*'s editor, Piaras Béaslaí, a marked man. He would have quite a few close escapes over the next few years, along with the man who printed the journal, Dick McKee, O/C of the Dublin Brigade. A printer by trade, McKee printed off thousands of copies of this Irish Volunteer journal at the premises of *Gaelic Press* in Liffey Street. The premises were owned by Joseph Stanley, a 1916 veteran from C and H Companies, 1st Battalion, Dublin Brigade.[89] The machine used to print *An t-Óglach* was an old one with a treadle, the sort used for printing handbills.[90] The premises were raided frequently by the police. During one raid an edition of *An t-Óglach* was laid out, ready in type, on a table but the detective officers did not notice it.[91] Stanley was continuously harassed by the police and eventually he was forced to close his premises. The printing operation was then moved to a more secret location, a tiny sealed room with no windows, at the back of a tobacconist's shop in Aungier Street.[92] This secret printing room lay 200 yards from Ship Street Barracks and Dublin Castle, under the noses of the British. As the popularity of *An t-Óglach* grew, Patrick Mahon from F Company 2nd Battalion and a young lad called Frank Boyce joined McKee's printing operation.[93] Tom Cullen and Joe O'Reilly, both trusted aides to Michael

Collins, ran copies from editor to printer from typist Bridie O'Reilly. Eventually, much to McKee's relief, a new printing machine was purchased to deal with increased demand for the paper.

It is easy to dismiss the vitriolic nature of some of the content of *An t-Óglach* as propaganda, but in an era when the only other sources of information were Irish and English national and regional papers, *An t-Óglach* assumed an almost mythic reputation. It was considered by Irish Volunteer GHQ to be vital in maintaining morale and educating the Volunteers in military organisation. The name itself, 'The Volunteer' in English, and the physical presence of the paper throughout the country was a challenge to British control. Also, the paper presented an alternative view of the nature of events along with some very seditious articles on munitions. In December 1918, the British war cabinet at Downing Street received a report on 'The State of Ireland'. This was a detailed weekly document containing reports from the Lord Lieutenant, Lord French, the General O/C of British Forces in Ireland Lieutenant-General Frederick Shaw and also Inspector General of the RIC, J. Byrne. In early December, Inspector General Byrne drew the war cabinet's attention to *An t-Óglach*. He acknowledged the power of the republican journal to inflame the Volunteer movement by circulating seditious literature.[94] To show the 'continued rebellious activity of this dangerous society', Byrne included an extract from the sixth issue, dated 15 November 1918, which contained the very report Michael Collins had given to the Irish Volunteer convention in 1917. The RIC now estimated Irish Volunteer strength to be in the region of 30,000. Inspector General Byrne reported that Irish Volunteer companies were not now appearing in public.[95] The 'popularity' of *An t-Óglach* among the British administration and military continued to grow. On 10 May 1919, Lieutenant-General Shaw wrote in his report to the war cabinet, that from '… careful reading of the different copies of *AN T'OGLAC* (the official secret Irish Volunteer organ) it would appear that the Irish Volunteer Headquarters so constantly speak of the necessity for courage and initiative that they realise that their units are only ill-trained troops. In consequence should they in any raid receive a serious setback the enthusiasm for this form of violence would quickly evaporate'.[96]

The British army was not the sole focus of Irish Volunteer attention. They had a particular antagonism towards the RIC and its Dublin city partner, the DMP. In 1919, Irish Volunteer GHQ decided, that in order to break Britain's control of Ireland, the RIC would have to be broken first. Where did this antagonism come from? Since its foundation in 1822, the RIC had been a highly professional police force. In maintaining law and order, the Irish police carried out their duties with rigour. The courts system, through resident magistrates and high court judges, supported the police through a variety of measures, from imposing financial bonds to ensure good behaviour to imprisonment or death by hanging. The RIC and DMP were also the first line of resistance against Irish men and women who sought to break the link with England through revolutionary means. The RIC was an armed police force: constables carried both revolvers and carbines should the situation warrant it. DMP constables were trained in firearms, but did not usually carry them. In Ireland the law was heavily associated with England's occupation of the country. The RIC crest featured a crown perched above the harp surrounded by a tribute of shamrocks. It was a constant reminder of where the allegiance of the serving Irish policeman lay. The RIC attended on bailiffs when they served notice of eviction and also arrested Irish Fenian revolutionaries and led them away to court and imprisonment.

The Easter Rising of 1916 and the subsequent War of Independence did not occur in a vacuum. In the 700 years Britain had occupied the island of Ireland there were a number of attempts made by the Irish to overturn British rule. But it was the American revolution of 1776 and the French revolution of 1789 that provided the Irish with a realistic political alternative to life as a subject of the British empire. The idea of Ireland as a republic was adopted by successive groups as the way forward. While the majority of Irish people would have been content with a measure of Home Rule, a minority of the population believed that British control in Ireland could only be broken by force of arms. By the end of the nineteenth century the political and social atmosphere in Ireland was highly charged. In 1897 Queen Victoria visited Dublin in celebration of her diamond jubilee. Her Majesty was warmly received by the majority. However, there was a growing minority who were not happy with the reminder of British imperial control over Ireland. Boisterous behaviour of students from Trinity College in support of the queen led to a riot with Irish nationalists in College Green. Up to 200 civilians and between sixteen and twenty policemen were taken to hospital.[97]

The following night, in protest at the baton charges by the DMP at the preceding night's rioting, the Dublin dockers marched to a rally at Rutland Square [Parnell Square]. Houses and businesses that flew a Union Jack along the route of the march had their windows smashed. The dockers' march came to a halt at the Orange Order Rooms at Rutland Square where Joseph O'Connor, a future lieutenant in the Irish Volunteers, saw shots fired by members of the Orange Society. Another riot ensued. As a result of their robust responses the DMP received the nickname the 'Jubilee Butchers' from nationalists. The visit of Queen Victoria was followed by the centenary of the 1798 Rising led by the United Irishmen. A commemorative ceremony in Dublin was attended by a French delegation. Joseph O'Connor was among a welcoming party of Irish republicans to meet the French visitors. The DMP were ordered to break up the commemorative ceremony and did so with the blows of their batons.[98] The commemorations held in 1898 reminded Irish people that an Irish republic had once been fought for by a mass movement led by men like Wolfe Tone. The names of those who had died in an attempt to win a republic in 1798 were inscribed on memorials dedicated throughout Ireland during the centenary. A second revolution had occurred in 1803 when Robert Emmet led a small group in an attempt to seize Dublin. This had also failed and ended with Emmet being tried, found guilty and executed by hanging and beheading. There followed two more attempted risings, one by the Young Irelanders in 1848 and the other by the Fenians in 1867. Each one provided a new generation of the hopeful with its heroes and marytrs.

The Boer War of 1899–1902 had demonstrated that Britain's empire could be challenged and stretched. While Irish regiments of the British army, such as the Royal Dublin Fusiliers, fought the Boer guerrilla army at the battles of Colenso and Tugela Heights, Irishmen of a different political persuasion raised an Irish brigade and fought with the Boers. On returning to Ireland, nationalists viewed the pro-Boers in awe because they had fought the British on the field of battle. Events like these encouraged a new generation to envisage an Ireland separate from Britain. This view was supported by the emphasis on a unique Irish culture through language, sport and music. The Gaelic Athletic Association (GAA), founded in 1884, promoted the Gaelic sports of hurling and football as distinctly Irish. A ban was imposed on anyone who played any 'British' sport like soccer or rugby. The Gaelic League was founded in 1893 by Douglas Hyde to promote the Irish language. The movement proved very popular among young Irish men and women searching for a break with the Victorian and

Edwardian society. The Irish language introduced them to an entirely different way of seeing themselves and their country. Living through Irish was an open door to a completely different way of thinking. Learning and writing in the old Irish script was in part a first step in defiance and a small step towards revolution in that it was an abandonment of England, its language and imperial control. With its clarion call of 'Ireland Sober and Ireland Free' the Gaelic League sought to focus the energy of its members and awaken their concept of what Irish nationality meant.[99] The nationalistic emphasis had not been Douglas Hyde's intention but the IRB had seen the advantages of controlling this movement and directing its energy towards the cause of Irish freedom. What the GAA and the Gaelic League provided in sporting and cultural distinction for Irish people, a new political party, Sinn Féin, provided in politics.

Min Ryan was attracted to the Sinn Féin movement through her older brother, Martin, who was studying to be a priest at the national seminary in Maynooth, County Kildare. When Martin came home on holiday he would always 'talk tremendously about the language movement and Sinn Féin'.[100] Sinn Féin was founded by Arthur Griffith in 1905. He proposed that Ireland should have a political arrangement with Britain akin to that of Austria-Hungary. It was a form of independence based on dual monarchy. Listening to her brother's enthusiasm, Min Ryan began to read anything she could find on Arthur Griffith and Sinn Féin. Support for the fledgling Sinn Féin was restricted to small groups of intellectuals at that early stage as most people were satisfied with the Irish Parliamentary Party. Min Ryan said that 'if you talked about Sinn Féin and tried to bring up a new idea, people looked on you as being a bit queer, with "notions"'.[101]

Patrick J. Little, a solicitor with offices at 22 Eustace Street, edited an evolving series of Irish nationalist and republican papers called *New Ireland, Éire, Sinn Féin* and, after 1916, *An Phoblacht*. He believed these papers articulated the views of Sinn Féin, the Gaelic League and the Irish Republican Brotherhood. Together, he said, they sowed the seeds which came to fruition much later when the public had ceased to trust British promises.[102] Little believed the public were prepared over the years for the attempt at independence in 1919, through speeches, meetings, by-elections, formative journals and papers and the drilling of the Irish Volunteers. While editing *New Ireland*, Little was approached by his neighbour in Dundrum, W. B. Yeats, the Anglo-Irish poet and playwright. Yeats asked Little if he would consider adopting a more moderate, but more passionate, advocacy of domestic home rule in *New Ireland*. If so, Lord Wimborne,[103] the Lord Lieutenant of Ireland and cousin of Winston Churchill, would be prepared to subsidise the paper to the tune of £2,000.[104]

It is not surprising then that in the first decades of the twentieth century Irish people were willing to act to shape their future and destiny. The first form of resistance was trade unionism, through the work of Jim Larkin, who formed the Irish Transport and General Workers' Union (ITGWU) in 1909. James Connolly also provided strong leadership for workers in advocating the establishment of a socialist Irish republic free from Britain as the only way of securing equality for all Irish people. The brutality of the DMP during the Great Lockout of 1913 did a great deal to unify Dubliners in opposition to Dublin Castle. Workers who had joined the ITGWU were locked out of work by their employers, led by William Martin Murphy, proprietor of Independent Newspapers. Joseph O'Connor witnessed what he called 'shocking brutality' on the part of the DMP during the Lockout. It was the foundation of the Irish Citizen Army by Jack White on 19 November 1913, which aimed to protect Dublin workers from the police, that further increased the tension in Ireland. The Irish Volunteers were also founded in November while The Ulster Volunteer Force had been founded the previous January. Armed conflict looked an increasing possibility.

The discussion of ideas over a decade or more resulted in a diversity of opinion about the future that lay in store for Ireland. The proposed introduction of Home Rule towards the end of the nineteenth century and the beginning of the twentieth century brought with it significant divisions in Irish society. By 1900, two attempts at Home Rule through democratic means in Westminster had failed. The first Home Rule Bill had been introduced by William Gladstone's Liberal government in 1886. Gladstone appealed to the House to 'think not just for the moment but for the years that are to come'.[105] The House of Commons did not listen and Home Rule was defeated by 343 to 313 votes. The second Home Rule Bill was defeated by 419 to 41 votes in the House of Lords on 8 September 1893. The movement for Home Rule was the central aim of the Irish Parliamentary Party under Charles Stewart Parnell in the late nineteenth century. The movement split due to Parnell's lengthy affair with Katherine O'Shea. This split in the Home Rule movement was healed by the work of John Redmond. His skilful and tireless efforts brought Home Rule into the British political arena for a third time in 1912. Defeat for the Liberal government's budget in 1909 led to the removal of the veto of the House of Lords on acts of law passed by the House of Commons.

The proposed introduction of Home Rule activated a large pro-unionist section of the population in Ireland to prepare to resist the imposition of Home Rule, by arms if necessary. The Unionist movement saw membership of the British empire as crucially important in maintaining the religious, cultural and financial life of mainly Protestant Ulster. Different expressions of Unionism in the Orange Order, Ulster Unionist MPs and the Ulster Volunteer Force found common cause in facing down the nationalist threat of Home Rule. The Unionists, led by Edward Carson and James Craig, had strong support among the British establishment. An alliance of Conservative Party MPs and Lords along with some very influential titled and business supporters in Britain ensured Unionist Ulster's resistance. Lord Randolph Churchill, a Conservative politician and Winston Churchill's father, had encouraged the use of the 'Orange Card', or Unionism, as a means to defeat the Liberal Party over earlier Home Rule Bills. The 'Orange Card' had ensured the protection of Protestant Ulster and would introduce the gun into the modern historical era. As 1914 drew closer, it looked as though Home Rule would have to be enforced in Ulster. General Hubert Gough, of the 3rd Cavalry Brigade of the British army stationed at the Curragh in County Kildare, mutinied. Out of seventy officers, fifty-seven said they would refuse to order their troops to enforce Home Rule on Ulster Unionists who wished to remain British and an integral part of the British empire.[106]

The Ulster Volunteer Force, founded in January 1913 to resist the imposition of Home Rule, illegally imported a substantial weapons shipment to Ireland from Germany. The shipment arrived aboard the SS *Clyde Valley* at Larne on 24 April 1914.[107] The Unionists were now armed and prepared to defend their place within the British empire. Any situation could lead to conflict. In August 1914, the RIC began receiving reports of provocative drilling by Viscount Jocelyn on the Tullymore–Bryansford Road in County Down. Sergeant Patrick McGovern of the RIC reported that the Viscount had marched his detachment of twenty-three men, armed with Martini-Enfield rifles with fixed bayonets, on a new route past the United Irish League Hall in the nationalist quarter where a detachment of unarmed Irish Volunteers were parading at the same time. A row would have ensued had it not been for the calming counsel of their leaders.

On another occasion, Viscount Jocelyn marched the Bryansford UVF to Newcastle. This time they numbered forty-two and were again armed with Martini-Enfield rifles with fixed bayonets. They did not enter the nationalist quarter on this occasion but each man was given ten rounds of ball cartridge and instructed to shoot anyone who attempted to take his weapon from him. These weapons were the British army rifle of the Zulu Wars and, while obsolete by 1914, they still cut an impressive sight to the Irish Volunteers who had no weapons at all. All of the men carrying arms were noted by Sergeant McGovern, who confirmed in his report that of the forty-two noted, thirty-nine were not licensed to carry arms. He did not intervene. Local Home Rule MP Jeremiah MacVeagh wrote to the Lord Chancellor accusing Viscount Jocelyn of grossly provocative conduct in parading his UVF force and asking if County Inspector Wallace was even aware of the situation.[108]

By August 1914, however, events in Ireland paled in comparison to events in Europe. Britain had declared war on Germany on 4 August. The Home Rule Bill was placed on the statute book at Westminster and its introduction suspended until after the war. Disagreements over Home Rule were put aside in support of Britain. On 20 September 1914 John Redmond made a speech at Woodenbridge, County Wicklow, in which he appealed for the Irish Volunteers to support Britain's fight wherever the firing line extended. This speech split the Irish Volunteers. In all, 170,000 followed Redmond's call to arms and joined the British army. Of these, 49,000 became casualties, including Redmond's own brother, MP for East Clare Captain Willie Redmond. The remaining 11,000 stayed in the Irish Volunteers. Few could have expected the Rising in Dublin and the executions that followed in April and May 1916. The political landscape that emerged from the experience of the First World War years was unrecognisable. W. B. Yeats' description of Ireland after the Rising as 'changed, changed utterly' was most apt.

In 1914 the RIC had regarded Sinn Féin as 'a negligible political force'.[109] By 1918, the RIC were reporting Sinn Féin as 'very industrious' and strengthening their organisation through 1,341 clubs with 111,000 members.[110] Sinn Féin looked forward to the general election of December 1918 and opened their campaign in November with a rally at the Mansion House attended by 8,000 people. This was the first opportunity since the 1916 Rising for the Irish people to express their support for the direction Ireland's future would take. A general election had not been held since

1910. Since then, the introduction of the Representation of the People Act had permitted women over thirty years of age to vote, which had trebled the electorate.[111] Sinn Féin nominated candidates for 102 of the 105 constituencies. RIC Inspector General Byrne observed that 'making allowance for the heated atmosphere of an election contest, language used, though disloyal and bitterly anti-English, [it] was, on the whole, not worse than might be anticipated'.[112] He also reported that at election rallies, Sinn Féin speakers were confident their claim to independence would be granted by the Peace Conference at Versailles or through the personal intervention of the president of the United States.

In Dublin city, DMP Superintendent Owen Brien reported that Sinn Féin electioneering activity was in full swing. Sinn Féin had twenty-four active clubs in the city with a membership of 4,700. The RIC believed that 'practically the entire Nationalist youth of both sexes in the Country had become obsessed with the idea of an Irish Republic and with the policy of abstention from the House of Commons'.[113] A number of attempts were made to dampen republican enthusiasm. One evening a group of soldiers attempted to enter Sinn Féin headquarters at 6 Harcourt Street, Dublin. Anticipating such an eventuality, the Dublin Brigade of the Irish Volunteers had posted a guard of forty men armed with sticks inside the building. The Volunteers beat off the soldiers from the front steps and closed the door. The soldiers then hurled a volley of stones and other missiles, smashing all the windows. The Volunteers retaliated, throwing bricks down on the heads of the soldiers from the upper storeys of the building. Three or four revolver shots were then heard. The DMP and a detachment of British military arrived to restore order. Four policemen were injured by stones thrown by the soldiers.[114] On the morning of 20 November 1918, the DMP raided the Sinn Féin HQ in Harcourt Street. As expected, the DMP 'seized a large quantity of seditious literature'.[115]

Throughout November, the DMP kept close surveillance on meetings of Cumann na mBan and Sinn Féin gatherings in Dublin. The Irish Volunteers were less conspicuous. Richard Mulcahy and Dick McKee were noted as attending a number of meetings, along with upwards of fifty named people already known to the DMP. The RIC also reported that a 'reliable informant' had visited Sinn Féin HQ to explore the building and speak with those present. The informant specifically mentioned the presence in the Sinn Féin HQ of 'an extreme section which in time of excitement might plunge the country into serious trouble'. The future of the country hung in the balance. Campaigning was intense and the atmosphere highly charged. Lieutenant-General Shaw, commander-in-chief of British forces in Ireland, ordered his troops to support the RIC strictly in accordance with the King's Regulations and not the Defence of the Realm Act. As such, all soldiers were to avoid coming into contact with civilians and were confined to barracks during the election proceedings on 27 and 28 December.[116] The result of the general election on 28 December was a landslide victory for Sinn Féin. The Irish Parliamentary Party was wiped out, winning only six seats. Sinn Féin won seventy-three seats and the Unionists twenty-two.

Sinn Féin's strategy to have Ireland's status as an independent nation recognised at the Versailles Peace Conference was one it pursued vigorously. Representatives of the United States and France viewed events in Ireland as a domestic affair and were reluctant to interfere in the affairs of their ally. The claim to independence as proclaimed in 1916 was to be endorsed by the meeting of the first Dáil Éireann, or Irish parliament, held on 21 January 1919. The newly elected TDs abstained from attendance at Westminster in favour of the Dublin-based independent Dáil.[117] The Act of Union was symbolically broken. In the hours before the Dáil met, eight members of the South Tipperary Brigade of the Irish Volunteers lay in wait to ambush a transport of gelignite at Soloheadbeg in South Tipperary.[118] In less than a minute, the two constables guarding the transport, James McDonald and Patrick O'Connell, were shot dead.[119] Volunteer Patrick Dwyer, who took part in the ambush, said it was their intention to disarm the constables and seize the gelignite without bloodshed if possible. Dan Breen gave a different account, stating that the action at Soloheadbeg was taken deliberately and with prior discussion and thought. Seán Treacy had said to Breen that the only way to start a war was to kill someone and so they intended to kill some of the police. Breen addressed the 'moral aspect' of the decision and knew they were branded as murderers by both the British and their own people on that fateful day. However, from Breen and Treacy's standpoint, they 'were merely continuing the action taken for the establishment of an Irish Republic that had begun on Easter Monday 1916'.[120] While Soloheadbeg would always be marked as the beginning of the War of Independence, that is not how matters appeared in 1919.

After the consistent call to arms in *An t-Óglach* one would have expected the editor to make the most of this ambush. *An t-Óglach* was generally silent on the ambush at Soloheadbeg. The only reference to it was a quote from a letter *An t-Óglach* had received from a Tipperary Volunteer who was in prison. Part of the letter ran as follows: 'The men who seized the explosives at Soloheadbeg risked their lives for Ireland in order to get war material to assist and defend Ireland's freedom. In self-defence they had to slay two of the armed enemy, and the true men and women of Ireland are proud of their bravery. By such deeds are tyrants and bullies held in check.'[121]

An t-Óglach concluded the article and the edition with a coded message in Irish in which the editor said that it is likely the good Irish Volunteers had been reading their books and studying their history. It advised the reader to study maps of their local area and pick out locations for combat: roads, junctions, railways, bridges and rivers.[122] The reaction by *An t-Óglach* to the Soloheadbeg ambush appeared to be mixed. On the one hand the killing of two policemen was applauded indirectly and the reference to it was carefully positioned at the back in a column headed 'General Notes'. On the other hand it was advising Volunteers to study their maps and prepare for combat.

Behind the scenes tensions among the Tipperary Volunteers and Irish Volunteer GHQ ran high. Dan Breen said that in the aftermath of Soloheadbeg, GHQ put considerable pressure on both himself and Seán Treacy to leave the country. Breen claimed that Chief of Staff Richard Mulcahy's argument for wanting them out of the country was that the Irish Volunteers were not yet ready and the South Tipperary action could not be supported.[123] The tension with GHQ would not dissipate in the coming years. Treacy and Breen were henceforth on the run. Whether GHQ was prepared or not, war was upon them and they would now have to deal with the situation as best they could. The words of Piaras Béaslaí, written in 1918, echoed through to January 1919: 'The day of the baton charges unassisted by military forces are ended. Where bodies of Volunteers meet them on anything like equal terms, force must be met by force.'[124]

The British response and the collective response of the nations attending the Versailles Peace Conference would determine the course of events in Ireland. Either way, both Sinn Féin and the Irish Volunteers prepared for an unclear future.

2

'Dublin: the Heart of the Whole Conspiracy'

Irish and British Forces – the Order of Battle 1919

'Dublin was and is the heart of the whole conspiracy. It was the principal military base for all Ireland, also the headquarters of the Viceroy and the Commander in Chief, as well as the site of large and important military stores of explosives and arms'.[1]

This description of Dublin by the British military revealed its importance to both the British and Irish. It was this fortress and its policing, military and administration that the Irish Volunteers were directed to defeat through a variety of operations during the War of Independence. The primary instrument for this monumental feat was to be the Dublin Brigade of the Irish Volunteers and its GHQ intelligence department.

By 1919 Dublin was a small city by European standards. The physical layout of the city resembled a spider's web bisected by the River Liffey running through the centre on an east–west axis. It was also ringed by two canals at a distance of two miles from the city centre: the Royal Canal to the north and the Grand Canal to the south. The British army considered Dublin city to be difficult territory to operate in for a number of reasons: 'There is little definite residential area, slums and tenement houses are found everywhere, and in the older part of the city there are many ramifications of underground cellars in which men, munitions and munitions factories can be hidden. There are innumerable small shops and comparatively few large stores. It is in fact an ideal town for guerrilla operations.'[2]

The Dublin of 1919 was a city of great contrasts. In the inner city, the north side in particular, were some of the worst slums in Europe. In the eighteenth and nineteenth centuries, Henrietta Street, for example, had been a fine development of grand Georgian houses owned and lived in by earls, viscounts, lords, bishops and MPs. By the early twentieth century, the street was in a dreadful state of disrepair while housing hundreds of impoverished families. In 1911, No. 14 Henrietta Street alone was home to more than 100 people. Conditions were cramped and damp, and rooms were subdivided by blankets hanging from rope. There was limited running water, while sanitation was poor. In such conditions consumption, as tuberculosis was then known, ran rife. In Dublin there were also the more affluent suburbs inhabited by the rising business and middle class. These better-off areas were in Drumcondra to the north and Rathmines, Ranelagh and Rathgar to the south. Substantial numbers of people were employed in the traditional brewing company Guinness. Others worked in shops like Eason and Clerys. The printing industry employed hundreds in the offices and print works of Independent Newspapers, *The Irish Times* and *The Freeman's Journal*. Hundreds worked for the railway companies – the Great Southern & Western, Dublin & South Eastern, Midlands & Great Western and Great Northern railway companies ran a comprehensive rail network from Dublin to the rest of the country. The Dublin United Transport Company provided electric tram and bus transport within the city and to outlying areas in greater Dublin. The dock at Dublin's North Wall facilitated trade and the transport of British military personnel and equipment to and from Ireland. Kingstown provided the official mail and passenger service to England.[3] Kingstown was popular with Dublin city day trippers, as were Howth and Skerries on the north of the county.

Dublin Castle, the heart of the British administration in Ireland, also provided highly prized pensionable employment in the form of the British civil service, military and police. British government administration at Dublin Castle was enhanced by the all-important Revenue Offices at the Custom House on the quays. The legal system centred on the Four Courts on King's Inns Quay completed the necessary administrative and social requirements of a city in the British empire of the post-war period. Supplying and supporting this hive of activity were hundreds of small businesses, from solicitors to painters and plumbers. Restaurants like Jammet's, Kidd's or the Cairo Café were popular eating places. Throughout the city was a range of hotels and guesthouses such as the Mayfair and Wicklow hotels. The upmarket Gresham or Shelbourne were beyond the reach of most living in Dublin. Working Dublin men and women obtained basic accommodation in 'digs', which provided a bed and a daily meal. The luckier ones rented a single or shared room or flat. Socially, Dublin of 1919 was quite mixed by Irish standards. Working and living side by side were Irish people from almost every county and a number of English, Scottish and Welsh citizens and soldiers who worked mainly for the British civil administration and military garrison of Ireland. There were also a number of returned Irish emigrants from the USA and parts of the global British empire. It was in the city and county of Dublin that the significant events of the Irish War of Independence would be played out, on a number of key fronts, such as intelligence, propaganda and guerrilla operations, shaping the future of Ireland and the nature of its relations with Britain for the next century.

The War of Independence fought by the Irish Volunteers in Dublin would be a combination of urban and rural warfare. The initial phase saw the Irish Volunteers issuing death threats, intimidating particular police officers, boycotting the RIC and raiding for arms, ammunition, explosives and equipment. This phase escalated quite quickly with the Dublin Brigade engaging in more aggressive tactics that aimed to neutralise the RIC and DMP while stretching the British army garrison to the point at which they could no longer effectively control the city as their platform for controlling Ireland. Individual Irish Volunteer companies carried out measures to hamper the movement of British Crown forces throughout Dublin, including the blocking and trenching of roads, and destruction of the telegraph network by cutting poles and wires. More aggressive Dublin Brigade tactics were similar to those employed by the Irish Volunteers across the country and included attacks on RIC barracks with the intent of capturing arms and burning them out. The more active detective officers of G Division in the DMP were singled out for assassination. Individual resident magistrates, senior police officers and constables were also picked out for assassination. The Irish Volunteers, or, as they would become, the Irish Republican Army (IRA), also carried out sniping and ambush attacks on British army patrols, routine supply transports and dispatch riders. A series of kidnappings of suspected spies, soldiers and police were carried out. There were also many opportunistic killings of RIC, DMP or British

A Dublin Brigade
Irish Volunteer
cap badge 1916.
(Image courtesy of
Whytes.com)

soldiers who happened to meet an Irish Volunteer patrol or company on
active operations. Some of the measures employed by the Irish Volunteers
were aimed at the level of intimidation and robbery, which sometimes
led to a brutal execution and a lonely death.[4] Supporting all this activity
was a comprehensive intelligence system aided by an extensive network of
established intelligence officers, agents, spies and sympathisers among all
creeds and classes of Dublin people working and living in just about every
conceivable job in the city and county.

The Dublin Brigade was organised on the Order of Battle drawn up
after the split in the Irish Volunteers caused by John Redmond, leader of
the Irish Parliamentary Party. Those who chose not to join Redmond's
National Volunteers retained the name the Irish Volunteers. Led by the
secret IRB, they staged the Easter Rising of 1916. After the Rising and
the experience of prison, the leaders of the Volunteers returned to Dublin
determined to reorganise and strike again. To implement their tactical
campaign they needed a comprehensive structure. A structure evolved,
which was an improved model based on the experience of 1916. This
reorganisation of their military forces responded to tactical requirements
during the War of Independence and also to the numbers of personnel
available.

The Irish Volunteers organisation in Dublin was run by the Dublin Brigade headquarters staff. The HQ held a weekly brigade council meeting that all battalion commanders were expected to attend. The Dublin Brigade HQ staff changed considerably during the War of Independence. This was mainly due to imprisonment and casualties. For the most part the Dublin Brigade HQ staff were as follows:

Dublin Brigade HQ Staff 1919–20 Located at Typographical Institute, 35 Lower Gardiner Street, 1919 & at La Plaza, 6 Gardiner's Row, 1920–21		
Position	**Name**	**Additional Positions**
Brigadier	Commandant Richard McKee	Printing of *An t-Óglach* Director of Organisation
Vice-Brigadier	Commandant Michael Walsh Succeeded by Peadar Clancy	Director of Munitions Succeeded by Peadar Clancy Succeeded by Seán Russell
Adjutant	John Shouldice Christopher 'Kit' O'Malley	
Quartermaster	Peadar Breslin & Seán Russell	Seán Russell: organisation of Bloody Sunday operations and taking of after-action reports.
Intelligence Officer	Liam Tobin promoted to GHQ intelligence & succeeded by Joseph Griffin	

The Dublin Brigade consisted of four city battalions, a 5th Battalion of Engineers with 6th and 7th Battalions situated in south County Dublin. The 1st and 2nd Battalions were assigned north of the River Liffey. The 1st Battalion, with 1,306 men listed on 11 July 1921, were to the west of the line and also included Blanchardstown and Castleknock. The 2nd Battalion, with 786 men listed on 11 July 1921, were to the east and also included Santry and Howth.[5]

The 3rd and 4th Battalions were assigned south of the Liffey. The 3rd Battalion, with 944 men listed on 11 July 1921, were assigned to the area east of the dividing line while the 4th Battalion, with 934 men listed on 11 July 1921, covered the area to the west of the line and also the country villages of Terenure, Templeogue and Rathfarnham. Killakee was included in the Rathfarnham area.[6]

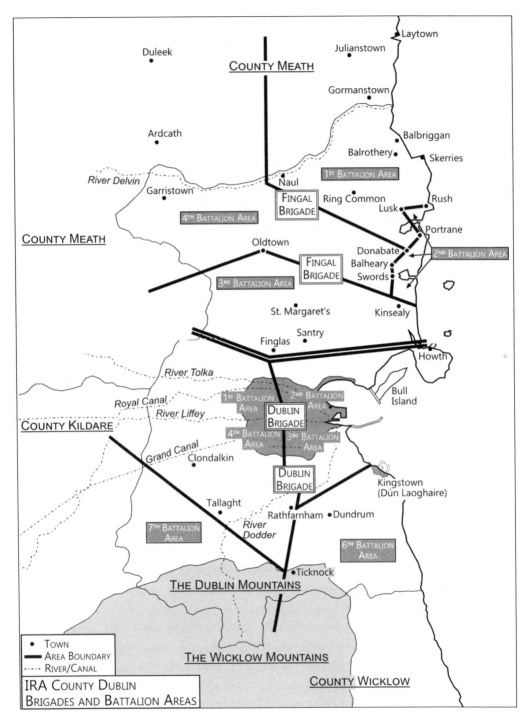

IRA brigades and battalion areas Dublin City and County. (With thanks to Eoin Brennan)

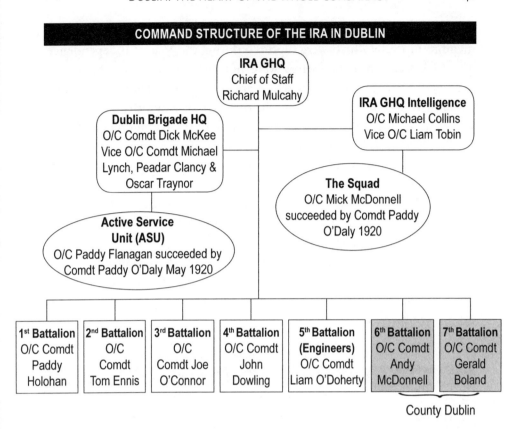

COMMAND STRUCTURE OF THE IRA IN DUBLIN

IRA GHQ
Chief of Staff
Richard Mulcahy

IRA GHQ Intelligence
O/C Michael Collins
Vice O/C Liam Tobin

Dublin Brigade HQ
O/C Comdt Dick McKee
Vice O/C Comdt Michael
Lynch, Peadar Clancy &
Oscar Traynor

The Squad
O/C Mick McDonnell
succeeded by Comdt Paddy
O'Daly 1920

**Active Service
Unit (ASU)**
O/C Paddy Flanagan succeeded by
Comdt Paddy O'Daly May 1920

| 1st Battalion O/C Comdt Paddy Holohan | 2nd Battalion O/C Comdt Tom Ennis | 3rd Battalion O/C Comdt Joe O'Connor | 4th Battalion O/C Comdt John Dowling | 5th Battalion (Engineers) O/C Comdt Liam O'Doherty | 6th Battalion O/C Comdt Andy McDonnell | 7th Battalion O/C Comdt Gerald Boland |

County Dublin

The 5th Battalion, with 340 men listed on 11 July 1921, was an engineer battalion assigned to special operations requiring their expertise in both city and county areas. The 6th Battalion, with 252 men listed on 11 July 1921, covered south County Dublin. The 7th Battalion, which covered south-west County Dublin, was listed with 241 men on 11 July 1921.

North County Dublin and parts of County Meath were assigned to the newly formed Fingal Brigade in 1920.[7] The Fingal Brigade, consisting of four battalions, was formed in October 1920.[8] Battalion O/C was Commandant Michael Lynch, former vice O/C Dublin Brigade. Lynch's vice-commandant was Michael Rock, originally O/C of the Naul Battalion District.

In the fluid situation which was the War of Independence, the numbers of men in the IRA organisation varied considerably. Men were constantly captured or killed. Officers or men with specific abilities were transferred to Battalion HQ staff or Brigade HQ staff. Despite the difficulties, by 1921 the IRA Dublin Brigade strength was estimated by the British to be 201 officers and 4,160 men.[9] This estimate was based on a comparison of numbers of imprisoned IRA men and the numbers on the Dublin Brigade membership rolls which were captured during the War of Independence. The IRA leadership themselves were not sure exactly how many men they had. Even in the 1930s when an attempt was made to establish a definitive list for each company in the IRA Brigades the actual count was contradictory depending on the opinion of the battalion or company O/C. Ultimately, individual company officers or battalion commanders had a specific small number of men upon whom they relied for almost all activities and engagements.

Irish Volunteer Battalions were initially instructed to have six to eight companies with just over 100 men in each. Each company HQ was assigned to a given geographical location of the city or county. E Company (later redesignated H Company) 4th Battalion, situated in the Rathfarnham area in south Dublin, offers an insight into the standard organisation of an Irish Volunteer Company. The company HQ listed the following officers on the command staff:

HQ Staff, E Company, 4th Battalion, Dublin Brigade.[10]		
Position/Rank	Name	Location
O/C Captain	F. X. Coughlan	Rathfarnham
1st Lieutenant	Thomas Kearney	Rathfarnham
2nd Lieutenant	Christopher Andrews	Terenure
Adjutant	John J. Tully	Terenure
Quartermaster	Patrick Donnelly	Whitechurch
Assistant Quartermaster	Thomas Higgins	Rathfarnham

Companies were also expected to have in place an O/C of each of the following positions: first aid, communications, training and intelligence. E Company did not have a number of these positions filled. The reasons may be varied, perhaps due to casualties, imprisonment or a lack of trained personnel to take the post. According to E Company's Official Roll for 11 July 1921, twelve Volunteers, three of whom were officers, had been interned. A captain was the company O/C. An Irish Volunteer company was divided into left and right halves, each with a lieutenant in charge. A half company was itself composed of two sections. A section typically contained twenty to thirty men; individual sections frequently contained whole families of brothers. Within each section a number of positions were appointed from section commander to machine-gunner.

A 1871 'Howth' Mauser single-shot rifle used by the Irish Volunteers in 1916.
(Courtesy Dave Swift, Claíomh – Irish Living History & Military Heritage)

A Short Magazine Lee-Enfield (SMLE) .303 Mark III, bandolier and 18-inch steel
bayonet. (Courtesy Dave Swift, Claíomh – Irish Living History & Military Heritage)

In order to carry out operations in Dublin, the Irish Volunteers required
up-to-date weapons. While rebuilding the organisation after 1916,
the leaders of the movement encouraged their Volunteers to 'acquire'
new weapons. Previously, the Irish Volunteers had been armed with the
German Mauser 1871 rifle. Containing no magazine, this rifle was a bolt-
action, single-shot weapon firing an 11mm black powder round or bullet.
These rifles had arrived in Ireland on 25 July 1914. Erskine Childers,
his wife, Molly, and Mary Spring Rice had smuggled a shipment of 900
Mausers into Howth Harbour on board the yacht *Asgard*. A further 600
rifles were landed at Kilcoole in County Wicklow the following day.[11]
By 1916, the Mauser '71 was already obsolete, having been replaced by
the Gewehr '98, a five-round magazine-fed rifle. By 1919 the weapon of
choice for the Irish Volunteers was the bolt-action, magazine-fed Short

Magazine Lee-Enfield No. 1 Mark III or SMLE for short. The SMLE fired a .303 round. The magazine had a ten-round capacity. This weapon was the standard British infantry rifle of the First World War. A proficiently trained soldier armed with an SMLE could fire up to fifteen aimed rounds per minute. The weapon was described as 'extremely powerful, the bullet being capable of penetrating 18in. (457mm) of oak, 36in. (914mm) of earth-packed sandbags, as well as a double thickness of house bricks at 200 yards (185m)'.[12]

The rifle also came with a 17in (431mm) steel bayonet, which gave the soldier armed with one a formidable appearance and considerable influence over unruly civilians. The SMLE was difficult for Irish Volunteers to obtain. It was down to the ingenuity of individual Volunteers to steal a rifle or arrange to buy one from a British soldier willing to sell, despite it being a criminal offence to do so. In 1918, G Company 1st Battalion. Dublin Brigade managed to smuggle out four SMLEs with 150 rounds of .303 ammunition from Islandbridge Barracks using a military car. The driver was paid £3.[13] Another source of rifles was a British soldier nicknamed 'Mouse', who was stationed at Portobello Barracks (now Cathal Brugha Barracks). Paying 'Mouse' £3 for each weapon, Captain Laffan's men of G Company managed to smuggle fifteen rifles and six .38 revolvers through the railings at the back of the barracks. The smuggling was done in small lots to avoid suspicion. Laffan tied two planks of wood on either side of his bicycle and put the rifles in between the planks. On other occasions, Irish Volunteers wore overcoats with slit pockets and thus were able to hold the rifles inside their coats.[14] Unable to procure as many rifles as they wanted, the IRA had to make do with shotguns and revolvers.

The handgun, be it revolver or automatic, was ideal for the kind of warfare the Irish Volunteers would favour in Dublin city. The Volunteers had no difficulty obtaining as many as they required. Among the most common were the British standard Webley Mk. VI .45, the short-barrel Webley RIC .44 or .45 and the Webley Bulldog.[15] Also popular was the US army standard sidearm, the Colt 1911 semi-automatic .45, and any number of Smith & Wesson revolvers. The German automatic pistols, Mauser C-96 7.63mm and the Luger 7.65mm, were highly prized by Dublin Brigade officers. The IRA also sought to use the hand grenade as part of their attacks on British vehicles and patrols. The standard British hand grenade of the First World War was the No. 5 'Mills' bomb and could be thrown accurately up to 30 yards (27.43m).[16] The Irish Volunteers and

British army at this time referred to the hand grenade as a 'bomb' and grenadiers as 'bombers'.

Even before the War of Independence began, it was obvious to Dublin Brigade HQ that adequate quantities of hand grenades and other explosive devices would be hard to obtain. In 1919, Commandant Dick McKee ordered his Vice-Commandant Michael Lynch to establish a munitions factory. Lynch selected his men and they attended lectures in explosive and bomb manufacture in a small tobacconist's shop owned by Martin Gleeson at 10A Aungier Street. McKee used the rear of the premises to print *An t-Óglach*. Lynch maintained that the team who worked on making munitions and hand grenades were the 'forgotten men' of the War of Independence. While attending and giving lectures, Lynch located a suitable site for his 'factory', a secret room in the basement of a bicycle shop run by Vice-Commandant of the Fingal Brigade, Archie Heron, and Joseph V. Lawless. In the basement of the bicycle shop at 198 Great Britain Street (now Parnell Street), Lynch's team worked away. There was only one way into or out of the basement. The place was packed with explosive materials. Michael Lynch was well aware of the dangers faced by his men, especially if caught in a British raid:

> To be caught in there by the enemy meant, in the early stages, imprisonment and, in the later phase of the struggle, certain death. In the beginning, they relied on their ingenuity to outwit any visits that might be paid by their [DMP] detectives. In the end, they worked with a loaded automatic on the bench beside them, determined to shoot the enemy until they themselves were shot.[17]

The equipment for the 'factory' came from a number of places. Lynch wanted a four-inch screw-cutting lathe. The British had confiscated a lathe from Leo Ganter, who ran a watch and clock manufacturers in South Great George's Street. The British later paid Ganter for it. After the First World War was over, Ganter bought back the lathe in a sale and gave it to the Dublin Brigade. Along with the lathe they put in a blacksmith's forge. In charge of the workshop was Matt Furlong, who had used a lathe at the National Shell Factory, Parkgate. This factory later burned down in suspicious circumstances. Tom Young operated the crucibles for casting the grenade casings. The furnaces were ordered through a sympathiser at Brooks Thomas Building Supplies. The grenades were manufactured on a

German 'egg' design. Foundry coke was used for the casing of the grenades while Dublin Gas Company soft coke was used for making brass necks for the grenades. The springs came from McQuillan's in Capel Street and the detonators were initially obtained from any number of county councils. When the British cut off the supply of explosives and any related material, Seumas O'Donovan then designed his own detonators, consisting of a copper tube filled with a fulminate, chlorate and mercury mix sealed with solder. The testing of standard grenades was carried out by O'Donovan and Seán Russell in a shed at the Bottle Tower in Churchtown, south County Dublin.[18] Seán Russell was appointed Director of Munitions in January 1921. He wisely ordered the scattering of the work and duplicating the premises to avoid losing everything in one enemy raid.[19] While the main munitions 'factory' was at 198 Great Britain Street, Crown Alley, Luke Street and Peter Street were also used.

Gelignite was the main explosive used. Most of it came from raids on quarries, chemists or sympathetic workers in various county councils. The most unorthodox hand grenade manufactured by the Dublin Brigade was about the size of a pineapple or turnip and contained 8 oz (0.22 kg) of gelignite. Vice-Commandant Michael Lynch and Tom Kehoe of GHQ intelligence cycled out to the open land at the Christian Brothers' O'Brien Institute in Marino to test it for the first time. The blast was enormous and every animal for a mile around sprang into life yelping, barking and squawking. Lynch and Keogh quickly departed. On the way back to the city they called into Lynch's home on Richmond Road, about a mile from the blast. Lynch's mother addressed them directly: "'What were you men up to? 'Oh nothing very important – just a little test,' Lynch replied. 'Well,' she said, 'about a half an hour ago, I heard a bang. It almost blew me out of the bed, and shook all the windows in the house.'"[20]

The test was not just about the size of the blast but also to check for fragmentation of the grenade itself to ensure it did not split along the casing weld. Complete disintegration of the grenade's metal casing in the explosion caused even greater damage as well as inflicting death or serious injuries on enemy troops. The grenade designer, Seumas O'Donovan, was hoping to cause a grenade to fragment into about forty-eight parts, producing a significant shrapnel effect.[21] Most of the Dublin Brigade grenades were manufactured in the shop-basement munitions factory on Great Britain Street. Over the year and a half Vice-Commandant Lynch was in charge, his factory turned out over 5,000 grenades. He never understood how they were able to get away with it as the smells emanating from the furnace were evident on the street above.[22]

Hand grenades were not the only weapon of war manufactured by the munitions unit. They also manufactured explosives. Seumas O'Donovan and Des Dowling, both qualified chemists, along with Bill Hogan,[23] a student for the priesthood with the Jesuits, developed and then manufactured a series of 'home-made' explosives for use by the Irish Volunteers during the War of Independence. O'Donovan was instructed to develop an explosive which could be easily manufactured from simple ingredients by any Irish Volunteer brigade in the country. This was to make it possible for Irish Volunteers to set up an explosives factory in any shed or farmhouse without 'blowing their heads off'.[24] The bomb makers then developed two explosive materials. The first was called 'Irish cheddar' and was based on a cheddite mix. The second was known as 'war flour' and was made from potassium chlorate, Chilean saltpetre and paraffin oil. These materials were not used for landmines due to their 'instability and dangerous unpredictability'.[25] The materials for the development of explosives came from England. Desmond Fitzgerald, TD and head of the Sinn Féin Propaganda Department, had a brother, Francis, who owned a chemical factory in Greenwich. The raw material, potassium chlorate, was dispatched to Dublin in bags marked 'bicarbonate of soda' or 'cream of tartar'. Until Francis Fitzgerald organised shipments of ingredients for explosives, O'Donovan was producing low-grade bombs. With Fitzgerald's help, the Irish Volunteers were able to receive dinitrobenzene and dinitrotoluene. These were then mixed with the potassium chlorate to make a better explosive.

The acquisition of high-explosive materials was important for O'Donovan and the munitions factory. Writing a series of articles for *An t-Óglach* in March 1920, O'Donovan explained the impact of high explosives: upon detonation, the explosive blast spreads rapidly in every direction reaching a speed of 17,000 to 21,000 feet (5km to 6.4km) per second or 12,000 to 15,000 miles per hour (19,000 to 24,000 km/h). This is the case for high explosives such as trinitrotoluene (TNT).[26] O'Donovan also warned his readers on the treatment of explosives. With such dangerous chemicals as picric and sulphuric acids and home-made thermite bombs containing aluminium powder and black oxide of manganese, accidents happened. Some IRA companies attempted to boost an explosive charge with petrol. Attempts like this usually had terrible consequences which could be fatal or leave any Volunteers caught in the blast with lifelong injuries.

As well as developing grenades and explosive charges, Seumas O'Donovan was also instructed to work on specialist weapons. For the attack on the London Midland & Scottish Railway building on the North Wall he produced a mix of phosphorus in carbon bisulphide packed in small bottles. He obtained the materials from Nobel's, an explosives factory where he was employed. O'Donovan also developed two gases: mono-bromo-methyl-ethyl-ketone and di-bromo-methyl-ethyl-ketone. He considered both of them good tear gases. During one of the experiments the gas exploded in his face. Luckily, O'Donovan was blinded for only twenty minutes. He did, however, get a week off work, as his face was a mass of water blisters.[27] The leadership of the Irish Volunteers believed that as poison gas had been used in the First World War, it might be used by the British against them in the coming conflict. The Irish Volunteers wished to be in a position to retaliate if necessary.[28] O'Donovan never questioned any of the orders he received from GHQ. Some of the most serious weapons he was ordered to develop lay in the field of biological warfare. O'Donovan was ordered to develop a means of infecting the horses of various British cavalry regiments with glanders or some similar infectious disease. O'Donovan also wrote a number of articles during the conscription crisis of 1918 about the possibility of spreading botulism.

As the Dublin Brigade began acquiring weapons, ammunition and explosives there was an urgent need to secure all of this war material in safe locations. The Irish Volunteers could not make use of fixed barracks or magazines. Instead, the Dublin Brigade turned to the ingenuity of their own tradesmen to build and conceal their arms and ammunition. What they produced was sheer genius.

Each company had its own munitions dump and sometimes a number of dumps. The locations of these dumps varied considerably from mountain hideaways to sub-basement armouries. Andy McDonnell, of E Company 3rd Battalion and later O/C of the 2nd Dublin Brigade, had a dump in 'Netley', Cross Avenue, Blackrock, the home of Eoin MacNeill TD and former chief of staff of the Irish Volunteers. It was a little risky because MacNeill was well known to the British. Professor MacNeill's son Niall was quartermaster of the 6th Battalion, south County Dublin. He had a special dump built into the wall in the kitchen. Despite the house being wrecked during a number of British army raids, the special dump was never found.[29] The 6th Battalion also had a dump near a Holy Well on Con Mulligan's land at Ticknock in the Dublin Mountains. This dump contained revolvers, rifles, ammunition and grenades. The grenades had been made in the 6th Battalion's own munitions factories at Jim Kavanagh's in Dundrum and T. Horan's in Blackrock. The dump at Ticknock also included gelignite that McDonnell's men had taken from the RIC magazine at Balally. It was an impressive haul including eight boxes of gelignite (with approximately fifty sticks per box), 400 detonators and 50 yards of fuse.[30] The gelignite had been temporarily put in biscuit tins and buried. When it was recovered, it had frozen. To thaw it out, McDonnell and his men put the gelignite under their clothes next to their skin. This made them ill, necessitating visits to their doctors. Clearly, it was incidents like this which were the reason for Seumas O'Donovan's article on thawing out gelignite in *An t-Óglach* in March 1920.[31]

Con Mulligan knew the 6th Battalion dump was on his land. He caused consternation by joining the British army. McDonnell and his men immediately moved the dump across the mountain to Jim Courtney's land at Kellystown. Using Courtney's kitchen, they counted their stores by candlelight into the small hours. Two loaves of brown bread lay cooling on the hob. McDonnell quietly put one under his coat. As the squad of men left the house and were walking down the mountain, he began to share the loaf, only to discover that P. J. Brennan had taken the other loaf. The Courtneys were to have no breakfast that morning.[32]

Dublin city provided a veritable rabbit warren of places to conceal the Dublin Brigade stores. In an era of horse-drawn transport, stables were commonplace at the rear of businesses and houses. The IRA made good use of them as real dumps or as effective decoys. An intelligence officer for IRA GHQ described one dump built by A Company 1st Battalion, who were also known by their nickname 'The 40 Thieves'[33] after the band from the Arabian Nights story of Ali Baba:

> A Coy had a number of very ingenious individuals ... [who] built at 6 Blackhall Street a perfect arsenal which was underneath the cellars. The way into it appeared to be an ordinary sewer trap door and they concreted it. To get into it, you had to go on your hands and when inside you could stand up. They erected shelves in this place and used it as a dump for all the weapons of the Company. Though the

Hall was raided several times that dump was never discovered by any raiders.[34]

On the outskirts of the city, F Company 4th Battalion had a number of dumps: one in Miss Flood's at Port Lester House, Bluebell, one in Miss Ellen Sarah Bushell's in Ring Street, Inchicore, one in the Brickworks at Drimnagh and another in an old mill at the Lansdowne Valley, also in Drimnagh. Inchicore and Drimnagh were important locations for the Irish Volunteers as they lay opposite the Great Southern & Western railway yards, Richmond Barracks and the main road from Dublin to Cork and Limerick. The dump held twenty-one revolvers, twenty-five shotguns and ammunition and was in the care of a local man, John Gannon, who was not a member of the Irish Volunteers. In 1919, Gannon and a young member of Na Fianna, John Kelly, took weapons from the dump and raided Moore's Pub at the third lock on the Grand Canal. They got away with a sum of money and some cigarettes. The loot was discovered by Gannon's employer, who notified the RIC and, in a follow-up raid, F Company's dump was discovered. Gannon was caught and sentenced to a term in Mountjoy Gaol. While there, Gannon joined an Irish Volunteer hunger strike. Kelly had fled to England but on his return to Ireland was confronted by the O/C of F Company, Christy Byrne, at the Brickworks dump. Kelly was shown a letter he himself had written that the Volunteers had intercepted. His guilt was proven beyond all doubt. Condemned by his own hand, John Kelly was deported. He was extremely lucky this occurred at an early stage in the War of Independence. If it had been in 1921 Kelly could have been shot for such a deed.

In the city itself, dumps were sometimes discovered quite literally by accident. On the morning of 25 January 1920, the Catholic church in Rathmines was destroyed by fire.[35] A few nights later, Vice-Commandant Michael Lynch was conducting a Dublin Brigade council meeting at 144 Great Brunswick Street (now Pearse Street) when a message arrived from O/C A Company 4th Battalion. They had been using the crypt of the church as an arms dump and had lost their stores in the blaze. Apparently hundreds of rounds went off as the church burned down but no one appeared to notice. A Company offered to assist the Dublin fire brigade in the clean-up to clear away any evidence of the rifles and revolvers sure to be lying among the debris. Lynch gave a written order to O/C A Company to stay away from Rathmines church and the fire brigade. He was afraid that if the British authorities got wind of the Irish Volunteers using churches to store weapons and ammunition it would cause a scandal. The next day Commandant Lynch went to see Captain Myers, O/C of the Dublin fire brigade looking after Rathmines, and nothing was ever heard of any weapons being found among the debris of the ruined church.[36] The O/C of A Company kept the note from Lynch and it was discovered among the officer's personal effects during a British army raid on his house four months later. As a result, the British then hunted Lynch, dead or alive.[37] Lynch was then transferred to north County Dublin to build up the newly established Fingal Brigade.

The Irish Volunteers GHQ knew from the practical experience of 1916 that they could not hope to win a conventional war against the British army. Instead, they intended to apply the lessons of other conflicts where smaller forces of volunteer armies took on conventional troops. The Irish Volunteers studied the Cuban War of Independence of 1895–1898, the 2nd Boer War of 1899–1902 and the campaign of German General Lettow-Vorbeck against the British in East Africa during the First World War. British cavalry officers of the 4th Hussars Lieutenant Reggie Barnes and his friend Lieutenant Winston S. Churchill witnessed the Cuban and Boer Wars at first hand. Barnes wrote an account of their observations on the Cuban War.[38] In March 1920 *An t-Óglach* carried part of these observations:

> Although the Spanish Government maintained in Cuba an army numerically far stronger than the insurgent forces, much better armed and organised, they were utterly unable to subdue or even check the revolt which spread rapidly ... an insurgent was distinguished from the peaceful negotiator only by a badge which could speedily be removed and by his rifle which was speedily hidden. Hence, the Government forces, whether in garrison or operating in the country were closely surrounded by an impalpable circle of fierce enemies who shot stragglers, intercepted messages, burned stores and maintained a continual observation.[39]

The Irish Volunteers' GHQ studies of General Lettow-Vorbeck's four-year undefeated guerrilla campaign against British forces in East Africa strongly influenced the Dublin Brigade strategy. GHQ wrote in *An t-Óglach*: 'The

secret of Lettow-Vorbeck's success was that he never allowed himself to
be forced to fight on ground that favoured the enemy ... Lettow-Vorbeck's
achievements prove to the hilt that enormous things can be accomplished
by quite small units of first class troops.'[40]

Applying the lessons learned from other conflicts required training
and experience. The Irish Volunteers aspired to put well-trained units in
the field. These units would eventually become known as Active Service
Units (ASUs) or flying columns. In Dublin the most experienced Irish
Volunteer operatives would emerge from the Squad and the ASU. These
two units would be amalgamated to form an elite and highly feared unit
called the Dublin Guards. But in 1918 those developments lay ahead.
For the present, one thing was certain: the Irish revolutionary forces
would not conduct a conventional war as in the past. As far as the GHQ
leadership were concerned, fighting as a standard field army of the early
twentieth century had only led to defeat, the execution of their leaders and
the imprisonment of their army. Fighting a war 'by the rules' was never
going to win the Irish republic they sought to make a reality. The wearing
of Irish Volunteer uniform had been declared a criminal offence and the
carrying of arms or ammunition punishable by death under the terms of
the Defence of the Realm Regulations Act and the Restoration of Order
in Ireland Regulations Act, which were in force in Ireland during the
period 1914–1921.[41]

After 1918 the Irish Volunteers generally dispensed with wearing
formal uniforms in favour of civilian clothes, or 'civvies', in order to
blend in with the local population. Those on active service in the country
districts wore a trench coat, leather gaiters and leather boots. They carried
their ammunition in a cloth or leather bandolier. Hats worn reflected
the various fashions of the period. Irish Volunteers around Dublin wore
the civilian attire of their trade. Vinny Byrne, a member of the Squad,
moved around the city as a cabinetmaker, complete with wood shavings
and ruler in his pocket. Tradesmen such as Byrne also wore the traditional
flat cap. Others masqueraded as businessmen and wore a smart suit and
tie, complete with homburg hat and briefcase. In a class-conscious society,
British troops and policemen frequently allowed 'respectable' gentlemen
on 'urgent business' to pass through their search cordons, little realising
these men were the very IRA activists being sought. While on active service
in Dublin, Irish Volunteers frequently wore a muffler or scarf wrapped
around the lower part of the face with a cap pulled down over the eyes.

Such suspicious-looking dress prevented men being identified by witnesses in after-action round-ups by the British army. Weapons would be supplied for an operation and otherwise stored in a dump. The weapons were often carried by Cumann na mBan or Na Fianna members to an agreed location prior to an action. They were collected afterwards and safely stored. Some Irish Volunteers carried weapons on a full-time basis but this was very dangerous in a city where search patrols were commonplace. The British army referred to full-time Volunteers who carried weapons as 'Grade A ... the worst type ... a real bad hat'.[42]

Quite a number of the leading members of the Irish Volunteers in the War of Independence had been experienced members of the youth organisation, Na Fianna Éireann. This organisation was founded in 1909 by Bulmer Hobson (president), assisted by Countess Markievicz (vice-president), at 24 Lower Camden Street, Dublin. Helena Molony and Seán McGarry were also key members of the organisation. At the inaugural meeting, the first secretary, Pádraig O'Riain, said that Na Fianna should be a national boy scout movement with a dual purpose: to 'counteract the anglicising influence of the British Boy Scouts [Baden-Powell's scout movement] and fight for the Independence of Ireland'.[43] Markievicz designed and painted the flag of the movement, a 1798 pike over a Celtic sunburst. Each branch of the movement was called a 'Sluagh'. Training was comprehensive and based on British army training manuals and the Baden-Powell handbook, *Scouting for Boys*. The uniform was designed by Michael Lonergan, who worked in Clerys.[44] It consisted of a smart double-breasted green shirt, riding breeches, boots and slouch cap or 'acquired' Baden-Powell hat. Na Fianna spent a great deal of time training. Seán Kavanagh, an ex-British soldier, introduced the boys to marching and drilling and laid the foundations of a strong military movement in Na Fianna and subsequently the Irish Volunteers.[45] Na Fianna Éireann frequently camped in the grounds of St Enda's in Rathfarnham, the Irish-speaking school founded by Padraig Pearse, signatory of the 1916 Proclamation and leader of the Rising. From St Enda's, the boys of Na Fianna would go on tough route marches across the Dublin Mountains, taking in Three Rock Mountain, Kilmashogue, Tibbraden and the Hell Fire Club.[46] Na Fianna also engaged in cultural pursuits, staging dramas such as *The Saxon Shilling* by poet Padraic Colum. They also formed a pipers' band and among their members was the future composer of 'Amhrán na bhFiann', Peadar Kearney.

The boys of Na Fianna were also trained to shoot. Countess Markievicz owned a large country house, south of Malahide, called Belcamp. It was here the boys received training in firearms. They were delighted at the prospect, as Gearóid Ua h-Uallacháin recalled: 'I remember getting a real gun in my hands for the first time while on sentry duty. It was a great sensation.'[47] At Belcamp, Countess Markievicz had .22 rifles and a plentiful supply of ammunition available to Na Fianna for shooting practice. Raffles were held to raise funds, with the top prize being a rifle and 100 rounds. Revolvers were also given as prizes for good conduct and performance on duty. John Price, a corporal in Na Fianna, received a Smith & Wesson .45 revolver from his senior officer, Con Colbert.[48] A rifle cost the princely sum of £7 and it took Ua h-Uallacháin two months to raise the money to buy one.[49] Having a rifle and a revolver, or both, meant a great deal to these young men. Ua h-Uallacháin began to build up a personal arsenal by first obtaining a 'Howth' Mauser and later on paying five guineas for an SMLE with 100 rounds of ammunition. He also bought a Savage .32 automatic with 100 rounds for £2 5s.[50] Na Fianna were not just trained to shoot, as Ua h-Uallacháin revealed: 'We were taught to be aggressive to the RIC, and the boys in Camden Street would avail of every opportunity to attack the Protestant Church Boys Brigade who at that time were very strong and would always carry the Union Jack.'[51]

They were not afraid to act upon this aggression. In 1911 there was a demonstration held in Beresford Place in protest at the coronation of George V. In the ensuing fracas, which involved members of Na Fianna, the DMP were showered with stones and required mounted police to clear the streets of the protesters. This willingness by Na Fianna to take on the police continued after the Irish Volunteers were founded in November 1913. Ordered to take part in the Howth gunrunning in July 1914, members of Na Fianna, like their older counterparts in the Irish Volunteers, carried pickaxe handles or hurleys for self-defence.[52] During the 1916 Rising, a sluagh of Na Fianna were detailed to capture and destroy the British army Magazine Fort in the Phoenix Park. O/C of the operation was Paddy O'Daly, who had infiltrated the magazine as a workman in the months prior to the Rising. Among his detachment of Na Fianna were Eamon Murray and Gearoid Ua h-Uallacháin. During the raid, which failed, Ua h-Uallacháin did not hesitate to act when he considered it necessary to shoot anyone who interfered with their instructions. He shot two people: one was a British soldier on sentry duty at the magazine who had advanced on him with rifle and bayonet, the other a boy of seventeen called George Playfair. Playfair had initially been detained and was then released by O'Daly along with his mother and brother. Upon his release, Playfair ran to a DMP constable at Islandbridge to raise the alarm. Ua h-Uallacháin saw Playfair speak with the constable and then run to a nearby house for safety. He followed the boy and shot him just as the door opened.[53]

After 1916, Na Fianna continued their aggressive operations against the British presence in Ireland. On Sunday evening 10 July 1917 Count George Plunkett and Cathal Brugha were arrested as they attempted to address a public meeting at Beresford Place. As they were led away by the DMP a full-scale riot ensued between Irish republicans and the DMP. Stones and bottles were fired at the police, while they responded by drawing their batons and advancing into the crowd. Approximately 200 policemen were on duty. During the rioting, District Inspector (DI) Mills of the DMP, who had charge of four sergeants and forty constables, arrested both Plunkett and Brugha. As the inspector led his prisoners away from Beresford Place the policemen were kicked and punched by a large crowd who moved in around them. Na Fianna officer Eamon Murray suddenly stepped out of the crowd and gave DI Mills a ferocious blow with a hurley to the back of the head. Mills, bleeding profusely, collapsed onto the ground, blood pouring from his wound. In the confusion Murray made his escape and ran up Abbey Street. He was followed closely by Constable J. J. Dooley. Dooley grabbed Murray but the crowd closed in on him and knocked him to the ground, forcing him to release his grip on his prisoner. As Murray walked away, he pulled a revolver and pointed it at the constable.[54]

The 51-year-old DI Mills was taken to Jervis Street Hospital where doctors tried to save his life. The Westmeath man, with thirty-one years' service in the DMP, had suffered a fractured skull. He died of his injuries the following day, leaving behind a wife and three children. In November of the same year Ua h-Uallacháin and a party of boys raided a pawnbroker's shop on Ellis Quay. They got away with twenty revolvers.[55] Another operation involved holding up a DMP constable and burning down a British army recruiting banner hung across the ruins of the GPO. Na Fianna used lead weights tied to sods of turf soaked in paraffin oil. The blazing turf made short work of the recruiting banner.[56]

Members of Na Fianna who demonstrated leadership and the qualities of a soldier dedicated to Irish independence were sworn into the IRB.

When the Irish Volunteers organisation was reorganised in 1917 the leadership was provided by former Na Fianna members in leading a national military movement. Na Fianna also had its share of martyrs to inspire a new generation. Both Seán Heuston and Con Colbert, officers in Na Fianna, were executed by firing squad after the 1916 Rising. The young men who stepped forward to lead the revolutionary movement had been through 1916 and the experience of prison in Britain. They had established a bond of friendship through the anti-conscription campaign and had provided crucial logistical support for Sinn Féin in the various by-elections of 1917 and the general election of 1918. This bond would become even stronger in the coming War of Independence. In 1918, the Dublin Na Fianna was reorganised, with the older boys forming four groups called Commandos. These groups were distributed throughout the city. Their activities were similar to those of the Irish Volunteers and ranged from intelligence gathering to smuggling arms. Some members of Na Fianna would even engage in sniping British patrols. The Dublin Brigade could not have functioned as effectively as it did without Na Fianna. It was the experience of former Na Fianna members and experienced Irish Volunteers which Commandant Dick McKee was to draw upon to rebuild the Dublin Brigade. With McKee's leadership, the Dublin Brigade would become a formidable military outfit.

Commandant Richard McKee was behind the reorganisation of the Dublin Brigade after the 1916 Rising. By 1917, 25-year-old McKee was living with his widowed mother, Bridget, and younger brother, Patrick, in Finglas in north Dublin. His sisters, Johanna and Máire, were at boarding colleges. McKee was a printer by trade and worked at M. H. Gill & Son.[57] Pat McCrea, driver and member of the Squad, got to know McKee in 1913 when they both joined the 2nd Battalion of the Irish Volunteers. McKee was quick to rise through the ranks, becoming a lieutenant in E Company.[58] Their parades were held at Father Matthew Park in Fairview. Dick McKee was over six feet (1.8 metres) tall, which made him an imposing figure, even taller than the 'Big Fella' himself, Michael Collins. McCrea described McKee as the heart of the Dublin Brigade: 'He was outstanding, a wonderful military man and he had a wonderful word of command. He could handle any number of men ... There was no one like Dick ... he was tense and vibrant ... he was a great disciplinarian ... nor did he have any qualms about shooting G men or getting that work done.'[59]

Dick McKee, O/C Dublin
Brigade 1918–1920,
photographed when he was
nineteen or twenty. (Courtesy
the Military Archives)

McKee knew the risks he faced: three of his senior officers from the 2nd Battalion garrison at Jacob's biscuit factory had been executed in the aftermath of 1916 (Tomás MacDonagh, Major John MacBride and Michael O'Hanrahan). In June 1918, after a four-month stint in Dundalk Gaol, McKee left employment at the printer's to take up a full-time position as Dublin Brigade Commander. Like all Irish Volunteer officers he was elected.

Dick McKee was well known to the DMP and the detectives of G Division and endured a number of terms in prison. While incarcerated, he did not waste his time: he organised his fellow Volunteer inmates and gave them lectures on Irish history, military tactics and sniping. The content of his lectures was based on *The Art of Command* by Colonel Von Spohn and *Memoirs of Miles Byrne*.[60] Von Spohn's treatise reveals much of McKee's concept of battlefield command in handling the Dublin Brigade. Von Spohn argued for the establishment of a sharply defined command structure on precise and formal lines while allowing subordinate commanders independence and initiative in the field.[61] McKee would give his men their orders but recognised they had the right to independence of action while on operations, 'where bullets alone are enough to decide right and wrong'.[62] This was an important aspect of guerrilla warfare as carried out in Dublin and introduced the level of flexibility necessary to deal with the unexpected. The *Memoirs of Miles Byrne* told the life story of a veteran of the 1798 Rising and Robert Emmet's rebellion of 1803. Byrne left Ireland for France on Emmet's orders, where he joined an Irish regiment in the service of Napoleon Bonaparte and rose to become a battalion commander. His exploits were an inspiration to a younger generation. McKee also hoped to teach the lessons of the failures of the past so they would never be repeated. He especially emphasised the dangers of spies and informers.

In 1918, McKee took on the additional position of Director of Training at GHQ. He was still Dublin Brigade Brigadier and responsible for printing *An t-Óglach*. He was paid a salary of £25 per month.[63] He tirelessly walked the streets of Dublin, from meeting to meeting, sporting a distinctive thin black moustache and wearing his black leather coat.[64] He was assisted by a hardworking and dedicated vice-commandant called Michael Lynch, who had been elected at the same time as McKee.[65] Both men served in 1916 and worked with Irish Volunteer companies in confronting Unionist mobs during the South Armagh by-election in 1917.[66] McKee knew the men in his command and personally chose key individuals to undertake posts crucial to the success of the Dublin Brigade.

An influential officer who served on the Dublin Brigade staff with McKee was Peadar Clancy. In Dublin, Clancy worked in partnership with Commandant Tom Hunter, who had served as second in command to Tomás MacDonagh's 2nd Battalion at Jacob's biscuit factory in 1916.[67] Together they ran a shop called The Republican Outfitters at 94 Talbot Street.[68] This shop became an important communications centre for the Irish Volunteers but it came under close observation from DMP G Division and also British intelligence. Peadar Clancy organised and took part in a number of important raids, which supplied the Irish Volunteers with weapons. The planning and daring required to carry out such raids indicate Clancy was a man of action with a clear understanding of what was required if Ireland was to win her freedom. Clancy never shirked from that duty, nor from making some of the very difficult decisions associated with it.

Clancy also took considerable risks in some of the operations he undertook. Some operations were in pursuit of arms while others were dangerous reconnaissance missions. He contacted Captain Nicholas Laffan, who was a district inspector with the Dublin Alliance Gas Company and, as such, could gain access to any building in Dublin city, be it civilian or military, under the pretence of inspecting the gas company's installations. Clancy told Laffan that he needed to get into Arbour Hill Prison to reconnoitre the layout of the building and possibly arrange an escape attempt for Irish Volunteer prisoners. Together, they entered the prison and proceeded to check a gas meter. A military policeman approached Laffan and asked who was in charge of the work detail. When Laffan said he was in charge, the soldier pulled him aside and told him to get Clancy out as quickly as possible before he was recognised by someone else!

This close shave did not deter Clancy from his risk-taking. Laffan later brought Clancy, dressed as a gas company fitter, to both Islandbridge and Portobello Barracks.[69] Clancy sent a note to Laffan to meet him at Kingsbridge Station (now Heuston Station) and to bring a 'sandwich' – the code word for a gun. Laffan showed up on time with his 'sandwich' and joined Clancy in a car driven by a British army officer, who was secretly smuggling weapons to the Irish Volunteers. The three men drove to Islandbridge Barracks where they picked up two heavy cases containing revolvers and .38 ammunition. The consignment was then brought to a dump at Rutland Place. The 'sandwich' remained 'wrapped' on this occasion.

McKee and Clancy played a perpetually dangerous game of cat and mouse with the British in Dublin. They sought to avoid and evade the constables and detectives of the DMP and RIC who watched the republican circles as they went about their work.

The British system of control in Dublin consisted of the Royal Irish Constabulary, the Dublin Metropolitan Police and the British Army garrison. The DMP HQ was located in Dublin Castle. Established by the Constabulary of Ireland Act 1836,[70] the DMP was commanded by a chief commissioner. In 1919 Chief Commissioner Lieutenant Colonel Edgeworth Johnstone was in charge of seven divisions of the DMP identified by the letters A through to G. All of the divisions were assigned a Dublin city district save one: G Division, the detective division. A and B Divisions were positioned south of the River Liffey with A to the south-west and B to the south-east. C and D Divisions were positioned north of the Liffey

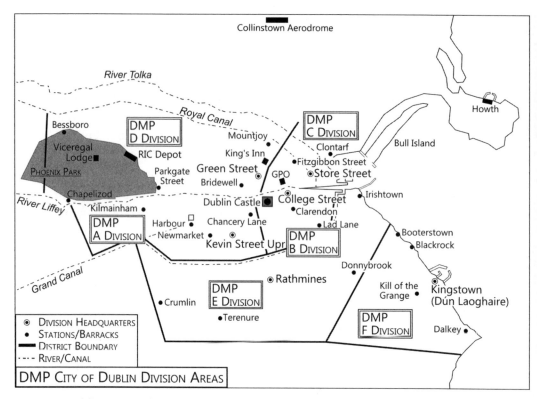

Dublin Metropolitan Police Divisions in Dublin city and suburbs. (With thanks to Eoin Brennan)

with C to the north-East and D to the north and north-west. E Division was assigned to the area directly south of the Grand Canal and ran from south of the Liffey at Chapelizod to the Merrion railway crossing on the coast. F Division encompassed the area surrounding Kingstown.

Each division was commanded by a superintendent under whom served a number of inspectors. Officers in the DMP were promoted from the ranks. In each divisional area were a number of police stations or barracks. A principal barracks served as the division HQ. The other ranks were sergeants and constables. As the political situation became more volatile in 1918 and into 1919, detectives of G Division began to carry guns and, in some cases, wore body armour.[71] DMP constables carried out traditional policing duties and were required to keep certain records of incidents in specific books which included: constables' tours of duty, bail book, prisoners book, habitual drunkards book, lost property book, military prisoners book, pedlars book, general dealers book, street cleaning by-law book and a refused-charges book.[72] In addition to these policing duties, the DMP also had the unenviable task of maintaining surveillance and keeping records of such on leading Irish revolutionaries and their associates likely to cause what was termed in official documents as 'disaffection' and 'sedition'. The surveillance operations fell to perhaps one of the most important divisions of any police force in the United Kingdom, G Division.

The detectives of G Division did a good job in keeping the leading members of Sinn Féin, the Irish Volunteers, Cumann na mBan, the Gaelic League, the GAA and the ITGWU under surveillance. In time they amassed a considerable amount of information about their movements and activities. The British war cabinet received a weekly report from the Lord Lieutenant, Lord French. This report included a typed briefing from the British military, the RIC and the DMP. In early December 1918, the British war cabinet, chaired by Prime Minister Lloyd George, were reading about the arrest of brothers Seamus and Peadar Breslin at the Columbcille branch of the Gaelic League and Sinn Féin Club after a five-chambered revolver and two field telephones were found in a police search. Peadar was charged and sentenced to two months in prison. Although it was not mentioned in the official report to cabinet, Peadar Breslin was O/C A Company, 1st Battalion, Dublin Brigade. The cabinet also read of the arrest of John McCluskey, caretaker at 44 Rutland Square, after thirty sticks of gelignite were found in the basement. The house was a meeting place for a section of Irish Volunteers and also The O'Rahilly Sinn Féin Club.[73]

The detectives of G Division were also watching all Sinn Féin offices and any political rallies held, particularly in the run-up to the general election of December 1918. A number of names began to appear with a certain regularity at all Sinn Féin events. Eoin MacNeill, Hanna Sheehy Skeffington, Rev. Fr Michael O'Flanagan, Harry Boland, Seán T. O'Kelly, Count Plunkett, Alderman Tom Kelly and P. J. Little were among the most prominent. But there were also a small number who, despite trying to go unnoticed, were spotted by the eagle-eyed G-Men. These included chief of staff of the Irish Volunteers Richard Mulcahy, O/C Dublin Brigade Dick McKee and the captain of Fingal Battalion Joseph V. Lawless.[74] Michael Collins was nowhere to be seen. The G-Men also had any number of valuable informers who kept watch in a less conspicuous manner than the detectives. The RIC Crime Special Branch had listed 105 'official' spies or informers working with them in 1890 for a price of £3 for significant

Royal Irish Constabulary
helmet and crest. (Courtesy
Dave Swift, Claíomh – Irish
Living History & Military
Heritage)

information or a sum of £100 per year. There were undoubtedly numbers
of touts who gave information or leads, for a variety of reasons.[75] With
all of the Sinn Féin and Irish Volunteer activity ongoing for a number of
years, coupled with the active surveillance of the detectives, the leading
members of the Irish Volunteers in Dublin were known to the DMP by
sight. This fact did not escape the attention of the Irish Volunteers GHQ,
with serious consequences for the G-Men in the early phase of the War of
Independence.

While the DMP policed the city, law and order in Dublin county
was kept by the Royal Irish Constabulary. The national training courses
for the RIC were carried out at the Depot in the Phoenix Park. Training
for police recruits, mounted police, officer training courses and firearms
training were run from here. Recruits at the Depot were also joined by
police officers from different parts of the British empire to undertake the
high standard of training delivered by the instructors. Of the recruits in
1913, 86 per cent were Catholic with 98 per cent of the force having been

born in Ireland.[76] This reflected the demographic of the Irish population at the time. While RIC officers tended to come from an Anglo-Irish Protestant and military background there was a continuous attempt to make the officer class more representative of the rank and file. By 1920, 40 per cent of the officers were Catholic. Officers, no matter what their social background, had life comparatively easy compared to their constables. The officers in general 'led a relaxed life attending theatres, tennis parties, hunting and shooting, and balls hosted by the gentry'.[77]

Life for the RIC constable began as a recruit in the Phoenix Park Depot and it was tough. Tom Carney joined the RIC on 1 October 1914, undertaking an initial six months' training at the Depot. There were a couple of companies of recruits in training when Carney arrived in Dublin. Conditions were spartan and resembled life in a military barracks. The recruits slept on straw mattresses but at least when they became constables they got an allowance of 3 shillings a year for the straw![78] The recruits received a great deal of foot drill for which there was a large barrack square. Later, they were trained in the use of revolver and rifle. On completion of their training they took an oath of allegiance to King George and to his successors. They also swore they would not belong to any secret society except the Society of Freemasons. This reference to the Freemasons was later removed from the oath.[79] Tom Carney completed his training in March 1915. His starting pay was just £80 12s per annum and would rise to £117 if he served for twenty years or more.[80] Constable Carney was dispatched to Dovea in County Tipperary for his first posting. His description of his duties would have been familiar to any RIC policeman beginning his service in County Dublin or indeed any county in Ireland.

On arrival in Dovea, Constable Carney was decked out in the distinctive dark green RIC uniform with patrol peaked cap. A snake-clasp black leather belt worn around the waist held a wooden baton and, more often as the occasion demanded, a revolver and holster with ammunition pouch. RIC constables also had a bolt-action six-round box magazine carbine available to them. A carbine was considered to have a barrel 20 inches (50.8cm) long or less. With the short barrel and a flattened bolt, this weapon was initially designed for cavalry use. By 1914 approximately 11,000 had been produced.[81] Carney patrolled with a senior constable or a sergeant until he got to know the people and the locality. Carney really enjoyed his early days in the RIC. He describes ploughing and harrowing with the local people. The local hurling team used to store their hurleys in the barracks. Carney would leave 'a sedate countryman' in the barracks to look after the rifles while he joined the locals playing hurling and Gaelic football.[82] If on duty as barrack orderly a constable slept in the day room and recorded events of the garrison in a diary. The orderly was up at 8 a.m. and his bedroll put away. The sergeant would parade the garrison, with or without equipment, at 9 a.m. Parade included an inspection of uniform and equipment and a period of drill in the barrack yard. An easy-going sergeant would just hold the parade in the day room and there would be no foot drill afterwards. RIC men were also rostered to have half an hour of daily education on police duties and Acts of Parliament. A daily duty lasted six hours and this included three patrol routes.

Some sergeants put their newly assigned constables through their paces, rostering them for a midnight patrol followed by an inspection at the end of their beat. Carney also related how, after 1916, extra 'Rising Patrols' were introduced between the hours of midnight and daylight. The local DI had to be informed of the times of these patrols as he might wish to show up for a surprise inspection. The RIC also introduced Mills bomb training for constables after 1916. Carney lamented the low pay and the five- to six-year wait before he could sit Civil Service examinations. The local DI had to recommend a constable as physically and mentally suitable for these exams. If a constable passed he went to Dublin for more training in police duties and drill.[83] Promotion and better pay were then possible but not certain.

In the rural Ireland of 1919 the RIC constable was responsible for a number of duties which included: collecting agricultural statistics, estimating the size of the potato crop, monitoring the sale of food and drink, assisting the coastguard in protecting wrecks from looters, escorting patients to asylums, undertaking the collection of data for national censuses, prosecution of illegal poteen distillers, checking lights on carts and bicycles, preventing animals from wandering on public roads, noting speeches at political meetings, preventing attendance at the wake of someone who had died of an infectious disease, and arresting beggars and tramps. By 1913, the RIC were responsible for the recording of twenty-nine official records.[84] All this policing was overseen by the head constable and the station or barrack sergeant. Eamon Broy, a detective with G Division DMP, who became an agent for Michael Collins, offered this assessment of the RIC: 'by and large the members of the RIC were personally honest and decent men with discipline and self-respect, and in peaceful times were influences for good in small communities. This applied particularly to Sergeants, who were often the most exemplary citizens in these communities.'[85]

The sergeant was the linchpin of the RIC. Well known throughout the locality in which they served and generally highly respected, sergeants patrolled with ease throughout their districts. This openness would make them particularly vulnerable throughout the War of Independence. The British military were to comment frequently on the lack of awareness among policemen of the danger they could be in. Even in districts that had been quiet for a time, the RIC would revert to the habits of a lifetime and patrol in the open along the roads and boreens, often stopping at a local shop or pub for cigarettes or light refreshment. This often led to an opportunistic IRA assassination of the unsuspecting policeman. A total of 425 policemen were killed during the War of Independence. Of the thirty-nine killed in Dublin city and county, nine were members of the DMP, twenty-three were members of the RIC and seven were members of the Auxiliary Division of the RIC. Another two were killed after the truce was agreed on 11 July 1921. Thirteen of those killed were from England, while the other twenty-six were from Ireland.[86]

In County Dublin the RIC was organised into three districts. The county HQ was at Howth. The senior RIC officer in a county was the county inspector (CI). In 1919, the honour fell to an astute and experienced officer, CI Andrew A. Roberts. RIC county barracks were not really military barracks but rather single- or two-storey houses. Two stations in south County Dublin, one DMP and one RIC, give an insight into the nature of RIC 'barracks'. Kill of the Grange was a DMP station in the F Division area. Built in 1849, it offered comparative comfort for the constables of the DMP. It was a two-storey building with a single-storey annex and a collection of outhouses. There was a sergeant's bedroom, four other bedrooms, a sergeant's room, a mess room, a reserve room and, downstairs, a kitchen. The single-storey annex housed two cells, a men's washroom, a drying room and toilet. There was also a ball alley, a rainwater tank and a well in the middle of the yard. In 1911 Kill of the Grange was stationed by three sergeants and eleven constables.[87] Four miles (6.4 km) from Kill of the Grange was the RIC barracks of Ballybrack. This station was the former Ballybrack Workmen's Club building and was policed by Sergeant Hurst and just three constables. The sergeant's wife and four children also lived at the station.[88] In an

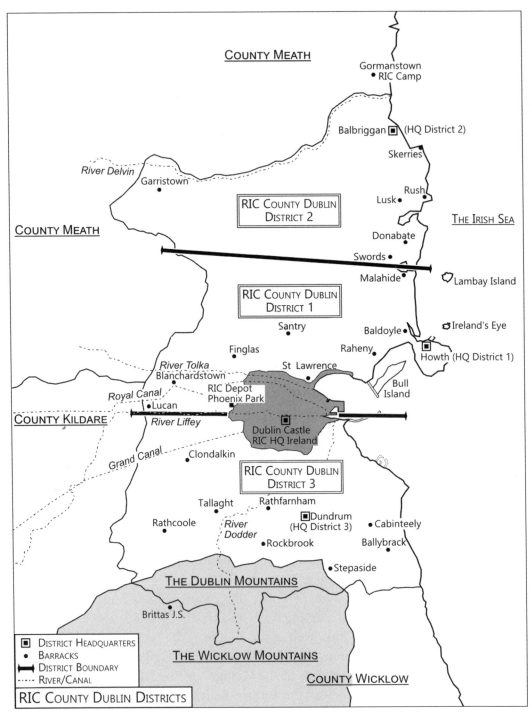

Royal Irish Constabulary County Dublin Districts. (With thanks to Eoin Brennan)

era with no radio, musicians were highly prized and Mrs Hurst's piano playing would have brought much enjoyment to the small barracks during the long winter evenings in the countryside of Ballybrack. By the end of 1918 the years of more relaxed country policing by the RIC were at an end. Troubled times were upon Ireland and nothing signified this more than the increased presence of the British Crown forces working in ever closer cooperation with the RIC.

Assisting the DMP and the RIC were the British army or Crown forces, as they referred to themselves, whose Irish GHQ was based at Parkgate on the western boundary of Dublin city adjacent to the Phoenix Park. This British army divisional HQ was officially formed on 1 January 1920 in response to increasing IRA activity. In December 1918, the recently appointed commander-in-chief of British forces in Ireland, Lieutenant-General Shaw, provided the British war cabinet with a list of troop requirements for Ireland during the expected substantial post-First World War demobilisation period. In the years after the First World War the British army was under considerable pressure as it faced a number of demands for its services. In spite of the pressure, its war-footing strength of 3.9 million in 1918 would be reduced to 250,000 by 1921 due to financial constraints.[89] After the armistice in November 1918, garrison duties for British troops in Germany tied down numbers of battalions while others were needed to oversee plebiscites in parts of the newly emerging countries from the former empires of the defeated Germany, Austria-Hungary and Ottoman Turkey. British troops were also serving in the Baltic states and in Russia as partial support for the Imperialist White Russians who faced the Bolshevik Red Army in the Russian Civil War. In addition to these duties, the British would soon be facing an Egyptian revolt and a Turkish fight for independence. Despite all of these demands placed on the Crown forces, the British cabinet began the demobilisation of the wartime forces. This places Lieutenant-General Shaw's request for more troops in a context of severe restrictions on British resources. Shaw considered the following should be retained in Ireland:

(a) 15 Infantry Battalions each at full peace establishment of 800. 24 Cyclists Units each at an establishment of 460.
(b) 3 Infantry Battalions for guarding Railways, Cable Landings, Forts, and 5 R.D.C. [Royal Defence Corps] Coys or their equivalent number of Infantry for guarding Vulnerable Points and Naval Stores.

(c) Artillery, R.E [Royal Engineers], Armoured Cars, Tanks, and R.A.F. [Royal Air Force] as at present. 2 Cavalry Regiments to be stationed at the Curragh. R.G.A. [Royal Garrison Artillery] to be reduced to peace establishment.'[90]

The British troops stationed in Ireland in December 1918 numbered 94,034. This number was not intended to occupy Ireland but rather was a mix of regiments intended for various purposes. Included were the Irish regiments of the British army such as the Royal Dublin Fusiliers, the Inniskilling Fusiliers and the Connaught Rangers, who had recruiting and training depots in Ireland. There were also British battalions stationed in Ireland for home defence or training prior to being shipped overseas. Finally, there were British battalions assigned to garrison duties throughout Ireland. Of the 94,034 listed by Lieutenant-General Shaw, 43,156 were preparing for overseas postings, 9,418 were Home Defence units. A surprising 27,284 were listed as temporarily unfit while 14,176 were certified 'non-effective' due to hospitalisation or awaiting discharge from such.[91] In 1918 the Dublin area was garrisoned by nine battalions of infantry and some RAF units. In support of the British infantry battalions were also cavalry, field and garrison artillery. Initially three and then two RAF units or 'Flights' operated to the north at Collinstown (which would become Dublin Airport) and to the west and south-west of the city, at Cookstown (Belgard Road, Tallaght) and Baldonnel (Casement Aerodrome). The Dublin District was a large British army-garrisoned area of Ireland. In 1918 it included Dublin county and city and also Carlow, Drogheda, Galway, Kildare (including Curragh and Newbridge), King's County (Laois), Leitrim, Longford, Mayo, Meath, Queen's County (Offaly), Roscommon, Sligo, Westmeath and Wicklow.[92]

The British war cabinet responded to Shaw's request for troops by sending reinforcements of five infantry battalions, one machine-gun battalion and four tanks to Ireland in May 1919. Shaw immediately requested a further three infantry battalions and one machine-gun battalion. Clearly responding to the now escalating trouble in Ireland, he wished to have a small reserve on hand which could be dispatched to a 'disaffected area without seriously weakening the garrison of the more important towns'.[93] Shaw's listing for the 'strength of effective troops in the Command on 30 April 1919' undoubtedly was cause for concern at British HQ at Parkgate. Of the 34,274 troops listed as the 'Total Effective

Strength' only 6,634 were stated to be 'available for Garrison in Ireland'.[94] Within a year, Shaw would be facing a major crisis in Ireland, the wrath of the war cabinet and a major shift in British policy in Ireland. What would cause this shift in British policy was the expansion of a military campaign by the Irish Volunteers. This campaign was spearheaded by a new Irish Volunteer intelligence department and two 'Special Duties' units answerable directly to Michael Collins alone. These units would be amalgamated to form a group known as 'the Squad'.

3

Collinstown, Assassinations & Ashtown

IRA operations in Dublin, 1919

On 21 January 1919, at 3.30 p.m., Dáil Éireann sat in session for the very first time. The Sinn Féin Party had campaigned throughout the election on the basis of withdrawing from Westminster and establishing an independent Irish parliament. The Dáil assembled in a packed Mansion House in Dawson Street, Dublin. Cathal Brugha, as the newly elected TD for Waterford, was proposed and seconded as Ceann Comhairle or Speaker. Having emphasised the important work which lay before the Dáil and asking Rev. Fr Michael O'Flanagan to give a blessing, Brugha called the roll of TDs for the island of Ireland. Of the seventy-three Sinn Féin elected members of the new parliament, only twenty-seven were present on this momentous day, the rest being imprisoned by the British. The Unionist TDs, or MPs as they preferred to be called, refused to attend the breakaway Irish parliament.

The new Irish parliament reaffirmed its commitment to achieving recognition for Ireland as a free and independent nation. The Dáil called upon all the free nations of the earth to support Ireland's claim to nationhood at the Paris Peace Conference at Versailles.[1] Among the gathering of the new TDs were some of those elected for Dublin, city and county. A number of them were members of the Irish Volunteers. One, the President of Cumann na mBan, Countess Markievicz, was the first woman ever elected in a parliamentary election in Britain and Ireland. Ten others out of the fourteen TDs elected for Dublin in the 1918 general election were Sinn Féin, of whom five were senior officers of the Irish Volunteers/IRA.

This first session of Dáil Éireann lasted only two days. In that short inauguration eleven departments were established to begin the process of the government of Ireland by her own people. It would be April before they met again. After the assembly departed, the Secretary to the Dáil and a member of the Irish Volunteers, Diarmuid O'Hegarty, drew up a report.[2] This document, dated 20 February 1919, despite being intended for TDs, soon found its way onto the desk of the RIC County Inspector for Dublin, Andrew Roberts. It drew attention to the strong international interest in the opening of the first Dáil by pointing out the presence of up to sixty foreign press representatives who attended the first sitting. Since then, however, English propaganda had cut Ireland off from the outside world. The Secretary declared: '... the British Army of occupation now stands between the People's freely elected Government and the Laws Dáil Éireann make. That obstacle cannot be removed at present due to the strength of the superior armed force. England hold Ireland against the clearly expressed will of the people.'[3]

With Dáil Éireann having its first sitting and the shooting of two RIC men in Tipperary on the same day, it was clear to CI Roberts that the republican movement had not only lost its fear of British power structures in Ireland but was now actively undermining it. January in County Dublin had started badly for Roberts when the clock tower of the Church of Ireland church in Swords was daubed with paint in protest at the local population's association with the British military. Matters improved later in the month when Roberts reported that the British Crown forces in Rathfarnham were working with the local RIC to prevent illegal drilling by the Irish Volunteers. The relative calm introduced by the British troops did not last long. On 19 January, just two days before the Dáil had its first session, two parties of RIC constables patrolling the Dublin Mountains were attacked by a force of fifty Irish Volunteers engaged in manoeuvres at Three Rock Mountain. Sergeant Lawton and Constable Jones were injured and were 'badly treated, disarmed and deprived of their equipment'.[4] CI Roberts stated his concern that this incident marked a serious change in the attitude of Sinn Féin towards the RIC and DMP, who they were now demanding should be driven out of the county and country. He added: 'Driving such dangerous ideas into the heads of the youth I am sure will lead to further outrage.'[5]

By the end of February, Roberts had ordered all RIC constables in County Dublin to be on the alert against surprise attacks and had issued

Inspector-General Byrne's instruction that, from now on, all RIC patrols were to be armed. Roberts concluded his January report: 'Altogether I consider we are passing through critical times.'[6] Just how critical would soon emerge, as threats and intimidation moved into a more lethal phase of pinpointed armed attacks. The 'obstacle' identified by the Secretary in his report to the Dáil was, however, not just the British military. The real threat to Irish independence as perceived by Michael Collins was not the British army but the RIC and, in particular, G Division of the DMP. Before any action could be taken against the enemy, however, weapons and ammunition would be required. The Dublin Brigade of the Irish Volunteers were first to strike.

By March 1919 over 800 men were employed building the RAF base of Collinstown Aerodrome. Among those employees were a number of tradesmen from the Dublin Brigade of the Irish Volunteers, namely Peadar Breslin, Christopher 'Kit' O'Malley and Paddy Holohan. Tom Byrne, O/C of the 1st Battalion at the time, was planning a 'big stunt' to raid the aerodrome and capture the seventy-five rifles in the guardroom. Michael Lynch told Byrne to see Brigade O/C Dick McKee because this large operation required careful planning.[7] From then on it was a Dublin Brigade 'job' planned by Kit O'Malley involving up to forty men from A and F Companies 1st Battalion with Captain Paddy Holohan as O/C of the operation. A number of cars were requisitioned for the night. Alderman Corrigan's car was driven by Owen Cullen while Pat McCrea took a car from Murphy Brothers of South Great George's Street.

McKee ordered Holohan not to engage in gunfire if possible, 'to endeavour to have a bloodless victory'[8] and so the Volunteers were given knuckledusters and stiletto blades attached.[9] Morphine was administered to the two large Airedale dogs that patrolled the guardhouse at about 4 p.m. by some of the 'workers' on the site. It only made them drowsy but they presented no problem to the Volunteers. Paddy Holohan assembled his men at Rutland Square at 10.30 p.m. Changing into British uniform, the unit headed north out of the city to Collinstown. At midnight the Dublin Brigade began their first major operation of the War of Independence.

Lieutenant Breslin approached the rear of the guardhouse while Captain Holohan's unit crawled towards the front. To avoid revealing their identity, the Volunteers were masked and had been assigned numbers. Volunteer Dan McDonnell had pulled a stocking over his head with two slits for eyes. He was armed with a five-chambered Iver Johnson revolver and, of course, his knuckleduster with stiletto blade.[10] When the sentry on patrol went into the guardhouse, the Volunteers rushed the building. The fourteen soldiers inside were mostly asleep and taken completely by surprise. They were unable to alert the garrison of 500 only a few hundred yards away. The Volunteers tied up each soldier with his hands behind his back and suspended him by the feet from the rafters.

The weapons haul – 75 SMLEs, 73 bayonets, 4,000 rounds of ammunition and some webbing kits – was hurriedly transferred to two of the waiting cars.[11] One driven by Owen Cullen travelled to the Naul in north County Dublin while the other made for Dublin city. Pat McCrea, driving a Model T Ford, was last to leave the aerodrome. Twelve Volunteers were packed into and hanging off the car as it sped back to Dublin.[12] The Volunteers had intended to take some of the British Army Crossley Tenders but could not get them started. Instead, they used crowbars and sledgehammers to smash up the engines. The rest of the Volunteers dispersed into the darkness from which they had emerged.

For driver Owen Cullen, the excitement was only just beginning. In his car were forty-nine rifles and about 2,000 rounds of ammunition. Altogether it weighed nearly three quarters of a ton. After five miles or so, the weight caused one of the tyres to burst. Cullen continued until he met with the Fingal Brigade Vice-Commandant Michael Rock and Battalion QM William Rooney who transferred the rifles to the dump at Walshestown. The boxes of ammunition were placed in a derelict cottage between St Margaret's and Duncoghley.[13] Owen Cullen drove the car, with one wheel on a bare rim, westwards for a few more miles until the car could go no further. He abandoned Alderman Corrigan's car on the side of the road and walked the 16 miles (27 km) back to Dublin. The Alderman was informed and duly reported his car as 'stolen' to the police, who had located it in the meantime. Over the course of the following month, QM of the 2nd Battalion of the Dublin Brigade, Mick McDonnell, transferred most of the weapons back into the city using his motorcycle sidecar. In a concerted effort to locate the missing weapons, RIC County Inspector Roberts ordered his constables on constant searches, but not a rifle nor a round was to be found. In his monthly report for March, Roberts stated that it was impossible to make any headway in the investigation. He wrote: 'In fact if any one of them [locals] were known to give us any helpful information, his life would be in danger so strong is the intimidatory influence of Sinn Féin.'[14]

For the Dublin Brigade, the Collinstown Raid was an outstanding success. It enhanced the already growing reputation of Dick McKee and a few others, such as Mick McDonnell. The element of surprise had been achieved, the weapons and ammunition captured with no casualties save the pride of the British troops in the guardhouse. For ranking Volunteers who took part, like Mick Magee, it was a real boost for morale. Volunteers like him would face significant danger in the coming war and they would not always be so fortunate.

While the Dublin Brigade were active in arming themselves and preparing for the inevitable conflict with the British and the RIC, Michael Collins was in the process of establishing an intelligence department within the Irish Volunteers. Through the actions of detective officers in G Division of the DMP, Joe Kavanagh, Jim McNamara and Eamon Broy, Collins received police documents and files relating to Sinn Féin and the Irish Volunteers. Kavanagh, who worked in Dublin Castle, also passed on revolvers and ammunition.

The connection Collins established with Broy was to be of major importance. After 1916 Broy had read captured documents from the Volunteer movement. While he studied the reasons behind the failure of previous insurrections in Ireland he came to the conclusion that he wanted to assist in the regrowth of the Volunteer organisation. The detective got his cousin Patrick Tracy to approach Harry O'Hanrahan and his sisters, who owned a shop at 384 North Circular Road and whose brother Michael had been executed in 1916. Through this shop, Broy passed on hundreds of documents from G Division, from official secret reports to orders for raids and arrests. Eventually, after he had more than proved his worth, Broy was called to a meeting with Michael Collins at the home of Mrs Micheál Ó Foghludha at 5 Cabra Road, near Phibsborough.[15] During the meeting Collins expressed the view that if the Volunteers did not employ violence the movement would collapse. He was also aware of the 'extreme risks' associated with such a policy. Tim Healy, a future governor general of Ireland, had already told him that the Volunteers were all 'stark raving mad' and 'had not the ghost of a chance by physical force'.[16] Collins believed the opposite: that nothing would be obtained from the British through constitutional means. Broy agreed with Collins and, no matter how dangerous things might become, was willing to continue his support for the Volunteers. The two began a long discussion.

Focusing on the psychology of training methods used by the RIC on young recruits and how it changed their outlook in a short time, Collins and Broy decided 'it was necessary to melt down the RIC'.[17] The ruthless campaign against the RIC about to be waged by the Irish Volunteers was the brainchild of Michael Collins. It would feature a combination of physical and psychological warfare by attacking RIC barracks and burning out vacated sites. This would force the RIC to withdraw to larger towns. Psychological pressure would be employed by boycotting the RIC in towns and communities while encouraging family members of RIC men to undermine individual constables' loyalty to the police. After these tactics had been initiated those who remained with the RIC would be considered a 'hard core'.[18] A pitiless war would be waged on them. As for the DMP, Collins ordered that uniformed members were not to be attacked. This order did not always hold. Any DMP member of G Division or any other Division who showed any zeal against the Volunteers would be open to attack.[19] Collins believed that through the actions described both the RIC and G Division of the DMP could be neutralised and the British hold on Ireland seriously weakened. Collins stated:

> To paralyse the British machine it was necessary to strike at individuals. Without her spies England was helpless. It was only by means of their accumulated and accumulating knowledge that the British machine could operate. Without their police throughout the country, how could they find the man they 'wanted'? Without their criminal agents in the capital how could they carry out that 'removal' of the leaders that they considered essential for their victory? Spies are not so ready to step into the shoes of their departed confederates as are soldiers to fill up the front line in honourable battle. And, even when the new spy stepped into the shoes of the old one, he could not step into the old man's knowledge.[20]

The tactics used against individual RIC men, G Men of the DMP in particular, were described by Adjutant Harry Colley of the Dublin Brigade: 'Those who did not desist were again warned and those who continued to act after that were man-handled. Following this when they persisted they were shot.'[21] Denis O'Brien was the first detective of G Division to receive the manhandling treatment. As part of his duties, O'Brien noted the movements of various Volunteers. He was accosted one evening by a group of Volunteers and tied to railings.[22]

The 'manhandling' tactics were applied by the members of the Dublin Brigade to just about anyone who they perceived would not fall into line with the aspirations of the Irish republic. One evening Pat McCrea, driver with Dublin Brigade Transport, met Michael Collins at the Brigade HQ in the Dublin Typographical Institute, 35 Lower Gardiner Street. Collins asked McCrea what had been done with the two painters at the Post Office who had refused to join a one-day strike in sympathy with hunger strikers in Mountjoy Gaol. McCrea related how three Irish Volunteers attended the Painters' Union meeting in Rutland Square and 'arrested' the painters. They were brought for a night-time drive in the country out past Artane, taken into a field and tied back to back. Their heads were painted with red lead paint. McCrea and his fellow Volunteers rubbed it well into their hair. McCrea added: 'Otherwise, we did not ill-treat them in any way.'[23] According to McCrea, Collins enjoyed hearing about this incident very much and approved of the methods used. The two non-striking painters were found and freed the following morning. They were not seen in Dublin again.

In mid-April 1919 an IRB meeting was arranged for Vaughan's Hotel at Rutland Square. This was a well-known haunt for Collins, Sinn Féin and IRA GHQ Staff. When the meeting concluded, Collins said to one of his old Irish Volunteer colleagues from London, Seán Nunan, 'Let's go for a walk'. Nunan was now a member of C Company 2nd Battalion of the Dublin Brigade. Collins had arranged a visit to the G Division Offices at 1 Great Brunswick Street with Detective Eamon Broy. Collins and Nunan arrived at 12.15 a.m. Only Detective Broy was on duty. It was the night shift, from 10 p.m. till 6 a.m. Broy led the two men upstairs to Inspector Neil McFeely's office and gave them access to large steel safe, which was really a secured room. There was no electric light so Collins produced some candles from his pocket. The two men spent the small hours studying the G Division files on the Irish Volunteers.[24]

Collins was looking to find out exactly what the British knew about the Irish Volunteers, to discover who the British knew and, more important, who they did not know. This would allow him to choose people unknown to the police and thus more difficult to track down. Collins also wanted to understand the mentality behind the records. He aimed to adapt and improve upon RIC structures and techniques and incorporate them into Irish Volunteer intelligence and military units. As Collins left the 'secure' room in Inspector McFeely's office around 4.30 a.m. he took with him one book. Collins was not after souvenirs: this book was a list of phone messages received by DMP stations during the Rising, including calls from loyalists reporting the positions of Irish Volunteer snipers around the city. He now had in his hands a list of families, houses and businesses that the Irish Volunteers could not trust. This book was a potential list of spies and informers. Collins took this book with him everywhere for the next year and a half until it was reclaimed by the Auxiliaries in a raid.[25]

Collins and Nunan stepped out into the early morning Dublin air, much to the relief of Broy, who must have been a near nervous wreck. The timing of the visit to the G Division Offices was fortunate: the files and books viewed by Collins and Nunan were removed to a more secure location at Dublin Castle shortly afterwards. Inspector McFeely himself fell under suspicion from his superiors of not being robust enough in the application of his duties.

While Collins was in the early stages of gathering intelligence on the RIC and DMP, diplomatic efforts were afoot to secure recognition for an independent Ireland at the Paris Peace Conference. This was the implementation of the Sinn Féin political strategy developed in 1918. At the meeting of the first Dáil, Seán T. O'Ceallaigh, TD for Dublin College Green, had been sent to Paris with the tall order of securing a hearing for Ireland's case for independence and to be recognised and admitted to the League of Nations. Because American President Woodrow Wilson had declared that every nation had the right to self-determination, Dáil Éireann appealed directly to him. There was considerable pressure on Wilson to recognise the Irish claim. An American delegation from the Friends of Ireland had arrived in Dublin on a fact-finding mission in May 1919. Both the US Senate and Congress had passed resolutions requesting the American representation at the Paris Conference to secure a hearing for the Irish diplomatic mission. Letters were sent by Irish government ministers and by Sean T. O'Ceallaigh to President Wilson and to French President Georges Clemenceau rejecting Britain's claim to represent Ireland. Finally, on 11 June 1919, President Wilson met with the American delegation in Paris. The meeting dealt a blow to Irish hopes. Wilson quoted the agreement that no small nation should appear before it without unanimous consent of the Committee of Four: the USA, Britain, France and Italy. The British had blocked agreement on Ireland's diplomatic effort. The apparent double standard of this stance was not lost among the British themselves. Hugh Martin, journalist with *The Daily*

News in England, wrote on 14 May 1919: '... and in the end we shall have to give up either the hypocrisy of pretending concern about freedom in Czechoslovakia or the infamy of stamping on freedom in Ireland. The issue may be delayed but it is not in doubt.'[26] The Sinn Féin government did not concede. Seán T. O'Ceallaigh continued his efforts in Paris.

In June 1919 de Valera departed for the United States. He had escaped from Lincoln Gaol on 3 February in an operation organised and led by Michael Collins. In going to America de Valera was hoping to use the Irish vote as leverage in the coming US presidential election to gain recognition for the Irish republic. He also planned to use his tour of American cities to raise important funds for Dáil Éireann. This funding would be used by Michael Collins as Minister for Finance to run the government of Ireland, establish its civil service and implement its legislation. In America, de Valera, as President of the Irish republic, attracted large audiences and gave voice to the Sinn Féin government.

Diplomatic efforts and intrigue also took place in Rome in an attempt to prevent Pope Benedict XV from condemning the Irish attempts to achieve independence. In Rome, the Irish College and, in particular, Monsignor John Hagan[27] proved instrumental in facilitating Irish efforts in presenting their case to the Holy See. The diplomatic efforts would continue as an attempt to secure an Irish republic. But for now, the window for a diplomatic solution had been lost.

After carrying out an assessment of RIC and British intelligence operations, Michael Collins moved to act decisively. He assembled a group of young men from the Dublin Brigade. They were called in to take on the 'hard core' of the RIC. In mid-July 1919 Commandant Dick McKee called a meeting at 35 North Great George's Street. Any policeman observing those entering the building would have thought it was a tradesmen's union meeting. Walking up the steps were painters, printers, bakers, electricians, carpenters, grocer's assistants and clerks.[28] The men all had one thing in common: they were all members of the 2nd Battalion Dublin Brigade. Out of this assembled group McKee and Mick McDonnell selected a number of men. McKee then asked those selected if they had any objections to shooting enemy agents. A number objected and left. Those who remained were told they would be assigned to 'special duties'. This meeting was the origin of two independent part-time Special Duties Units that would eventually amalgamate to form a full-time unit called the Squad.[29]

Members of IRA GHQ intelligence and the Squad photographed during the truce in 1921. Photograph was supplied by Captain Seán O'Connell, member of D Company 2nd Battalion Dublin Brigade who joined IRA GHQ Intelligence in March 1921. Identified are: *Back row (l–r)*: Sean O'Connell, Joe Dolan, Jim Slattery and Paddy Griffin; *front row, on left*: Charlie Byrne (aka 'The Count'). (Courtesy the Military Archives)

Unit One was formed in mid-July 1919 under the command of Mick McDonnell or 'Mick Mac' as the men called him. His men, Tom Kehoe, Jim Slattery and Vinny Byrne, were all from E Company. Mick McDonnell was a close friend of Michael Collins. He also knew Dick McKee very well, having served in 1916 and been in Knutsford Prison together. McDonnell was a tense and excitable character who put a great deal of effort into every order he was given. Jim Slattery found McDonnell a hard taskmaster: 'Mick Mac was first stiff with us and strict. When I was holding up the mail van I caught the horse and naturally he slipped on the cobbles as I held on to him. He groused at me for that for he had to have his grouse even though he got a good haul of mails that day.'

Pat McCrea, who worked closely with Mick McDonnell, said he 'only believed in hard work and no amusement.'[30] McDonnell had gone to a great deal of trouble getting two cars for exclusive Squad use. One Saturday, Collins asked McCrea to get the use of one of the cars for a trip to County Meath. McCrea was given a note from McKee seeking

McDonnell's permission to release the cars. McDonnell was ill and in bed at the time. He read the note three or four times and then said 'I hope this is not a bloody joy ride.' After some haggling McDonnell agreed to give Collins the use of the car on condition that it was used only for official business and that it be returned safely. McCrea was assigned as driver while Collins took Dick McKee and Austin Stack on the journey. They went to Dunshaughlin to meet Seán Boylan O/C of Dunboyne area and to Maynooth to meet local O/C Paddy Colgan.

On the return to Dublin the back axle broke at Islandbridge, just down from the British army barracks. There was nothing for it but to abandon the car. McCrea went straight to McDonnell to get the expected telling-off over with. McDonnell greeted McCrea with a frosty 'Are you only coming back now?' When McCrea told McDonnell where the car was, he jumped up in the bed and swore, cursing Collins, McKee and Stack, saying that he went to a lot of trouble to get the cars for the use of the Squad and not for driving the brass hats around the country on a Sunday joyride. McCrea contacted Joe Lawless the following morning. They drove to Islandbridge and fitted a new axle on McDonnell's car. McCrea reported it to McDonnell who said he realised it was not his fault but that of 'the other G------s.'[31]

Just after the formation of McDonnell's Special Duties Unit, the first order was issued. They were to shoot Detective Sergeant Patrick Smyth. The Volunteers referred to him as 'The Dog'. Orders to kill particular members of the RIC and DMP were issued by Collins but usually delivered by Liam Tobin or Tom Cullen. McDonnell ordered Jim Slattery to go to Drumcondra Bridge and to take Tom Kehoe and Tom Ennis. Mick Kennedy, who knew Smyth by sight, was also to go as he would identify the man to be shot. Slattery related how they waited for Smyth for five nights and when Smyth eventually passed, Mick Kennedy was not sure if it was him and the opportunity passed.

A few nights later on 30 July, McDonnell's unit was waiting for Smyth again. It was after 11 p.m. when the detective sergeant stepped off the tram at Botanic Avenue and walked across Drumcondra Bridge. When he reached the corner of Millmount Avenue, the Volunteers opened fire. In spite of being hit in the back, Smyth ran for his life. Slattery was astonished that Smyth could keep running as another ten or eleven shots rang out, zipping all around him. Smyth was hit again in the leg and hip. He was unarmed at the time of the attack so could not return fire. His young son and daughter came to his aid after hearing the gunfire from their home at 51 Millmount Avenue. McDonnell's unit melted away and an ambulance was called. Smyth lingered on in the Mater Hospital until 8 September, when he died of his wounds.[32] The day after the attempt on Detective Smyth, Mick McDonnell angrily rounded on his men for making 'a right mess' of it.[33]

In early September Mick McDonnell had another 'job' for his unit. Detective Constable Daniel Hoey was providing strong inspiration for the other detectives in G Division and had himself narrowly missed catching Michael Collins one evening. Hoey had spent a number of years following and noting the movements and activities of leading Volunteers. Collins believed Hoey's detailed notes on Seán Mac Diarmada and his identification of him in Richmond Barracks were the main factors responsible for the IRB leader's execution in 1916.[34] Consequently, Mick McDonnell received his orders to shoot Hoey. After the botched attempt on Detective Smyth, McDonnell's unit had dispensed with their .38 revolvers and acquired .45s, which had much greater stopping power. The Special Duties Unit did not intend leaving any more of their intended targets alive. Thus, on the night of 12 September, McDonnell, Slattery and Ennis hovered around Townsend Street waiting for Hoey to report back to Great Brunswick Street DMP station at the end of his duty. As the detective approached the garage door of the station Mick McDonnell opened fire. His first shot cut Detective Hoey's watch chain. The 32-year-old Offaly man died instantly.

With two detectives now assassinated, Michael Collins increased the pressure on G Division further and ordered the formation of a second Special Duties Unit under the command of Captain Paddy O'Daly. Born Patrick Daly in 1888, he also went under the names Paddy O'Daly and Pádraig Uá Dálaigh during his lifetime. His father was a retired policeman and the family lived on Belview Terrace, Clontarf.[35] After leaving school Paddy became an apprentice carpenter. In 1907, at nineteen years of age, he joined the IRB. O'Daly was strongly influenced by his brothers Seamus and Frank, who were already members. Paddy also joined the Colonel John O'Mahony Hurling Club at Dollymount and this introduced him to the Gaelic language and culture of music and dance.[36] In 1910 O'Daly married Margaret Gillies, known as Daisy.[37] He joined Na Fianna Éireann and was involved in the Howth gunrunning in 1914. In 1916 he demonstrated the determination, resolute conviction and ability to organise others that

IRA GHQ Squad 1919–1921[38]

Name	Rank/Position	Original company and battalion of origin in the Dublin Brigade
1st Phase 1919–1920 (part-time)		
Mick McDonnell	**Brigade QM & O/C Squad**	1916 veteran & QM 2nd Bn (formerly E Coy); had a breakdown in health
(Special Duties Unit 1)		
Tom Kehoe	E Coy, 2nd Bn	
Jimmy Slattery	Section Commander, later promoted to Lieutenant	E Coy 2nd Bn; lost a hand on the Custom House job.
Vinny Byrne	Volunteer	E Coy 2nd Bn
(Special Duties Unit 2)		
Paddy O'Daly	**Captain & O/C Squad (succeeded Mick McDonnell)**	B Coy 2nd Bn
Joe Leonard	Lieutenant	B Coy 2nd Bn
Ben Barrett (transferred from 1st Bn)	Volunteer	B Coy 2nd Bn
Tom Kilcoyne	Lieutenant	B Coy, 2nd Bn; was promoted to Captain and remained an O/C B Company eventually Battalion Commander arrested on the Custom House operation

Seconded to assist the Squad while on the run in 1919 and 1920 were senior officers of the 3rd Tipperary Brigade: Seán Treacy; Dan Breen; Seamus Robinson; Seán Hogan.

2nd Phase 1920 (full-time Squad with five additional members)		
Seán Doyle	Lieutenant	2nd Bn. Mortally wounded in Custom House operation, 25 May 1921.
Paddy Griffin		No information has been found
Eddie Byrne		No information has been found
Mick Reilly		Dead by 1940s
Jimmy Conroy	Volunteer	F Coy 2nd Bn

3rd Phase 1920–21 (full-time Squad with additional members selected to strengthen the unit)		
Ben Byrne		D Coy 1st Bn
Frank Bolster		No information has been found.
Mick Keogh		C Coy 2nd Bn

3rd Phase 1920–21 (full-time Squad with additional members selected to strengthen the unit) *(continued)*		
Mick Keogh *(continued)*		C Coy 2nd Bn
		Comdt D. Lyons O/C 38th Mallow, Co. Cork witnessed the death of Capt. Keogh. A grenade exploded in Keogh's hand during live grenade exercise: 'He fell and I caught him just as his knees were touching the ground. I pulled him into the door. Just as he fell into my arms he said three times "The Crucifix is in my back pocket." I tried his back pocket and could not find it. I then placed my own Beads in his left hand and said an Act of Contrition. The Doctor and the orderly arrived then and attended him. The Priest arrived and attended him before he died'.[39]
Mick Kennedy		A Coy 3rd Bn
Bill Stapleton		B Coy 2nd Bn
Sam Robinson		No information has been found
M. O'Reilly		No information has been found
Pat McCrea		B Coy 2nd Bn
Joe Byrne		No information has been found
Seamus (James) Brennan		No information has been found
Paddy Drury		F Coy 1st Bn
Sean O'Connell		D Coy, 2nd Bn

became the hallmarks of his character in the following years. He was a very tough Volunteer and did not hesitate when making decisions. During the Rising he led an attack on the Magazine Fort in the Phoenix Park. It was only the error of lighting a fire in the wrong part of the magazine that thwarted Na Fianna's efforts to destroy it. O'Daly was wounded later in the week defending the Four Courts from British attack. After the Rising he spent time in Kilmainham Gaol before being sent to Frongoch. After his release in December 1916, O'Daly continued to work as a carpenter. By 1919 Paddy and Daisy had four children.[40]

On 29 January 1919, O'Daly was arrested along with eleven of his men from B Company while holding a meeting at Clonliffe Hall. They were sentenced to six months' hard labour at Mountjoy Gaol. While he served his sentence, O'Daly's wife became seriously ill and was transferred to a hospice. O'Daly was granted a few days' intermittent parole to attend to Daisy. He used the time during his brief release to arrange a jail break through Vice-Commandant Peadar Clancy and Chief of Staff Richard Mulcahy.[41] On his return to jail O'Daly informed the prisoners and selected warders who were sympathetic to the Volunteer cause. On the evening of the escape a snowball fight among twenty-seven prisoners in the exercise yard turned into a melee involving Warders Kelly and Murphy. Warder Jones got a punch in the face for resisting the prisoners' attempt to escape. Peadar Clancy and his men threw a rope ladder over the prison wall. Piaras Béaslaí, J. J. Walsh and Paddy Fleming were among the twenty prisoners who climbed over the wall and off into the warren of Dublin's streets.[42] O'Daly remained behind. He wife died two days later. He attended her funeral and then returned to Mountjoy to serve the remainder of his sentence.

Paddy O'Daly was released from prison along with Joe Leonard on 2 August 1919. The following month, on 19 September, O'Daly formed the second Special Duties Unit from fellow B Company, 2nd Battalion Volunteers Joe Leonard, Ben Barrett and Seán Doyle.[43] O'Daly and Leonard were inseparable and would go through hell and high water together for the rest of their lives. Whether Collins intended to introduce an element of competition among his units is unlikely. The operation of two small Special Duties Units more likely indicated the urgency of the task at hand. At this time Collins preferred to operate with small numbers of trusted men and women.

On 20 August 1919 Cathal Brugha stood before Dáil Éireann and proposed that an oath of allegiance should be taken to the Irish Republic and the Dáil by the Irish Volunteers. The wording of the oath was read aloud to the assembly:

> I, A.B., do solemnly swear (or affirm) that I do not and shall not yield a voluntary support to any pretended Government, authority or power within Ireland hostile and inimical thereto, and I do further swear (or affirm) that to the best of my knowledge and ability I will support and defend the Irish Republic and the Government of the Irish Republic, which is Dáil Éireann, against all enemies, foreign and domestic, and I will bear true faith and allegiance to the same, and that I take this obligation freely without any mental reservation or purpose of evasion, so help me, God.[44]

After a short debate on the matter, the motion was carried by thirty votes to five. Thus the Irish Volunteers became the standing army of the elected government of the Irish Republic. They were from then on officially known as the Irish Republican Army or IRA. Mick McDonnell and Paddy

O'Daly's assassination units were no longer Irish Volunteers but members of the IRA under the control of Dáil Éireann.

Quite a number of the Volunteers did not easily accept taking the oath. They had no doubt about their commitment to an Irish Republic but believed some of the Dáil had yet to prove their loyalty. The following month, Dáil members began to get a taste of the pressure the Volunteers had been under for years. On 10 September 1919, Dáil Éireann was declared a dangerous association and banned. TDs were now officially on the run. Many of them were to be arrested and imprisoned. The Dáil continued to meet in secret and established a number of safe houses in the city. They were constantly on the move from place to place as continuous British raids captured individuals, files and documents from Sinn Féin and the IRA. In 1919, the Dáil had four public sessions and ten in private.[45] Michael Collins was one Dáil member who experienced life on the run more than most.

Collins at this time wielded enormous influence over the republican movement. It was his work behind the scenes that secured acceptance of the oath. He was TD for the Cork South constituency, Minister for Finance, Director of Organisation and Director of Intelligence IRA. On top of all that he was also a member of the Supreme Council of the IRB. With an enormous workload and the capacity to match, Michael Collins moved around, directing different affairs from different locations.

Working for him was Eveleen Lawless, sister of Joe V. Lawless of the Fingal Brigade and who also ran the bicycle shop with the munitions factory on Great Britain Street. Eveleen was present when the offices at both 6 and 76 Harcourt Street were raided. On one occasion she hid Collins' gun down her stocking. It was in a raid at No. 76 that Dick McKee was arrested and imprisoned in October 1919. He was released in January 1920. Michael Collins only just escaped onto the roof and into the Standard Hotel next door. Inspector Neil McFeely of G Division was on both raids but did not recognise Collins even though he came face to face with him. Eveleen believed McFeely was secretly sympathetic to the republicans. Perhaps the climate of fear pervading Dublin was more of an influence on the inspector.

Initially Collins worked at 6 Harcourt Street but after a number of raids moved to 76 Harcourt Street on 11 November 1919. After this, too, was raided Collins moved again, to Camden Street and thence to Mary Street over Robinson's Seed Merchants. One of Collins' key offices was at

5 Mespil Road. In June 1920, Eveleen Lawless left Collins' employment to take up a religious life as a nun with the Sisters of Charity.[46] As Collins continued his work for the government of the Irish Republic, he directed Paddy O'Daly to begin active operations.

O'Daly received his first order from Collins early in November 1919: to seek out and kill one Detective Officer Wharton who was seen regularly in Harcourt Street. On 10 November O'Daly and Joe Leonard spotted Wharton with three other detectives, including Michael Flanagan, heading down Harcourt Street. Joe Leonard was unarmed at the time. As the detectives crossed Cuffe Street O'Daly moved in behind them, drawing his automatic and opening fire. Luckily for Wharton, O'Daly had fired only one shot when the gun jammed. The bullet entered Wharton's back near the right shoulder blade, passing cleanly though his body and exiting through the right side of his chest.[47] One of the other detectives stepped into the line of fire, preventing O'Daly and Leonard being shot at in return by the other two detectives. O'Daly and Leonard made their escape along Cuffe Street.[48] While the shooting was taking place, the scene was being observed by a British officer, Captain William Kearns Batchelor. He claimed he saw Wharton shot through the lung and a girl standing nearby hit with the same bullet. Detective Flanagan never mentioned the girl who was shot in his statement. Batchelor gave chase, but lost the men after they disappeared down Camden Row. Detective Flanagan called an ambulance for Wharton, who remained in hospital until mid-January 1920. In the subsequent investigation launched by G Division DMP, Captain Batchelor claimed he could identify one of the guilty men whom he had seen around St Stephen's Green.

On 19 November 1919 James Hurley, an ex-British soldier and newspaper street vendor, was arrested by Detective Sergeant John Barton and imprisoned in Mountjoy. He was picked out and wrongly accused of shooting Detective Wharton on the evidence of Captain Batchelor. At Hurley's court martial, held at Ship Street Barracks on 6 February, Batchelor recalled that he had seen two men standing at the junction of Harcourt Street and Cuffe Street for a number of days from 5 November onwards. He was certain Hurley was one of them. Hurley was sentenced to fifteen years' penal servitude. In April 1920 Batchelor received a threatening letter in the post. It was dated 1 April 1920 with the postmark Kiltimagh, County Mayo.[49] It declared Captain Batchelor guilty of police spying and added that Hurley had been wrongly punished. The letter finished with a menacing: 'Your doom is sealed x.x.x.x.x'[50]

The typed Xs were not intended as affectionate but rather marked the intention to deliver the kiss of death. In June 1920, Captain Batchelor applied for and received a £1,000 reward for the conviction of one of Collins' 'murder gang' and also a colonial appointment to get him out of Ireland for his own safety. Some of the letters written supporting Batchelor's applications were signed by Brigadier-General John Brind, O/C British Army GHQ intelligence, Dublin. It appeared that Collins' intelligence department had been right all along about Captain Batchelor being a spy. The evidence on James Hurley may even have been fabricated in order to give British army intelligence and the beleaguered G Division some taste of victory, if not among their own comrades then in the eyes of their superiors and the general public. James Hurley remained in prison until released during the truce. He was killed assisting a wounded soldier during the fighting in Dublin at the outbreak of the civil war in 1922.[51]

Just ten days after arresting James Hurley, Detective Sergeant John Barton was mortally wounded as he entered Great Brunswick Street police station. Collins had ordered no fewer than three Special Service Units – McDonnell's, O'Daly's and the Tipperary 'Big Four' of Seán Treacy, Breen, Hogan and Robinson – to join in the hunt for Barton.[52] He never stood a chance. The IRA nearly hit some of their own men in the heat of the moment. Barton died of his wounds a few hours later in Mercer's Hospital.[53] In 1917 Barton had been awarded the King's Police Medal for 'conspicuous gallantry and exceptional ability and devotion to duty'. Those very qualities were what made Barton and his colleagues marked men for Michael Collins' Special Duties Units.[54] The 'hard core' of the RIC now found themselves in a vicious war with little room for error.

Michael Collins realised after a number of operations that his Special Duties Units were under a great deal of pressure in carrying out their own intelligence prior to an operation. Joe Leonard, second in command to Paddy O'Daly, was not alone when he commented:

> In our small beginnings we patrolled the streets all day long until we were fagged out, as we had to do our own intelligence work, finding out where the enemy could be located, talking to them and finding out their latest devilment, but eventually we pointed out to Mick Collins that if we were to continue through the whole day in the city, we could not be of use for very long, as we would be picked up by the G Division Men and hanged by the neck while it would be good for us.[55]

IRA GHQ intelligence department, located over Fowlers, 3 Crow Street
Principal officers & background

Name	Pseudonym	Rank/Position	Profile
Michael Collins	Mr Brennan	Director of Intelligence	1916 service as staff officer (Captain) & subsequently TD and Minister for Finance
Liam Tobin		Assistant Director of Intelligence	1916 service & subsequently C Coy 1st Bn
Tom Cullen		Intelligence Officer	Born 1891. 1913 2nd Bn Dublin Brigade & subsequently O/C Wicklow Coy 1917 (Captain)
Frank Thornton		Intelligence Officer	(Captain) Liverpool Irish Volunteer Unit, 1916 service in Dublin under alias Frank Drennan & subsequently GHQ Staff
Frank Saurin	Mr Stanley	Intelligence Officer	F Coy 2nd Bn IO with Vinny Byrne
Joe Dolan		Intelligence Officer	A Coy 1st Bn until transfer to GHQ intelligence
Charlie Dalton		Intelligence Officer	F Coy 2nd Bn
Charlie Byrne		Intelligence Officer	No information has been found
Lilly Mernin		Intelligence Officer	Agent of intelligence department under direct supervision of Director Michael Collins in November 1919
Joe Guilfoyle		Intelligence Officer	A Coy 3rd Bn, 1916 Service & subsequently QM A Coy 3rd Bn until transfer to GHQ intelligence Feb 1920. Interned in the Rath Camp, The Curragh Feb to May 1921
Paddy Caldwell		Intelligence Officer	Liverpool Irish Volunteer Unit, 1916 Service, F Coy 1st Bn, GHQ Intelligence Officer March 1920
Paddy Kennedy		Intelligence Officer	Irish Citizen Army 1917 until transfer to D Coy 2nd Bn & in mid-1920 to GHQ intelligence
Dan McDonnell		Intelligence Officer	A Coy 1st Bn until transfer to GHQ intelligence. Railway worker. Joined GHQ Intellience August 1920
Ned Kelliher		Intelligence Officer	C Coy 3rd Bn
George Fitzgerald		Intelligence Officer	A Coy 1st Bn until transferred to GHQ intelligence
Thomas Sweeney Newell		Intelligence Officer	Castlegar Coy, 1st Galway Bde, transferred to Dublin October 1920 to assist GHQ intelligence identify Sgt Igoe RIC & his RIC detectives
Peter McGee		Intelligence Officer	No information has been found
Christopher 'Kit' Farrell		Intelligence Officer	A Coy, 3rd Battalion Also QM 3rd Battalion

Something else was needed. Collins established an effective intelligence department and transformed the fortunes of an Irish army at war with the British. Initially Collins, along with Liam Tobin and Tom Kehoe, carried out some intelligence work. IRA GHQ intelligence in Dublin expanded slowly. In the autumn of 1919, Collins invited Frank Thornton, Frank Saurin, Joe Dolan and Joe Guilfoyle to become intelligence officers. One of the first to become an intelligence officer and IRA agent was not invited as the others were, but volunteered her services. Her name was Miss Lily Mernin.

Lily Mernin became an intelligence officer and IRA agent in December 1919. Born in Dublin in 1888, she had grown up with her grandmother, a confectioner in Waterford city. On finishing school, Lily returned to Dublin and lived with her sister Mary and their aunts, Mary and Hannah, at 113 Middle Abbey Street.[56] Her addition to IRA intelligence was to be absolutely crucial in giving Collins the edge over the British in the early phase of the War of Independence. Mernin worked as a shorthand typist for the British army at Dublin Castle. In 1919 she got in touch with Piaras Béaslaí to assist the IRA. Collins met Mernin at her home where she agreed to become an intelligence agent. She worked directly for Collins until September 1920 when Intelligence Officer Frank Saurin became her contact outside the Castle. Situated in the same building as Mernin was the British army's intelligence department. This gave her access to officially classified information such as official reports, troop strengths, British army raids and information on the identity and addresses of British secret service personnel. She also picked up a great deal of information on physical descriptions, social habits and activities of British and RIC personnel through friendships and general 'loose talk' among Castle employees. The Castle, like any organisational hierarchy, had its share of hard-working employees but also its careerists. It was a hive of gossip relating to the tension between the different arms of the British power structure in Ireland as each of them vied for control, influence and promotion.[57]

One of Mernin's first assignments was to get to the bottom of the issuing of typed death threats on official Dáil Éireann notepaper being sent to prominent republicans. The threats were being sent from Dublin Castle. Mernin actually discovered the room and the very typewriter on which the threats were typed. Her next assignment required a cool head. Her job was to accompany Tom Cullen of the IRA intelligence staff in attending various summer social events like the Sports Gala at the Royal

Dublin Society at Ballsbridge or the Phoenix Park Races. Events like these were attended by the British military, RIC, Dublin Castle civil servants and their wives. On occasion, Collins' men were also in attendance. Lily Mernin and Tom Cullen would stroll, arms linked, down Grafton Street or Dame Street, 'spotting' British officers.[58] Identification of a target was essential for IRA intelligence officers who, from 1920, would assist Special Duties Units in their operations.

While Lily Mernin was on various assignments under Michael Collins' orders, she was working a six-day week that included Sunday. After her long hours at the Castle, she went to Clonliffe Road and entered No. 118, a house for which she was given a key. Inside, there was a room with a table, chair and typewriter where she would type out copies of information she had uncovered that day and put them into a sealed envelope for Collins' attention. Mernin identified the following information, which was most important for Collins and the intelligence department:

(1)   To get him [Collins] the addresses and supply him descriptions of all British Officers, Intelligence Officers, and others in Dublin Castle, as far as possible, and also the addresses and descriptions of civilians both male and female, employed in the Castle, and, if possible, an account of their personal habits, their national sympathies (if ascertainable) and places in Dublin frequented by them.

(2)   To abstract, wherever possible, the carbons of any documents typed by myself or other typists, and forward them to Collins; also copies of any documents I could get hold of.

(3)   To forward to him the weekly 'Strength returns' of the garrison which passed through my hands.

(4)   To report any talk or rumours overheard in the Castle likely to be of interest or importance.[59]

Some intelligence officers and their agents worked completely independently of GHQ intelligence, having been ordered by Michael Collins to resign from the IRA or Cumann na mBan. This was done to make them less visible and reduce the chance of their detection by the British. This led to some IRA intelligence officers being accused of cowardice and desertion. Thomas Markham was sent by Michael Collins to work in Dublin Castle during the truce period and afterwards. He reported directly to Collins and went under the pseudonym Tom

Donovan. When applying for his pension after the Civil War, Markham was unable to prove many of the operations he had carried out as his work was so secret. In 1924 he wrote, 'No man alive now, knew all of Collin's many strings.'[60] Markham's version of events was not accepted at the time of his application but over the years other eyewitnesses have corroborated some of his claims.

Another of Collins' important contacts was Tommy Gay. A 1916 veteran, he served in A Company, 1st Battalion. After being released from prison in 1916, he dropped out of the Irish Volunteers and distanced himself from Sinn Féin. In later years his version of events of working closely with Collins would also be questioned. Yet Collins made great use of Gay's position as a librarian in Capel Street. Gay was a vital source and a conduit through whom information was both delivered and dispatched. Collins also used Gay's home at Haddon Road in Clontarf for meetings with Detectives Broy and Kavanagh and former G-Man and subsequently British secret service agent Dave Neligan, who worked at Dublin Castle.[61] These agents also sent information through Gay. Pat McCrea knew that Tommy Gay carried out secret operations for Collins personally. Eventually, Collins began to incorporate some of his contacts into GHQ intelligence. Introductions became necessary as Collins feared his contacts might be shot accidentally by their own side.[62] For example, Collins introduced agents Eamon Broy and Tommy Gay to Intelligence Officers Liam Tobin and Tom Cullen, who had been tracking them.[63] The life of intelligence officers was most secret: their families and friends knew almost nothing about their activities.

Intelligence officers of the early twentieth century had grown up in a world of apparent certainty and clear, guiding moral Christian principals. People understood right from wrong, lived by the Ten Commandments and applauded honesty, loyalty and integrity. The officers' activities turned the traditional sense of morality completely upon its head. They were to engage in lying, stealing, threats, intimidation, and executions and murder. Such attributes became an essential component of this war and were applied with the greatest skill of all, stealth. However patriotic such actions were portrayed, they had a grave effect upon the intelligence officers themselves. The nature of the work carried out by them meant they, above all, would face torture and eventual death if caught. The strain on them was enormous and led to mental breakdown during the War of Independence, with recurring episodes for the rest of their lives. Some of the officers seemed unaffected by their work and, in fact, proved very effective. Neither Irish nor British intelligence officers ever received the recognition due to them. Much of the truth behind their work died with them or remains in restricted documents withheld by both the Irish and British authorities.

Despite the danger of what the officers knew would surely face them, they volunteered willingly. They faced the most dangerous assignments of the entire period with great courage. The consequences of their work determined victory or defeat. The stakes for their respective nations could not be higher. Thirty years later, Dan McDonnell would write about the complexity of their lives during the War of Independence: 'During all this time we did not know whether we would be alive twenty-four hours or not. We had to mix with all the British Forces, get back again into I.R.A. outfits and fight them. It was an extraordinary situation. We owe our existence to-day to our wits.'[64]

As the War of Independence gathered pace the intelligence department grew in number and scope. They were soon joined by Charlie Dalton, Dan McDonnell, Ned Kelliher and Seamus Hughes. Each intelligence officer, or IO, was given a trial period and a code number to protect their identity. IOs also had a number of pseudonyms, which included Irish versions of their names and a number of English names. This tactic made it very difficult for the British to track them down and capture them. Even when the British had IRA and Cumann na mBan agents in custody, a positive identification proved most difficult. IO Frank Saurin was also known as Mr Stanley, while Michael Collins used, on occasion, Mr Brennan or Mr Field. The world of the IO was perhaps the most difficult and dangerous job undertaken by agents of both the IRA and the British army during the War of Independence. Agents on both sides lived a double life. They befriended people and got close to them to obtain information of value to their side, information that would often lead to betrayal and death. In some cases, it even led to betraying their own side to win the trust, albeit temporarily, of their enemies. IRA IO Dan McDonnell made contact with two British agents in Dublin Castle whom he knew as 'Fever' and 'Ashe' and admitted he gave these agents details of a certain number of IRA comrades' homes or places of refuge to raid.[65] This murky world of espionage nearly got McDonnell killed by his own side, as he revealed: 'We learned at this time that some of us had been followed and under observation to be shot by local I.R.A. Companies in Dublin because of our mixing around with British forces.'[66]

Frank Thornton joined the intelligence department at the end of 1919. At the same time IRA brigades down to battalion and company level were ordered to appoint an IO but the response was quite varied until after November 1920 when the value of such information was demonstrated with ruthless efficiency on a Sunday morning in Dublin. IOs were given a code number to identify themselves in reports and correspondence. Patrick Moynihan, who worked in the GPO, was known as 118, Dan McDonnell was 101, Ned Kelliher 102 and Paddy Drury 104.[67] Each IO developed his or her own series of contacts in certain locations across Dublin city and county. These contacts were street vendors and dockers, or worked in hotels, railway stations and trains, shops, mail boat companies and British army barracks. In other words, the IRA had contacts in every place it was possible to have someone divulging information. IO Paddy Kennedy established an interesting group of contacts, among whom were the British secret service agent David Neligan, an Auxiliary called Reynolds, a waiter in the Gresham Hotel, a porter in the Shelbourne Hotel and a civilian in the Telephone Exchange. Reynolds, in particular, was very helpful and handed in photographs of British officers, agents and policemen.[68]

James Hughes described a regular day for an IRA intelligence officer. It began with reporting to 3 Crowe Street, the intelligence HQ, to see if any special orders of the day were issued. Some IOs spent the morning carefully reading the daily newspapers to glean any possible information on individuals of particular interest. Then he set off patrolling a regular route and noting any unusual characters on the street. An important route took in the quays, Dublin Castle and the vicinity of various British army barracks. The general appearance and schedules of particular people's movements were noted. There were also a number of people in town who appeared to have nothing to do. Their appearance was especially recorded.[69] IOs also paid special attention to any cars giving rise to suspicion. The registration numbers would be recorded and the car's future movements monitored. Hughes also watched any cars outside Mitchell's Café. It was a favourite hangout for Auxiliaries and British intelligence officers.[70] Other cafés favoured by the British were Kidd's and Jammet's. IRA IOs frequented all of these cafés, sometimes establishing links with British double agents or British soldiers who were prepared to sell weapons or information. It was the simple observations that frequently led to greater discoveries. Some of the cars Hughes noted regularly pulled up at Mount Street where there were a number of residences of British secret service agents.

For James Hughes, the ability to hold one's nerve could be the difference between life and death. Very often it was simply waiting to see what would happen and not reacting that saved lives. Hughes experienced this crisis of decision one morning:

> I remember another morning when the Squad was given the job of covering Michael Collins's retreat from a house in Fitzwilliam Place. Frank Saurin and I were together on Fitzwilliam Square and, of course, we were armed. No sooner had we taken up position when we saw an armoured car approaching which caused apprehension on our part, but it passed on without stopping. Had we had taken premature action, it is doubtful if Collins would have escaped.[71]

While IOs patrolled the streets they were liable to be searched and questioned or even arrested. They regularly bluffed their way out of the situation. When all of their information had been sifted and leads exhausted on a particular case, the time would come to draw up lists for execution. IO Mick Kennedy assisted with that job. Collins was anxious to find out the identity of the British secret service agents in Dublin. The coordination of a number of IRA IO contacts was vital in building up a picture of their whereabouts. A careful check was kept on the residents of guesthouses, hotels and private houses through maids and caretakers. Orders would be sent to the Special Duties Units, or later the Squad, who would quickly organise and move out onto the streets of Dublin. They were under constant pressure: walking, watching, running, dodging and hiding. Orders would be received. They would collect their guns and go on a 'job'. Then after the gunshots, the blood, the screams and the running, it would begin all over again.

Initially, Mick McDonnell and Paddy O'Daly's Special Duties Units were based at 100 Seville Place, the offices of O'Toole's GAA Club. The Special Duties Units had separate munitions dumps from the Dublin Brigade. Pat McCrea, who did a lot of the driving for these units, called at dumps in Hardwicke Place, Temple Street, North Great Charles Street and Mount Prospect Avenue in Dollymount.[72] The dump at North Great Charles Street was in a stable that had been converted to a lock-up garage. Mick McDonnell stored his motorcycle combination there. This was the official dump for a long time but it was moved after a near discovery by a British army cordon and search operation. After a while they obtained a more central base in the city at George Moreland's Cabinet Making and Upholstering at Middle Abbey Street facing Stafford Street (Wolfe Tone Street). When both McDonnell's and O'Daly's Special Duties Units amalgamated to form the Squad their HQ was established at George Moreland's Cabinet Making and Upholstering at Middle Abbey Street. Vinny Byrne described the building as follows:

> The entrance to the premises was enclosed by two large gates, one with wicket opening. The area of the premises was about 75' [22 m] long by about 12' [3.6 m] wide, flanked on each side by a high wall. The ground floor was used as a cabinet-making shop, which was only a blind, of course. The second-floor consisted of two large stores ... A Volunteer bricklayer was brought in and instructed to remove the door and door-frame of the lavatory in the yard and the opening to be bricked up with old brick. The floor of the lavatory on the second floor was made moveable and into one of the joists we fixed a six-inch nail. We had a small registered mail bag to which was attached a light rope. Into this bag we used to put our guns and lower it into the lavatory underneath. The other end of the rope we fixed to the nail. It was a perfect job.[73]

Michael Collins visited Moreland's twice a week, which was, according to Vinny Byrne, great for the men's morale. Collins would ask them how they were and share a few jokes before moving on to his next assignment.[74] The bond of loyalty to Collins by his chosen Special Duties operatives established in these dark days became unbreakable.

The intelligence and Special Duties Units soon developed greater tactical awareness. This involved specific ways of moving through the city and positioning during an operation. The Special Duties Units that were eventually amalgamated to form the Squad developed a very effective system. They would meet in the open and go to a dump to collect their guns. While moving through the city they walked in pairs on both sides of the road with other pairs of operatives a few feet further back, also on both sides of the road. Once in the area selected for a 'job', a number of men would cover the two chosen to carry out the killing. The other members of the unit would step into the street with guns drawn to secure their intended escape routes, or what Jim Stapleton referred to as their 'gateway'.[75] The Squad preferred to operate in areas where they could blend in with a crowd and avoid the watchful eye of detectives or British intelligence agents. Some of their operations took place, however, in areas distant from the city. These operations left the Squad exposed as they desperately attempted to find the safety of the city streets once more.

As the number of assassinations increased, the British established regular checkpoints on all the main bridges in the city. Jim Slattery, an early member of the Squad, was well aware that these bottlenecks could lead to them being caught with their guns on them either before or after a 'job'. Slattery and Tom Kehoe met Mick Collins in a well-known republican meeting place, Phil Shanahan's Pub on Foley Street, to voice their concerns. They requested that he provide two separate sets of guns for his assassination units, one set on the north side of the city and a second set on the south side. Thus Special Duties Units could cross the Liffey bridges without being caught in the possession of their weapons before or after an operation. Collins listened to them and asked what they'd like to drink. 'Two sherries,' they said. Slattery didn't like to ask for something harder, like his usual whiskey, in front of Collins, who generally only had a sherry. Collins left the drinks for Kehoe and Slattery and disappeared. The Squad had their two sets of guns within a few days.[76] Jim Slattery had both Smith & Wesson and Colt revolvers. As he said himself, 'I never believed in those automatics.' Automatics, while offering a greater rate of fire and number of rounds, were liable to jam on occasion with all sorts of consequences. Slattery also found a 'Short .45' very handy as it would fit in a coat pocket and could be drawn with relative ease.

The initial British response to the killings of G Division DMP and RIC personnel across Ireland was implemented by the Lord Lieutenant, Field Marshal John French. Tough as old boots, this Irishman had a bullish attitude and was a vastly experienced soldier. He had served in the British army in Egypt, India, Africa and Europe. Lord French and the British War Cabinet, a coalition of Liberals and Conservatives, were preparing for a sophisticated fight, employing a combined political and military strategy underpinned with counterterror measures. The first step was to strengthen G Division of the DMP and instruct the British army to develop their secret service in Ireland. French intended to fight fire with fire. Charles William Forbes Redmond was brought in from Belfast as assistant commissioner, to take command of G Division. Alan Bell RM was also brought in to carry out a number of investigations.

In November 1919, Michael Collins decided on an assassination attempt on Lord French. Mick McDonnell was asked if he would be willing to accept the 'job' of shooting the lord lieutenant at the Armistice

Day Parade in Dublin. McDonnell was only given twenty-four hours' notice. He knew this would probably be his last day on earth but he agreed and, unsurprisingly, did not sleep much that night. The 'job' was called off the following morning as Cathal Brugha said the people would not tolerate it. The following month it was decided to go ahead with the assassination attempt. Lord French had a country residence at Frenchpark near Boyle, County Roscommon. On return to Dublin, the train usually stopped at Ashtown railway station from where Lord French made the short journey to the Viceregal Lodge at the Phoenix Park in a small convoy of cars. The IRA plan was to ambush the unsuspecting Lord French on the road from the railway station to Ashtown Cross at Kelly's Pub on the Navan Road.

The ambush exhibited the classic chaos of war: nothing went according to plan and confusion reigned. There were thirteen men in the unit assembled to make the attack: Mick McDonnell's men, Paddy O'Daly's men, the Tipperary 'Big Four' and also a Lieutenant from D Company, 2nd Battalion, Martin Savage, whom Joe Leonard brought along at the last minute.[77] Dan Breen and his Tipperary comrades had been on the run since Soloheadbeg and had come to Dublin to place themselves at the disposal of Mick McDonnell's unit. Breen knew Dublin well, having worked on the railways there since he was seventeen years old. He and his men welcomed the chance to join the 'job' at Ashtown.

The first attempt at Ashtown Cross was cancelled as French did not turn up. Then on 19 December Mick McDonnell received a phone call from Tom Ennis O/C E Company telling him the train had left Broadstone Station in Dublin earlier that morning and would return from Boyle later in the day. Lord French would be on board. McDonnell and O'Daly hurriedly assembled their men. With the taxi drivers on strike, the IRA men had to use bicycles to make it out of the city. On arriving at the crossroads, six of the men went into Kelly's Pub and ordered sherry, port wine and some minerals for the teetotallers. McDonnell reconnoitred the area briefly. He saw a cart in the pub yard and ordered Dan Breen, Tom Kehoe and Martin Savage to use it as a roadblock. Paddy O'Daly and four others took up position behind a hedge just up from Kelly's on the road leading from the railway station. They were armed with hand grenades and revolvers. They were to concentrate on the second car, which McDonnell had assumed would be the Lord Lieutenant's vehicle.

At about one o'clock, the party with Lord French left the station. As Breen and his detail struggled with the cart, a lead motorcycle and French's car passed swiftly through the position. With Lord French were Mrs Seymour, Captain De Pret (ADC to Lord French) and Detective Sergeant Hally of G Division. Six grenades came over the hedge and exploded on the road. On hearing the first explosion Sergeant Hally roared, 'Drive like the Devil'. Hally got off two shots at O'Daly and his men behind the hedge. He also fired three shots at the others beside the cart as the car drove on towards the Phoenix Park. Hally himself was hit in the right hand and had a finger broken. A constable on duty at the crossroads, Constable O'Loughlin was hit in the foot and went down as he attempted to draw his revolver. The second car was halted by the grenades.

Two British army lorries came on the scene but did not stop. As they passed, Sergeant Rumble of the Royal Berkshire Regiment fired off a few rounds. Martin Savage was hit, shot through the jaw. As the 21-year-old from Ballysadare in County Sligo fell, Dan Breen caught him and lowered him to the ground. His last words as his life ebbed away were barely audible: 'I'm done Dan. Carry on.' Breen himself was hit in the leg, but the bullet passed clean through. After the firing had ceased one of the Volunteers knelt beside Martin Savage and whispered an act of contrition in his ear. Two of his comrades carried Savage to the door of the pub but Bartholomew Kelly, brother of the owner Peter, closed the door on them. They had no option but to leave Savage's body on the ground and make haste to the city before British reinforcements arrived. While some of the men tended to Savage, others held up the driver of the second car, Corporal Appleby. They were disgusted to find the car filled with luggage. Breen was now bleeding profusely. Seamus Robinson jumped on the back of Seán Treacy's bicycle as his own bicycle's frame had collapsed and together they made for Dublin city, taking the Navan Road.[78]

Around a quarter past one, Michael Donohoe, an ex-sergeant of the DMP, was cycling past the Deaf & Dumb Institute on the Navan Road. He heard the reports of the explosions in the distance. Ten minutes later, seven or eight young men pedalling like blazes passed him, heading for the city. He later thought there were more than eight. They were followed four minutes later by two more young men sharing one bicycle. The two men were, of course, Treacy and Robinson. They held up Donohoe and took his bicycle, saying they would leave it for him at the Gresham Hotel.[79] His bicycle was returned to him via the DMP who found it not far from the Gresham.

At this time Breen realised he was leaving a trail of blood for the DMP to follow so he tied a bootlace around the end of his trouser leg, which did the trick. Paddy O'Daly got the wounded Breen to Mrs Twomey's at 88 Phibsborough Road. Breen was now very weak from the loss of blood and was put to bed. Dr J. M. Ryan, captain of the Dublin hurling team, came to attend to him.[80] As Paddy O'Daly walked away from Twomey's, he felt the assassination units had been extremely lucky to escape with only one dead. He believed if Breen had succeeded in blocking the road they would have been outnumbered and outgunned with nowhere to go. Fate had been on their side that day. Seán Hogan had dropped a grenade, causing O'Daly and himself to dive for cover as it exploded. At that very moment, the military escort passed by and thus they were both saved from a volley of fire from the British soldiers.

The DMP tried to determine in which direction the IRA unit had gone. The police were initially confused by a trail of mixed hand-grenade parts found on the Pelletstown and Ashtown Roads but a significant lead was soon discovered when a trail of blood was seen leading towards the city on the Navan Road. Soon after the ambush, Ashtown Cross was swarming with RIC and DMP senior police officers. In his December 1919 report, County Inspector Andrew Roberts acknowledged the attack on the Lord Lieutenant took place on the boundary of the jurisdiction shared between the RIC and the DMP but in a clear attempt to lay blame for not dealing with the IRA GHQ, he wrote: 'I am inclined to believe that the whole thing was planned by a gang of Extremists who had their Headquarters in the city of Dublin.'[81]

There was a good deal of frustration among the RIC at the lack of action on the part of the DMP to apprehend the key men behind IRA GHQ and the Dublin Brigade. However, the DMP were quickly on the case of the Ashtown ambush. Leads were followed and the trail led to Martin Savage's work place. Vice O/C Dublin Brigade Michael Lynch sent Tom Ennis on a highly urgent mission to get to Savage's workplace to recover important IRA documents. These documents contained the names of the Special Duties Units and Dick McKee's private papers. Ennis retrieved the documents. Just as he was leaving, British troops arrived to search the building. Ennis was fired on but managed to evade capture, escaping uninjured. Tom Ennis's bravery saved the lives of many men that day.[82]

In his statement to the subsequent investigation, Detective Sergeant Edward Hally was unable to identify any of the IRA unit in action that day.

Hally was not alone: neither could eyewitnesses Bartholomew Kelly, T. J. Roark, Patrick Rickards or Michael Donohoe identify a single member of the IRA unit. Apparently, the IRA men were wearing mufflers or caps pulled down well over their eyes and could not be seen.[83] Both Sergeant Rumble and Detective Sergeant Hally claimed to have shot Martin Savage, whose body was initially brought to the stables of the Viceregal Lodge. After examination by a doctor, it was taken to Bessboro DMP Barracks at the Phoenix Park.

Savage's identity was established by his employer, Mr William Kirke, the next day. A Smith & Wesson revolver and an automatic pistol, both fully loaded, were found on him. On the first finger of his right hand was the ring of a hand-grenade and a whistle. Also found and of considerable significance were eleven rounds of dumdum ammunition.[84] These rounds had the nose of the bullet deliberately flattened or hollowed to increase the damage upon impact. This style of ammunition was developed by the British army in India but had been outlawed by the Hague Convention in 1899.[85]

The IRA requested permission from the Catholic Pro-Cathedral to allow Martin Savage's body to lie at rest there prior to the journey to his home town of Ballysadare. Permission was refused and so the Dublin Brigade turned to Savage's local parish church of Saint Laurence's. Permission was also denied here so his body lay in a box car at Broadstone Station before the journey home to County Sligo.[86] The Dublin Brigade, and in particular the 2nd Battalion, wanted to march through the city's streets with their fallen comrade but Chief of Staff Richard Mulcahy advised that it was better to remain unseen. Secrecy protected them from detection and arrest. Frank Henderson, O/C of 2nd Battalion, realised that the Dublin Brigade would see more action. Mulcahy's instruction was accepted and the Volunteers 'silently vowed to regard their fellow soldier's death as an occasion for the strengthening of their determination to be steadfast no matter what the odds'.[87] For all those assembled it must have been a sobering moment as they faced into 1920.

For Collins, the attempt on French was daring and audacious. Casualties were always deeply felt and Lieutenant Martin Savage was no exception. Vice-Commandant Michael Lynch went to visit Tom Kehoe the afternoon of the ambush and found him sitting in a chair, his whole body shaking with grief for his fallen comrade.[88] The ambush sent shockwaves of a different sort through the British establishment. It exposed the now failed

DMP and the weakness of the RIC. The police were deeply embarrassed by the attempt on Lord French. The public reaction was generally silent, except for some people who made the odd loose comment. An old railway worker was heard saying derogatory things about Lieutenant Savage. Mick McDonnell decided to teach him a lesson 'to keep his mouth shut'.[89] One night he gathered together Tom Kehoe, Michael Brennan from Clare and Vinny Byrne. They went to Shamrock Cottages off the North Strand Road where the man lived. He was old and sported a fine beard. Michael Brennan used a pair of horse clippers to shave off the beard while the others held him down. The women of the house were in great distress. After his ordeal, the old man was told 'to watch his mouth in future'.[90]

The old man was not alone in voicing opposition to the IRA's ambush on Lord French. The national papers were scathing in their condemnation. The *Irish Independent* referred to it as 'Criminal Folly' and 'An Outrage'. The deceased Martin Savage was described as a 'Murderer'.[91] The Dublin Brigade had mostly been in prison in the aftermath of the 1916 Rising and had been unable to respond to the national papers' condemnation of their actions then. Now, however, they were determined to reply. The *Irish Independent* was singled out for special attention. Its editorial antagonism towards the ITGWU and national republicanism was long established by 1919. Gearóid Ua hUallacháin, Chief of Staff and QM General of Na Fianna Éireann, was chosen for this special 'job'. He selected IRA Volunteers from the Dublin Docks who were used to swinging a sledgehammer. Meeting at 46 Rutland Square, the men were addressed by Richard Mulcahy, Michael Lynch and Peadar Clancy. They then set off in small groups for the *Irish Independent*. As Ua hUallacháin arrived quite a scene awaited him: 'all the rooms were lit up and one could see the shadows of the members of staff standing against the blinds with their hands held over their heads. This gave us a most uncomfortable feeling as we entered the building. We made a thorough job of the machines'.[92]

Ua hUallacháin and his men wrecked the typesetting and printing machines so much that *The Irish Times* had to step in and print an abridged version of the *Irish Independent* until the plant was repaired.[93] Ua hUallacháin was chosen for this assignment as he had the expertise to identify where the most damage could be done. The *Irish Independent* responded to the IRA raid by printing editorials more favourable to the republican cause from then on.

The issues surrounding the printing of the news and the truth in the news were emphasised by the *Irish Independent* incident. Access to the world press and the skill of propaganda was a major concern to the republican government and the IRA long before the sitting of the first Dáil, however. In 1918, the Irish Volunteer paper, *An t-Óglach*, drew attention to the role played by a Dublin man in bringing about the collapse of Germany and her allies in the Great War.[94] Alfred Charles William Harmsworth left school at sixteen and rose to become a press magnate, owning the *Evening News*, *Daily Mirror*, *Daily Mail* and *The Times*.[95] Early in 1918, Harmsworth, by then Lord Northcliffe, was appointed Director of Propaganda in Enemy Countries.[96] He skilfully directed a campaign that undermined the morale of the Central Powers' home front[97] and made the populations in those countries more amenable to peace.[98] The editor of *An t-Óglach*, Piaras Béaslaí, was greatly impressed by Northcliffe's contribution to the Allied victory in 1918.

Two developments occurred that greatly aided the Irish independence movement. In 1919 the Sinn Féin government in Dublin realised that foreign countries were obtaining the news on the Irish situation from English sources. Director of Propaganda for the Sinn Féin government, Desmond Fitzgerald TD, travelled to London and made contact with the foreign press correspondents of many countries. They agreed to receive copies of a *Daily Irish Bulletin* carrying the news from an Irish government standpoint.[99] The impact was a change in the reporting of the War of Independence in countries across the world. George Gavan Duffy reported on this change in French papers and on papers from other countries while he was in Paris. *The Freeman's Journal* provided Fitzgerald's department with the use of a daily transmission of 300 words on their private telegraph wire, thus directly reaching many foreign news agencies and foreign correspondents in London in time for them to send their daily copy for print to their home countries.[100] The ability to counter the British control of the foreign press was a coup for Desmond Fitzgerald.

In 1920 the Black and Tans would arrive to reinforce a collapsing RIC. They would be supported by the more elite Auxiliary division of the RIC. The 'truth' in the news would be more vigorously debated than ever as the terror visited upon the DMP by Michael Collins' men was about to be returned with interest. In 1920, Ireland would know the true meaning of terror.

4

'Indomitable Spirit'

The War Escalates – January to October 1920

The year 1920 witnessed explosive confrontation between the British and Irish forces throughout Ireland. It was the year the Black and Tans and the Auxiliaries were introduced to Ireland as the British sought to counter the IRA attacks visited upon the RIC and British army. Substantial British military reinforcements also arrived in Ireland to impose martial law. This was also the year the IRA perfected its guerrilla tactics with the introduction of flying columns, otherwise known as Active Service Units (ASUs). In Dublin, the IRA increased its active operations to acquire arms and also began mounting attacks on British troops. In anticipation of the guerrilla warfare soon to be adopted by the IRA, the RIC implemented defensive measures at all RIC barracks. The measures initially involved placing barbed wire and sandbags at approaches to the entrances and at windows. Sandbags were later replaced by steel shutters.[1] DI Thomas Lowndes wrote the RIC report for County Dublin in February 1920. He was relieved no attacks on RIC barracks had yet taken place. The reason for this he put down to the close proximity of most RIC barracks in the county to Dublin city: a prolonged attack would surely lead to an engagement with the substantial British reinforcements in the city. However, Lowndes considered that the RIC barracks at the extreme northern and southern ends of the county were at risk of attack.[2] As a result of Lowndes' report, British troops were stationed at strategic RIC barracks to discourage the IRA from direct attacks. The actions implemented were part of a strategy to restrict the movement of IRA personnel by imposing the Restoration of Order in Ireland Act (1920) on counties Dublin, Louth, Longford, Sligo, Westmeath and Wicklow. Martial law was declared in counties Cork, Kerry, Limerick, Tipperary, Clare, Waterford, Kilkenny and Wexford in 1920 and 1921.[3]

Surprisingly, 1920 began with a diplomatic manoeuvre by Prime Minister Lloyd George. Just before Christmas 1919, he had attempted to isolate the Irish republican movement from perceived moderate Irish political opinion when he introduced his Better Government for Ireland Bill on 22 December, just four days after the ambush at Ashtown. The Bill would become the Government of Ireland Act 1920. Lloyd George recognised that implementation of the 1914 Home Rule Bill was no longer possible and he openly admitted that three quarters of the Irish population were governed without their consent and were bitterly hostile to a British government. He also stated that a considerable section of the population preferred British rule and were opposed to Irish rule. But, hidden within the delivery of another sublime performance from the 'Welsh Wizard' was the key phrase: 'Irishmen claim the right to control their own "domestic concerns", without interference from Englishmen, Scotsmen, or Welshmen'.[4] For the Prime Minister 'any arrangement by which Ireland is severed from the United Kingdom, either nominally or in substance and in fact, would be fatal to the interests of both'. This view was explained further by MP Benjamin Spoor on 23 February 1920 during a debate in the House of Commons on the British army estimates. He said: 'Evacuate the troops from Ireland. That is the only solution, in the opinion of some of us, of the Irish problem. If a policy of repression and coercion, whether in Egypt or Ireland, or any other part of the Empire, is to be continued, it seems to me that that is the direction in which madness lies, and ultimately the disintegration and smash-up of our Empire'.[5]

Secretary of State for War Winston Churchill was looking for £75 million to finance the British army for 1920 and needed to finance a garrison of 35,000 'effectives' with additional support troops of 5,000 in Ireland.[6] A smaller garrison was costing the exchequer £900,000 per month by August 1919.[7] The garrison and the cost would rise beyond Churchill's estimates and is an indication of the desire to keep Ireland within the empire. It was assumed by many in the Commons that an Irish republic would be hostile to the United Kingdom, the Easter Rising being a case in point. The solution to the hitherto intractable 'Irish Question' was to implement a more aggressive policy on the ground to make the eventual political solution workable. During 1920, the British political and civil administration would be reconstituted and the RIC and the British military reorganised and substantially reinforced. The British intelligence operation would also receive significant financial support, enabling them to deploy more agents and build an impressive network of informants. However, internal divisions within the British cabinet, the army and the police would undermine their military action on occasions when considerable gains were being made.

On 15 January 1920 Irish people went to the polls to elect Municipal and Urban Councils. Sinn Féin needed a substantial victory to secure political control on a local level. In spite of a campaign of coercion implemented by the RIC and aided by the British army, which saw Sinn Féin candidates arrested and imprisoned, support for the newly established Irish republic was overwhelming. Of twelve cities and boroughs in the country, eleven voted in republican administrations. Belfast was the only city to return a Unionist majority. Of the 206 councils in Ireland, 172 were now republican. Three of the lord mayors elected would be dead within the year: Michael O'Callaghan, Mayor of Limerick, and Tomás Mac Curtain, Mayor of Cork, were both shot dead in their homes by members of the RIC disguised with blackened faces. Terence Mac Swiney, who replaced Mac Curtain, would die on hunger strike.

Although Sinn Féin had a majority on Dublin City Council they were not able to press home their advantage. Mrs Kathleen Clarke, widow of executed 1916 leader Tom Clarke, was elected for two constituencies and only had one vote. Two Sinn Féin aldermen, Thomas Kelly TD and Seán O'Mahony TD, were in prison, while Seán T. O'Kelly TD was in Paris. Women representing Sinn Féin polled very well. Nationally, out of a total of 1,470 seats, Sinn Féin won 422, Unionists 297, Labour 324, Independent Nationalists 213, Independents 128 and Others 85.[8] The republican councils now broke off relations with the British Local Government Board and pledged their allegiance to Dáil Éireann.[9] Dublin Corporation voted in favour of the following resolution by 38 votes to 5:

> That this Council of the elected representatives of the City of Dublin hereby acknowledge the authority of Dáil Éireann as the duly elected Government of the Irish people, and undertakes to give effect to all decrees duly promulgated by the said Dáil Éireann in so far as same effect this Council. That copies of this resolution be transmitted to the Governments of Europe, and to the President and Chairman of the Senate and the House of Representatives of the U.S.A.[10]

Meanwhile, IRA GHQ Intelligence and the Squad continued their surveillance and operations against G Division. They also faced a new enemy. In November 1919, the DMP had been strengthened by a Belfast contingent of detectives led by the experienced Assistant Commissioner William Forbes Redmond. As part of this initiative, British intelligence at Scotland Yard, headed by Sir Basil Thompson, sent a number of specially recruited agents and key men to Dublin with the specific task of neutralising the leadership and men behind the IRA's campaign of assassinations. Among them were ex-Sergeant-Major Jack Byrnes (working under the alias of John Jameson), Captain Kearns Batchelor, a Sergeant Molloy and Alan Bell RM.[11] Bell, a former District Inspector in the RIC, was brought in to investigate the Ashtown ambush and also to track down the money from the Dáil Loan Scheme initiated by Michael Collins as Minister for Finance. If Bell could locate the money, the Dáil would be unable to finance and thus implement the new Irish Republic. Within three months, four of these five men would be dead, all assassinated on the instructions of IRA Director of Intelligence, Michael Collins.

IRA IO Frank Thornton entered a police station posing as the cousin of a DMP sergeant and managed to obtain a photograph of Assistant Commissioner Forbes Redmond.[12] From that moment, Redmond was a dead man. IO Joe Dolan, who was detailed to put Redmond under surveillance, said Redmond was a hard man to miss, being tall and wearing a hard hat (bowler). Both IRA Special Duties Units tried to kill the Assistant Commissioner a number of times but fortune intervened to save him.[13] On 21 January 1920 at 6.30 p.m., however, his luck ran out as he walked up Harcourt Street on his way to his lodgings at the Standard Hotel. On Harcourt Street were the two Special Duties Units: McDonnell's and O'Daly's. When Redmond reached Montague Street Paddy O'Daly and Tom Kehoe stepped up behind him and opened fire. O'Daly's shot was accurate and lethal, and Redmond went down with a bullet in the back of the head that severed his spinal cord. Kehoe hit Redmond in the back. He died instantly.[14]

As the killings continued, Lloyd George prepared the ground for his political strategy. At the end of January 1920 a secret report was written for the British cabinet at Downing Street which detailed the desire of Ulster Unionists for the whole province to be excluded from any form of Home Rule or settlement of the Irish Question. The report refers to 'inner circles', who, however, were in favour of the exclusion of just six counties: the other three, Donegal, Cavan and Monaghan, would 'provide such an access of strength to the Roman Catholic Party, that the supremacy of the Unionists would be seriously threatened'.[15] In the local government elections on 15 January, in the nine Ulster counties, twenty-three towns had elected a republican majority and twenty-two a Unionist majority. Of the six counties favoured by Edward Carson in establishing a Unionist Ulster, Fermanagh and Tyrone had majority Sinn Féin support.[16] The Unionists were eager to accept a deal under Lloyd George's government as a general election could see Labour gain power, resulting in a more favourable deal for Irish Republicans and less advantageous terms for Ulster. The report described the condition of Ulster as 'satisfactory' while the state of the rest of Ireland was considered to be 'appalling'. Dublin was even worse than anticipated. Fear was the prevailing factor: 'Everybody seems to suspect his neighbour; burglaries, assaults and raids for arms, take place every day. The majority of these cases are not reported in the press because people are afraid to give evidence to the police, fearing that if they do so worse will befall them.'[17]

The report included the results of discussions with barristers in the Four Courts. In what was a surprise to no one, they considered the establishment of a separate parliament for Ulster would be a great loss to the Bar from a financial point of view.[18] The writer of the report also believed that the Catholic hierarchy would support the establishment of partition and two separate parliaments because they greatly feared the spread of Bolshevism. This shows just how 'revolutionary' were considered the ideas of Sinn Féin and their plans for a new Irish Republic among 'the establishment' of the period. Also, the Church was anxious to support partition in order to end the terrible outrages. Tellingly, the report concluded that, if the British government were to implement a separate measure of Home Rule providing for a northern and southern Irish parliament, the people would be found in the south to make the bill work.[19]

There was concern that the discipline of the RIC was breaking down and that there might be a repetition of the indiscriminate firing which occurred in Thurles.[20] As the cogs of political machination began to move, Dublin Castle ordered the DMP and British army to step up their raids.

On 2 January 1920 Inspector Neil McFeely, to whose office Collins had paid a midnight visit, was ordered to lead a raid on the offices of the New Ireland Assurance Company at 56 Lower Sackville Street. He duly carried out the raid but did not report the presence of a cellar to his superiors, thinking it belonged to Kapp & Peterson who had a shop on the ground floor and had nothing to do with the offices he was ordered

Liam Tobin, Deputy Director IRA GHQ Intelligence Department. Photograph taken after surrender in 1916, when he was twenty-one years old. (Courtesy Kilmainham Gaol, OPW)

to search on the second floor. On 18 January, he received an order from the Chief Commissioner of the DMP to retire from the force for not carrying out his duties effectively. His pay was stopped on the same date. Inspector McFeely could not believe that after twenty-five years in the force his career was over. He appealed to the Chief Secretary at Dublin Castle in a heartfelt letter: 'Every Officer and man of the Force (past and present) who knows me is well aware that I always carried out my duties [in] a thorough and intelligent manner, and during all the strenuous and dangerous time through which we have passed, when men had reason to be uneasy, I never showed fear or shirked any work imposed on me.'[21]

McFeely's appeals fell on deaf ears. Whether he knew it or not, the raid on 56 Lower Sackville Street was strongly connected with the first attempt by British intelligence to capture senior IRA intelligence officers and Michael Collins himself. British intelligence agent Jack Byrnes, alias

John Jameson, had arrived in Ireland with impressive credentials as a social agitator and was recommended to Collins by Dáil Éireann envoy for London, Art Ó'Briain. Jameson posed as a jewellery salesman. He managed to meet with Michael Collins very soon after arriving in Ireland and reported back to his superiors the command system employed by the IRA in Dublin. It was out of his reports and observations of the IRA that the British began to focus on Collins.[22] Over time it would become an obsession.

Tom Cullen did not trust Jameson. On a number of occasions, premises where they had just met the British agent were raided. This led to Cullen voicing his concerns to his comrades. While Jameson attempted to set up Liam Tobin and Frank Thornton, those same IRA IOs decided to lay a trap for Jameson. Both Tobin and Thornton had worked for the New Ireland Assurance Company. Jameson said he could supply the IRA with weapons and the IRA men suggested the New Ireland offices as the drop-off point. Jameson met Tobin with a portmanteau filled with revolvers and proceeded to the hall of Kapp & Peterson on the ground floor. Frank Thornton met them and let Jameson see him go downstairs to the cellar. Tobin then took Jameson away. Thornton watched them leave before dashing aound the corner with the revolvers to Tom Cullen, who was waiting at 32 Bachelor's Walk, one of Collins' secret offices and the QM General's stores.

Detective Jim McNamara at G Division sent a message to Thornton that the New Ireland offices would be raided that day at 3 p.m. Thornton met up with Tobin and Cullen at McBirney's across the Liffey to watch events unfold. Sure enough, at 3 p.m. a large force of British soldiers and DMP led by Inspector McFeely pulled up and entered the building. Nothing was found and they left empty-handed. The raiding party returned later that night at 1 a.m. with picks and shovels to dig up the basement under Kapp & Peterson. Nothing was ever found save an old Irish Volunteer cap. As Inspector McFeely had not searched the basement on the first raid, the agent Jameson must have reported the first raid as a wasted opportunity.[23] Similar raids after meetings with Jameson followed and it appeared that Tom Cullen's suspicions were justified.

Jameson was staying at the Granville Hotel. His room was searched by Tom Cullen, who found incriminating documents among his possessions.[24] Jameson was now in great peril. He had met Collins and knew senior members of GHQ intelligence. Michael Collins issued an order for his execution. On 2 March 1920, Paddy O'Daly met Jameson in town and took him supposedly to meet Collins out in Glasnevin. He led Jameson down Hampstead Lane off Hollywood Road to where Tom Kilcoyne, Ben Barrett and Joe Leonard were waiting.[25] John Jameson was informed he would be shot. It is hard to believe he was not interrogated before his execution. The Squad had captured a British intelligence agent, who was at the time considered one of their very best. His knowledge alone on British intelligence in Dublin was worth a great deal.

The Squad made their getaway on three bicycles with one man standing pedalling and one seated behind him holding his shoulders. Jameson's body was found lying across the path that was Hampstead Lane at the back of Albert Model Farm. The only known description of perhaps one of Britain's finest agents was reported in the *Irish Independent* the next morning. Jameson was described as an 'unknown civilian' of 5' 9½" in height with dark hair, blue eyes and sharp features. He wore a gold ring with a red stone on his left hand and was well dressed. He also had a number of tattoos, from a butterfly to oriental designs. One tattoo bore the name 'Phyllis'. Jameson suffered a lonely death. His mission, to uncover the IRA and organise the capture of Michael Collins, had failed. Yet there is no denying this man's bravery nor his ability to arrange meetings with the IRA Director of Intelligence. The risks he took were evident from his injuries. He had a number of bullet wounds, one in the left side of the back exiting his chest through the heart, one in the back of the neck and one in front of the left ear. Jameson would have died immediately. When the RIC arrived, Jameson's body was surrounded by a group of children. A sergeant and two constables rushed the children away and quickly removed the body to a waiting ambulance and thence to the Mater Hospital.[26]

Another British agent was soon to follow Jameson into the hereafter: IRA IOs Paddy Caldwell and Joe Guilfoyle had a British agent called Molloy under surveillance. Molloy, whose real name was Bernie McNulty from Foxford in County Mayo, had been a sergeant in the Pay Corps and was now on the trail of Liam Tobin and Tom Cullen. By mid-March Molloy, posing as a double agent, had managed to establish contact with both Tobin and Cullen. He was perhaps unaware that as he met the key men of the IRA's intelligence department he was being watched by both Caldwell and Guilfoyle. A week later, on 24 March, the two IOs were ordered to meet Tobin and Cullen in Grafton Street. Cullen pulled Caldwell into a doorway and produced a .45 Webley revolver. Orders had been issued for Molloy's immediate execution. Joe Leonard, Paddy Caldwell and Joe Guilfoyle were ordered to act as cover while Mick McDonnell and Tom Kehoe moved in on the British agent.[27] Molloy was shot at the junction of Wicklow Street and William Street. On this occasion, the crowd on the street turned hostile and attempted to prevent McDonnell and Kehoe from escaping. A quick display of their weapons ensured people stepped away.[28]

Michael Collins next turned his attention to Alan Bell and his attempts to follow the trail of the Dáil Loan funds. As Minister for Finance, Collins had introduced the Dáil Loan Scheme and it brought in thousands of pounds as well as a great deal of gold. Collins deposited the monies with a number of different banks under fictitious names. Mr and Mrs Erskine Childers, Alderman Corrigan (whose car was so useful to the Dublin Brigade at Collinstown), Liam Devlin, Mr and Mrs Davin and George Nesbitt acted as trustees for large sums of money prior to the bank accounts being established. Solicitors Corrigan & Corrigan acted as a clearing house, especially for the large amounts from the USA. The money was deposited at the Munster & Leinster Bank (at the Dame Street, O'Connell Street and Phibsborough branches), the Hibernian Bank (at the College Green and Camden Street branches) and the National Bank at College Green. Some £203,000 of the Dáil Loan fund was used as capital to found the National Land Bank at Leeson Street Lower and further amounts were placed on deposit there.[29] Different locations were used so that if the money was uncovered in one bank the Dáil would not lose all of it. Gold in the form of sovereigns and gold bars (which came from Cork) were hidden in tins, between £250 and £500 in each, and buried at Corrigans' Undertakers at 5 Camden Street. The amount buried was worth over £25,500.[30] The National Land Bank initially had difficulty in getting its cheques accepted by other banks – they declined to do business with the Dáil Éireann initiative. Acting under instruction from Michael Collins, Daithí O'Donoghue, a Sinn Féin finance official, visited members of the Bankers Committee to deliver a 'message' from Michael Collins. National Land Bank cheques were accepted by the Irish banks within days.[31] Michael Collins was not the only one applying pressure to the Dublin banks, however. By March, Alan Bell RM was closing in on the Dáil money trail.

With his characteristic attention to detail, Bell had ordered the Dublin bank managers to attend the police courts as part of his inquiries. Michael

Collins ordered Sinn Féin and IRA solicitor Michael Noyk to see if he could gain access to Bell's sessions, but Noyk was denied access.[32] Mick McDonnell received orders to mobilise his men to kill Bell. Tom Cullen put Bell under surveillance and quickly established his daily routine from his home in Monkstown to his office at Dublin Castle. Every day at 9.30 a.m. Bell took a tram to the city centre to a stop opposite Trinity College.[33] The RIC had tried to impress upon Bell the danger he might be in and wanted to assign two detectives to accompany him as personal protection, but he would not hear of it. He eventually relented, allowing two detectives to meet him in the city and walk with him to Dublin Castle. With regular DMP patrols around Bell's home, the only clear opportunity to shoot the resident magistrate would be while he was on the morning tram.

On the morning of 26 March 1920, Mick McDonnell's Special Duties Unit assembled at Ailesbury Road. Tom Kehoe cycled behind the tram and signalled to the IRA men that Bell was on board.[34] When the tram stopped, Mick McDonnell, Liam Tobin, Jimmy Slattery, Vinnie Byrne, Tom Cullen, Joe Guilfoyle and Joe Dolan got on. A number of them went upstairs and McDonnell and Tobin sat opposite Bell. McDonnell leaned across to the unsuspecting man and asked: 'Are you Mr Bell?' No sooner had Bell said 'Yes' than a heavy hand landed on his shoulder, accompanied by the words: 'We want you.' Alan Bell was pulled out of his seat and dragged off the tram. McDonnell and Tobin shot Bell immediately on the pavement.[35] The Special Duties Unit then ran up Simmonscourt Road to escape. In the after-operation analysis, the IRA men observed the deserted open streets at the location and time of the shooting. They were used to operating in the crowded streets of the city centre. The open streets of the suburbs had left them exposed to any enemy counter-action. Fortunately for them, there had been no British military around on the morning of Bell's death. If there had been, Jimmy Slattery was convinced they would not have escaped. As he observed, 'That was a lesson that we took deeply to heart – remembered for future occasions.'[36]

The RIC investigation into the killing of Alan Bell RM followed the usual format: no one had seen anything nor could anybody identify any of the assailants. The British officials were infuriated by the lack of cooperation from members of the general public. Two civil servants, Mr Torney and Mr Francis, were interviewed by Sergeant S. D. Nixon of G Division. Both were on the top deck of the tram and had to have seen Alan Bell shot on the pavement. Torney said he was on the other side of the tram and saw nothing. He was very agitated about even being interviewed by the police. Mr Francis gave the following statement but refused to sign it, believing it would cast no light on the murder:

STATEMENT OF MR F.W. FRANCIS,

Accountant General's Office, Four Courts, re/

MURDER of MR ALAN BELL, R.M.

I travelled on the top of the Tram Car (Dalkey-Dublin) between 9 & 10 a.m. on Friday 26th inst. I was smoking a cigarette and reading a newspaper. At Sandymount Avenue I heard shots. I was very much upset, as I am not strong since my only son was killed in the late War.

I looked down on the Road and saw a man lying dead. I know nothing further.[37]

Assistant Commissioner Barrett of the DMP bitterly remarked that the statements from Mr Torney and Mr Francis 'show what little help poor Mr Bell received from parties whose position would lead one to expect something more. It shows what little assistance they intend giving (even confidentially) in the interests of society to track down these desperate assassins.'[38]

The view of the senior police officers was that these civil servants could not be relied upon nor should they continue in employment. One legal official suggested the men might actually have seen nothing. However, anyone who witnessed the Squad in action was simply terrified that they would themselves be killed if they were involved in an investigation. The IRA knew they had the power to instil absolute terror in the police, army, civil servants and the general public. But even though Irish people disapproved of murder, in general the greater part of the population was in sympathy with the cause of Dáil Éireann and the IRA, who they believed were fighting for the cause of the nation.[39] Fear of the agencies of the British state had been surpassed by fear of the IRA. It was one of the major factors used in paralysing those who might even think of assisting the British.

The ability to torture and kill people with impunity would have all sorts of consequences, both in the immediate future and in the long term. It was inevitable that killing people at very close range would have a serious effect on those carrying out such actions. Add to that the strain of intelligence work and living with the constant expectation of being caught and it should have been expected that people would crack sooner or later.

In April 1920, Mick McDonnell, the man with the responsibility for forming the first Special Duties Unit from B Company 2nd Battalion Dublin Brigade, suffered a breakdown in health. Dr Richard Hayes removed McDonnell to Jervis Street Hospital where he spent five weeks convalescing. McDonnell returned to duty but then his personal life became a cause for concern for IRA intelligence. McDonnell had married Ellen O'Toole on 9 October 1912.[40] They had a daughter, Sheila, in 1913. By 1919 McDonnell had become estranged from his wife, finding a new love with Eileen O'Loughlin, with whom he was spending a lot of time. Tom Cullen discovered Eileen's father was in the DMP and as a result did not trust her. Cullen also feared that McDonnell, because of his medical condition, might be talking a little too much about the IRA operations they had undertaken. One evening Tom Kehoe took Vinny Byrne for a joyride to the Phoenix Park on McDonnell's motorbike. Kehoe took a loaded gun and went looking for Eileen O'Loughlin but she could not be found. Byrne was sure Kehoe would have shot her if he had seen her that night.[41] Eileen had been very lucky but the incident indicates just how suspicion and fear went hand in hand, with the threat of death ever present. Mick McDonnell suffered a second breakdown in health in October 1920. By February 1921, Michael Collins was deeply worried about McDonnell's health and also that if he was captured he could reveal a great deal. Collins ordered McDonnell to the United States to recover,[42] but knew that McDonnell was beyond recovery.

It was during McDonnell's bouts of illness that Michael Collins decided that a full-time assassination unit was now necessary. The two small Special Duties Units were amalgamated and Paddy O'Daly was appointed O/C. New recruits were bought in to strengthen both IRA GHQ intelligence and the Squad. The new men were brought on operations and shown how actions were carried out. Each man 'had to prove his mettle and was detailed to do an actual job'.[43] In the intelligence department this might mean trailing a suspect, often an IRA operative. Unknowingly, while on this trial assignment, the new recruit would be under the surveillance of a seasoned member of IRA intelligence. If considered adequate the new recruit was brought on board; otherwise they were returned to the IRA unit from which they had come. For a prospective Squad member, a trial period meant an actual killing.

An Intelligence Officer always accompanied the Squad when assigned a 'job'. The usual locations were street junctions as this gave the assassins a number of escape routes. The Intelligence Officer would identify the man to be killed. Two men were always detailed to carry out the killing.[44] Paddy O'Daly or Jim Slattery always 'nominated' the two men and 'This was adhered to rigidly'.[45] The Intelligence Officer would often go up to the intended target and ask him a simple question (e.g. 'Are you Alan Bell?') or by making a prearranged signal like lifting their hat or taking out a handkerchief.[46] The intended target, thus identified, was then surrounded and either killed on the spot or taken to another location and shot. On a rare occasion, when there was some doubt about the target's guilt, he would be abducted, sometimes in broad daylight, and interrogated. If his answers were satisfactory he was released; otherwise, he was executed. The Intelligence Officer would also join in the killing, usually firing the first shot. In the earlier stages of the Squad's assassinations, victims were shot in the trunk of the body, this being the larger part of the target, making hitting the target more likely (unless you were Tom Cullen, who, according to Dan Breen, 'was a terrible shot'[47]). Jim Slattery said the key to a successful 'job' was 'getting close to your man'.[48] Slattery later admitted that he had missed a few times even when he was 'up close'.[49]

Some detectives were extremely fortunate. Detective Sergeant Richard J. Revelle, who lived off Phibsborough Road at 10 Connaught Street, found himself confronted by the Squad on Saturday morning, 8 May 1920, as he was cycling to work at Dublin Castle. Paddy O'Daly, Tom Kehoe and Joe Leonard secured the 'gateway' and covered the main unit. Four Squad members, Joe Leonard and Vinny Byrne among them, stepped off the path and opened fire, the repeated gunshots blowing Revelle off his bicycle and across the road. Revelle was seriously wounded and lay on the road with blood pouring from a neck wound, two bullet holes in his arm, which was fractured, and a leg wound. Sure of their kill, the men ran off towards Cross Guns Bridge. However, locals rushed to Revelle's aid and staunched the bleeding. He had been wearing a steel bullet-proof jacket[50] and survived. He was certain that one of the men who fired at him had been observing his movements. That man was Vinny Byrne. After this, the Squad required certainty of a kill and from then on a shot to the head was required, along with a number of shots to the body.

The Squad never questioned Collins' reasons for having someone killed. Mick Collins, as far as members of the Squad were concerned, 'was the kind of man it was easy to trust. He had a sense of purpose, confidence and dedication. If he ordered something to be done there was always a sound reason for having it done.'[51] Yet Collins also had the ruthless streak required of military commanders during war, to identify objectives and detail men and women to carry them out knowing there would sometimes be casualties. The risks and danger experienced by his operatives affected Collins greatly and he could visualise their suffering. Eamon Broy, who spent a lot of time with the Director of IRA Intelligence, related how Collins described events:

> Collins had such a remarkable power of description that, listening to him, one could form a vivid mental picture of the occurrences he described. For instance, in his account of the tortures of Hales and Harte in West Cork, the impression he created was as vivid as if one actually saw the pliers being used to tear the flesh from the victim. These tortures were inflicted by the British Army long before the Black and Tans came to the country. As a result of his treatment Harte went insane.[52]

It has been claimed that Collins was not vindictive and the Squad were not sent out to kill for revenge. There was always a reason for a killing. Yet it is difficult to argue that point when members of the RIC and British army were assassinated. In the early stage of the conflict members of the RIC were shot for being too diligent in their detective and police work against Sinn Féin and the IRA. Later, they were shot in retaliation for involvement in operations against the IRA. The assassination of District Inspector Lea-Wilson in Gorey, County Wexford, by members of the Squad was always said to be because Lea-Wilson had beaten Tom Clarke or Sean Mac Diarmada after the surrender of the Irish Volunteers in 1916. Paddy O'Daly denied this, writing:

> Captain Lea-Wilson was not shot because he had ill-treated Sean McDermott and other prisoners in 1916, because there were other British officers just as bad as he had been and no attempt was ever made to shoot them. I believe he was shot on account of the position he held at the time of his execution, and for no other reason. I am satisfied from my long experience with the Squad that no man was shot merely for revenge and that any execution sanctioned by Michael Collins was perfectly justified.[53]

O'Daly went on to relate how he once received a 'dressing down' from Collins. Rumours were put about at IRA GHQ that O'Daly was going to shoot Inspector Winters, who had treated O'Daly's disabled daughter harshly during a raid on his home after 1916. The girl had only one hand and was shoved to one side by Winters for making a sarcastic remark. The British officer in charge of the raid ordered Winters out of the house. Collins, who heard the rumours, was raging. He demanded to know if O'Daly intended to shoot Winters. O'Daly dismissed the accusation, saying it was only a joke. Collins gave O'Daly a lecture on revenge and how those who engaged in it were not fit to be Irish Volunteers. O'Daly's parting quip to Collins was that if Winters was ever marked for assassination he would like to be considered for the 'job'.[54] O'Daly certainly had a vindictive streak and frequently acted upon it.

There is evidence to support Paddy O'Daly's assertion in relation to Lea-Wilson. If Lea-Wilson was not shot out of revenge, why was he killed? On 20 March 1920, the Lord Mayor of Cork, Tomás Mac Curtain, a member of Sinn Féin and O/C of Cork No. 1 Brigade of the Irish Volunteers, was assassinated when a group of masked men with blackened faces stormed his home. IRA GHQ intelligence was given the task of tracking down those who had carried out the attack. According to Frank Thornton, Michael Collins received a report of a Crossley car that had gone to a large house at Tinneranny on the Kilkenny side of the rivers Nore and Barrow near New Ross in County Wexford. The car had come and gone from the house a few times and in it was a man described as small, dark, swarthy and carrying an ashplant. He also wore a distinctive signet ring on the little finger of his left hand. A man of similar description had arrived at Mac Curtain's home to carry out an interrogation. Mrs Mac Curtain had given his description to IRA intelligence and it matched that of Captain Jocelyn Lee Hardy of British army intelligence. This man, nicknamed 'Hoppy' by the Dublin Brigade because of his wooden leg due to an injury in the First World War, developed a fearsome reputation for terror on the streets of Dublin during the War of Independence.

On the night of Mac Curtain's killing, two cars left the house outside New Ross and went south. On 29 March, the night Thomas Dwyer was killed at The Ragg near Thurles, County Tipperary, two cars again left the house, this time travelling in the Tipperary direction.[55] Thornton, along with Phil Lennon O/C Wexford and some of his men, investigated the case, proving the stories to be correct, even discovering the tyre tracks of the Crossley cars. The house, owned by a Protestant family with Unionist sympathies, was raided by the IRA and the people interrogated and court-martialled. They admitted that British officers had used the house. The IRA sentenced the family to deportation. Frank Thornton maintained that the group using this house was a 'military gang' which preceded the later assassination units of the British secret service. The distance from Gorey to New Ross is only 37 miles (60 km). If Lea-Wilson was even suspected of being a member of the British unit operating from New Ross and involved in the killing of two IRA officers, it would have been enough to warrant an IRA investigation.

District Inspector Lea-Wilson was shot dead by members of the Squad on the morning of 15 June 1920 just outside Gorey, County Wexford. He had walked the short distance from his home into town to buy a newspaper. The Squad, feigning a car breakdown, waited for him on the return journey. The order to kill the policeman came from two IRA senior IOs, Liam Tobin and Frank Thornton. Tom Cullen, Jimmy Slattery and Pat McCrea were among the Squad members on this assignment. Joseph McMahon, Jack Whelan and Liam O'Leary from the Wexford Brigade provided local knowledge after the Squad had carried out a reconnaissance mission to New Ross and Gorey.[56] The mission ended in the usual manner with a hail of gunfire and the victim lying on the roadside covered in blood, the assailants departing the grisly scene as quickly as possible.

The British cabinet were not idle while the assassinations continued. Lloyd George now believed that the RIC and DMP were simply not able to face the IRA campaign. In January 1920, orders were dispatched to the British military in Ireland to actively assist the RIC.[57] The period after the republican victory in the local elections in January 1920 was followed by an intensification of raids by the British army. They were ordered to arrest members of Sinn Féin and the IRA who were considered to be 'important and really dangerous'.[58] In January alone the army carried out over 1,000 raids across the country in which 220 arrests were made.[59] The raids continued in February, numbering at least 4,000 with 296 arrested.[60]

Some of the raids in Dublin led to startling discoveries. On 21 February, a British raiding party was driving up and down Oakley Road in Ranelagh. They were looking for the IRA Chief of Staff's home, 'Cullenswood' at No. 4. Michael Collins also had an office there known as 'The Republican Hut'. The streets were dark and No. 4 had no number on it so the soldiers passed on by until they came to No. 44. This was the home of Áine Ceannt, widow of the executed 1916 Irish Volunteer Éamon Ceannt. Also living there at the time was Robert C. Barton. One of the numbers had fallen from the '44' on the gate and so the British entered the house. Barton, though not on the list, was arrested.[61] The British returned to Oakley Road a few nights later and this time they made no mistakes. Mulcahy's home was raided, he himself only just escaping out a back window in his pyjamas.

While searching the house, the British discovered many files, including the IRA rolls for the Dublin Brigade. A second tranche of Mulcahy's papers was discovered in another raid on 19 November 1920. The capture of his papers led to the location and arrest of leading IRA members in Dublin. The consequences of such captures were also felt far from Dublin. Seumus Robinson recorded for the Bureau of Military History:

> When Ernie O'Malley came to us he had a typewriter and a porter, trying to satisfy G.H.Q.'s insatiable maw for written reports, until after we had twelve of our most important houses burned after the Cullenswood House raid, when we told Ernie that we would stand for no more written reports from South Tipperary being sent to Dublin. Ernie very much sympathised with us. It was his dispatches that had been captured![62]

The British army raids continued as well as an increased presence of troops, patrols and sudden checkpoints on Dublin streets. A curfew was imposed on the city on 23 February 1920. It ran from midnight until 5 a.m. Twenty British army patrols, each consisting of one officer and twelve other ranks, moved around the city every night keeping order.[63] As the conflict increased, the British made tactical adaptations to their lorries. Some had cages fitted to cover the top of the lorry to prevent grenades being tossed inside the vehicle. Other lorries had steel plates welded to the outside as armoured protection for the troops. Captain Rymer-Jones of the 1st Battalion King's Own Liverpool Regiment served as an infantry officer in Dublin from 1920 to 1921. His duties included a posting as transport officer, exercising horses in parks, guard duties, night curfew patrols, raids and detachments to guard the isolated RIC barracks at Lucan.[64] Interviewed in 1989 by historian Peter Hart, the retired brigadier offered some operational and personal insights into his time in Dublin during the War of Independence:

How did you get on with the population generally?
Well, I was on raids and I appeared in one of the Irish papers described as 'A very polite young Officer'. I don't know whether that pleases me or not.

We were raiding for information. One of the people I had to raid was the house of one of the people who went over the top at Passchendaele, a Captain Redmond. He wasn't in and I had to go through the motions of searching the place. Considering his politics I had to take away his uniform. I took it away.

I did another one, daughters of a well-known gallant British officer ... Of course if Home Rule had been granted before the war there wouldn't have been any of this trouble. I did support Home Rule. Protestants were arming themselves.

Did you understand the politics then?
Yes. The Rising happened during the War. Very difficult to sort yourself out on these questions. That chance had passed. General Gough was one of the people who was very naughtily supporting the Ulstermen whereas he ought to have been put under arrest.

We had been trained in their searching work. 'Raid these places because these are the people who are causing the trouble.' When we raided the house the two girls were saying 'why don't you look under the carpet, why don't you lift the floor up?' I said 'It's all very funny to hear you, you know, but this is a very serious matter. It's to stop people being killed.'

When you found the Nominal Rolls ... how would you organise those raids?
We had six officers a night and six houses for each of them to raid. We didn't always manage it. I had a most interesting raid. They were all in Ship Street, slums, and Inchicore. From these rolls it was clear in Inchicore that they came from almost every house.

And how would you organise it? How would you gain entrance and secure exits?
Officer shot on his own as he tried to gain revenge for the death of his brother – door opened by a priest and a Sinn Féin shot him over the priest's shoulder.[65]

You took your house and detailed usually a Sergeant to cover the rear if anybody rushed out the back. I'd have the whole Platoon, Sergeant and a few men, rushed the house and got a hold of the senior member of the family and gather all the family in one room. 'You [the senior member], come with me so I don't destroy anything or make a nuisance of anything.' We went around and found the father of the family. We took him back and the Barracks were full but we put him in Mizzen [Nissen] huts. His sons were on the run. 'You'll stop and have a cup of tea before you go?'

If they didn't open the door we'd have to break it down. They'd usually open it. Weapons, information, the stuff we found in the drawers. You wouldn't find anything worthwhile like literature in these slum houses. Never found anything, didn't expect to. Really looking for the young men of the Sinn Féin but they had always left.

1916 was the first revolt but after that the trouble didn't stop and they were undercover. We were out there trying to keep things down. I was closely involved with the undercover Sinn Féiners. After Bloody Sunday everything changed.

We were out nearly every night because of the capture of the nominal rolls of Inchicore ...

Any sympathy with the Sinn Féin? No, but with the Irish yes. Carson and Gough were stupid people. Without them we'd have had Home Rule and none of this trouble.[66]

Captain Rymer-Jones had previously served as an intelligence officer with the British army in Germany after the First World War. Curiously, he also served in Egypt directly before his posting in Dublin. Rymer-Jones reveals the attitude of many of the British troops serving in Ireland: they had a job to do and had to make the best of a bad lot.

In March 1920 General Shaw was replaced by General Sir Nevil Macready as General Officer Commanding-in-Chief Ireland. A former chief of police from London, General Macready despised Ireland and its people even more than 'the Boche'.[67] He reported to the British cabinet how a posting to Ireland was received by British soldiers: 'While [...] all ranks are interested in the work and show increased keenness, the number of desertions and applications for discharge are heavy, which indicates that service in this country is not popular.'[68]

Active service for a British soldier in Ireland was a radically different proposition from conventional warfare. Dealing with an indifferent or hostile population was not easy. General Macready understood the difficulties of this situation for his troops:

> [U]nder the present conditions it is necessary for the troops to be on as good terms with the inhabitants as possible, and at the same time to be willing and ready to shoot if occasion requires. It is this that makes it so difficult to bring home to young lads the fact that they are liable to be attacked at any moment by people who pretend to be on good terms with them, or who seem to be carrying out their daily avocations (this was very marked in the attack on troops at Kingsbridge Station on 19th July, when the majority of the attackers were apparently railwaymen dressed in blue overalls).[69]

Ireland was divided into British army districts, in an east–west direction from coast to coast. General Strickland commanded the testing 6th divisional area in the south. This area was extremely challenging in terms of both IRA activity and topography, containing some of Ireland's biggest mountain ranges. The British army faced shrewd IRA commanders like Tom Barry, Liam Lynch and Michael Brennan, who would significantly stretch the British crown forces. The 5th divisional area was commanded by General Jeudwine and took in a vast swathe of Ireland from Wicklow to Galway. Also included were Mayo, Leitrim and Donegal. In this area the military faced IRA guerrilla commanders Seán MacÉoin, Michael Kilroy and Tom Maguire. Ulster was garrisoned by the Ulster Brigade, which became the 1st Division in August 1920. It took in the six counties which would form Northern Ireland, plus Monaghan. In Ulster, the IRA fielded a number of commanders of considerable ability: Commandants Eoin O'Duffy and Dan Hogan (brother of Michael Hogan, who was killed at Croke Park) in Monaghan, Captain Frank Aiken in Armagh, and Commandants Joe McKelvey and Roger MacCorley and IO Michael Carolan in Belfast.[70]

The British army Dublin District covered Counties Dublin, Meath, Louth and Cavan. Dublin city was divided into two distinct British military zones. The region north of the River Liffey was under the command of the 24th Infantry Brigade, while the area south of the Liffey was under the 25th.

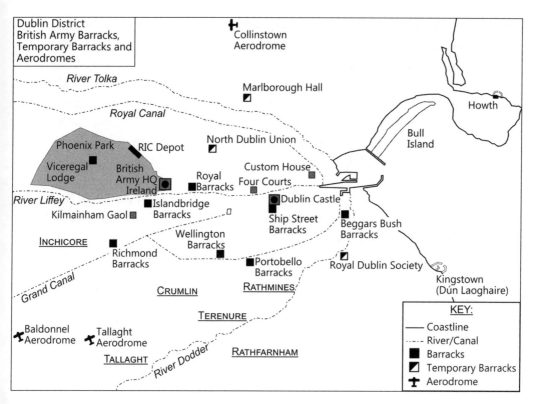

British army barracks and aerodromes in Dublin City and County.
(With thanks to Eoin Brennan)

The overall British commander of the Dublin District was Major-General Gerald Boyd. He was described as: 'a disciplinarian, a tremendous worker, at all times cheerful and optimistic ... he can, and does, breathe his own indomitable spirit into his men'.[71] He had joined the British army as a private and had risen through the ranks, receiving a battlefield commission during the Boer War. Major-General Boyd was given a tough assignment. He had command an army of battle-hardened officers and senior NCOs and young, inexperienced recruits while adapting to a new type of enemy engaging in urban and rural guerrilla warfare. His response to the situation in Dublin was rigorous and energetic.

General Boyd's initiatives paid off. A large number of Sinn Féin TDs and IRA officers and men were arrested during the early part of 1920. On 5 April, IRA prisoners at Mountjoy Gaol began a hunger strike. A strike by transport workers added pressure on the British government. On 12 and 13 April, huge crowds of up to 20,000 republican supporters began protesting outside the prison. General Boyd deployed more troops and called in an aeroplane to 'buzz' the crowd. The tactic worked and reduced the tension on the streets.

Lloyd George's cabinet then decided to release the hunger strikers.[72] The British army viewed it as a serious mistake to free IRA personnel. Agents and sympathisers who had assisted the British army and RIC were now vulnerable to retribution, which would certainly discourage others from helping the Crown forces in future.[73] The constant political interference from Downing Street undermined the military efforts to defeat the IRA.

At a cabinet meeting in Downing Street on Monday 7 June 1920, the British confirmed their decision to stand and fight in Ireland. This would be achieved by reorganising the Irish civil administration, reinforcing the police and increasing the military garrison. The cabinet believed it would also be necessary to strengthen the law.[74] To implement this strategy, a new team was put in place at Dublin Castle.

Sir Hamar Greenwood was appointed Chief Secretary to Ireland. A Canadian and a former King's Counsel, he served as parliamentary private secretary to Winston Churchill. Greenwood was noted for his decisive ability and was a teetotaller. During the First World War he became commander of the 10th Battalion South Wales Borderers, a unit he raised himself. Greenwood was a strong supporter of Lloyd George. He believed in restoring British rule in Ireland by defeating the IRA.[75] Greenwood became the public face of the British terror policy in Ireland and received much of the ire of opposition politicians, the British and Irish press and Irish public opinion. In spite of this opposition Greenwood performed well.

While Greenwood was the public face of British policy in Ireland, the real power behind the scenes at Dublin Castle was Under-Secretary Sir John Anderson, a Scotsman and graduate of Edinburgh University in mathematics, chemistry and geology. Recommended by Sir Warren Fisher, Permanent Secretary to the Treasury, Anderson was noted for his capacity to grasp the essence of a problem quickly, to determine how it could be solved and to establish an effective means of doing so. Anderson was also appointed Treasury Representative to Ireland.[76] This post was very important as it gave him insight into and control over British expenditure in Ireland, which included financing the Crown forces and secret service. Some of Anderson's papers and reports would refer to issues so sensitive that they are withheld from the scrutiny of historians almost a century later![77]

Anderson worked very closely with General Macready, and frequently tempered the general's desire for firm action in dealing with the Irish.

The final addition to this new British team at Dublin Castle was the appointment of Alfred Cope as Assistant Under-Secretary. Andy Cope, as he was known, was from Lambeth in London and had worked at Customs and Excise. George Chester Duggan, who was a civil servant in finance at Dublin Castle at this time, said of Cope:

> On him was to fall the difficult task of harmonising friction between police and military and between those quasi-military and too often sinister forces – Auxiliaries and Black and Tans ... He too was to try to secure contact with Republican leaders ... a strange personality ... and at first sight a curious choice for the post. But he was a man who revelled in work, who was never happier than when he held a dozen threads in his hand, and in the tangled web of Irish politic there were threads enough to spare ... He hated airs of self assumption, he hated intolerance, he breathed the spirit of a fighting democracy. His career in Ireland was a long struggle against militarism, which sought to impose itself on the life of the country.[78]

The British army did not understand the need for a political strategy running parallel with a military one. Just as the republican movement had developed a dual political/military strategy, so too had the experienced Lloyd George. Ultimately, the War of Independence would be settled through some form of negotiation and political settlement. For Lloyd George, the British army was one tool in accomplishing that end. The prime minister would use the Crown forces, the RIC and the Auxiliaries to defeat the IRA. If that could not be achieved, these combined forces would weaken the IRA enough to impose a political settlement as advantageous to the British empire as possible. The British cabinet gave approval for 'some plan whereby Irishmen were made to feel the effect of the campaign of murder and arson along economic channels'.[79]

In March and April 1920, the British government had applied pressure on the DMP and RIC to locate Michael Collins. RIC Head Constable for Clonakilty Michael Keany knew Collins' family and had pieced together some of Collins' routine in Dublin. Keany submitted a report from Clonakilty on 3 March in which he said he was 'reliably informed' that Collins was residing permanently in Dublin and was a constant visitor at the residence of John P. Twohig at 'Craigmeller' on Haddon Road in

Clontarf and also at Timothy Donovan's residence, 3 St Michael's, Sarsfield Road in Inchicore. He said these two men were married to aunts of Collins'. Keany concluded his report, stating: 'I am informed that Collins walks the streets of Dublin with two cousins of his, Hannah and Mary O'Brien.'

G Division followed up on Keany's report in locating Michael Collins and the family and friends with whom he was known to associate. Detective Officer Coffey's investigations came to nothing and he reported his findings as follows: 'As far as I can ascertain neither have been seen associating with a man answering Collins' description.' For his dedication to duty Head Constable Michael Keany was promoted to the rank of District Inspector in Clonakilty. He was shot and killed in broad daylight in front of his nineteen-year-old son on 11 February 1922, after the truce.[80] With the DMP offering no leads on the whereabouts of Michael Collins and the senior IRA leadership in Dublin, it was decided to expand the army's already developing intelligence department.[81]

The seizure of IRA documents gave army intelligence vital leads in identifying key IRA figures, organisational structure and home addresses. In early 1920 a small group of British officers began intelligence operations on their own initiative. By March, this group was assimilated into the Special Branch of Dublin District British Army Command. Brigadier-General J. E. S. Brind was appointed O/C, with Colonel Hill-Dillon of MI5 as second in command. However, working in the same building as Hill-Dillon's office was IRA IO Lily Mernin. Brind and Hill-Dillon worked to create a central registry at British army GHQ and with a card index system they attempted to filter information received from units at company and battalion level. Intelligence officers aimed to recruit informers and liaise with the RIC.[82] To run intelligence operations, British army divisions and the secret service received a substantial budget from which to draw funds. In the financial year 1 April 1920 to 31 March 1921, the 6th Division in the south drew down £2,032 while the 5th Division in the midlands, west and north-west drew down £320. The 1st Division spent just £14 on intelligence in the same period whereas the Dublin District disposed of the considerable sum of £20,000. The British believed if they could crack IRA resistance in Dublin they could win the conflict. The key to that was first to identify Michael Collins and his officers and then to capture or kill them.[83]

In May 1920 a training school for British intelligence agents and spies under the command of Lieutenant Colonel Walter C. Wilson was established at Hounslow, west of London. Graduating from this school, the British intelligence officers filtered into Dublin in increasing numbers.[84] They lived outside Dublin Castle, taking lodgings under assumed names. Dressed in plain clothes, these agents monitored ships, railway stations, cafés and restaurants.[85] The Cairo Café and Kidd's in Grafton Street were regular haunts. Posing as touts, IRA IOs Tom Cullen, Frank Thornton and Frank Saurin established contact with two of the British secret service agents, Lieutenant George Bennet and Lieutenant Peter Ames. According to Thornton the group became 'great friends'.[86] However, they would meet up one morning in November under far less cordial circumstances.

Some of the British secret service retained their former identity as regular British officers simply seconded to other units in Ireland. Such regular identities were not just a useful cover but also served as good propaganda when some of them became casualties of IRA counter-intelligence actions. They gathered information and moved under cover of darkness to carry out operations against the IRA, operations that included searches for documents, weapons and ammunition, and suspects. They also carried out assassinations. The British had now found an effective counterpart to G Division of the DMP.

The same month as the establishment of a secret service training school saw Hill-Dillon replaced by Colonel Ormonde de L'Épée Winter with the title Deputy Chief of Police and Director of Intelligence for Ireland. He was known as 'O'. The intelligence network heretofore established by the British army was removed from their control and handed to Colonel Winter, under the command of Basil Thompson as Directorate of Intelligence or 'London Bureau'.[87] There was a great deal of infighting among the British about methods and personnel. The British army were most definitely not impressed with Winter and his operatives. This hampered their efforts to some degree, enabling IRA intelligence to maintain the lead they had established early in 1919. During the summer months of 1920, 'O' flooded Dublin with his secret service agents. In June there were just seven secret service officers in Dublin. In July the number had increased to fifty-one; in August there were eighty-two and in November ninety-seven.[88] As the respective intelligence departments struggled for supremacy on Dublin's streets, the nightly raids by British troops continued. A description of such nights was provided by Erskine Childers and appeared in the *Daily News*, Monday 29 March 1920:

As the citizens go to bed, the barracks spring to life. Lorries, tanks, and armoured searchlight cars, muster in fleets, lists of 'objectives' are distributed, and, when the midnight curfew order has emptied the streets – pitch dark streets – the weird cavalcade issue forth to the attack. Think of raiding a private house at the dead of night in a tank (my own experience), in a tank whose weird rumble and roar can be heard miles away! ... A thunder of knocks: no time to dress (even for a woman alone) or the door will crash in. On opening, in charge the soldiers – literally charge – with fixed bayonets and in full war-kit. No warrant shown on entering, no apology on leaving, if, as in nine cases out of ten, suspicions prove to be groundless and the raid a mistake. In many recent instances even women occupants have been locked up under guard while their own property is ransacked. Imagine the moral effect of such a procedure on the young officers and men told off for this duty! Is it any wonder that gross abuses occur: looting, wanton destruction, brutal severity to women?[89]

While Childers refers to the effects of raids upon women, what could not be referred to was the central role played by women in supporting the Irish revolution. Women were involved officially as members of Cumann na mBan. They were also involved on an unofficial level, engaging in covert operations. Operations carried out by women included administrative duties, acting as couriers of dispatches, transport of weapons and ammunition, first aid and the storing of IRA intelligence documents and arms. The transporting of arms and ammunition involved moving weapons not just to different companies and battalions in Dublin but also to different parts of the country. Captain Eileen McGrane was O/C of the university branch of Cumann na mBan and joined after the Rising, when she came to Dublin to attend university.[90] Captain McGrane offered Michael Collins a room for storage in her lodgings, which she shared with Mary McCarthy and Margot Trench at 21 Dawson Street. Collins' No. 2, Tom Cullen, stored the handguns and ammunition used by IRA GHQ intelligence there, along with copies of highly classified DMP, RIC and British intelligence documents. Cumann na mBan also provided some comforts of home such as meals, clean clothes or lodgings for IRA men on the run. Offering them warm food, water to wash and shave and a clean shirt on their back sustained morale in stressful circumstances. For young men on operations of a very grim nature, the strong logistical support

Senior officers of Cumann na mBan with Lord Mayor of Dublin Laurence O'Neill at the Mansion House Dublin, c.1922. (Courtesy Sandra Shallow-Brennan)

and kindness of the republican women was undoubtedly critical to IRA success.

The Cumann na mBan organisation was founded on Thursday 2 April 1914 at a meeting in Wynn's Hotel on Lower Abbey Street, Dublin.[91] The organisation became well established in Dublin city and county. The spirit of their revolutionary intent was expressed through their adopted badge, the letters C[NA]MB presented with a rifle. Eileen McGrane got her uniform from Harry Boland's drapery store in Middle Abbey Street. The service provided by Cumann na mBan in the 1916 Rising had proved the case for the involvement of women in a revolution against British rule. Of the women who took part in the Rising, seventy-seven were imprisoned.[92] The women of this movement were fighting not just for the freedom of Ireland but also for the equality they believed an Irish republic would bring. Dublin was the seat of the Cumann na mBan executive, which ran the entire organisation in Ireland, Britain and further afield. Dublin city and county was run by a district council,[93] which was attended by a captain and secretary from each of the ten Dublin city branches. They met weekly and undertook the implementation of urgent assignments as well as ensuring training standards were maintained.[94] Each branch of Cumann na mBan was attached to a local IRA battalion. In Dublin city two or three branches were assigned to support each Dublin Brigade battalion. A captain was elected to take command of each Cumann na mBan Branch and was aided by a lieutenant and an adjutant.[95] Each branch was divided into three sections. Each section was subdivided into a right and a left squad.

CUMANN NA MBAN ORGANISATIONAL STRUCTURE 1919–1923[96]

President: Madam Markievicz TD

Dublin City District Council

Secretary Comdt Margaret (Loo) Kennedy

O/C Eilís Ní Ríain [Ryan]

Vice O/C Sorcha Bhean Mhic Ruaidhri [McMahon]

Vice O/C Eily O'Hanrahan

Cumann na mBan Branches assigned to 1st Battalion Dublin Brigade Area:	Cumann na mBan Branches assigned to 2nd Battalion Dublin Brigade Area:	Cumann na mBan Branches assigned to 3rd Battalion Dublin Brigade Area:	Cumann na mBan Branches assigned to 4th Battalion Dublin Brigade Area:
1. Ard Craobh O/C Capt. Eilís Ní Ríain (165 members)	**1. Ranelagh** O/C Capt. Phyllis Ryan (123 members)	**1.University** O/C Capt. Eileen McGrane arrested 1 Jan 1921 & succeeded by Capt. Dr Kathleen Murphy (62 members)	**1. Eamonn Ceannt** O/C Capt. Mary Twamley (50 members)
2. Columcille O/C Capt. Bridie O'Reilly (46 members)	**2. Fairview** O/C Capt. Judy Gaughran (39 members)	**2. Ringsend** O/C Capt. Áine Ellis (32 members)	**2. Inghinidhe** O/C Capt. May Byrne (90 members)
	3. Drumcondra O/C Capt. Brigid English (62 members)	**3. Inghinidhe** O/C Capt. May Byrne (90 members)	Note: **Inghinidhe** assigned to both 3rd & 4th Bn areas.

F Company Auxiliary Division RIC photographed at Dublin Castle.
(Courtesy the Military Archives)

One example of the work carried out by the women of Cumann na mBan was that of Máire Gleeson, or Mollie as she was known to her friends. She had arrived in Dublin in June 1916. It was said of her that she 'threw herself heart and soul into the activities around her'.[97] She initially assisted the South Tipperary Brigade in regularly transporting arms, or as Mollie referred to them, her 'golfsticks', on the train from Kingsbridge to Limerick Junction. The British military very courteously offered to carry her 'stuff'. Mollie always gratefully accepted their help.[98] Patrick Seely, a porter at Kingsbridge Station, acted as a courier for Molly due to the proximity of her restaurant, on Parkgate Street, called West End Café. This café became a hub for British soldiers and Auxiliaries who were off duty from the army HQ across the road and hungry for a bite to eat. She got to know two Black and Tans, Arnott and Rogers, very well. Apparently, Rogers 'was a real harum-scarum'. One of her more infamous, or famous, depending on which side you were on, diners at West End Café was RIC Head Constable Eugene Igoe. With so many Crown forces personnel dining in her establishment Molly 'was on the qui vive [alert] at all times and acted immediately on every cue', passing on very useful information which 'perhaps saved documents, arms or even lives'.[99]

There were a number of women who were not members of Cumann na mBan but who were committed to the Republican movement. One of them was Ellen Sarah Bushell of 2 New Street, Inchicore. Born in 1884 in Frances Street, Dublin, Ellen became involved in the republican movement through serving on the executive of Na Fianna. She began by making kilts for the Chead Sluagh of Na Fianna Éireann in 1910 and also for the students of Pearse's school in Rathfarnham, St Enda's. She took no money for doing the work, being content to assist children who could barely afford the cloth. She was a weaver of silk and poplin, like her father, Edward. She also made bandoliers out of mailbags for the Volunteers. Ellen then worked in the Abbey Theatre. She personally knew Pádraig Pearse, Tomás MacDonagh and Con Colbert, leaders in the 1916 Rising. Prior to the Rising her house was used for meetings and during Easter Week she was constantly on the move, acting as a courier for the different Irish Volunteer garrisons.[100] Later on, she hid weapons, ammunition and explosives in the Abbey Theatre for the 3rd Battalion. Wounded IRA men were treated in her home. Pádraig Ó Conchubhair received medical attention for a bullet wound in Miss Bushell's in June 1919.[101] Eventually, the British realised the importance of her house and became aware of her activities. Her home was raided by Black and Tans eight times in two weeks and was left so badly damaged in the process she was homeless for five weeks.[102]

It was Irish women like Ellen Bushell who all too often had to deal with the aftermath of IRA actions. On 14 April the RIC were withdrawn from isolated barracks that were vulnerable to attack by the IRA. The IRA responded by burning out the vacated barracks, thus preventing a return by the RIC at a later date. This tactical error strengthened the IRA's position across Ireland. The British had to attempt to control these areas by mobile patrols, which were exposed to ambush. The Dublin and Fingal Brigades responded immediately and organised the burning of these barracks in County Dublin. Commandant Dick McKee aimed to deprive the newly arriving Black and Tan reinforcements or British military of the use of these barracks as a tool for closing the net on the IRA. In May 1920 F Company 4th Battalion were ordered to destroy Crumlin RIC Barracks. As the building was being drenched with petrol and Volunteer Joe Larkin, a member of the Engineers, was setting the explosive charge, someone opened a lantern. The naked flame ignited the petrol vapour. Larkin was badly burned as he fought his way through the flames to the doorway.[103] Lieutenant George Dwyer took him to Miss Bushell's house in Inchicore before setting off with Paddy O'Connor on their bicycles to summon medical help. Eventually, Larkin was removed to Miss Flood's house nearby,[104] which was also the site of the company arms dump. Dr Rock treated Larkin for six weeks. He made a full recovery.

Other Volunteers did not fare so well. On 12 May 1920, a combined 6th Battalion unit of the IRA under the command of B Company Captain Peter O'Mara staged a raid to burn out the RIC barracks at Ballybrack in south County Dublin, which had been vacated six months earlier.[105] Another unit was to attack Kill of the Grange DMP barracks not far away. The area was now covered by combined police and British army patrols. Ballybrack was still occupied by the sergeant's wife, Mrs Hurst, and her children. Around 10 p.m. Captain O'Mara and his men arrived at the barracks, armed with revolvers and with their faces masked. They had cut the local telegraph wires in advance. O'Mara gave Mrs Hurst ten minutes to collect her belongings and leave the building. She pleaded with the IRA officer to give her time to remove her treasured piano but time would not allow it. The bed and some other possessions were all she could carry out with the help of her family. While Mrs Hurst was saving what she could, the IRA company placed straw, saturated with petrol, in different parts of the building. O'Mara then ordered the building evacuated before setting the fire, but someone prematurely struck a match, igniting the petrol vapour. Within seconds the place was an inferno. Lieutenant Tom Dunne and QM Pat Meaney were trapped inside. Desperate to get the men out, O'Mara ordered the protective steel shutters to be sprung from one of the windows on the ground floor. The men were rescued but both had received horrific burns.[106] A motorcyclist passing the scene was held up at gunpoint and ordered to bring the two badly injured men to a Dublin hospital. The IRA unit then dispersed.

As Tom Dunne and Pat Meaney were taken to the Mater Hospital on what must have been a nightmare journey, the RIC, the DMP and the British army set out to investigate the attacks. The Kingstown DMP arrived at Kill of the Grange to find the barracks in flames and not a soul in sight. Investigations proved fruitless. At 2.30 a.m. Sergeant John J. Flanagan, with a combined police and British army patrol from the RIC's Cabinteely barracks, arrived at Ballybrack. They were greeted by a distraught woman, a blazing RIC barracks and a trail of blood leading away from the scene. Lieutenant Leonard Rudge of the 2nd Battalion Worcester Regiment followed the trail to a fountain and on for 400 yards (365 metres). There he made the gruesome discovery of human skin and fingernails. Rudge also found a tobacco pouch with the letters PJM marked on it. Around the same time as Rudge made his discovery, reports were coming in of a shooting nearby. Mr McCabe, a gardener on the estate of the Right Hon. Laurence Waldron, had been shot dead in a most callous fashion at Strathmore Road. The reasons for McCabe's death are unknown. Perhaps he had stumbled upon one of the cordon of scouts established by Captain O'Mara. Maybe he panicked and ran to raise the alarm or perhaps his death was the settling of an old score. Either way, McCabe's killing was similar to those carried out by the Squad. He was found lying in a pool of blood with a bullet through the forehead and three gunshot wounds through his chest.[107]

Of the two IRA men who had been trapped in the conflagration, Thomas Dunne received extensive burns to the hands, forearms and head. He died on 14 May 1920. Patrick Meaney, who had extensive burns on the legs, hands, ribs and forearms, lingered on for a few days more, finally passing away on 21 May. Events such as this were common during the War of Independence. IRA Battalions were instructed not to use petrol but paraffin oil, which burned well but did not have the explosive capacity of petrol vapour. The instruction was not always heeded. Kill of the Grange and Ballybrack police barracks were just two of seventy barracks across Ireland to be destroyed on the night of 20 May 1920. Stepaside RIC barracks was burned out on 19 August 1920 with the aid of No. 3 Company Engineers Battalion.[108] Other RIC barracks burned out at this time were Rockbrook in south Dublin, and Raheny and Skerries north of Dublin city.[109]

By May 1920 morale in the RIC had reached an all-time low.[110] In 1919 just ninety-nine constables resigned but in 1920 the cumulative effect of boycotting, armed attacks, assassinations and burning of barracks was taking its toll: 1,647 constables resigned in 1920 alone.[111] The British, fearing the collapse of the RIC, began a recruiting drive in Britain to create two forces. The first became known as the Black and Tans (a shortage of RIC uniforms for the new recruits led to the new police wearing a mix of RIC dark-green and British army khaki uniforms, hence their name). In 1920, 7,869 Black and Tans would be recruited, with a further 5,834 in 1921.[112] The second drive sought to establish an elite force. Known officially as the Auxiliary Division of the RIC, to the IRA they were the Auxiliaries or Auxies.

The brutality that characterised the behaviour of both the Black and Tans and the Auxiliaries was designed and driven by the British cabinet. This policy of counter-terror was laid bare during a mutiny by RIC constables at Listowel, County Kerry, in June 1920.

The backdrop to this incident was the installation of a completely new British regime in Dublin, which was to implement the new counter-terror strategy. Inspector General of the RIC Sir Joseph Byrne was instructed to go on sick leave; as he was both Irish and Catholic he was considered not to have the stomach for what was to come. He was replaced by Major-General Sir Hugh Tudor who became initially adviser to the RIC and later Chief of Police. Tudor had earned a distinguished reputation in the First World War serving as an artillery commander. He developed the box barrage and smokescreen tactics that saved many British lives in fighting the Germans on the Western Front. Tudor met and struck up a friendship with Winston Churchill while serving in India. They met again while serving at the front during the First World War.[113] Churchill had taken to the trenches in an attempt to rebuild his shattered political career after the debacle of Gallipoli in 1915, for which he had been responsible. It was Churchill who secured Tudor's appointment to Ireland. Tudor personally recruited former British army subordinates to hold positions in the RIC throughout Ireland. On his advice, Ormonde de L'Épée Winter was appointed Chief of Intelligence at Dublin Castle. The IRA referred to Winter as the 'Holy Terror'. To his colleagues at the Castle, Winter was referred to as 'White Snake'. It was a fearsome reputation for a fearsome assignment. Winter would not disappoint.

Tudor soon found himself at odds with traditional RIC constables. Matters came to a head in Listowel, County Kerry. On 16 June 1920, the RIC at Listowel were ordered to turn over their barracks to the British military and, led by Constable Jeremiah Mee, they refused. RIC County Inspector Power-O'Shea travelled to Listowel to order the constables to comply but after his address, fourteen constables stepped forward to resign.[114] Two days later, in a further escalation of the situation, General Tudor, accompanied by District Commissioner for Munster, Lieutenant Colonel Gerard Bryce Ferguson Smyth, and Captain Chadwick, with a detachment of British troops, arrived to address the muntineers. District Commissioner Smyth was in full dress uniform complete with Distinguished Service Order and Bar with campaign medals, including the Mons Star.[115] Smyth addressed his constables, explaining a number of aspects to the new RIC strategy, as follows:

1. If a police barracks is burned, or if the barracks already occupied is not suitable, then the best house in the locality is to be commandeered, the occupants thrown out in the gutter. Let him die there, the more the merrier.

2. ... when civilians are seen approaching, shout 'hands up'. Should the order be not immediately obeyed, shoot, and shoot with effect. If the

persons approaching carry their hands in their pockets or are in any way suspicious looking, shoot them down. You may make mistakes occasionally and innocent persons may be shot, but this cannot be helped and you are bound to get the right persons sometimes. The more you shoot, the better I will like you, and I assure you that not one policeman will get into trouble for shooting any man.

3.   ... Inquests are to be made illegal so that in future no policeman will have to give evidence at inquests.

4.   ... Hunger strikers will be allowed to die in jail, the more the merrier. Some of them have died already, and a damn bad job they were not all allowed to die.[116]

After the address, Constable Mee stepped forward and said, 'By your accent I take it you are an Englishman. You forget you are addressing Irishmen.' Mee took off his uniform cap and belt. Placing them on the table, he said, 'These too are English and you may have them. To hell with you, you are a murderer.'[117] Mee was placed under arrest. At every stage Constable Mee was supported by his RIC colleagues.

Smyth had issued a number of official orders in June. The orders referred to defence of police barracks, open and covert movement of police patrols and instructions on when to open fire on suspected attackers. In his official orders Smyth stated that 'A policeman is perfectly justified in shooting any man *who he has good reason to believe is carrying arms* and who does not throw up his hands when ordered'. But he also stated in Order No. 5, dated 17 June 1920: 'I wish to make perfectly clear to all ranks that I will not tolerate any "reprisals". They bring discredit on the police. I will deal most severely with any officer or man concerned in them.'[118]

There is a radical contradiction between Smyth's official orders and his 'unofficial' ones. It seems out of character for Smyth to take the men into his confidence and make such a series of statements as he did. However, the apparent contradiction bears a great deal of similarity to the contrast between an official statement issued to the press and the usual off-the-record remarks that relate the reality of a situation. The unofficial briefing delivered at Listowel bears all the hallmarks of Major-General Tudor's suggestions for crushing the IRA's campaign. Tudor was a former commanding officer of Smyth's. He proposed, among other things, introducing identity cards and passports, deporting prisoners to Britain, levying fines and punishments on districts where the IRA were active and a special penalty of flogging for cutting girls' hair or other outrages against women.[119] After a series of discussions at Listowel the visiting parties left. An eyewitness account of events at Listowel RIC Barracks was written and sent to Sinn Féin HQ in Dublin. The American Commission on Conditions in Ireland 1920–21 took two sworn statements from Constables John McNamara (RIC No: 69,575) and Michael Kelly (RIC No: 68,147), who were also present at Listowel. For Sinn Féin it was a propaganda coup while for Smyth it was a death sentence. A month after the Listowel Mutiny, on 17 July, a Special Duties Unit of the 1st Battalion Cork No. 1 Brigade, led by IO Seán Culhane, entered the Cork Country Club and shot the District Commissioner a number of times in the head and body.[120] His funeral at Banbridge, County Down, led to days of Unionist rioting in which Catholics were driven from their jobs and their property targeted for destruction. Damage throughout the town totalled £40,000. Anti-Catholic pogroms in the proposed Home Rule area of a six-county Ulster would become a familiar scene throughout the War of Independence as IRA activity led to the deaths of highly respected officers and men in the British military and the RIC from local Protestant communities. One of the worst outbreaks of anti-Catholic violence was incited by a Twelfth of July speech from Sir Edward Carson and supported by an orchestrated anti-Catholic campaign in the *Belfast Newsletter*. A week later, Belfast erupted into days and nights of continuous sectarian violence aimed at Catholic workers, their families and homes.[121]

The order justifying a shoot-to-kill policy resulted from assassinations of RIC and DMP members by IRA men dressed in civilian clothes. But a much darker influence was at work. Orders such as those issued by Smyth reflected the British cabinet policy from this point on in the War of Independence. The RIC became a real paramilitary force; any suspect could be shot accidentally, shot deliberately or, as would become increasingly more common, 'shot while attempting to escape'. Strip searches, severe beatings and floggings as a prelude to more rigorous and prolonged torture became common. Lloyd George bore responsibility for placing a police force in the front line and recruiting British officers along with thousands of ex-servicemen to impose a cloaked paramilitary solution on the Irish situation. The British cabinet would not acknowledge they were in a war and preferred to present the situation in Ireland outwardly as a campaign of terror instigated and maintained by a group of 'extremist gunmen' who were little better than 'paid assassins' or a 'gang of terrorists'.[122]

Casualties in Ireland, both civilian and IRA, were carefully compiled by Dáil Éireann. A list of those captured, arrested and imprisoned was also carefully compiled and the whereabouts of each prisoner noted. Such details were regularly published in the press and also in the Dáil's official daily news-sheet, *Irish Bulletin*, considered even by Unionists to be 'accurate and fair'.[123] Figures did not include casualties occurring in armed conflict between British Crown forces and the IRA. In 1920, it was reported that over 200 unarmed Irish civilians had been killed by the British military and police.[124] These numbers included six women, twelve children, ten elderly men and two Catholic priests. Each case was also documented and reported in the press. One of the children was eight-year-old Dubliner Annie O'Neill. She was playing outside her home when a British army officer gave chase to two young men. He fired, killing the child accidentally. One of the priests was Fr Michael Griffin from Galway. Abducted by Auxiliaries on the night of 14 November 1920, he was interrogated and executed with a bullet through the temple. His body was secretly buried in a bog near Barna outside Galway city. His remains were discovered four days later.[125] Fr Griffin may have been killed by the Auxiliaries in revenge for the disappearance and murder of Pádraig Joyce, a national school teacher at Barna, by the IRA the previous month.[126] The Catholic bishops in Ireland also began to record incidents in their dioceses perpetrated by the Auxiliaries and the Black and Tans.

The American Commission on Conditions in Ireland[127] recorded eyewitness accounts of numerous distressing attacks and violence against civilians and their homes and businesses. They could not verify numbers of casualties but there was certainly a dramatic increase on the numbers of civilians killed previously: eight in 1919, six in 1918 and seven in 1917.[128] The brutal nature of the war was repugnant to many Irishmen in the RIC and so accelerated the rate of resignations in an already beleaguered force. The terror visited upon Irish people convinced them that peace would only be realised if the British left Ireland. British rule as implemented by the RIC, Black and Tans, Auxiliaries and the British army was soon to encourage statements like that made by Unionist landlord O'Conor Don, who said, 'If "they" don't turn these ----- Black and Tans out of the country we'll soon be all ------ Republicans!'[129]

One of the first towns in County Dublin to experience the wrath of the Black and Tans was Balbriggan. It lay in RIC District 2 of County Dublin, which was also the 1st Battalion Fingal Brigade IRA area. Tensions were high following the mortal wounding of RIC Sergeant Patrick Finnerty on 14 April 1920. The sergeant and three constables had been tailing a republican parade through Balbriggan to a bonfire in celebration at the release of hunger strikers that same month. Captain John Gaynor, of the Balbriggan Company 1ˢᵗ Battalion Fingal Brigade anticipated that Sergeant Finnerty would attempt to remove a tricolour flag from those parading on their return to town. Gaynor indicated his intent to 'plug' the sergeant if he tried to seize the flag. Gaynor described the subsequent events: 'We had just reached Clonard St., which is the entrance to the town on that side, when Sergeant Finnerty made a dash to seize the flag, which was in the centre of the procession. I immediately pulled a revolver from my pocket and dropped him.'[130]

Captain Gaynor was later arrested along with a number of his IRA comrades and interrogated for over a week. They were released as no evidence could be brought against them. The RIC account stated that Sergeant Finnerty was attacked by a group from behind. He was badly wounded, having been shot in the back and the abdomen. After the shooting, the group responsible melted back into the larger crowd. A Galway man from Clonkeen, the sergeant died on 16 April at the Mater Hospital. He was buried in his home county.[131] In the weeks after Finnerty's death, an RIC depot was established at Gormanston for training Black and Tans and Auxiliaries. Balbriggan pubs became important social hubs for Black and Tans looking for a release from the restrictions of depot life. An RIC sergeant called McNamara was responsible for keeping order among the Black and Tans when they went to Balbriggan. Captain Gaynor said the RIC sergeant did not use 'kid gloves' and it was not unusual to see him employing fist and boot to keep order among those who had consumed too much drink.[132] On Sunday 19 September 1920 the IRA held a public sports day in Balbriggan as a secret fundraiser for the IRA. The event was well attended, even by Black and Tans. All was calm that Sunday night prior to the ferocious storm about to break.

On Monday evening, 20 September 1920, two Galway men, Head Constable Peter Burke and his brother Michael, an RIC sergeant, were returning to Gormanston depot after a trip to Dublin. They ordered their taxi to drop them at Mrs Smith's pub in Balbriggan. According to IRA reports, the constables refused to pay the taxi fare. Neither man was in uniform. They had a few drinks with some of the Black and Tans already in the pub. Mick Rock, Vice-Commandant of the Fingal Brigade, and

Captain Gaynor were also in town that night as they were writing up the accounts after the sports day on Sunday. Rock asked Lieutenant William Corcoran to get some weapons and he returned with revolvers for all of them. Rock, Gaynor and Corcoran went off with revolvers to Mrs Smith's to confront the RIC men. They entered the pub and as they spoke with Head Constable Burke about the taxi fare he drew his gun. The IRA men opened fire and 'the place was quickly in bedlam'. The RIC account states that Rock entered the building and simply shot the two RIC men using dumdum ammunition. Burke died immediately. His brother Michael was wounded. The IRA men left the pub and ordered that none of the local IRA company were to sleep at home that night.[133]

Within a few hours of the shooting, Black and Tans from Gormanston assisted by Auxiliaries from Collinstown Aerodrome rolled into Balbriggan bent on reprisal. Councillor John Derham was an eyewitness: 'Two grocery stores they looted and razed; threw the tea and sugar and soap and candles and everything on the floor about three feet high; tramped over it; and pulled things out in the passage to destroy what they did not set fire to.'[134]

Two IRA Volunteers, Seán Gibbons and Jim Lawless, were found in their homes by the Black and Tans. They were taken to the RIC barracks in the town and beaten mercilessly. They were interrogated all night and finally bayonetted to death around 5 a.m. Their bodies were dumped in the main street. Councillor Derham saw the bodies the following morning. His home was one of thirty burned down by the Black and Tans. One of his sons was beaten unconscious.[135] Jack Straw (referred to as William Straw by the RIC), a Scot and an ex-Royal Navy serviceman, was reported by locals as having led the Tans around the town that night. Captain Gaynor spoke with him the following morning. He disappeared the next day and showed up in Skerries where two local IRA men, John (Terry) Sherlock and Tom Hand, put him out of town. Shortly after that, both men were shot dead by the Black and Tans. Within a week, the Fingal Brigade had seized Jack Straw, arrested him and taken him to Willie Dempsey's Mill. A court martial followed, the result of which was a dispute between the Brigade O/C Commandant Michael Lynch and Staff Officer Dan Brophy. Lynch was not convinced the evidence was enough to prove Straw was a British agent or spy. After some discussion, however, a sentence of death was passed on Straw.[136] He was executed by Dan Brophy and Joe Kelly, a Fingal Brigade IO, and his body buried in a ditch. Straw was found by the

RIC on 21 October 1920.[137] The newly appointed RIC County Inspector for County Dublin, Hugh M. Lowndes, said Straw was innocent of any involvement in the reprisals at Balbriggan.[138] What CI Lowndes made of the sacking of Balbriggan is to this date unknown. His report for Dublin for September 1920 is still withheld from analysis by historians. Also withheld are all County Inspector reports for every county in Ireland for the months of March, April and May 1920. This coincides with the arrival and initial establishment of the Black and Tans in towns and villages in Ireland.

The details of the sacking of Balbriggan were communicated to the American Commission. The Commission was of the view that the British High Command considered the killing of Head Constable Burke to be a corporate crime perpetrated by the citizens of Balbriggan. Based on the evidence presented to the Commission this was found to be untrue. In a harsh judgement of the death of Head Constable Peter Burke, the Commission report stated: 'The deaths of Burke and others would appear to us to prove that at least some of the slain Imperial British force were victims of their own carelessness and drunken aggression.'[139] However, the American Commission reminded the British, as signatories to the Hague Convention of 1907, certain actions were forbidden, stating Article 23: 'In addition to the prohibitions provided by special conventions, it is especially forbidden – (g) To destroy or seize the enemy's property, unless such destruction or seizure be imperatively demanded by the necessities of war.'[140]

The evidence gathered by the American Commission concluded that Ireland was experiencing a campaign of orchestrated terror for which the British cabinet was directly responsible.

The difficulty in defining the conflict experienced in Ireland can be seen in the correspondence between British army GHQ at Parkgate and the War Office in London. It revealed the difficulty the British army had in awarding suitable medals for services rendered by RIC and British Crown forces personnel in Ireland. The RIC Medal was awarded in the initial stages but this was not viewed as appropriate for the army or navy. The War Office recognised that whatever was decided to be awarded to the Crown forces should also be awarded to members of the RIC as the risks were equally shared. The Meritorious Service Medal (MSM), awarded to NCOs for gallant conduct in the performance of military duty, was excluded as a form of reward for services against the IRA. Instead, the medal of the OBE was specially approved as a substitute for the MSM for 'the special conditions obtaining in Ireland'.[141] A military division and a civil division of the award for the British army and RIC respectively was suggested. The directions for such awards emerged from correspondence between King George V at Buckingham Palace and Secretary for War Winston Churchill at Whitehall in October and November 1920. Churchill had advised the king that the Crown forces would not be happy with the OBE and requested 'His Majesty's sanction to the bestowal of all Military Orders, Decorations (the Victoria Cross excepted) and gallantry and other medals in recognition of services in Ireland'. The reply, penned by the King's private secretary, left Churchill with no misunderstanding about the issues at stake: 'The King feels that this proposal involves an important question of policy, as its adoption would be an admission that the Army in Ireland is engaged in War, and not as His Majesty supposes, in the restoration of law and order. In these circumstances the King desires that you will bring the substance of the above letter before the Cabinet.'[142]

Awards for gallantry such as the Military Medal, Military Cross and the Distinguished Service Order were bestowed on soldiers fighting the king's enemies. The rewards could not be 'conferred in connection with rebellion of His Majesty's subjects'. The War Office were also concerned that a medal ribbon for services of gallantry in Ireland would make the officer or soldier a 'marked' man, especially in the event of capture by the enemy.[143]

The debate over medals to be awarded to members of the British Crown forces and the RIC make it clear that a war was being fought but without formal recognition. The American Commission would expose the reality of the conflict. It heavily criticised Chief Secretary Sir Hamar Greenwood for the marked contrast between the tone of regret noted in his public statements and his failure to ensure justice in a number of actions perpetrated by the RIC, Auxiliaries and British Crown forces: 'We would particularly emphasize his explanation of the death of Mrs Ellen Quinn, the expectant mother who was shot wantonly by the military; of his inquiries by military tribunals into the crimes ordered and committed by the military; of his failure to arrest the miscreants who sacked Balbriggan, and his condonation of the Croke Park massacre.'[144]

The House of Commons debated the Balbriggan outrage and other disturbing events of the War in Ireland on 20 October 1920. Arthur Henderson, Labour Party MP for Widnes, Cheshire, called for 'an independent investigation ... into the causes, nature and extent of reprisals on the part of those whose duty is the maintenance of law and order'.[145] The anger and fury of some MPs had not dissipated in the intervening month. Henderson expressed the shock and anger of many in the House when he stated: 'a policy of military terrorism has been inaugurated, which, in our opinion, is not only a betrayal of democratic principles and not only a betrayal of the things for which we claimed to stand during the five years great world War, but is utterly opposed to the best traditions of the British people.'[146]

According to the information possessed by Henderson, the raid on Balbriggan was carried out by approximately 150 Black and Tans. Quoting the *Manchester Guardian*, Henderson related what had happened in Balbriggan regarding the deaths and the burnings of houses and a hosiery factory. He described the random shootings and destruction carried out by the RIC and British army in Ireland. He pleaded with the Prime Minister, reading from a telegram he had received from a former MP, William O'Brien:

> 'As one who spent twenty arduous years in the struggle for peace between the two countries I solemnly tell all men of goodwill that the most peacefully minded men of the Irish race will be filled with horror of the English name unless some stop is speedily put to this atrocious campaign of vengeance, and to the blood – guilty incitements from high quarters to which it is directly traceable.'

Chief Secretary Hamar Greenwood was at his very best in defence of British government policy and in justifying what they saw as legitimate actions by the Crown forces in Ireland. Referring to the republicans as a 'gang of terrorists', Greenwood regretted the happenings at Balbriggan and elsewhere. He described many incidents where members of the RIC were ambushed and received terrible wounds from 'expanding ammunition' (dumdum rounds). One such case he mentioned was the ambush of District Inspector Brady at Tubbercurry in County Sligo.[147] Brady was hit three times with dumdum rounds and was so badly injured that his clothes had to be cut off for medical treatment to be administered. Greenwood singled out the drivers of RIC patrols for special mention. Due to their job they could not return fire when ambushed and were often badly wounded or killed during ambushes. At Tubbercurry, the driver was wounded in the legs but kept going and returned his fellow RIC constables to their barracks. Greenwood, in defending the actions of the RIC, argued that when constables saw the bodies of their colleagues so badly injured, as was the case at Tubbercurry and Balbriggan, it was inevitable they 'saw red' and unfortunately 'things got out of hand'.[148] As for indiscriminate firing by RIC constables as they travelled through the countryside, Greenwood's explanation was that ditches and walls often concealed a republican ambush consisting of parties of up to fifty men. Random shots were deliberately fired into walls and hedges to provoke an enemy response if present.[149]

What occurred next was unexpected. The MP for Central Hull, Lieutenant Commander Joseph Kenworthy, stood to address the House. Among those facing him were Prime Minister Lloyd George, Secretary for War Winston Churchill, Leader of the House Andrew Bonar Law and Chief Secretary of Ireland Hamar Greenwood. Kenworthy said that 'The whole of the Sinn Fein organisation does not consist of a gang of murderers, and anyone who holds that it does is a stranger to the truth.'[150] Drawing on the facts he said that the IRA had captured 269 armed police and soldiers in the four months ending August 1920. All the prisoners had been released unharmed. In contrast, republicans captured by the RIC and British Crown forces were treated shamefully. Kenworthy described the systematic torture of prisoners, who endured floggings and sustained beatings in 'third degree' interrogations to exhort a confession. He then challenged the cabinet, stating 'If we claim to be civilised we would not ill-treat even the vilest murderer'.[151] He accused the British government of 'openly encouraging lynch law'. Referring to the existence of a state of war denied by Lloyd George, Kenworthy said many of the casualties suffered by the RIC and British army occurred in open fighting whereas spies were shot or assassinated. He then offered a surprising insight into the Irish republican mindset and spirit, saying: 'the history of the last century shows that suppressed nationalities always in the end win if the people have the courage to fight on'. Drawing on the example of three hunger strikers – Michael Fitzgerald, Joseph Murphy and Terence MacSwiney,[152] Kenworthy then rounded on Winston Churchill: 'The War Secretary jeers at the fasting of the Lord Mayor of Cork. Will he go for three days without food? Will he go one day without drink?'[153]

Kenworthy concluded by saying an honourable settlement was required which would not embitter the relations between the two peoples of

Ireland and Britain. When the vote on the Motion of Censure proposed by Arthur Henderson was taken, it was overwhelmingly defeated, 346 to 79.[154] It was evident that those sympathetic toward the Irish struggle for independence were a minority in the House of Commons. At the end of 1920, Arthur Henderson MP would chair a British Labour Party mission to Ireland to investigate the conflict. Assisted by the Irish Labour Party, the Commission toured counties Dublin, Cork, Kerry and Tipperary, receiving reports and eyewitness testimony, and published its findings. Its report was even more shocking than that of the American Commission and detailed dreadful atrocities carried out by Black and Tans and Auxiliaries.

Internationally, Britain's reputation was badly damaged by events in Ireland. Archbishop of Dublin William Walsh received a letter from Pastor James B. Curry, Church of the Holy Name on 207 W 96th Street, New York. It contained £71/4d from their friends in America, who had been touched by the story of the ruin suffered by the people of Balbriggan.[155] Archbishop Walsh also received a letter from Rev. M. J. Foley, president and editor of the *Western Catholic*, Quincy, Illinois. Rev. Foley said his soul was in agony because of the suffering of Erin's children. In response to the violence in Ireland, Rev. Foley started a boycott on English produce while visiting the Springfield Armory where he addressed over 6,000 people.[156] The efforts of many people in Ireland, Britain, America and elsewhere could not bring about a peace. The IRA and the British Crown forces in Ireland were fully engaged. It would take some time before the belligerent parties would be ready for peace.

5

Bloody Sunday

The Conflict Defined – June to November 1920

During 1920, McKee and Clancy continued their efforts to arm the Dublin Brigade. On 1 June 1920 they carried out another spectacular success by raiding the King's Inns. A small British guard of an NCO and twelve other ranks were surprised and deprived of the weapons in the armoury.[1] The captured haul contained twenty-five SMLEs, two Lewis guns and several thousand rounds of ammunition.[2] H Company 1st Battalion were all on the 'job'. H Company were given eight SMLEs for their part in the raid and an eighteen-year-old Volunteer named Kevin Barry was well pleased to have captured a Lewis gun, his second such weapon. A Lewis gun was a serious piece of kit for any company, British or Irish. It looked like a section of drainpipe with a metal dinner plate sitting on top of it. Nicknamed 'The Belgian Rattlesnake' by the Germans during the First World War, the Lewis gun fired a .303 round from a magazine pan holding either forty-seven or ninety-six rounds. Firing at a rate of 600 rounds per minute, it had a range of 1,870 yards (1.7 km).[3]

As well as raiding for arms, the Dublin and Fingal Brigades also began to develop tactical units. After the 'Sacking of Balbriggan' Vice-Commandant Mick Rock of the Fingal Brigade was on the run. He was now shunned in the Fingal area. People who had once been glad to see him turned their backs and moved away when they saw him coming.[4] Rock then established an Active Service Unit (ASU) made up of others in the Fingal Brigade who were also on the run. ASUs were more commonly known as flying columns. Rock's Fingal ASU had twenty men and also trained members of the battalions in Fingal on a rotating basis. Their weapons were provided from Lee-Enfield rifles Rock had secretly kept back from the Collinstown raid. Compared with other IRA flying columns, Mick Rock's men were

(L–r): A Luger (Parabellum) and Mauser C-96 (also known as a Peter the Painter or a Broomhandle), automatic pistols favoured by the Squad. (Courtesy Dave Swift, Claíomh – Irish Living History & Military Heritage)

spoiled: each man was armed with a Lee-Enfield rifle, a bayonet and 150 rounds of ammunition.[5] Ammunition for IRA units was generally sparse. The average for a flying column Volunteer was twenty to thirty-five rounds.[6] Ernie O'Malley, a former medical student, now a training officer in guerrilla warfare with IRA units in the field, worked with the Fingal Brigade before he was transferred to County Kilkenny.

In the city, the Dublin Brigade, encouraged by the relative ease with which they had pulled off the Collinstown and King's Inns raids, were lulled into a false sense of security. All these raids had been meticulously planned with plenty of IRA personnel on hand who were decisive and experienced. Michael Douglas of G Company 1st Battalion approached H Company with news that a British supply detail of the 2nd Battalion Duke of Wellington Regiment showed up a number of mornings a week between 8 and 9 a.m. at Monk's Bakery on Upper Church Street. In this British army detail there were usually seven to eight soldiers led by a sergeant and a corporal. The NCOs would go into the bakery to organise the flour and supplies while the soldiers would go into the shop for minerals and cakes.[7] The company members approached both Peadar Clancy and Dick McKee for permission to carry out an operation to seize the detail's rifles and ammunition. The O/C of H Company, Seamus Kavanagh, was unaware of the plans.[8] Permission for the operation was granted. This IRA raid would change the nature of the conflict in Dublin.

In planning the operation, four men were assigned to cover the rear of the lorry. Three men were posted on the right-hand side near the bakery. Five men would take up position on the left-hand side of the lorry while another four were to cover the driver's cab. Two outposts armed with grenades were placed nearby. H Company Transport Officer Davy Golden with C Company's Jimmy Carrigan waited in a Ford van at the Spinning Wheel pub. Kevin Barry was with the two men covering the right-hand side of the lorry near Monk's Bakery. He turned up late as he was serving Mass. The Company QM gave him the only weapon left, a Parabellum.[9] Seán O'Neill recalled that Barry was not happy with this weapon and would have preferred a .45. H Company 1st Battalion Dublin Brigade moved into position early on the morning of Monday 20 September. Anxiously they waited; 9 a.m. came and went and still the British detail did not arrive.[10] Hanging around an ambush site for up to two hours prior to an action was tactically unwise. It left ASUs exposed, with the likelihood of being outmanoeuvred by British forces. In other actions around Dublin IRA Volunteers would pay a heavy price for such inexperience. Finally, at around 11 a.m., the British army lorry arrived.

Right from the outset there were problems with this operation. When the lorry pulled up, it was obvious there were more on this detail than usual. In the back, there were seven soldiers on both left and right sides with another four behind the cab. In the front alongside the driver were two sergeants and one other rank. The tailgate of the lorry was dropped down. An NCO and three privates went into the bakery. Seán O'Neill stepped up to the back of the lorry and shouted, 'Hands up. Drop your rifles.' Everyone froze. The British soldiers looked at each other and, seeing only one IRA man covering them with a pistol, released the safety catches on their rifles, quickly put one round in the breech and opened fire.

Pandemonium ensued, with no shortage of targets on either side. Seán O'Neill, terror-struck, found himself looking into the barrel of a Lee-Enfield six feet above him. How he was not killed was down to nerves or overexcitement on the part of the British soldiers. Bob O'Flanagan was hit in the side of the head. Others had their hats shot off their heads and O'Neill was eventually wounded from a ricochet striking a brick wall beside him. When O'Neill had discharged all his rounds, he made a run for North King Street. The other H Company men followed him with the British still firing. The IRA unit kept moving until they reached Cathedral Street, quite some distance away. It was only then they realised Kevin Barry was missing. During the action Barry had fired only one round before his gun jammed. This was a common occurrence for IRA men using automatics and was put down to mixing ammunition of different marks and dates.[11] In quite a number of cases, rather than fighting as a unit, it was literally every man for himself. Barry found himself taking fire and unable to return it. He rolled under the British lorry for cover while trying to free the action of his weapon. As he lay there, the firing petered out and Barry was now completely isolated.

A British soldier, twenty-year-old Private Marshall Whitehead,[12] was killed after being hit with three rounds.[13] Three other soldiers were wounded. Kevin Barry was taken prisoner by a detachment of Lancashire Fusiliers and taken to the North Dublin Union, their temporary barracks, where he was beaten. Barry had important information regarding the organisation of his IRA company, brigade personnel and the whereabouts of weapons dumps. He was also part of an action that saw a British soldier killed, the first such casualty in Dublin since the 1916 Rising. Barry was placed in a cell and at first threatened by two officers and three sergeants. He was told if he did not talk he would be turned out on the barrack square to face the anger of soldiers who had just witnessed their own man killed. He was also threatened with being run through with a bayonet. Barry, who was only eighteen, was pushed onto the floor and held down by the hobnailed army boots of two NCOs while a third grabbed him by the hair, pulling his head upwards and twisting his arm at the elbow joint at the same time. Barry refused to talk, even to a man dressed in civilian clothes who offered him a pardon if he would reveal the names of his companions. Barry refused to give in. He received medical treatment from an officer of the Royal Army Medical Corps (RAMC) after the NCOs were finished with him.[14] Kevin Barry was court-martialled and sentenced to death by hanging at Mountjoy Gaol. He received notice of the sentence on Wednesday 27 October, just a few days before the execution was to take place. William Walsh, Archbishop of Dublin, appealed to the British authorities for clemency due to Barry's young age but no reprieve came. The Dublin Brigade planned a number of attempts to rescue the young Volunteer but they came to nought. John Ellis, the English hangman, came over from Britain to carry out the sentence on Monday 1 November 1920.

The hanging of Kevin Barry was a major turning point in the conflict in Dublin during the War of Independence. Up to this, IRA raids on the British army had been bloodless, and smacked of a boy's adventure story. The Dublin Brigade felt a lot of guilt over Barry especially because of his age. The British army had now suffered casualties and had captured an IRA Volunteer who was partly responsible for those casualties. Under the Hague Convention, of which Britain was a signatory, Kevin Barry was a prisoner of war, and should have been treated as such and incarcerated for the duration of the conflict. By executing him as a criminal, the British were equating the IRA with criminals. It was nothing new. They had refused even to use the name IRA openly lest it confer national status upon their enemies. The execution of someone so young as Barry was also about sending a clear message: no one who took up arms against the British empire was above retribution, regardless of age. Up to September 1920, 156 members of the RIC had been killed by the IRA, 105 in 1920 alone.[15] The 'Sinn Feiners', as the British called them, would now be pursued to a bloody finish.

The Dublin Brigade also learned lessons from the Monk's Bakery attack. In future, IRA companies would not engage with the warning, 'hands up'. The action would be opened with grenades exploding followed by a volley or two of rifle and handgun fire. Afterwards, the IRA men would melt back into the Dublin streets or alleys.[16] This form of action would also evoke a British response. With significant reinforcements arriving in Dublin, the British were beginning to turn the screw on the IRA and the republican movement. In the autumn of 1920 Dublin experienced more British army raids and intense activity on the part of the British secret service and the newly arrived Auxiliaries. The British army patrols, raids and a curfew would place the city on lockdown, while the secret service, working on captured IRA documents, would attempt to track down leading IRA leaders and Sinn Féin political figures. The Auxiliary division would strike real fear into Irish hearts.

The Auxiliaries could be considered as the tip of the British spear. They were a heavily armed elite force. Brigadier-General Frank Crozier, who spent a good deal of his youth in Ireland, was appointed first O/C of the Auxiliaries. His second in command was General Edward A. Wood. Crozier did not last long. He sacked twenty-one of his officers for conduct unbecoming. After being injured in a crash on 23 November 1920, Crozier went on medical leave. On returning to duty in January 1921 he discovered the cadets he had sacked had been reinstated. Crozier resigned in disgust the following month. General E. A. Wood replaced him and remained Auxiliary Division O/C for the duration of the War of Independence.

There were a number of Auxiliary companies stationed in Dublin. All of them took their orders from their HQ at Beggars Bush barracks with the exception of F Company, which operated exclusively under the orders of the Chief of Police and Intelligence at Dublin Castle.

A Major Reynolds was one of the Auxiliaries at Dublin Castle who worked for IRA intelligence. Interviewed by the Bureau of Military History in the 1950s, he gave an insight into the organisation and command structures of the Auxiliary division (see Appendix C). A description of the temperament of the Auxiliary combatants of F Company was provided by Ernie O'Malley, who had good cause to observe them closely over a period of time:

> The Company was made up of soldiers of fortune: men of private means, clerks, journalists and a few from universities. Many had probably been drawn by the good pay and the swaggering efficiency of an elastic discipline. They were all officers, therefore, gentlemen. They elected their own officers. The men had been specially selected as they were a guard company for part of the Castle. They had permission to carry out raids in areas beyond that one which they nominally controlled. They had seen service in France, Mesopotamia, India, Russia, Gallipoli, and held rank from major down. Some were boys, the majority were mature. A few had greying hairs. There was a sense of individual assurance; lusty animals, conscious of their strength after hard fighting; they had been tested in command, their morale was good. In an emergency they would stand out, but they might be worn down by the lack of organized warfare that suited them. When they sat at the fire I could see brooding bitterness in many faces. The World War had left its mark; behind organized efficiency and a sense of comradeship was a glum and swarthy melancholy.
>
> In the daytime they did not talk much; sometimes they would watch us as if to resolve their impressions as to what kind of strange animals we might be, but we were an unknown quantity, save judged in the pattern of their hereditary contempt and the current interpretation of the papers they read.[17]

The Auxiliaries were tough, experienced and resolute. Generally respected by the British and feared by the IRA and the Irish population, they were not afraid to stand and fight. Quite a number of Auxiliaries came to Ireland with exceptional military records. In answer to a question by Lieutenant Colonel Hilder on 11 April 1921, Mr Henry, MP for Derry South, stated that, between them, the members of the Auxiliary Division had received numerous awards for gallantry, including 130 Military Crosses, 63 Military Medals, 23 Distinguished Conduct Medals and 22 Distinguished Service Orders, and 350 had been mentioned in dispatches.[18]

IRA units were frequently instructed to avoid attacking Auxiliaries and instead target British lorries: army drivers were instructed to keep going, if possible, to get out of an ambush situation.

The combined actions of Ormonde Winter's secret service, General Boyd's curfew patrols, pickets and raids and the close attentions of F Company Auxiliaries led the British to grow in confidence. They received added legal support for their occupation and control of Ireland through the enactment of the Restoration of Order in Ireland Act on 13 August 1920. The British army succeeded in capturing two IRA units, one comprising thirty-five men and the other fifteen. Both units had surrendered without a fight when confronted by RIC and British army patrols respectively.[19] The former incident took place at Kilmashogue in the Dublin Mountains. Numbers 3 and 4 Companies of the 5th Engineer Battalion were on manoeuvres when they were surprised by a combined Black and Tan and British army patrol. One of the Volunteers, John Doyle, was shot dead. He was the son of Alderman Peadar Doyle, Inchicore.[20]

The British also benefited from information revealed in IRA document seizures. On top of IRA Chief of Staff Richard Mulcahy's papers being captured, the British had raided 32 Bachelors Walk and made an astonishing discovery. In Michael Collins' office on the third floor, they discovered an 'ingenious trolly arrangement opening in a different room'. The mechanism lay beneath the floorboards of one room and could be rolled under the wall beneath the floor into the adjoining room.[21] It was the discovery of caches of documents like this which led the British to develop lists of names, home and 'work' addresses and the identity profiles of leading Sinn Féin, IRA and Cumann na mBan personnel. In these lists, the British also included anyone they suspected of being a republican sympathiser. Kitty Doyle of 12 Grace Park Avenue was described as an 'Important member of the Cumann-na-mBan. Acts as a letter box for

Dáil Members.'[22] Notes on Miss Margaret Dunne of 5 Chelmsford Road, Ranelagh, stated: 'This person runs a S.F. Post office which is a covering for various members of the Dáil. House was raided and a great quantity of seditious literature taken.'[23] The British also added twenty TDs or Sinn Féin councillors from Dublin city and county to the 'C List'. The TDs' and councillors' home addresses were noted, so from then on it was unsafe for them to remain at home.[24] On the British 'A List' of the captured IRA membership rolls were Pat McCrea, Tom Cullen, Joe Leonard and Vincent Byrne, all of them members of Michael Collins' Squad. Of intriguing significance was Vincent or Vinny Byrne of Anne's Cottages, South Anne Street. The British knew he was a member of E Company, 2nd Battalion of the Irish Volunteers. They had also traced him to 3 Crow Street where they noted Byrne was working as a 'cabinetmaker'. This was the HQ of the IRA intelligence department! Increased British pressure may have precipitated its move from Crow Street to Great Brunswick Street. A sign over the door read 'O'Donoghue & Smith, Manufacturing Agents'.[25]

The British net was seriously restricting the freedom of movement of the IRA operatives in Dublin. The capture or killing of some of their key figures was looking increasingly likely.

In September and October 1920 there were significant reverses for both Sinn Féin and the IRA as the 'Cairo Gang' began to exert real pressure on the IRA in Dublin. The 'Cairo Gang' was a group of British intelligence agents who socialised at the Cairo Café, 59 Grafton Street. Paid informers supplied them with accurate information. On 22 September 1920, just two days after the death of Private Marshall Whitehead in the Monk's Bakery operation, Limerick County Councillor and Sinn Féin Director of Elections, John Lynch, had just arrived in Dublin with Dáil Loan subscription funds for Michael Collins. Alerted to Lynch's presence, a unit of British agents descended on the Royal Exchange Hotel. The agents may have mistaken John Lynch for Commandant Liam Lynch, O/C Cork No. 2 Brigade. The error was enough to seal the Limerick Councillor's death warrant. The agents went to Lynch's room and shot him dead. DMP Detective David Neligan, one of Collins' IRA agents still working for G Division at this point, consulted the Occurrences Book at College Green DMP station, B Division Area. As Neligan scanned the book he came across reference to a telephone message from a British officer stating that he and others, including Captain Baggallay,

Lieutenant Angliss (operating under the assumed name of Mahon)[26] and some RIC officers, had raided the Exchange Hotel at 2 a.m. and killed a republican named Lynch.[27] The British claimed the Sinn Féin official had resisted and so they killed him.

The British officer who had made the telephone call was Captain Hardy. He was responsible for a number of killings during the period, including that of 66-year-old Peter O'Carroll on 16 October 1920. O'Carroll was a member of the IRB and secretly bought weapons from British soldiers for the IRA. His daughter Mary (Dolly) was a member of the Colmcille Branch of Cumann na mBan. Two of his sons were members of the IRA, Liam (William), Adjutant of the 1st Battalion, and Peadar (Peter), a Volunteer with A Company, 1st Battalion. O'Carroll had a visit from Captain 'Hoppy' Hardy and his fellow officers. After refusing to give any information, he was executed on his doorstep, 92 Manor Street, with a bullet to the head. Captain Hardy and his men pinned a note to the body O'Carroll, which read: 'A Traitor to Ireland. Shot by the IRA.'[28]

More bad news followed. Michael Collins lost one of his top agents in Dublin Castle when DMP Detective Joe Kavanagh died of an embolism caused by a gastric ulcer on 21 October 1920.[29] Kavanagh had supplied Collins with valuable information, weapons and ammunition on a regular basis.[30] His loss was a bad blow to the Dublin IRA at a difficult time. Things did not improve for the republican movement: a number of Volunteers on hunger strike were fading fast. Michael Fitzgerald, O/C 1st Battalion Cork No. 2 Brigade IRA, died on Monday 17 October after sixty-seven days on hunger strike. He was followed by Volunteer Joseph Murphy on 25 October after seventy-six days on hunger strike. Both Fitzgerald and Murphy died at Cork Gaol. On Monday 25 October 1920 Lord Mayor of Cork Terence MacSwiney also died after seventy-four days on hunger strike.[31] The bravery of Fitzgerald and his fellow Volunteers was referred to in the House of Commons by the MP for Central Hull, Joseph Kenworthy. Fr Dominic OSFC, who was with MacSwiney when he died, sent a telegram to the Deputy Lord Mayor of Cork. It read:

> The Lord Mayor Completed his sacrifice for Ireland at 5.40 this morning. Please inform Bishop. Respectfully request his fellow citizens will maintain the same calm, dignified, noble bearing as on the assassination of Thomas MacCurtain. My deepest sympathy to his friends, fellow-citizens, and fellow soldiers.

No vain regrets, but fervent prayers; no useless sighs, but stern resolve to emulate his patient and heroic endurance in bearing all that God requires of us in establishing the Republic on a firm basis. May his noble spirit be with us always to guide and guard. Ar Dheis Dé go raibh a anam.[32]

In the midst of all this, Seán Treacy and Dan Breen returned to Dublin. Both were also on the British 'A List' after their exploits at Soloheadbeg, Knocklong and Ashtown, to name but a few. Treacy and Breen were very close friends. They held no secrets and discussed everything. Treacy was courageous and a natural leader. Breen said Treacy was the kind of person for whom nothing was impossible and any problem could be overcome with vision and will. These qualities made him a natural leader.[33] Treacy's strength of character was inspiring. His father, Denis, had died when he was only three and he grew up an only child with his mother, Bridget, and a tough, domineering aunt, Mary Anne Allis.[34] In 1911 Treacy was sworn into the IRB by Eamon O'Duibhir. This led to his meeting with Dan Breen and together they took the path to revolution. Breen, too, had lost his father as a child, when he was only six. His mother, Honora, a midwife, worked hard to raise her eight children. Breen inherited his nationalism from her and from having witnessed the eviction of Michael Dwyer Bán, less than a mile from his home. Michael Bán died on the side of the road after being thrown out of his house. This event 'left a deep and lasting impression' on the young Dan.[35] At school, a number of future Tipperary revolutionaries, Seán Treacy, Dan Breen, Dinny Lacey and Packy Deere, were taught by Kerryman Cormac Breathnach. After leaving school Breen worked on the railways. It was Seán Treacy who swore Dan into the IRB and together they joined a company of Volunteers formed in their home townland of Donohill in Tipperary in 1913.[36]

A British captain named George Osbert Smyth had also arrived in Dublin, from Egypt. Captain Smyth had returned to Ireland to avenge his brother, Gerald, who as divisional commissioner for Munster had been assassinated at the Cork Country Club in July 1920. Captain Smyth was part of the Cairo Gang, or 'Murder Gang' as the Dublin Brigade referred to them. The British believed that Breen was involved in Gerald Smyth's killing and were determined to deal with him once and for all. With so many agents and spotters posted around Dublin, it was inevitable that Treacy and Breen would be identified. One evening Dan Breen was confronted by a number of British agents on a tram and was lucky to escape without a shootout.[37] Breen got to 140 Drumcondra Road that night, home of the Fleming family, who, along with the Bolands and a few others, provided Treacy and Breen with food, lodging, clothes and some extra cash from time to time.[38] Without the kindness of families like this the Volunteers from Tipperary would have faced an impossible existence. But with a more systematic system of British surveillance emerging, the number of safe houses for Treacy and Breen was growing thin. The Tipperary comrades were priority targets for the British and on the night of 11–12 October 1920 they finally caught up with them at Fernside, the home of Professor Carolan.

The night had begun with a trip to the cinema for Treacy and Breen with Kay and Dot Fleming. On taking the tram to Drumcondra they were seen by one of the men who had confronted Breen on the tram a few nights earlier. After a cup of tea at Flemings, the two IRA men moved on to Fernside, on the main road out of Dublin across the Tolka Bridge at Drumcondra. Breen and Treacy had a latchkey to the Carolan home. Not wanting to disturb the household they let themselves in and went to a room upstairs at the back of the house overlooking a conservatory. They shared the one bed in the room. Seán slept with a loaded Parabellum under his pillow. Breen put his loaded Mauser automatic pistol on a chair close to the bed. After chatting a little they drifted off to sleep.

At about 1 a.m. the front door of the house was burst open and British soldiers entered the house. Directed upstairs by the owner of the house, John Carolan, the British officers began to search the building. On reaching the landing, a ferocious gun battle began as Seán Treacy and Dan Breen, now cornered, fought desperately to escape. Breen, though wounded, held the British unit at bay while Treacy, having lost his glasses, made good his escape out the back window. Breen then charged onto the landing, firing as he went, shooting two British officers and wounding a number of others. The dead were Captain George Osborne Bryce-Ferguson, who was killed instantly, and Captain Alfred White, who died of his wounds. In the ensuing confusion, Breen followed Treacy out the bedroom window, crashing through the glass roof of the conservatory. Falling heavily, Breen broke some of his toes. He was now very badly wounded and drenched in blood, having been shot in the hand, the lower back, the right lung and twice in the right calf; he also had a graze to the forehead.

Unable to find his comrade in the dark, Breen crossed the Tolka River and struggled up the bank to a house on Botanic Avenue where he finally collapsed. Breen was rescued the following morning by the Dublin Brigade and brought to O'Donnell's Nursing Home alongside the Mater Hospital. This nursing home was used to treat wounded IRA Volunteers in secret.

Professor Carolan was not so fortunate. He was threatened by the British officers and when the firing in the house ceased he was brought upstairs at gunpoint and shot through the neck, which severed his spinal cord. He collapsed onto the body of Captain Bryce-Ferguson. John Carolan lived for another two and a half weeks before succumbing to blood poisoning and congestion of the lungs on 27 October.[39] While in hospital he made a sworn statement to a solicitor. It was afterwards published as part of the Labour Party (Great Britain) Commission Report on Ireland in 1921. The professor said there was no one else on the landing apart from the British officers when he was shot.[40]

In the aftermath of this raid, the IRA carried out an investigation into who could have informed the British of the whereabouts of Treacy and Breen. Suspicion fell on an British ex-serviceman named Robert Pike, who lived at Tolka Cottages near the back of Fernside. Suspicion was enough in the latter stages of the War of Independence and Pike was executed by the IRA as he stood outside Fleming's shop on 18 June 1921.[41]

In the ensuing days, the British surrounded the Mater Hospital and began a search of the hospital looking for Breen, whom they were certain was there. In the process they found the body of an Irish Volunteer, Captain Matt Furlong from the IRA Munitions Department. Furlong had been in County Meath with a group including the new O/C of Munitions, Commandant Peadar Clancy, Captain Patrick McHugh, Tom Young and Seán O'Sullivan. They were testing a newly manufactured trench mortar that they hoped to use for attacks on army barracks. Furlong insisted on clearing away the group and dropping the shell down the barrel of the mortar by hand. The result was a muffled explosion as shrapnel flew in all directions. Furlong was seriously injured but still conscious. After administering first aid to slow the bleeding, Peadar Clancy travelled with the badly wounded Volunteer to the Mater Hospital in an ambulance. Clancy got out before arriving at the Mater in case he was recognised. Matt Furlong had his left leg amputated and initially there was hope he might recover.[42] Unfortunately, he weakened and died from his injuries the following day, 14 October.[43] That afternoon, Clancy arranged to meet up with a number of senior officers of the Dublin Brigade at his shop, Republican Outfitters in Talbot Street. It was a dangerous place to meet at the best of times as it was always under surveillance from British agents. Seán Treacy could not have picked a worse place in the entire city to show up.

After escaping the raid at Fernside, Treacy had walked to Finglas in search of a safe house.[44] The Squad were mobilised to protect him but were unable to convince him to lie low for a few days. Treacy was very concerned for his comrade-in-arms and went to attend the Dublin Brigade meeting at Peadar Clancy's shop. The gathering of IRA top figures Liam Tobin, Tom Cullen, Dick McKee, Frank and Leo Henderson and Peadar Clancy was noted by Dublin Castle spotters[45] and a raid on the premises was quickly organised. The following account is unsigned but ascribed to the O/C of the Dublin Brigade, Commandant Dick McKee.

> Report on the Death of V. Com. Sean Treacy, Tipp. No. 3
>
> On Thursday, October 14th at about 3.45 p.m. a party of enemy raided 94 Talbot St. They came in two lorries preceded by an armoured car from the direction of Nelson's Pillar. There were four men in the shop at the time together with the shopman. Seán was one of the four and was standing midway up the counter talking to the shopman. The remaining three were conversing in a group near the door and away from the counter. The approaching enemy cars were heard some distance off and one of the three men near the door looked out to see what they were; he turned back and said: "They are coming – get out." And then walked out of the shop. At this time the enemy cars were just stopping before the door. Seán Treacy followed the man who gave the alarm and walked to the edge of the footpath where a bicycle was standing and mounted it. He had not properly mounted when two men in civilian clothes pushed at him and knocked him off the machine and then grappled with him. When Seán was clear of the bicycle and while the two men were still grappling with him, he drew his pistol, and holding it by the barrel with his left hand and steadying it between his knees, he fired twice at another man in civilian clothes who was coming to the assistance of the two who were holding him. This man jumped back into cover. The struggle with the other two continued and in the course of a few seconds they had moved up some yards and on to the pathway and against the window of Speidel's Porkshop. While there Seán got one

of his assailants between him and the window and got the muzzle of his pistol against the man's stomach and fired from a revolver at about 5 yards range. This man (believed to be Lieutenant Price) was falling and another Seán was turning towards the second when a man, also in civilian clothes, came up behind him and fired from a revolver at about 5 yards range. Seán's head immediately sank backwards and while he was falling fire was opened from machine-gun, rifles and revolvers and he with the two men who were struggling with him fell almost together and lay motionless on the pathway.

Lt. Price was killed outright, and Sergt. Christian (the second man who grappled with Seán) has since died.

Another officer, Captain Le Grand was wounded. Whether he is the man at whom Seán first fired, or was hit by some of his own men is not known. Seán Treacy, in that fight, displayed soldierly qualities of the very highest order. He was not for an instant dismayed. Every action of his was deliberate – even to the end.[46]

The British army's historical record, written after the War of Independence, has an interesting view on the events. It reads: 'On arrival the alarm was given and it has since been ascertained that one of the rebels deliberately exposed himself in the street, opening fire to divert our attention.'[47]

Treacy's remains were returned to Tipperary on Sunday 17 October 1920. The republican tricolour was placed over his coffin. As it was lifted from the train, British troops on duty surprised everyone present by coming to attention and presenting arms. After the funeral Mass at Soloheadbeg Catholic Church, Seán Treacy was laid to rest at Kilfeacle. Con Moloney, 3rd Tipperary Brigade, delivered a resolute speech at the graveside: 'Seán Treacy is dead. His death is a great blow to us and to Ireland. But his loss must not unnerve us. Rather must it strengthen our resolve to continue on the path he opened for us; to strive for the ideals for which he gave his life, if necessary, to die fighting as Sean did.'[48]

In his last moments, Treacy was cut off and isolated from his comrades just as Kevin Barry had been. Even worse, in Treacy's case, some of them watched as he fought for his life and did not or could not intervene. It was often a similar situation for members of the RIC. The nature of guerrilla warfare was cruel in the manner in which death was delivered to both sides. Anxious to discover if the body at the Mater Hospital was either Treacy or Breen, the authorities at Dublin Castle brought RIC Sergeant Daniel

Roche from Tipperary to Dublin to view the body. Roche knew both of them by sight.[49] On seeing Furlong's broken body, the sergeant knew it was neither. On 17 October, Sergeant Roche set out from Dublin Castle with a Constable Fitzmaurice and Detective Dave Neligan. They were heading for the Phoenix Park Depot – known in Dublin simply as 'The Depot'– via Capel Street. As they walked across Essex Bridge [Grattan Bridge], the sergeant was completely unaware he was now a target for the Squad. Neligan's account of this event contrasts with that of the Squad: he claimed he pleaded with the Squad not the kill the sergeant.[50] Joe Dolan, a member of the Squad, claimed that Neligan had set Roche up and had given the IRA men a signal identifying the intended victim when they were en route to the depot.[51] As the shooting started, both Neligan and Fitzmaurice ran hell for leather leaving Sergeant Roche to meet his end alone. Joe Leonard fired six rounds from his revolver into the sergeant as he walked up Capel Street. Jim Slattery and Tom Kehoe also fired a few more rounds into the already dying man.[52] As repeated so many times on the streets of Dublin, a killing was not just about making sure the man was dead. It was also about sending a message to the enemy.

As October drew to a close, the IRA and the republican movement in Dublin were in a very difficult situation. British military pressure was beginning to tell and from a British perspective it looked as if the Irish were beginning to buckle. It was at this very time the Prime Minister's office in Downing Street received an indirect contact from Dublin regarding a peace initiative. The message was carried by Patrick Moylett, who claimed he was acting on Arthur Griffith's express instructions, but this was understandably denied at the time. Moylett was a committed republican whose home had been taken over and his businesses ransacked by the Auxiliaries. Using his extensive business connections in London, Moylett established indirect contact with Lloyd George through George Cockerill MP and John Steele, a journalist with the *Chicago Tribune*. The outcome was a proposal for a conference of plenipotentiaries representing both countries to negotiate rather than dictate a peace. Also addressed was the particular word 'republic': as Cockerill suggested, what other word could be found to describe a nation in revolt that had always had a regent and never looked elsewhere for a king? Perhaps in Cockerill's suggestion lay the origins of the concept of *Saorstát Éireann* or Irish Free State.[53] When Michael Collins heard of the approaches made by Moylett, he was furious. O'Hegarty, secretary to Dáil Éireann, wrote of the Moylett discussions:

The negotiations in which Mr Moylett was concerned with Mr Steele were all nonsense ... Moylett was the paw, Steele was the cat and Sir Philip Kerr was the monkey ... in other words Steele is a tool of Lloyd George. I think Michael Collins has somewhat the same opinion ... It is not easy to get over Moylett who is quite anxious to do good and cannot see that he does harm by allowing himself to be used as a tool.[54]

It is hardly credible that Patrick Moylett went to London to propose peace negotiations between Dáil Éireann and the British government on his own and with absolutely no authority from members of the Irish government.

However, the approach for peace from Moylett was confirmation for the British that the counter-terror strategy was bearing fruit. Irrespective of the criticism levelled at Moylett, the proposals put forward during his 'unofficial' approach to the British government in October and November 1920 formed the basis for the treaty negotiations a year later. While Moylett was busy in London, Michael Collins and his intelligence department were planning something much more decisive and much darker.

For a number of months, IRA intelligence had been trying to establish who the members of the British secret service in Dublin were. The threat they posed to the IRA was so serious it now meant they had to be killed and the threat removed. The orders issued by Michael Collins for the assassination of British secret service agents were planned and implemented by IRA intelligence, the Squad and the Dublin Brigade. The British agents lived in hotels, guesthouses and private lodgings on the south side of the city. Each morning a car from Dublin Castle picked some of them up and brought them to Dublin Castle or British army HQ at Parkgate. Other agents lived a nocturnal existence, only going out after curfew had begun. The Squad and Dublin Brigade carried out raids on mail deliveries to the Castle and on the temporary GPO at The Rink in the Rotunda. The captured documents and letters revealed that certain British officers were linked with the killings of Sinn Féin officials and IRA Volunteers around the country.[55]

In November 1920, with the courageous efforts of IO Lily Mernin, the IRA's intelligence department received the names and addresses of the agents. Mernin also passed on very sensitive information obtained as a result of a friendship she had established with a Miss Dunne, daughter of a retired RIC superintendent, who worked in the Castle as a typist. Miss

Dunne had got to know two of the British agents, Lieutenant H. Angliss (who used the alias Mahon) and Peel. Mahon drank a lot and talked too much when he did so, revealing much of what he got up to during the hours of darkness.[56] A planned assassination of these two British agents was called off in favour of an operation to remove the threat of British intelligence in Dublin entirely. According to IRA IO Dan McDonnell, 'There were at least, to my knowledge, anything between fifty-five and sixty agents marked down for destruction that morning.'[57] This operation would take place on 21 November and would be known as 'Bloody Sunday'. The British would refer to it in their official documents as 'Black Sunday'.

The intelligence reports were submitted to Frank Thornton, Collins' No. 3, who presented the final report to the Dáil cabinet and the army council.[58] Liam Tobin, who was suffering from his nerves in the weeks prior to the operation, was on rest.[59] In their surveillance, the IRA IOs also managed to locate the HQ and two sub-HQs of the British secret service agents in the city. Liam Tobin recalled that copies of the lists of British agents were made out and assigned to the Dublin Brigade battalions. The Squad was ordered to 'do the Special Ones in Pembroke Street in which we were interested'.[60] Once the operation was cleared by the Dáil cabinet, Seán Russell, O/C 2nd Battalion, was appointed to plan the operation. Russell carefully selected the units to carry out the executions of the British agents. (Of the operations carried out, twelve are recorded to date.) Four operations were assigned to A, C, D and K Companies of the south-side 3rd Battalion. Two operations were assigned to E and F Companies of the south-side 4th Battalion with one operation to the north-side 1st Battalion. The majority of the operations, five in total, would be carried out by Seán Russell's own B, C, D and E Companies of the north-side 2nd Battalion. The members of the Squad and IRA intelligence were also assigned to join company units on operations of particular interest to Michael Collins. The IRA units allocated to each target's house were divided into those who would take holding positions outside and those who would go inside. IRA scouting parties would also be posted to strategic positions at key junctions nearby. Members of Cumann na mBan provided support by being in prearranged locations to take weapons and ammunition from operational members after they had completed their orders and were returning to their respective battalion areas.

The operations were all coordinated to take place around Dublin city at 9 a.m. on Sunday 21 November 1920. The targets of paramount importance for the IRA were Lieutenant Ames and Lieutenant Bennett at 38 Upper Mount Street. These two British officers had been identified as the commanding officers of the British intelligence unit. They had moved here from their previous lodgings a few days before and were only located after considerable effort. Captain Tom Ennis, Squad members Lieutenant Seán Doyle and Vinny Byrne, IO Frank Saurin and E Company 2nd Battalion were on this operation. The second target for the IRA and possibly what has been described as one of the sub-HQs, was Lieutenant H. Angliss (working under the pseudonym Mahon) and Mr Peel (also a pseudonym) at 22 Lower Mount Street. This mission was assigned to Squad members Tom Kehoe and Jim Slattery. Supporting them was a detachment of E Company 2nd Battalion.

A major operation was assigned to Captain Paddy Flanagan, IO Charlie Dalton and C Company 3rd Battalion at 28 Upper Pembroke Street. This may have been the original British intelligence field HQ but with the movement of Ames and Bennett, the concentration of agents was being dispersed. Dalton was to locate two agents in particular who lived on the third floor, Major Dowling and Colonel Montgomery. It transpired that 28 Upper Pembroke Street was, in fact, two houses joined into one, with up to seven British officers staying there, possibly more.

Senior IRA IO Frank Thornton described the importance of the operation as the men of the Dublin Brigade set out that sunny morning: 'This was one of the most critical moments in the history of our Movement. Men were asked to do something on that day which was outside the ordinary scope of the soldier, but realising their duty to their country and always being ready to obey orders, all jobs were executed.'[61]

Written after the event, Thornton captures how precarious a time this was in the war. He emphasises the sense of duty felt by the Volunteers sent on these operations. What he does not describe, nor do many of the veterans, was the shocking nature of what they were about to engage in. The Volunteers on active service that day had not experienced anything like this type of operation before. The Squad members were a different matter, however. As Detective Broy wrote: 'these men had a complete mastery of the situation from an Irish nationalist point of view, and were sufficiently case-hardened to meet the new situation created by the arrival of the Tans, Auxiliaries and British Intelligence Officers.'[62] Vinny Byrne was ordered to take an elderly Volunteer first-aider with him, should anyone be wounded. Having no first-aid equipment, Byrne took a detour to a Squad dump at Jackie Dunne's in Denzille Lane near Holles Street. Byrne asked Dunne if he had any first-aid kits or bandages. He rummaged around and came back with a .38 revolver saying, 'Will this be of any use to you?' Byrne gave it to the first-aider.[63] The message was clear. Some of the Volunteers also brought sledgehammers or axes to break in any doors barred to them.[64] As they moved across the city towards their assigned targets, groups of Volunteers saw others moving into position also. There was a look of recognition as they passed on nervously, with the clock ticking towards nine.

At 9 a.m. Tom Ennis's unit walked briskly up the steps of 38 Upper Mount Street. After the maid opened the door they stuck their foot in to prevent her from closing it. The woman was ordered to take them to the rooms of Ames and Bennett. Ennis went to a back room where Lieutenant Ames was sleeping. Seán Doyle, Vinny Byrne and Herbie Conroy got into Lieutenant Bennett's room via a back parlour and folding doors, which the maid obligingly pointed out. Bennett was in the act of going for his gun when the IRA men rushed into the room. They ordered him to put his hands up. Doyle searched under his pillow, removing a Colt .45. Frank Saurin, the IRA IO accompanying them, began a quick search of the room looking for papers. Among the items he collected was Lieutenant Ames' notebook. It revealed an intelligence system very similar in its operational structure to the IRA's.[65] As he stood there in his pyjamas, Bennett was clearly worried and asked, 'What will happen to me?' Byrne, trying to keep things calm, lied and said, 'Ah, nothing'. Bennett was marched down to Ames' room where Tom Ennis was holding the other British agent. An exchange of shots in the street outside was heard and a British dispatch rider was forced into the house at gunpoint.

This British soldier had already experienced the grim scenes occurring in the Dublin streets nearby. He had already passed 119 Lower Baggot Street and had seen a group of about twenty men of Captain T. Burke's C Company 2nd Battalion, which included Volunteer Seán Lemass, running from the building. They had just shot Captain Baggallay. Further up the Street, at 92 Lower Baggot Street, the dispatch rider had seen the body of Captain W. Newbury hanging out of a window, bleeding profusely. Newbury's wife, though heavily pregnant, had tried to shield him in his attempt to escape but Squad men Joe Leonard and Bill Stapleton had pushed her to one side as they opened fire on the British officer. His body was left half in and half out of the window. Mrs Newbury was understandably hysterical when the police arrived. The official British army account of the event recorded, 'woman's resolution and her subsequent grief strongly affected police party'.[66] Mrs Newbury lost her baby and died giving birth to her stillborn child.[67]

The dispatch rider had continued up Baggot Street and turned into Herbert Place where he was stopped by an IRA scouting party strung across the road. His Triumph motorcycle combination was taken off him and Volunteer Michael Lawless ordered him into 38 Upper Mount Street where Captain Ennis, Lieutenant Doyle, Byrne and Conroy were in the process of shooting Ames and Bennett.[68]

The dispatch rider was terrified but Vinny Byrne decided not to shoot him and instead had him placed under guard in the hallway. Lieutenants Ames and Bennett were put standing facing the bedroom wall. Vinny Byrne then said, 'The Lord have mercy on your souls.' A hail of gunfire struck the two prisoners. Bennett was discovered with ten bullet wounds in him, Ames with seven.[69] Ennis's unit then left the building via the hallway, leaving the dispatch rider in the hallway unharmed. This man would later swear Captain Paddy Moran was one of those who killed Lieutenants Ames and Bennett.[70] His testimony would be confirmed by a British officer's batman who was staying in the house opposite and had watched events unfold. Despite this convincing evidence, Captain Moran could not have been involved in the killings in Mount Street because, at about the time Ennis's unit was moving into Mount Street, Moran was walking speedily across Sackville Street with his unit, D Company 2nd Battalion, making for the Gresham Hotel. A newspaper boy, seeing the unit of fifteen to twenty men converging on the entrance, said, 'There's a job on. Best clear out of this.'[71]

Moran dispersed his groups in the Gresham. They were looking for three British agents. The head porter was held at gunpoint and ordered to identify the rooms in which the agents were staying. Mick Kilkelly took one group to Room 14, Lieutenant Wilde's room. As Wilde spoke with Volunteer James Cahill at the door, Volunteer Kilkelly opened fire, shooting Wilde three times in the chest and killing him instantly. Cahill and Nick Leonard then went to Captain Patrick McCormack's room. Entering the room, they were fired on by McCormack, The Volunteers returned fire, killing the captain. In the House of Commons the following day Sir Hamar Greenwood said of Captain McCormack's brutal death: 'Party then moved to Room 24, entered room, and found McCormack sitting in bed reading paper. Without word, five shots were fired into his body and head as he sat there. Bed saturated, body and especially head horribly disfigured. Possibly hammer was used as well as shots to finish off this gallant officer.'[72] The third British agent at the Gresham escaped, having gone out to Mass early. His religious devotion saved his life.[73]

As the bells continued to toll across the city of Dublin the shots continued to ring out. After entering 22 Lower Mount Street, Tom Kehoe's men forced the maid to show them Lieutenant Hugh Angliss' room. She tried to alert Angliss by calling out loud as she walked up the stairs that there were men here who wanted to see him. Kehoe led five of his men into the room, surprising Angliss and a friend of his who was staying with him. While the Volunteers kept the British agent and his guest covered, Kehoe opened a bag belonging to the officer. It contained a number of pistols: a Colt, a Webley-Scott and a .32 automatic. Angliss was understandably evasive about his identity when asked. But Kehoe, looking at Angliss' wallet, declared, 'you're a liar!'

As this exchange continued, gunfire was heard: a section of Auxiliaries was attempting to force entry to the building. A Volunteer from the stairway shouted, 'Are you all right there, boys? They're surrounding the house.' Kehoe and his men opened fire on Angliss immediately. Angliss lifted his arm to cover his face but it was a hopeless attempt to shield himself from five assailants. He yelled as he was hit and tried in vain to get cover under the bed. His friend was left unharmed as he was not on the list.[74] Peel, the other British agent in the house, barricaded the door to his room. Unable to get in, the Volunteers had fired over seventeen shots through the door but Peel was unharmed. A serious confrontation was now developing at 22 Lower Mount Street between Tom Kehoe's twenty-man unit and a section of seventeen Auxiliaries who happened upon the scene.[75]

The Auxiliaries were walking down Lower Mount Street on their way to Kingsbridge Station when they heard gunshots coming from No. 22. Going towards the house, they saw a woman shrieking from the basement window. The Auxiliaries attempted to enter the house but the door was held on the inside by Volunteer Billy McLean. As they pushed against the door their weight told and it began to give. McLean stuck his revolver out through the gap and fired on them. They returned fire through the letterbox, wounding McLean in the trigger finger. The section leader divided his men into groups to attempt entry to No. 22 via the houses on either side. He also detailed Cadets Frank Garniss and Cecil A. Morris to double back for reinforcements to Beggars Bush Barracks, less than a half a mile away. The front door of the house then opened and ten or twelve IRA men led by Tom Kehoe charged out into the street, firing as they went. Turning left, they crossed the road and disappeared down Grattan Street. Squad member Jim Slattery and Volunteer Jack Dempsey had escaped over a wall into a lane at the rear of the house. Volunteer Frank Teeling was fired on and hit as he tried to climb the wall. He was captured by the Auxiliaries who, upon discovering the body of Angliss, wanted to exact immediate revenge. They were prevented by their senior officer, Brigadier-General Frank Crozier, who had just arrived and taken charge.

The Auxiliary section leader at 22 Lower Mount Street had also telephoned Beggars Bush for reinforcements. It then emerged that Cadets Garniss and Morris had not arrived at the barracks and their whereabouts was unknown. Brigadier-General Crozier was inspecting a company of Auxiliaries on the square at the barracks at the time, when a nurse and a dispatch rider came running in breathless, with the news that they had discovered the bodies of the two Auxiliaries in the back garden of 16 Northumberland Road. Wearing civilian clothes, Garniss and Morris had run into an IRA scouting party under the command of Captain Francis Casey of D Company 3rd Battalion at Mount Street Bridge.[76] Once their identity as Auxiliaries was established, they were taken to the back garden of a house and shot in the head.[77] They were the first Auxiliary casualties in the conflict in Ireland.[78]

After escaping from 22 Lower Mount Street, Jim Slattery and Jack Dempsey went to Golden's in Victoria Street to wash. James Carrigan and Patrick Kelly, drivers of a Hudson-Six for Captain Paddy Flanagan's operation on 28 Upper Pembroke Street, also stayed at Golden's. Captain Flanagan's assignment turned out to be one of the worst experiences for all involved.

From the outset, Captain Flanagan's unit from C Company 3rd Battalion had the toughest assignment. Flanagan was given the task of killing two British agents, Captain Leonard Price and Major 'Chummy' Dowling, in rooms on the second floor of 28 Pembroke Street. There were also two other British intelligence agents, Captain R. D. Jeune and Lieutenant Randolf Murray, living on the third floor. It is worth nothing that the IRA units assigned to the different locations on Bloody Sunday were given the identities of the British agents they were to assassinate, but not the names of all people in the building. This led to considerable confusion for the

IRA in houses where a number of people were staying. In this instance, matters were further complicated by the presence of four British infantry officers – Colonel Woodcock O/C Lancashire Fusiliers and his adjutant, Captain Keenlyside, and Colonels Montgomery and Day – and their wives, who were also residing at this address.[79] IRA IO Charlie Dalton had prepared the ground. He had got to know a maid in the house, Maudie, and through her had identified the rooms of agents Price and Dowling. At 9 a.m., between fifteen and twenty men of D Company 2nd Battalion entered the building. Leo Duffy came in over the back wall and was seen by Mrs Woodcock, who was sitting at her dressing table preparing to go down to breakfast. The IRA also had assistance from the house porter, James Greene.

As soon as the unit entered the building, Flanagan, Dalton and a small group of Volunteers went up the stairs, their footsteps muffled by the plush carpet. They wasted no time. On reaching the second floor they located Captain Price and Major Dowling. Both were shot in the chest. Dowling was killed instantly. Price lay gasping until an officer rushed down from the top floor to help. Price was beyond aid and the life slipped from him. Dalton wanted to search the room for British military papers but Flanagan said, 'Wait be damned. Get out of here as quickly as you can.'[80]

On seeing the IRA man come over the back wall, Mrs Woodcock had called her husband. He rushed to warn Lieutenant Colonel Hugh Montgomery on the ground floor but ran straight into the C Company covering party waiting downstairs. They had already run into Lieutenant Murray and were holding him against the wall at the stairs to the basement. The shots fired by Flanagan and Dalton caused the C Company party downstairs to open fire also. The primary target was Colonel Montgomery, who surprised the IRA party by coming out of his room unexpectedly. Hit once and fatally wounded, he made it back to his bed. He died of his injuries on 10 December 1920.[81] Colonel Woodcock turned to run up the stairs and was also hit twice but managed to escape back to his room where he collapsed on the bed in front of his wife. Lieutenant Murray was badly wounded but survived due to the panic-induced shooting of the IRA men. Captain Keenlyside, on hearing the gunfire, had emerged from his room with his wife. She bravely struggled with those attempting to kill her husband, distracting them sufficiently to affect their aim. Keenlyside was wounded but survived.[82]

All across the south side of the city combined units of IRA intelligence, the Squad and the Dublin Brigade carried out Michael Collins' orders to neutralise the British intelligence operation in Dublin. There were a few cases of mistaken identity, as in the case of a Captain Fitzgerald, shot in place of a Colonel Fitzpatrick at 28 Earlsfort Terrace by a unit from A Company 3rd Battalion. There was another horror story at 'Briama', 117 Morehampton Road, where Captain Larry Nugent's K Company 3rd Battalion killed three men (one a civilian) and wounded a fourth. A ten-year-old boy saw his father dragged to a room to be shot after Captain Maclean implored the IRA men not to shoot them in front of their families.[83] Three of K Company's unit never returned to duty after this operation.[84] At some of the addresses the British agents were not there, as happened at 7 Ranelagh Road. Rathfarnham's E Company 4th Battalion under Captain Francis Coghlan were ordered to shoot a Captain Noble and his wife (or paramour – accounts differ) as they were both considered to be agents. The captain was not in but Joe Dolan, a member of IRA intelligence, beat the woman who was present in the house and stole her rings. He then set the house on fire. Captain Coghlan ordered his men to wait and put the fire out.[85]

After the operations concluded, the different IRA units separated, some leaving the city altogether. The 2nd Battalion units made for the south quay opposite Common Street on the north quay. It was here that Tommy Kilcoyne had commandeered a boat to ferry the IRA men across the Liffey and thus avoid any British checkpoints on the bridges.[86] Charlie Dalton got to the south quays after passing three DMP constables at Oriel House on Harcourt Place who took no notice of him. He found Frank Saurin already there but the ferry was gone. These two stragglers were now in grave danger and knew the consequences should they be caught. Dalton later told Ernie O'Malley, 'I got the wind up rightly. I was thinking of the tenders swinging up from Beggars Bush. But Tom Kilcoyne rowed back and took us across the river. Tom Kilcoyne was always very cool. He was a big lump of a fellow, and Captain of B Company 2nd Battalion in the end'.[87] Once across the river they got back to the dump safely, hid their weapons and made for the IRA's field HQ for that day, Peter and Catherine Byrne's at 17 North Richmond Street. Two of the Byrnes' daughters, Catherine and Alice, were members of Cumann na mBan Central Branch. They were ordered to feed the Volunteers who arrived and also to treat any of the wounded. Catherine Byrne's codename was 'Splash'. She regularly carried weapons and ammunition for the IRA in Dublin. She treated Billy McLean's gunshot wound while Paddy O'Daly went through captured British intelligence papers.

Pat McCrea and his men had arrived back from Baggot Street. While they were at the Byrne household, different units arrived to make their after-action reports.[88] These reports were given first to O/C of the Squad, Paddy O'Daly, and then to 2nd Battalion O/C Seán Russell.[89] As the morning passed Catherine Byrne was already thinking of the afternoon. She and her fiancé were looking forward to a trip to Croke Park to see Tipperary play Dublin. Quite a number of those involved in operations that Sunday morning were planning on going to the match, too. McCrea returned home at 11 a.m. and cooked his breakfast. His wife up to that point had not suspected he was deeply involved with the IRA. To cover up his absence earlier that morning, he told his wife he had been 'out fishing with the boys'. His wife asked him had he not caught any fish, as there were none in the kitchen. McCrea went back into town and saw intense British military activity all over the city. He was in the habit of going to a Gaelic football match at Croke Park on a Sunday but decided to stay away that afternoon as there could be trouble. He went home and fell asleep on the couch. At 4 p.m. he was woken by his wife who was in floods of tears. She handed him a copy of a 'Stop Press' edition of the paper, which detailed the killings that morning. She asked him if this was the fishing expedition he had been on. McCrea told his wife the truth and there followed an emotional exchange between them:

> 'Yes, and don't you see we had a good catch', or words to that effect. She then said 'I don't care what you think about it, I think it is murder'. I said: 'No, that is nonsense; I'd feel like going to the altar after that job this morning', and thus I tried to calm her. I don't think she put out any lights in the house during the following winter. I did not stay at home then for about a week. That Sunday night I slept in a grove in the Demesne known as St Anne's which was nearby.[90]

The table on page 172 shows the command structure and personnel of the Dublin Brigade involved in the operation to assassinate British IOs on Bloody Sunday. While not a definitive list, it shows the key IRA personnel who led operations and what companies and battalions the majority of the IRA Volunteers came from. It also shows which British IOs they were detailed to attack and the outcome of those attacks. It demonstrates the enormous undertaking of the operation and how it could not have been undertaken without an effectively functioning military organisation.

News of the events that morning was even more distressing to the British troops in the city. It was their friends and colleagues, with some of whom they had shared four years in the trenches during the First World War, who were now dead. Captain Rymer-Jones and his platoon of the 1st Battalion King's Own Liverpool Regiment were on a raid of the Great Southern railway yards in Inchicore. According to intelligence he had received, the IRA had weapons and ammunition stored in the area. On this particular morning nothing was found and the captain and his men returned to Richmond Barracks. With them was British intelligence officer Captain Jeune. Had he not been on duty at Inchicore he would have been in his bed at 28 Upper Pembroke Street when Captain Flanagan began his operation. Rymer-Jones and Jeune's disappointment at finding no IRA arms was nothing compared to the shock that awaited them on their return to barracks. News was just coming in of an unprecedented IRA operation across the city. 'The raiding boys of the Sinn Féin, we called them then, they weren't IRA, Sinn Féin, in their uniform of dirty mackintoshes and black homburg hats, went to all these places, killed the officers, dragging them out of bed with their wives and families watching.'[91] As more details came in, Captain Rymer-Jones had great difficulty in restraining his men from going into the city to take revenge.[92] Jeune hurried back to his lodgings to find his brother officers lying dead on the floor.[93] As news of the killings reached Dublin Castle, panic spread among those of the British officers' families who were living out in the city. Accounts were circulating of up to fifty British officers being shot. Eventually, more accurate figures emerged and the official British report read: '14 deaths, 6 injured including one Shinner and 4 prisoners captured.'[94]

The four prisoners were Volunteers Frank Teeling and Conor Clune and Commandants Peadar Clancy and Dick McKee. Teeling was sent to King George V Hospital at Parkgate to have his wounds treated. The others were now in Dublin Castle. The atmosphere in the city was highly charged. Michael Collins expected a response from the British. Worried that the proposed Gaelic football match between Tipperary and Dublin could become a focus for conflict, it was suggested, albeit late in the day, to cancel it. The GAA said it was too late as the city was filled with

Combined IRA GHQ Intelligence, The Squad & Dublin Brigade operations on Sunday 21 November 1920[95]

Pre-Operational Planning: IRA GHQ Intelligence Department.
Operational Planning: Seán Russell O/C 2nd Bn Dublin Brigade.
Operational Briefing: Dick McKee & Peadar Clancy 20 November 9–10 p.m. at Dublin Brigade HQ, Typographical Institute, 35 Lower Gardiner Street, Dublin.
Company Briefings: Various Battalion & Company Commanders at different locations in Dublin, e.g. E Coy 2nd Bn meeting held Saturday night 20 November at 100 Seville Place.

Locations of Lodgings	British intelligence officers	IRA OC and IO	IRA companies, battalions & Volunteers assigned	
38 Upper Mount Street	Lt. A. Ames (executed) Lt. Bennett (executed) Unnamed officer also resident (survived)	O/C Capt. Tom Ennis E Coy & the Squad IO Frank Saurin	Lt. Seán Doyle	The Squad
			Vol. Vinny Byrne	The Squad
			Johnny McDonnell	E Coy 2nd Bn
		20–30 men on this operation (15–20 entered the house)	Willie Maher	E Coy 2nd Bn
			Herbert Conroy	E Coy 2nd Bn
			Seán Daly	E Coy 2nd Bn
			Michael J. Lawless	E Coy 2nd Bn
22 Lower Mount Street	Lt. H. Angliss (pseudonym Mr Mahon – executed)	O/C Tom Kehoe	Jim Slattery	The Squad
			Billy McLean (wounded)	E Coy 2nd Bn
			Frank Teeling (wounded and captured)	E Coy 2nd Bn
	Mr Peel (survived unwounded)		Andy Monahan	E Coy 2nd Bn
			Valentine Bennett	E Coy 2nd Bn
			Denny Begley (wounded)	E Coy 3rd Bn
			Scouting party	D Coy 3rd Bn
28–29 Upper Pembroke Street	Capt. Leonard Price MC (executed)	O/C Capt. Paddy Flanagan IO Charlie Dalton	Lt. Albert Rutherford	C Coy 3rd Bn
			Lt. Joe O'Connor	C Coy 3rd Bn
	Major C.M.G. Dowling (executed)		Mick O'Hanlon	C Coy 3rd Bn
	Col. Montgomery (died of wounds 10 December 1920)		Seamus Gaugin	not listed on official C Coy Roll
			Jack Egan	not listed on official C Coy Roll
	Col. Woodcock (wounded)		Andy Cooney	C Coy 3rd Bn
			George P. White	C Coy 3rd Bn
	Capt. Keenlyside (wounded)		Jim (Seamus) Doyle ('The Shelmalier')	C Coy 3rd Bn
	Capt. Robert D. Jeune (on a raid – not present)		Michael Davis	C Coy 3rd Bn
			Leo Duffy	C Coy 3rd Bn
			James Carrigan	Driver, C Coy 1st Bn
			Patrick Kelly	Driver, G Coy 1st Bn
			IO Ned J. Kelleher, O/C of cover party at front entrance	C Coy 3rd Bn

Locations of Lodgings	British intelligence officers	IRA OC and IO	IRA companies, battalions & Volunteers assigned	
92 Lower Baggot Street	Captain W.F. Newbury (executed)	O/C Joe Leonard The Squad	Bill Stapleton	The Squad
		IO Hugo MacNeill B Coy 2nd Bn	Jack Stafford	B Coy 2nd Bn
			Pat McCrea	The Squad, Brigade Transport & B Coy 2nd Bn
			Paddy Griffin	The Squad
			Eddie Byrne	The Squad, B Coy 2nd Bn
			Mick Fleming	The Squad, B Coy 3rd Bn, Brigade Transport
16 Northumberland Road	Cadet Cecil A. Morris ADRIC (executed) Cadet Frank Garniss ADRIC (executed)	O/C Capt. Francis Casey	D Coy Scouting Party on Grand Canal Bridge, Upper Mount Street	D Coy 3rd Bn
			James F. Cullen	D Coy 3rd Bn
			M. Kavanagh	D Coy 3rd Bn
			Peter Murphy	(not listed with D Coy)
			William Reilly	(not listed with D Coy)
			M. Scanlon	(not listed with D Coy)
28 Earlsfort Terrace	Captain Fitzgerald (executed)	O/C Lt. Paddy Byrne IO Mick Kennedy (20 Volunteers in this unit entered the house)	Lt. John Doyle	A Coy 3rd Bn
			Leo O'Brien	A Coy 3rd Bn
			John Timmons	A Coy 3rd Bn
			Joe Timmons	A Coy 3rd Bn
			Covering party: Christopher 'Kit' Farrell	A Coy 3rd Bn
			Mick [P] Kennedy	A Coy 3rd Bn (a P. Kennedy only listed in Official A Coy Roll)
			Joe Lynch	A Coy 3rd Bn
			Jim O'Donnell	A Coy 3rd Bn
			Christopher 'Kit' O'Donnell	A Coy 3rd Bn
'Briama' 117 Morehampton Road	Captain Maclean (executed) Mr Smith (executed) Lt. Donald (executed) Mr Caldow (wounded)	O/C Capt. Larry Nugent (10 Volunteers entered the house)	SL James Bird	K Coy 3rd Bn
			Edward Devitt	K Coy 3rd Bn
			J. F. O'Donnell	3 Bn Armourer
			J. Norton	K Coy 3rd Bn
			Daniel Finlayson	K Coy 3rd Bn & B Coy 2nd Bn
			Vol. J. Young	K Coy 3rd Bn
			Vol. Michael White	K Coy 3rd Bn
			Vol. P. Brennan	K Coy 3rd Bn

Locations of Lodgings	British intelligence officers	IRA OC and IO	IRA companies, battalions & Volunteers assigned	
Gresham Hotel, Sackville Street	Lt. L.E.W. Wilde (executed)	O/C Capt. Paddy Moran	James Cahill	D Coy, 2nd Bn
	Captain P. J. McCormack (executed)	IO Paddy Kennedy	Adjutant Mick Kilkelly	D Coy, 2nd Bn
	Third British officer unnamed & not present during IRA operation		SL Arthur Beasley	D Coy, 2nd Bn
			SL James Foley	D Coy, 2nd Bn
			Michael Noone	D Coy, 2nd Bn
			Nick Leonard	D Coy, 2nd Bn
			Joe Glynn	D Coy, 2nd Bn
			William Hogan	D Coy, 2nd Bn
			Richard McGrath	D Coy, 2nd Bn
			Morgan Durnin	D Coy, 2nd Bn
			George McCann	D Coy, 2nd Bn
			Joe Doyle	D Coy, 2nd Bn
			John Cullinane	D Coy, 2nd Bn
119 Lower Baggot Street	Captain G.T. Baggallay (executed)	O/C of operation unidentified	Capt. T. Burke	C Coy 2nd Bn
			Lt. Matty McDonald	C Coy 2nd Bn
			Lt. M. Fleming	C Coy 2nd Bn
			Acting Lt. F. Cotter	C Coy 2nd Bn
			IO J Sexton	not located in official coy roll
			SL Jack Keating	C Coy 2nd Bn
			Seán Lemass	C Coy 2nd Bn
7 Ranelagh Road	Capt. Noble (unharmed – not present when operation took place)	O/C Capt. Francis X. Coghlan IO Joe Dolan IO Dan McDonnell	Christopher 'Todd' Andrews	E Coy 4th Bn
			James Kenny	E Coy 4th Bn
Eastwood Hotel, Lower Leeson Street	Lt.-Colonel Jennings (escaped unharmed – had left these lodgings a few days prior to the operation)	O/C Capt. Christy Byrne SL Ned Bennett went into the hotel	Lt. Jimmy Donnelly	F Coy 4th Bn
			Lt Ned Bennett	F Coy 4th Bn
			SL Pádraig Ó Conchubhair	F Coy 4th Bn
			Jimmy McGuinness	F Coy 4th Bn
			Joe McGuinness	F Coy 4th Bn
			George J. Dwyer	F Coy 4th Bn
			Jerry Gannon	F Coy 4th Bn
			Capt. Bob Byrne	B Coy 4th Bn

Locations of Lodgings	British intelligence officers	IRA OC and IO	IRA companies, battalions & Volunteers assigned	
Eastwood Hotel, Lower Leeson Street			Adj. Annie Cooney	Inghinidhe Branch Cumann na mBan attached to 3rd & 4th Bn
			SL Lily Cooney	Inghinidhe Branch Cumann na mBan attached to 3rd & 4th Bn Dublin Brigade IRA
			Ellen Bushell	Civilian sympathiser working for the IRA
Phibsborough (address not given)		O/C Capt. Paddy Holohan (6 detailed for this operation) Operation called off	Patrick Lawson	1st Bn
Escape Route: O/C Capt. Tommy Kilcoyne B Coy 2nd Bn commandeered a ferry to move the various members of the Squad and 2nd Bn units back across the River Liffey to their own battalion area. Other units dispersed throughout the city with some Volunteers even taking the first train available out of Dublin.				
After Action Reports & First-Aid Station: Peter and Catherine Byrne family home at 17 Richmond Street, Mountjoy, on the north side of Dublin.				

thousands of people on their way to the pitch at Croke Park.[96] Among the IRA present were Captain Paddy Moran, Tom Kehoe, Joe Dolan and Dan McDonnell. Harry Colley, Tom Kilcoyne and Sean Russell actually visited the ground in an attempt to have the GAA disperse the crowd. They had received information from their agents in the DMP that a British military operation, including Auxiliaries, was planned for some time during the match that afternoon.[97]

The first the crowd at Croke Park knew of any British operation was the appearance of a plane over the ground. It circled a number of times and then flew off. The British forces, under the command of Lieutenant Colonel Robert Bray, were to establish a cordon around Croke Park. Then Auxiliaries, under Major E. L. Mills, and about 100 Black and Tans of the RIC were to filter the crowd as they exited the ground in an attempt to capture IRA men from the morning's killings.[98] Shortly after the plane disappeared, Tipperary were awarded a penalty against Dublin. As Tom

Ryan, the Tipperary captain, stepped up to take it, the air was suddenly filled with rifle and machine-gun fire. Ryan described the sheer terror of those moments:

> [T]he crowd of spectators immediately stampeded. The players also fled from the field in among the sideline spectators, except six of us who threw ourselves down on the ground where we were. The six of us who remained – [Michael] Hogan and I and four of the Dublin team – were I think all Volunteers. I suppose it was our Volunteer training that prompted us to protect ourselves by lying down rather than by rushing around. From where we lay, we could see sparks flying off the railway embankment wall where the bullets struck the wall, and we saw people rolling down the embankment who presumably were hit. There was general pandemonium at this stage between the firing, people rushing and a general panic amongst the crowd.
>
>   Two of the players who were lying on the field at this stage got up and made a rush for the paling surrounding the pitch on the Hill Sixty [now Hill 16] side, which was nearest to them. One by one we followed their example, and it was while Hogan was running from the field to the paling that he got hit by a bullet. I think Josie Sinnott and myself were the last to leave the field. Going across to Hogan, I tried to lift him but the blood was spurting from a wound in his back and I knew he was very badly injured. He made the exclamation when I lifted him, 'Jesus, Mary and Joseph! I am done!', and died on the spot. My hands were covered in his blood.[99]

The Tipperary captain escaped to a house in Clonliffe Road where he was captured and his tricoloured Tipperary football kit ripped off him with bayonets. A British officer intervened to save his life. Ryan was taken back to Croke Park where the dead and dying were being attended to by spectators, priests and soldiers.[100] The ninety seconds of firing resulted in eleven dead and over fifty injured. Three were mortally wounded and died a few days later.[101] Three of the dead were boys: Jeremiah O'Leary (ten), William Robinson (eleven) and John William Scott (fourteen). One of those killed was a woman, 26-year-old Jane Boyle. She was with her fiancé at the halfway line when she was killed. The other fatalities were all men: James Burke (fourty-four), Daniel Carroll (thirty), Michael Feery (forty), Michael Hogan (twenty-four), Patrick O'Dowd (fifty-seven), Thomas

Ryan (twenty-seven), James Teehan (twenty-seven), Joe Traynor (twenty-one), Tom Hogan (nineteen) and James Matthews (forty-eight).[102]

Dublin city was convulsed with violence. All through that day, Clune, Clancy and McKee were held in the guardroom at Dublin Castle awaiting the retribution they knew was coming.

The Labour Party Commission investigating conditions in Ireland began working in Dublin in early December. Part of their extensive investigations included what they termed 'The Massacre at Croke Park'. Their starting point was the statement of Sir Hamar Greenwood in the House of Commons on 23 November, in which he said the military had encircled the ground and had attempted to calm the crowd in advance by making announcements through a megaphone. Greenwood claimed that as the police approached the grounds they were fired upon from two locations. The resulting panic among the spectators caused a stampede. He claimed that the firing lasted three minutes and that thirty revolvers thrown away by men in the crowd were found afterwards by the police.[103] The Labour Party Commission made every effort to 'bring to light' evidence to support the Chief Secretary's statement. In spite of their efforts, the mass of evidence available not only contradicted his account but supported claims that the police had opened fired once their lorries had come to a halt.[104] Of the many witnesses who told of their experiences before the Labour Commission, eleven were included in the final report in Appendix II (1). The eyewitness accounts tell of an aeroplane, lorries, armoured cars, rifle and machine-gun fire. They tell of the terror-stricken crowd, those who were shot and the acts of mercy from others, including British army officers, who tried to help the wounded. The accounts reveal the cruelty and malice of the Black and Tans of the RIC and the Auxiliaries in killing, preventing medical aid being given to the injured and also the robbery of the takings at the turnstiles.[105] After carrying out their investigation, the Commission concluded that:

> [T]he indiscriminate shooting of panic-stricken men cannot be even partly justified or defended on the ground that there might have been 'gun men' among them trying to escape ... Not even panic, itself a sufficiently serious reflection in the case of a disciplined force, can excuse the action of the police amongst whom there appears to have been a spirit of calculated brutality and lack of self-control which, as has been officially admitted, resulted in twelve innocent persons

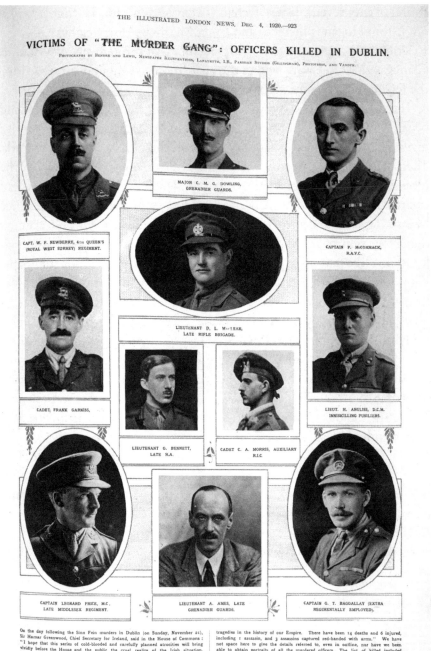

The Illustrated London News, 4 December 1920, published the names and photographs of 11 British officers killed by the Squad and Dublin Brigade on Bloody Sunday. Both sides called the other's assassins 'The Murder Gang'. (Courtesy National Library of Ireland)

losing their lives [two more died later], eleven being seriously injured enough to be detained in hospital, and fifty others being more or less slightly hurt – a grand total of seventy-three victims. According to the evidence furnished to the Commission, the operations were conducted by the R.I.C. and Auxiliaries. The soldiers took no part.[106]

On Monday morning, 22 November, Pat McCrea went into the city and straight to the Squad HQ at George Moreland's cabinet-making premises in Abbey Street. He received bad news. James McNamara, one of Collins' DMP detectives in Dublin Castle, had sent news to the Dublin Brigade that Commandant Dick McKee and Vice-Commandant Peadar Clancy had been captured by the British and were being held by the Auxiliaries of F Company at Dublin Castle. Their capture had happened after the briefing of the various Dublin Brigade operational units on Saturday night. After the briefing, McKee and Clancy had gone to a late meeting with Piaras Béaslaí in Vaughan's Hotel. They had only just left when the hotel was raided. Volunteer Conor Clune was captured. Piaras Béaslaí, editor of *An t-Óglach*, only just managed to escape over the back wall of the hotel. McKee and Clancy went to Seán Fitzgerald's in Gloucester Street, their lodgings for the night. They must have been followed because witnesses of that night reported seeing a white cross marked on the door of Fitzgerald's.

Between 1 a.m. and 2 a.m. on 21 November, the British raided the house on Gloucester Street, after cordoning off the surrounding area. A revolver McKee had on him was shoved into a grandfather clock in the hall. It was not discovered during the raid.[107] When Collins found out the captured men were in Dublin Castle he ordered any proposed rescue units to stand down. There was nothing they could do but wait. Shortly afterwards, Collins received the news that they had been dreading: their comrades were dead. The official version released by the British, which included convenient photographs of the attempted escape, stated in each case that: 'Cause of death was due to shock & haemorrhage due to bullet wounds fired by members of the Auxiliary Division R.I.C. in self-defence & in execution of their duty in preventing the escape of deceased who was in their lawful custody.'[108]

It soon became clear from the medical evidence that this version of events was far from the truth. The bodies of Clune, Clancy and McKee were removed to King George V Hospital. Michael Collins sent a message to Oscar Traynor, Vice O/C Dublin Brigade, that a number of Volunteers, not prominent in the movement, were to be sent to retrieve the bodies. According to McCrea, Collins did not want the bodies handled by the Tans. McCrea was told not to go on the mission himself but ignored this order and went with Tommy Gay and one other Volunteer. On arriving at the hospital they went to the mortuary. The Tans on duty turned their backs, in what McCrea interpreted as a spirit of decency.

Accompanying McCrea and the IRA Volunteers were Dick McKee's mother, Bridget, his sister Maire and Dick McKee's fiancée, May Gibney. The sight that awaited them was truly dreadful. Conor Clune had been shot through the chest but had not been tortured.[109] Peadar Clancy had a large hole in his temple between the eye and ear which was plugged with cotton wool. His throat was also badly injured and was also covered with cotton wool.[110] Dick McKee's body was in a bad condition. His hands and all along his arms had been opened with thrusts of a bayonet. There was an extensive wound in his side, 11 inches (28cm) long, and a gunshot wound in his neck.[111] There was no doubt that they had been tortured.

Such torture as this was to become a regular experience for Volunteers who fell into the hands of the Auxiliaries of F Company at Dublin Castle. The evidence of bayonet wounds was confirmed in two interviews carried out by Ernie O'Malley: with McCrea and Maire McKee. Both of them saw the bodies in the hospital mortuary. The evidence provided by Detective David Neligan said the bodies were not bayonetted or mutilated; he also said he did not see the bodies.[112] McCrea said the bodies of the Volunteers were taken to the Pro-Cathedral on Marlborough Street. Doctors, on Michael Collins' instructions, examined the wounds at the Pro-Cathedral, after which photographs were taken and sent to the press in the USA. The bodies of Peadar Clancy and Dick McKee were then dressed in Volunteer uniform for the last time. After the funeral Mass, two hearses, each drawn by four horses and covered with floral wreaths, led the cortège to Glasnevin Cemetery. Conor Clune's body was claimed by his employer Edward MacLysaght, the famous Irish genealogist. He returned the body to County Clare where, after a funeral Mass, Conor Clune was buried at the old Franciscan Abbey at Quin.[113]

John 'Shankers' Ryan was later identified by the IRA as being responsible for tailing and betraying McKee and Clancy. He was shot by IRA IO Paddy Kennedy at a pub in the Gloucester Diamond in early 1921.

Just a week later, on Sunday 28 November 1920, Commandant Tom Barry's west Cork flying column annihilated an Auxiliary patrol at Kilmichael. This ambush was an important boost in morale for the IRA and the republicans. Barry's victory at Kilmichael, which left only one Auxiliary alive, had demonstrated that this formidable foe could be defeated. The ambush was also controversial as the British claimed the bodies of the dead Auxiliaries were mutilated. The IRA denied this, claiming the Auxiliaries had pretended to surrender, only to begin fighting again.[114] What is clear is that there was little quarter expected and little quarter given in this war. Survival was down to individual acts of mercy by IRA Volunteers or British soldiers. However, as the island entered the final month of 1920, mercy was now in short supply. In Dublin, there was relative calm after the violence of 21 November, but it was short-lived. IRA GHQ and the Dublin Brigade awaited the British storm that they knew was sure to break. It was only a matter of when.

6

'Knee-Deep in Gelignite'

December to July 1921

On the day of the assassinations of British secret service officers, Under-Secretary Sir John Anderson held an important meeting with the British army's Dublin District senior officers, Generals Boyd, Tudor, and Brind, at Dublin Castle. They decided all roads out of the city were to be picketed by British troops and all steamers from Dublin and Kingstown were to be searched. All British officers living outside Dublin Castle were to be brought within barracks immediately. Instructions were issued to the army, as follows: 'arrest as many known officers of IRA and extremists as possible with a view to detention in special camp already constructed at Ballykinlar near Newcastle [County Down]. Extensive searches throughout Dublin already in progress. Curfew hour will be advanced from midnight to ten o'clock as from tomorrow'.[1]

On receiving details of the measures, Chief Secretary Hamar Greenwood sent a telegram to Anderson, saying: 'I shall support you and the Police, and military in every and most drastic actions you take. The whole power of the Govt is behind you. Keep me informed. These awful deeds of assassination might [serve] to wake up Great Britain and the Empire to the facts of the Irish situation.'[2]

The bodies of the fallen British secret service agents and military officers were taken in procession through the streets of Dublin with full military honours. Each coffin was draped with a Union flag and placed on a gun carriage, which was flanked by troops from the various British army regiments of the Dublin District. Captain Rymer-Jones described being on duty with the funeral cortège:

[T]here was an enormous parade next day. This is typical of the Irish and thousands lined the route over the Liffey down to the docks. I had to march alongside one of the vehicles with a dead body ... tens of thousands of people turned out to watch and they kidded themselves they were sympathetic. I think they were in an Irish way. At the back were the Black and Tans most of whom became Palestinian Policemen later ... if the Irishmen didn't take their hats off as the corpses went by they seized them and threw them in the Liffey.[3]

One of the first major successes for the British after Bloody Sunday was the capture of Joseph Lawless on 8 December.[4] This was followed a few days later by the discovery of the Dublin Brigade's munitions factory on the premises owned by Lawless at 198 Parnell Street. The Auxiliaries of F Company raided it on the night of 11–12 December and lay in wait inside the building for the IRA men to arrive the following morning. Tom Young was first to arrive but when he called in to the newsagents next door for his usual paper, he received a warning of what lay in store. Mick Keogh, who started his day with a pint for breakfast, was told of the night raid by his barman. Both men stayed in the area and alerted anyone else arriving.[5] The loss of the munitions factory was bad enough but without the quick work of these two Volunteers it could have been a lot worse. The IRA munitions unit simply watched as the Auxiliaries carried out their coup and hauled away the IRA's much-needed explosives and equipment.

Captured in the British sweeps following Bloody Sunday were a number of very important IRA, Cumann na mBan and Sinn Féin members. One of the very first was the leader of the Squad. On 23 November Captain Paddy O'Daly was visiting the house of Michael Love, a member of F Company 2nd Battalion at 10 Bessborough Avenue. Paddy's eldest son, also called Paddy, was staying there. The house was raided by a combined British army and RIC detachment. One of the policemen was Constable Dick McCarthy from Clontarf RIC Station. McCarthy covered for O'Daly, saying he was a hard-working carpenter, and O'Daly was not arrested.[6] Michael Love, however, was taken away. After an hour, a second raiding party arrived at the house also looking for Michael Love. They were not inclined to depart empty-handed and took O'Daly with them, depositing him in the prisoners' cage at Portobello Barracks (now Cathal Brugha Barracks). O'Daly eventually ended up at Mountjoy Gaol where he was put through a number of identity parades.[7] The warders knew him

Funeral cortège of British secret service officers leaves King George V Military Hospital on its way through the streets of Dublin in the days after Bloody Sunday, November 1920. (Courtesy the Military Archives)

as he had been released from his last stint in the prison only in August 1919. The warders, perhaps for their own safety, kept pulling O'Daly out of the line-up and placing him at the back of successive rows of prisoners. Charles Monroe, governor of the prison, came in to observe one of the identity parades. He saw O'Daly change places with another prisoner but quickly looked away. In other parades, the warders let O'Daly and other prisoners take toilet breaks or exchange places with other prisoners. While he was in Mountjoy, Arthur Griffith arrived, arrested on 26 November for his own safety on the orders of General Boyd of the Dublin District. The British were worried Griffith might become the target of a reprisal and that isolating him might produce a peace deal more quickly.[8]

From the beginning of December, the British implemented a persistent raid strategy nationwide. Brigadier-General Brind at British army GHQ was beginning to understand that 'Being ceaselessly harried and hunted day and night, has more effect on the morale of irregular levies [IRA Volunteers] than anything except the infliction of heavy casualties'.[9] The city was flooded with British troops who undertook seventy-two raids on 2 December alone. For the three days from 2 to 4 December there were

Crowds watch the gun carriages bearing the coffins of murdered British intelligence officers crossing O'Connell Bridge. From *The Illustrated London News*, 4 December 1920. (Courtesy National Library of Ireland)

136 raids in total. It did not stop there. After a brief respite, there followed over fifty raids between 9 and 13 December. As British intelligence, thanks mainly due to the Auxiliary F Company at Dublin Castle, began to collect and collate information received, the raids became more effective. There were some notable raids in which the British hoped to capture a major figure. Lieutenant Howse of the 1ˢᵗ Battalion Lancashire Regiment led a raid on 174 St James' Street hoping to arrest Dáil Minister for Local Government W. T. Cosgrave or 'Mr Burke', his alias. Just Mrs Louisa Cosgrave and her sister-in-law were at home, however.[10] After Bloody Sunday, Cosgrave had dyed his hair 'a flaming red' and gone into hiding. He used the pseudonym Brother Doyle and stayed at the Glencree Reformatory run by the Oblate Order near Enniskerry, County Wicklow.[11]

On 9 December, Captain Crane with his platoon NCO, Sergeant William Lowder, and a detachment from the 2ⁿᵈ Battalion Duke of Wellington Regiment raided 8 St Columbus Road Upper in Drumcondra. This address was the family home of Charlie Dalton, a member of Michael

Collins' intelligence department. Captain Crane had orders to arrest Charlie's father, James, but also apprehended his older brother, Emmet. There was little incriminating evidence in the house except documents and some of Emmet's British military equipment, consisting of a dagger, bayonet and helmet. Both father and son were arrested and taken to the prisoners' enclosure at Collinstown Aerodrome. Lieutenant Emmet Dalton's impressive service record as an officer in the British army in the Middle East and in France secured their release on 18 December 1920. Among the prisoners they met while in custody were Joe Lawless and Peadar Kearney (who wrote 'Amhrán na bhFiann' or 'The Soldier's Song').[12] Upon his release, Emmet Dalton was approached by his brother, Charlie, to see if he would be willing to assist the Dublin Brigade in a training programme. Newly appointed O/C of the Dublin Brigade, Commandant Oscar Traynor, asked Emmet to give a series of lectures to Dublin battalions of the IRA.[13] Despite being only twenty-two, the elder Dalton's vast experience in leadership, tactics and discipline were a valuable asset.[14] His cool head and experience were soon put to the test. One evening, while he was giving a lecture to Dublin Brigade senior officers at The Plaza, 6 Gardiner's Row, the building was raided. Dalton calmly led O/C Oscar Traynor and Adjutant Kit O'Malley through the British cordon after a brief, friendly chat with the British officer in charge.[15] Over a period of months, Emmet Dalton, apart from giving lectures, became something of a specialist for important IRA operations. His complete dependability brought him to the attention of Michael Collins.

By the end of December 1920, the British had captured nearly 500 men and women of the IRA and Cumann na mBan. The huge number of prisoners made it difficult for the British to determine their real identities. The refusal of the British to admit that a state of war existed in Ireland meant every prisoner's case had to have legal preparation.[16] This tied down numbers of officers and men in an administrative capacity who would otherwise have been deployed more effectively in the battle against the IRA. An additional complication was the transfer of Dublin District intelligence from British army control to General Sir Hugh Tudor's key man, Ormonde Winter. The new organisation was called D Branch. The budget allotted to D Branch in January 1921 was a mere £655 while the British army's secret service received £3,380. By June 1921, Winter would be allocated £10,000 per month for his department and an undisclosed sum from RIC sources.[17] With better intelligence came even more captures of IRA personnel. If the British were to win this war in the time allotted by Lloyd George, they had to capture and kill Michael Collins and his intelligence staff. This increased the pressure on D Branch to provide the information which was held by prisoners falling into British custody. Interrogation, more than ever, became a battleground.

In the written accounts of their capture, IRA personnel always state they refused to cooperate or give any information to their interrogators. This is most unlikely to be true. British intelligence reports for 1921 state quite clearly that their information came from reliable informants and from captured prisoners. With an ever-increasing number of prisoners in custody, it was inevitable that the British would attempt to obtain information either with or without the cooperation of the captured. This interrogation process had already been experienced by quite a few Irish republicans. British interrogation techniques, which were developed during the First World War, were markedly different from that of the Germans, who generally treated captured prisoners well, giving them food and cigarettes. The German approach produced a compliant prisoner who generally revealed anything asked of him. The British approach was considerably more direct and robust. On the instructions of Lieutenant-General Sir Aylmer Hunter-Weston the following notice was given to captured German prisoners on the Western Front.

> Guidelines given to captured German prisoners to consider carefully prior to questioning:
> **To Prisoners:**
> **Important Warning**
> 1. Answer questions quickly, clearly, shortly and <u>truthfully</u>.
> 2. Remember, we already <u>know</u> the correct answers to many of the questions, which are only put to test your good faith.
> 3. True and satisfactory information is remembered to the credit of prisoners.
> 4. Those who give untruthful or unsatisfactory answers will be dealt with <u>specially</u>.[18]

Irish republicans, whether civilians or members of the IRA or Cumann na mBan, were generally not given a document warning them to cooperate. For specific republican suspects, fear and a general 'softening-up' process marked the introduction into custody of the Crown forces.

Some republicans would escape with a beating, eventually being released, whereas others faced torture and the added possibility of the session ending with an extrajudicial execution.

Gearóid Ua h-Uallacháin was a 1916 veteran of the attack on the Magazine Fort in the Phoenix Park, QM and Acting Chief of Staff of Na Fianna Éireann. In November 1920 Dick McKee and Peadar Clancy ordered Ua h-Uallacháin to travel to England to work on IRA plans for blowing up Stuart Road Power Station in Manchester. The plans were suspended in favour of an operation on the night of 27–28 November 1920, when eight cotton warehouses and four timber yards in Liverpool Docks were burned down by the local IRA battalion.[19] Plans submitted by Ua h-Uallacháin for the destruction of the power station had been captured by the British in a raid on Richard Mulcahy's home on 19 November 1920. As a result, Ua h-Uallacháin changed his name to Gerald O'Dea and carried faked identity cards. The British may have suspected Ua h-Uallacháin of involvement in the Liverpool operation. On Christmas Eve he was working in the Clontarf Pumping Station when it was raided by Auxiliaries. Ua h-Uallacháin was roughed up and taken to the North Dublin Union. There he received the 'softening-up' treatment. A big six-footer rolled up his sleeves and set to work, slapping and punching the IRA man in the head. Ua h-Uallacháin said a British soldier standing at a guardroom watching the beginning of the proceedings winked at him. This convinced Ua h-Uallacháin that his interrogators were only bluffing and he refused to talk. Ua h-Uallacháin was court-martialled and found not guilty. He was released, only to be rearrested and imprisoned at Arbour Hill for a few months before being released again. For the rest of the War of independence he lived in fear of being arrested again or killed.[20]

Ua h-Uallacháin's experience was very mild when compared with that of some other republicans, such as Ernie O'Malley, an IRA officer who had trained flying columns and led operations in Monaghan and Cork. O'Malley's experience sheds a great deal of light on the procedural norms for interrogation at Dublin Castle. Captured in a raid on 9 December by A Company ADRIC at Hanrahan's farmhouse in Cappagh, County Kilkenny, he was first beaten and tortured at Woodstock House in Inistioge before being taken to Dublin Castle. The British knew from the diary and weapons in his possession that they had captured an important prisoner.[21] After some time in the Auxiliary guardhouse he was put in a cell with Fr Dominic, a Capuchin friar who ministered to republicans.

They were fed well with food from the officers' mess. Fr Dominic was suspicious, likening the good meals to fattening a turkey for Christmas.[22]

O'Malley was then introduced to Major King and Captain Hardy, an experienced interrogation team at the Castle. Then began the 'softening-up' process. O'Malley was asked a question followed by a punch in the face and a number to the body. The questioning continued, with O'Malley giving insufficient information or none at all. Major King landed repeated blows to the prisoner's head – left and right alternately. What was an ordeal for O'Malley was routine for Hardy and King. His refusal to reveal anything seemed to encourage his interrogators even more. A hot poker was pulled from the stove and held before his eyes, burning his eyebrows and eyelashes. King then throttled O'Malley, digging his thumbs deeply into his throat. Still the pair were not finished. They placed the barrel of a revolver against his temple, telling him that if he did not answer by a count of three, his brains would be all over the wall. It was a mock execution and Major King fired a blank round. O'Malley was then returned to his cell and later, when he could stand, was permitted some fresh air in the Castle precinct. Áine Malone and Maire McKee were passing by O'Malley and he called out to them. They were in the Castle to recover the belongings of Dick McKee and Peadar Clancy. It took Áine a few moments to recognise O'Malley.[23] He was in a terrible state. Badly beaten, he now faced being hanged for an ambush at Kilmichael, an event at which he was not even present.

Áine Malone later returned with a parcel of clean clothes and some sweets. She also got word to Michael Collins. This moment of kindness brought great relief and hope to O'Malley.[24] On Christmas Day he nearly got himself beaten again for refusing to salute the King during a toast at Christmas dinner with Auxiliaries in the guardroom. O'Malley also met Major King that day but refused to drink with him. O'Malley, like many IRA men and Cumann na mBan women, did not drink alcohol. After Christmas, O'Malley was taken to Kilmainham Gaol to await his fate.[25]

While British Crown forces carried out their raids in November and December, moves were afoot to broker a peace deal. Christmas Day was a little better for Sinéad de Valera as her husband had arrived back from his tour of the United States. The tour had raised the considerable sum of approximately $5 million for the republican cause in the form of bonds. Much of the money was the generous financial sacrifice of hard-working Irish Americans who longed to see Ireland a free and independent country. De Valera's attempts to secure Republican and Democratic recognition of the Irish Republic during the US presidential campaign of 1920 caused a great deal of division between Sinn Féin and the Irish-American Clan na Gael. New York Judge Daniel Cohalan believed de Valera's interference would cement British–American ties in a post-war world, which would in turn strengthen the position of the Anglo-Americans while weakening that of the Irish-Americans.[26] Michael Collins, Arthur Griffith and Dáil Éireann demonstrated absolute loyalty to de Valera in the interests of national unity and to prevent the British from capitalising on any division among Irish ranks.

De Valera received generous financial support from the Dáil. Up to $1.5 million was made available to him to fund the gaining of recognition for the Irish Republic and also to support lobbying in the US presidential election. His fundraising in aid of the Friends of Irish Freedom 'Victory Bond' and the Irish Republic Bond Certificates was a major success, with the latter drive raising $5,123,640.[27] De Valera also raised public awareness of events in Ireland by speaking to thousands of people at mass rallies across the US. The numbers attending were staggering: 70,000 at Fenway Park in Boston and 50,000 at the Cubs' baseball ground in Chicago, to mention but two.[28] De Valera did not, however, manage to gain formal recognition for an Irish Republic from the US president. While there was significant popular support for the Irish republican cause, the US government, it seemed, was not prepared to undermine its wartime allies.

Michael Collins was convinced the success of both the political and military campaigns for Irish independence depended on events in Ireland and not in America. For 700 years, events concerning all of the people in Ireland had been decided in London and Collins was determined that that centuries-old dynamic would be settled in London and Dublin.[29] At the close of 1920, there were a number attempts to organise a peace. The Archbishop of Tuam suggested a 'Truce of God' but while it attracted a lot of civilian support in Ireland and Britain, it did not have the support of the combatants or their respective governments. The best chance was through the involvement of Archbishop of Perth, Dr Patrick Clune CSsR, as he understood both the Irish and British mindset very well. Born in County Clare in 1864, he was the uncle of Volunteer Conor Clune, killed in Dublin Castle on 21 November 1920. Archbishop Clune had served as a military chaplain to Australian troops on the Western Front during the First World War.[30] In November 1920 he was in Ireland, visiting Tipperary and Limerick before returning to Dublin via Galway.

In Dublin, the mood was menacing. Cyril Bryan, a journalist travelling with the archbishop and writing for *The Western Australia Record*, offered this description of the approaches to the seat of British power in Ireland:

> Dublin Castle is a queer old place these days. There never was a great deal of it to be seen, but all the visitor glimpses nowadays is one enormous tangle of barbed wire all over the place, and almost hiding massive steel plates that completely cover huge gates. Over all is some 20 or 30 feet of bomb-proof wire, and it is amusing to see the passers-by stare at this in wonder. It resembles a big hoarding without any advertising.[31]

In early December Dr Clune met with Lloyd George at the House of Commons. Invited to act as an intermediary, he travelled back to Dublin where he visited Arthur Griffith at Mountjoy Gaol and afterwards had talks with Michael Collins. The Sinn Féin and IRA political leadership expressed their desire for a truce but there would be no surrender of arms.[32] On 10 December Lloyd George addressed MPs in the House of Commons, saying that the majority of Irish people were 'anxious for peace and a fair settlement' while the section that controlled 'murder and outrage' in Ireland were 'not yet ready for peace'.[33] To prove his point Lloyd George referred to two messages he had received from Ireland, one from a vice-president of Sinn Féin, Rev. Fr O'Flanagan, and the other from 'Galway County Council'. This latter message had been drawn up by six of the council's thirty-two members.[34]

Lloyd George now believed the campaign orchestrated by the Black and Tans and the Auxiliaries was taking effect. He also believed the messages received represented moderate Irish public opinion. He therefore rejected the efforts at peace conducted by Dr Clune by making conditions impossible for negotiations to take place. In a hardening of the British stance, Lloyd George said there would be no recognition of Dáil Éireann, no safe conduct for anyone who was 'guilty of crimes of violence, of murder, of very brutal murder'.[35] There was no attempt to rein in the Auxiliaries and the Black and Tans in their pursuit of violence and mayhem. The Prime Minister's speech gave a green light to a continuation of the terror.

The night following Lloyd George's speech, K Company of the Auxiliary Division of the RIC set fires in Cork city resulting in a huge blaze that destroyed some of the city's most valuable businesses and properties. Also destroyed were the Municipal Hall and the Carnegie Library. The fire brigade had their hoses cut and firefighters were shot at as they attempted to extinguish the blaze.[36] The inferno was so bad that the Dublin fire brigade was called upon to journey to Cork to assist in putting out the flames.[37] The fires were reportedly a reprisal for an IRA ambush on an Auxiliary patrol at Dillon's Cross, in which one Auxiliary was killed and eleven were wounded.[38]

Archbishop Clune continued his efforts but in such a climate of violence no one was of a mind to make peace. The considerably influential 'War Party' of the British cabinet argued for and got their way to continue the war in Ireland. Dr Clune concluded his peace mission in London on Christmas Eve 1920.[39] At the same time, Captain Rymer-Jones, attached to the 1st Battalion King's Own Liverpool Regiment, found himself in Lucan RIC barracks in west County Dublin. He had been sent to Lucan with a detachment of troops to protect the isolated village barracks from IRA attack. The captain was taken with the beauty of the village and went out for a stroll at Christmas 1920:

> We took it in turn of course to cover it [Lucan RIC barracks] the whole time. I had the misfortune to be sent out there at Christmas to cover it. It was a dazzlingly pretty village and of course it had the Irish who I am very fond of ... In a way it helped in a study of the Irish character, quite impossible at times. They're a very fascinating race. I'm getting away from it, so in my turn I went out to Lucan and it was lovely weather, it was Christmas coming and they seemed very pleased to see you everywhere and of course you weren't supposed to go outside otherwise there was no point in the barbed wire. But one day I felt that it deserved some look, it was so quiet there. I thought I'm going to have a look this lovely village. And so I walked down the road and as I was passing one of their little shops, it went back through the shop another couple of steps and there was another room behind. It sounds very Irish but at any rate sitting out there at a table with a large loaf and a mound of butter in front of him was a little man who, seeing me, called out 'Come in, dear.' So I went in and he gave me bread and butter and tea and we discussed the horrors of this fratricide and how terrible it was. And he got down a book and read me something out of the bible as well as another goody goody book. And we both decided how terrible it was that

this should be happening. And I left him with thanks and went back to the barracks.

And the Inspector met me, he was in charge of the place, he said, 'Can I have a word with you, sir?' I knew what that meant. Out came the bottle of whiskey and he always drank it neat, which I couldn't do in those days. And so you had this large tumbler of neat whiskey and I said 'What a lovely place this is.' I said, 'I've been down in the village and who would be that charming little man, who we got on so well together.' 'Oh that's so-and-so. He's a terrible fella. He's got two sons on the run and each Saturday he goes into Dublin gets drunk and challenges the police to arrest him.' And I thought well that's Ireland, that's Ireland.[40]

As Captain Rymer-Jones sipped his whiskey in Lucan RIC Barracks, Captain Paddy O'Daly, O/C of the Squad, was being driven at high speed through the Dublin streets in an armoured car. At Kilmainham Gaol, he was questioned for an hour by a British intelligence officer, during the course of which he denied any question put to him about involvement with the IRA and Bloody Sunday. O'Daly was not released. Mrs Holland, the lady looking after one of O'Daly's children, got a British soldier to bring in extra food to him in the jail. As the soldier downed a few gulps of whiskey and smoked a few cigarettes, he couldn't believe O'Daly did not drink or smoke. After three weeks in Kilmainham, O'Daly was moved to Ballykinlar Camp in County Down. A Royal Navy destroyer brought the batch of prisoners to Belfast where they received a hot reception from the shipyard workers. The prisoners were showered with nuts, bolts and pieces of metal.[41] Eventually, the prisoners reached Ballykinlar. O'Daly was to remain in the camp until March 1921.[42] Paddy O'Daly, commander of the Squad, was protected by policemen and warders. The British suspected his involvement in Bloody Sunday, but the fact that he had not led an operation to assassinate any of the British officers meant he could look their intelligence officers in the eye and say with conviction that he had not shot anyone that day.

The option of protection was not open to Captain Eileen McGrane of Cumann na mBan.[43] On New Year's Eve, she got the shock of her life when the flat she shared with Margot Trench and Mary McCarthy on the top floor at 21 Dawson Street was raided by fifteen Auxiliaries of F Company, led by District Inspectors Crang and Simpson. They were looking for

Eileen McGrane's apartment at 21 Dawson Street after a raid by F Company Auxiliaries on 31 December 1920. (Courtesy the Military Archives)

Tom Cullen of IRA intelligence. Discovered in the apartment was a specially kitted-out room for use as a temporary office, crammed with IRA intelligence papers. The office had been used from time to time by Michael Collins and Arthur Griffith. It was, however, also an arms dump. Eileen McGrane, the British discovered, 'was fully acquainted with the contents and nature of all of them. They would have enabled her to be tried under practically every Regulation of the R.O.I.R. In addition 6 revolvers and a large quantity of dum-dum ammunition were found. There can be no doubt that these weapons were in her custody and that she was fully aware that they were there.'[44]

The weapons included three automatic pistols and three revolvers along with 250–300 rounds of ammunition. Eileen McGrane was in serious trouble. The files found in her flat were submitted to the chief of police, General Sir Hugh Tudor, and also to the head of British intelligence, Colonel Ormonde Winter. How the British got her to admit she knew the contents of the documents and the presence of the weapons is unknown. Captain McGrane suffered a great deal in prison. She was eight stone (50.8 kg) on admission to prison but quickly lost a half a stone. She went on hunger strike at different times and was removed to hospital for medical treatment.[45] The contents of the files captured contained British intelligence and RIC documents along with IRA intelligence papers. The telephone record book, which Michael Collins had removed from Inspector McFeely's office at Great Brunswick DMP station, was also recovered. The British believed that Captain McGrane was Collins' private secretary.

After keeping her in jail for six months without charge, the British decided to prosecute their prisoner under section 9AA, which, among other things, prohibited the carrying of arms. The British did not want the contents of the captured files disclosed, given the highly classified nature of their contents. Included were photographs of suspected British agents and plans to introduce a typhoid bacillus into the milk of British army garrisons. Eileen McGrane was watched very closely while in prison. All her letters were censored and any addresses referred to in them were raided by the Auxiliaries of F Company. McGrane was given a sentence of four years' penal servitude. The British considered this sentence quite lenient. Michael Collins instructed the Dublin Brigade to organise her escape from Mountjoy but the British discovered the plans, which McGrane admitted to her captors. As a result of this and a threat on the life of the chief wardress Miss McGlynn, Eileen McGrane was removed to prison in England.[46]

In January 1921 General Boyd, O/C of the Dublin District, received much-needed reinforcements to deal with a fresh outbreak of IRA activity. General Boyd's command was now the largest concentrated command in Britain and Ireland, quite an achievement for a man who joined the British army as a private. Finding a place to billet the incoming battalions proved difficult. The 2nd Battalion East Surrey Regiment, under Lieutenant-Colonel Baldwin DSO, arrived in Dublin on 14 January 1921. The nineteen officers, a sergeant-major and 613 other ranks were billeted at Marlborough Hall in Glasnevin on the north side of Dublin, in the 24th Provisional Brigade Area. The battalion's main duties were curfew patrols, raiding parties, escorting political prisoners and providing a protective guard at important buildings such as the Viceregal Lodge and the Bank of Ireland. There was also a guard on the Custom House but this was

3rd Battalion Rifle Brigade Band, British Army, photographed in the Phoenix Park, Dublin, June 1921. (Courtesy the Royal Green Jackets (Rifles) Museum Archives, Hampshire Record Office, Peninsula Barracks, Winchester, UK)

withdrawn, a decision which had dramatic consequences.[47] The battalion suffered their first casualty on 20 January when twenty-year-old Private Albert Manley was mortally wounded when a comrade accidentally discharged a Verey pistol at Mountjoy Gaol.[48]

The 3rd Battalion Rifle Brigade also arrived in Dublin in January 1921. C Company had been sent as a vanguard in December 1920 to prepare the way. The battalion was billeted in the main hall at the Royal Dublin Society showgrounds (RDS) in Ballsbridge. The officers used the restaurant as a dormitory. This unit served in the 25th Provisional Brigade Area on the south side of Dublin. The RDS was cold and uncomfortable. Raids and other duties were constant.[49] C Company 2nd Battalion were considered to have got the most unpleasant duty, being posted as detachment at Dublin Castle for the month of March.[50] During its tour of duty, the Rifle Brigade's perseverance in raiding paid off with the capture of one of the largest hauls of IRA weapons and ammunition ever seized. The 3rd Battalion letter to the editor, which appeared in *The Rifle Brigade Chronicle for 1921*, recorded the following as part of the haul:

Revolvers & automatic pistols:	54
Rounds of ammunition (rifle):	10,739
Swords:	54

Rounds of ammunition (revolver):   703
Rifles (mostly broken):   4
Shot gun cartridges: 127
Shot guns: 6
Ordnance maps: 24
Dirks & scabbards: 24
Bombs (grenades):   34
IRA Uniform: 1
Detonators: 8,993
IRA Caps: 10
Tubes of ammonite: 59
Tins of high explosive: 18

Also included were aluminium powder, roman candles, rifle bolts, tripods and gun cases.[51]

The officer compiling the report of the capture wrote of the triumphant return to barracks:

> And the sight of that lorry returning with the swag was one to be remembered. The raiding party were all young soldiers immensely interested in the articles captured. Knee-deep in gelignite mixed with loose detonators, and shod in hob-nailed boots, they trampled about the lorry examining the different arms and throwing them down on the mass of explosives rattling on the bottom of the lorry, which was driven at the usual breakneck speed, bumping over the cobbles of the Dublin streets. They were happy in their ignorance, for there were enough explosives there to blow up the whole of the RDS Showgrounds.[52]

The 2nd Battalion Rifle Brigade also experienced IRA attacks on their lorries. On 15 April, an A Company patrol was returning from Portobello Barracks to the RDS when a grenade was thrown into their lorry by an IRA Volunteer standing on the pavement. The grenade was caught in mid-air by Rifleman Partridge, who quickly threw it away. Partridge was awarded an OBE for saving his comrades from death or serious injury.[53] In early 1921, the British resorted to carrying republican prisoners in the lorries as hostages to protect against grenade attack. One of their most prestigious prisoner hostages was Colonel Maurice Moore, a former officer in the British army's famous Connaught Rangers and Inspector General of the Irish Volunteers prior to the 1914 split in the movement.[54] Colonel Moore was brought from his home at Seaview Terrace in Donnybrook to the RDS after a raiding party discovered Sinn Féin documents in his house. The colonel was locked into a horsebox, the standard accommodation for prisoners at this venue. When informed that he would be a hostage on a British army lorry patrol, he submitted his protest in writing, but it did him little good. The lorry took Moore on a fine tour of Dublin, visiting both north and south sides of the city. General Boyd intervened and ordered the colonel's release after a few days on account of his age and former position.[55]

As part of his aim to improve the protection of motor transport for his troops, General Boyd managed to acquire a steady increase in the number and type of armoured cars available to support operations. Up to December 1920, the British army in Dublin had two Rolls Royce, four Austin and a few Jeffrey Quads and Peerless armoured cars.[56] In 1921, the new Peerless armoured car began to arrive in significant numbers and dramatically improved defence against attacks by the Dublin Brigade. The British described the Peerless as 'practically unstoppable'. Fast and highly manoeuvrable, it was ideal for Dublin streets. Peerless armoured car sections were formed by both the 24th and 25th British Infantry Brigades. The IRA, lacking any heavy weapons except a stationary landmine, feared armoured cars and encountering one nearly always led to the abandonment of an operation. Michael Rock's Fingal flying column were planning an attack on the Auxiliaries at the train station near Gormanston Camp. They had acquired two cars and a Lewis gun from IRA GHQ. The Lewis gun was mounted on the dashboard of the first car and was to spray the Black and Tans with fire as they came up the road from the railway station. Commandant Rock and the Brigade O/C Commandant Michael Lynch followed in the second car. While moving up to the train station they ran straight into what they thought was a Rolls Royce armoured car. The IRA drivers slammed the gears into reverse and rapidly withdrew from position. While the 'armoured car' turned out to be a hackney cab, the incident serves to demonstrate how the presence of such armoured support served to protect the Crown forces from IRA attack.[57] Rock's flying column did not have much luck with their operations. Either intelligence was poor or his men did not adhere properly to orders issued. Rock planned to release typhoid into the water supply of Gormanston Camp but sanction was denied by IRA GHQ. Where Rock's men were more successful was in shooting individual policemen.

The Dublin Brigade was now called upon to respond to the increase in British army and D Branch operations in the city. The first move followed quickly on the heels of Bloody Sunday. A series of documents with comprehensive detail were issued to IRA brigades by IRA GHQ on 27 November 1920.[58] These orders covered how to establish effective intelligence operations. Separate instructions were issued on 18 December 1920, covering all aspects of intelligence, from the appointment of intelligence officers to surveillance and the submission of reports. The second initiative introduced by IRA GHQ in Dublin was to order the Dublin Brigade to form a full-time, paid Active Service Unit (ASU). Each city battalion was ordered to assemble 'a section of hand-picked fighting men'.[59] It was intended that the ASU sections would operate independently of their battalions but would also come under a unified command to enable them to engage the British or RIC as a larger fighting unit.[60] The Squad and Dublin Brigade battalions would continue their operations independently of the ASU.

The Dublin Brigade ASU was formed at the end of December 1920. Captain Paddy Flanagan was appointed O/C. Four sections of twelve IRA Volunteers were formed with each numbered and located in a battalion area. Each section had an O/C, a sergeant and a QM. The men were to be paid £4/10 per week. Captain Flanagan personally chose many of the men who formed the ASU. The unit went on active service in January 1921.[61] The ASU HQ was established at Flanagan's office (17 Eustace Street) but after a raid by British troops moved to 17 Little Strand Street. In establishing an ASU, Commandant Oscar Traynor, O/C of the Dublin Brigade, sought not just to stretch British Crown forces but also to inflict casualties and destroy stores and transport. The ASU was to become the cutting edge of the Dublin Brigade. Every Volunteer of the Dublin ASU was issued with a .45 automatic pistol and twelve rounds.[62] The main operations were assassinations, sniping, raids, burning Crown forces' stores and ambushing patrols. The tactics for carrying out such operations were refined over a period of months. With regard to ambush sites, positions were quickly established and proved to be very dangerous for British transports. Pádraig Ó Conchubair and Paddy Rigney described the ideal location for an ambush in Dublin: 'To be of any use, a position should have the following requirements: a large number of lanes or bye-streets leading off the main street, and leading to a rallying point in the rear; it should be extensive enough to contain the section without crowding, and it should be straight so that the men could see one another.'[63]

The Dublin Brigade quickly established their regular spots for ambushes. Among the locations favoured by the ASU on the north side were Ormond Quay, Ryder's Row, Findlater's Church on North Frederick Street, Dorset Street, Liberty Hall and Amiens Street, while on the south side the ASU regularly hit the locations of Thomas Street, Camden Street (called the Dardanelles by British troops because the buildings on both sides of the street were so close together and presented great danger), Grafton Street, Dolphin's Barn, the Halfway House at Drimnagh Castle and Blackhorse Bridge.[64]

In early January, the Dublin Brigade ASU Nos. 1 and 2 Sections carried out their first combined ambush on two lorries of Auxiliaries at the junction of Bachelor's Walk and Liffey Street.[65] Traynor wanted to test the Auxiliaries and how they would take it. Unsurprisingly, 'they took it bad'.[66] ASU Volunteers were armed with revolvers and grenades and were posted in twos and threes at intervals along the quay. As the Crown forces' lorry appeared, the Volunteers would step out to the edge of the footpath and throw their grenades,[67] signalling the beginning of an attack. Volunteer Jim Cahill, No. 2 Section ASU, observed that the cages and the sloping armour on some of the British lorries presented a problem for the ASU men. With a five-to-six-second fuse on most of their grenades it meant the majority would bounce back off the lorry, presenting more of a danger to themselves than their intended targets. Seán Quinn of No. 1 Section was severely wounded by fragments from his own grenade. Joe Gilhooley received wounds from both rifle fire and grenade splinters. Cahill began reducing the fuse timing to 2½ seconds, which meant the grenades would explode over the cage and shower the soldiers or police in the lorry with bomb fragments.[68] This was followed by a few volleys of revolver fire. The explosions over the cage also increased the likelihood that the IRA men would escape in the confusion. Such actions brought the Volunteers of the Dublin Brigade ASU up close to their enemy. Casualties were inevitable and Volunteers were killed in action or captured, court-martialled and executed by hanging.[69] The method used by the ASU in their first ambush at Bachelor's Walk in early January became standard operating procedure for Dublin Brigade ambushes, so much so that civilians and even the DMP came to recognise the signs of an impending ambush and would attempt to disappear.

As the British forces and the Dublin ASU battled it out in the streets it was difficult to avoid civilian casualties. In an attack on an Auxiliary lorry on Grafton Street on 18 April 1921, three civilians were wounded. More shocking was another attack, also in Grafton Street, on 12 May 1921, in which three grenades were thrown at an Auxiliary lorry. At least fifteen civilians were wounded, three critically. Another seven civilians were injured in an attack on an Auxiliary lorry on North Frederick Street on Monday 17 May 1921.[70] The wounds of civilians presenting at Dublin hospitals included gunshot and shrapnel wounds in all parts of the head and body, with victims suffering any combination of shock, lacerations, fractured bones, internal and external bleeding. All ages of children, women and men were among the victims.[71] Civilian casualties occurred throughout the fighting in Dublin but particularly in 1921.

The grenade explosions caused panic among civilians and soldiers. The confusion induced by the exchange of gunfire that accompanied the explosions coupled with the civilian attire of the Dublin ASU meant it was difficult for Crown forces to identify targets in the split seconds of an action. Anyone who appeared to be a threat was likely to be shot and innocent bystanders were usually hit. Oscar Traynor explained that the element of surprise was vital to give the Dublin ASU an edge. He said the explosion of the grenades was usually the first indication an attack had begun and was for civilians 'a signal to take cover, an art in which the citizens soon became expert, thus leaving the Volunteer soldiers and the enemy troops shooting it out in semi-isolation'.[72] The civilian casualties named and listed in the Dublin newspapers are, however, at odds with Commandant Traynor's account of events on the streets of Dublin in 1921.

These attacks also took their toll on the men carrying them out. On 18 January 1921, Commandant Joe O'Connor's E Company 3rd Battalion lay in wait to ambush a British army lorry at the junction of Clonskeagh Road and Bird Avenue. There were two men armed with grenades and five riflemen in the party. When the lorry came through the position the grenades landed a direct hit, disabling both the occupants and the lorry. P. J. Brennan described the effects on one of his men during an attack: 'One of the party became violently mentally deranged and the remaining 5 members of the party had a very difficult job disarming and restraining him and getting him to a place of safety so that he would not fall into enemy hands and be a source of danger to himself and his comrades.'[73]

On 21 January 1921, No. 1 Section of the Dublin ASU, led by Lieutenant Frank Flood, set out for Binn's Bridge over the Royal Canal in Drumcondra. They had been ordered to attack one of the RIC lorries which took this route each day. The ambush turned into a disaster, ending up in the destruction of the section. The consequences were severe. The section was in place from 8.30 a.m. and when, after an hour, there was no sign of any lorry of the Crown forces, Lieutenant Frank Flood decided to move north, out of the cover of the city streets and beyond the Tolka Bridge, to a field on the right, Clonturk Park. While on their way, the RIC lorry they were to ambush passed them on the road. The new ambush position lay opposite St Patrick's teacher training college. Flood directed Tommy Bryan and Dermot O'Sullivan to stand at the corner of Richmond Road. The rest of the section were ordered to take up position behind the cover of a stone wall facing the main Drumcondra Road. They prepared loopholes in the wall as firing positions. All they could do now was wait for another RIC lorry to appear. DMP Sergeant Thomas Singleton from Clontarf RIC Station passed by. Flood let him carry on patrolling his beat without interference. However, the sergeant saw the ASU Volunteers and returned with Constables Patrick Kennedy and Martin Hegarty. A third constable dressed in plain clothes, Owen D. Murphy, came along on a bicycle. The Auxiliaries at Dublin Castle had also been alerted and had organised a counter-ambush.

Around 11 a.m. Lieutenant Flood decided to call in his section to disperse them as it looked as if no RIC lorry would appear that day. At that very moment, however, one came into the ambush position from the direction of Gormanston Camp. Grenades were thrown and fire was opened on the RIC. But just as the ambush began, the IRA men saw an armoured car and a lorry of Auxiliaries approaching from the city. It was DI Johnston and his I Company Auxiliaries from the North Dublin Union. Major King's F Company men, in two tenders and an armoured car from Dublin Castle, completed the encirclement by approaching up Richmond Road from Ballybough. The ASU section were now in an exposed position and facing substantial enemy numbers. Lieutenant Flood decided to retreat. As they pulled back over a wide, open field they came under rifle and machine-gun fire from the RIC and Auxiliaries. Flood's men tried to escape through the back gardens of the houses on Richmond Road but this route was cut off. As they ran, Lieutenant Michael Magee, a 1916 veteran, was hit and fell. He rose and was hit again. This time he did not get up.[74] He died of his wounds the following day.[75]

Four Volunteers followed Lieutenant Flood as he ran up Grace Park Road and into Grace Park Gardens. After a futile attempt to force entry to a house, Frank Flood, Tommy Bryan, Dermot O'Sullivan, Paddy Doyle, Bernard Ryan were captured along with their weapons and ammunition. Meanwhile, Volunteer Seán Burke had got separated and escaped into a house on Richmond Road. With the help of a maid, he managed to bluff his way out of an interrogation by an Auxiliary search party.[76] Lieutenant Flood and his men were charged under Regulation 67, ROIR. Thus charged with 'High Treason by levying war contrary to the Treason Act 1351 (25 Edward III. St. C. 2) as made applicable to Ireland by Poyning's Act 1494 (10 Henry VII. C. 22)', the five men were court-martialled, found guilty and sentenced to death by hanging.[77]

Just over two weeks after the ambush at Clonturk Park, Major King and two of his Auxiliary cadets, H. Hinchcliffe and Frederick Welsh, returned to the scene. This time they had with them two men they had arrested in Talbot Street earlier that day, James Murphy and Patrick Kennedy. The pair were brought into the field at Clonturk Park and made to stand against the same wall from which No. 1 Section of the Dublin ASU had attempted an ambush a fortnight before. Old tin buckets were put over their heads and they were then shot in the head and body a number of times. Major King thought he had left two dead men behind but, incredibly, one of them was still alive. Two DMP Constables from Clontarf Station arrived on the scene to investigate the shots they had heard. They found Patrick Kennedy dead and James Murphy lying propped up against the wall, grievously wounded. The constables called for an ambulance and transferred the two men to the Mater Hospital where Murphy made a sworn statement to his brother and a commissioner for oaths,[78] which was read into the record of the House of Commons by the MP for Belfast Falls, Joseph Devlin, on 21 February 1921.[79]

In the weeks that followed, Major King and Cadets Hinchcliffe and Welsh were arrested and charged with murder.[80] (Welsh was eventually acquitted as witnesses could not say for certain whether he was in the car with King, Hinchcliffe and the two prisoners.) During the trial, a witness, who was on the police adviser's staff, gave evidence that in Dublin Castle both Murphy and Kennedy were beaten and punched by a number of men in the Intelligence Room.[81] Witnesses saw the two prisoners being driven through the gates of the Castle after the interrogation. The barrister for the prosecution of the Auxiliaries was denied permission to read the dying declaration of James Murphy. The military court argued that the statement of a dying man could not be accepted as legitimate. Both King and Hinchcliffe pleaded not guilty. King claimed he was on another raid and could not have left the Castle with the prisoners at the time witnesses claimed he did. There was also an attempt to intimidate witnesses to the 'Drumcondra affair' in Dublin Castle made by Captain Hardy.[82] King claimed a sergeant released the prisoners from the Castle onto the street at 10 p.m. The beatings of the prisoners and the taking of a bloodied prisoner to the water pump to have him cleaned up in front of many witnesses were all denied. The events were put down to a row among the RIC over a game of cards. This version of events was supported by evidence from other Auxiliaries at the Castle.[83] King and Hinchcliffe were found not guilty on 15 April 1921.[84] Major King was transferred to D Company ADRIC in Galway and served out the rest of the War of Independence there.

After their arrest, King had been brought to Arbour Hill Prison where he came face to face with a recently arrested Eamon Broy, an agent of Michael Collins in G Division. In the raid on Eileen McGrane's apartment at 21 Dawson Street, the Auxiliaries had found reports that had come from Broy's office. He was questioned about the papers and, in the third week of February 1921, was arrested and imprisoned. Life in Arbour Hill was not unbearable for Broy. Behind secure doors and bars he felt safe and, while the breakfast of porridge, bread and tea was basic, at least there was one. The commandant of the prison was a Major Curry and the warders were mostly Royal Garrison Artillery personnel. They treated the prisoners well.[85] He spent some time talking with King on their trips to the exercise yard. Major William Lorraine King had grown up in England. He had served as a volunteer in the 1st Middlesex Royal Engineers before leaving Britain to become a detective in the South African police. During the First World War he joined the 2nd Regiment 1st South African Infantry and was awarded the MC and DCM for gallantry.[86] His wife Isabella died of cancer in the Rotunda Hospital in Dublin on 13 September 1917.[87] King remarried on 29 November 1920, to Helen Sophie Gilbert at the Church of Ireland Monkstown.[88] The Major had no time for politicians, saying, 'All Governments are the same. They utilise the services of people like you and me and are then quite prepared to hang us if it suits their purpose.'

Broy, afraid he might be hanged himself, was of the opinion Major King feared he too would hang as 'politicians' were anxious to make an example of him to show how 'fair-minded' they were.[89]

At the end of 1920, the RIC had reorganised and established a highly efficient and ruthless team of detectives-cum-assassins at Dublin Castle. Frank Saurin, IRA IO, referred to them as 'a plain-clothes RIC posse'.[90] This unit was formed from the 'hard core' of the RIC and run by Eugene Igoe, a 31-year-old head constable. Igoe carefully selected committed RIC constables around Ireland who could identify leading members of Sinn Féin and the IRA on sight. He and his men moved between the Castle and the RIC depot at the Phoenix Park. They also patrolled in pairs on both sides of the street and kept a close watch on the Dublin ports and railway stations. Igoe had made a careful study of the operational methods of the Squad and adapted their methods: his men always altered their routes and were always unpredictable. This made tailing them extremely difficult.[91]

The Squad at this point were commanded by Tom Kehoe as Paddy O'Daly was still in Ballykinlar Camp. Michael Collins continued to issue orders for assassinations. On his return from America, Éamon de Valera had tried to get Collins to go to the USA on Dáil business but Collins would have none of it. He managed to find ways to remain in Dublin and eventually de Valera gave up on the idea. There is no doubt, however, that de Valera was uncomfortable with the manner in which the Dublin Brigade had to fight the war in the city.

The killing continued. The Squad had shot dead DI Philip O'Sullivan on 17 December 1920 while he was walking with his fiancée on Henry Street. In January 1921, Collins, who dined at the Wicklow Hotel quite often, became aware that a porter, one Peter Doran, was a British informer. Collins issued orders for the Squad to act. Dan McDonnell knew Doran on sight and was detailed to carry out the killing. Doran was shot through the head and chest by McDonnell and Joe Dolan as he was leaving his workplace. The assailants' 'gateway' was secured by the usual Squad covering party.[92] The Squad became even more confident as the War continued. Regardless of the increasing number of British army and Auxiliary patrols, they carried out one of their most audacious attacks almost on the doorstep of the Castle.

The Squad had been observing RIC personnel who regularly left Dublin Castle and made their way to the Ormond Hotel across the River Liffey.

They believed they had identified three members of Igoe's unit. They made their plans and on 23 February Constables Martin Greer, Daniel Hoey and Edward McDonagh walked into an ambush on the junction of Parliament Street and Essex Street.[93] Greer and Hoey were shot dead on the spot. McDonagh, though wounded, ran for his life. As he approached Wellington Quay, he ducked into a shop and jumped over the counter but one of the Squad was close on his heels and fired into the already wounded man to make sure he would not tell any tales. Charlie Dalton said the 'Igoe Gang', as the IRA referred to them, never ventured out much after those killings except in a Ford touring car. So good were Igoe's protective measures that IRA intelligence never fully established the identity of the members of his unit.[94]

Michael Collins continued to employ the Squad in their traditional role throughout the conflict but as the war entered its final few months, changes became necessary. Emmet Dalton, Michael Collins' specialist, entered the frame to carry out a combined operation to rescue the captured 'Blacksmith of Ballinalee', Commandant Seán MacEoin. The commandant had been taken prisoner after a trip to Dublin for a meeting with Cathal Brugha. MacEoin had ambushed a two-lorry patrol of seventeen Auxiliaries from M Company ADRIC, destroying the first lorry with a mine explosion and catching the survivors in the subsequent firefight with fifty men of the Longford flying column (ASU) in place. Four Auxiliaries died, two in the action and two from their wounds. Some of his men wanted to shoot the survivors but MacEoin allowed them to go unharmed.[95] This did not save MacEoin, however, and after his capture it was likely he would face the death penalty. Michael Collins had great respect for the commander of the Longford flying column and ordered a rescue attempt.

The Squad held up a British provisions detail at the Dublin Corporation abattoir, capturing the escorting Peerless armoured car. One British soldier was mortally wounded in the hectic seizure. Emmet Dalton and Joe Leonard dressed in British army uniform, and Tom Kehoe, Pat McCrea, Bill Stapleton, Sean Caffrey and Peter Gough, in British army caps and dungarees, got into the Peerless.[96] With McCrea at the wheel, they entered the outer gate at Mountjoy Gaol. Then Emmet Dalton and Joe Leonard, dressed as British officers, proceeded to Governor Monroe's office to demand the handover of MacEoin, saying he was required at the Castle for interrogation. When the governor attempted to phone the Castle to secure confirmation, Dalton and Leonard whipped out their revolvers and tied up the governor, the chief warder and a doctor who were also present. Seán MacEoin could not be reached so a rescue was impossible.

Meanwhile, Áine Malone, a member of Cumann na mBan, brought a fictitious parcel for a prisoner to a wicket door in the main gate. When a soldier opened it, he was rushed by a party of Dublin Brigade Volunteers. The manoeuvre was spotted by a British sentry who opened fire and wounded one of the Volunteers. Tom Kehoe returned fire, killing the sentry.[97] The IRA unit made good their escape, heading north out of the city on the Malahide Road into the Fingal area. Pat McCrea had forgotten to open the steel plate covering the radiator vent at the front of the armoured car and eventually it overheated.[98] The armoured car was stripped of its equipment and guns and left on the side of the road under the cover of some trees. McCrea took this precaution as he knew the British would have aircraft up looking for their lost Peerless.

The operations carried out by the Squad and the Dublin Brigade demonstrated a capacity to take the fight to the British while also showing an inventive and unpredictable streak. On 14 February, Pádraig Ó Conchubhair and Paddy Rigney of No. 4 Section Dublin ASU with F Company 4th Battalion, O/C Jimmy Donnelly and his Volunteers organised the spectacular jailbreak of captured IRA Volunteers Ernie O'Malley, Frank Teeling and Simon Donnelly from Kilmainham Gaol.[99] Paddy Moran, who was on trial for involvement in Bloody Sunday at the time and facing a possible death sentence, could have gone with them but remained behind. The decision cost him his life.[100] General Macready, Commander-in-Chief British forces in Ireland, was devastated by the news of the escape. Writing to Sir John Anderson at the Castle he gave vent to his anger and frustration:

> We have had a real disaster. The man Teeling and two other unimportant men escaped last night from Kilmainham Prison and got clean away. It is about the worst blow I have had for a very long time, and I am naturally furious. I will not make any remarks about it till I get the Inquiry which is being held, but it is perfectly obvious that the escape could not have been made without the collusion of the men of the Welsh Regiment who were on duty there. I will certainly take the most drastic action against those responsible ...[101]

The fact that the general could not fully rely on the loyalty of his own troops was a serious problem and a strong indicator of the discontent that was general among British forces during the conflict in Ireland. The Welsh soldiers concerned, Privates Roper and Holland,[102] got long prison sentences.

Macready was an enigma in his own right. Some of his ideas were positive but with an imperial purpose. In early April he gave an interview to Carl Ackerman for his paper *Public Ledger Philadelphia*, in which he said: 'Education alone will cure this country ... but it will take at least a generation of teaching history in Ireland before there is a cure, before there is an understanding in this country of Great Britain.'[103] This was from the same 'enlightened' general who would, by 30 May 1921, be calling on Sir John Anderson to introduce flogging, imprisonment, penal servitude and 'a little bit of the "cat"'(cat-of-nine-tails)! If this was implemented, Macready wrote to Anderson, they would be successful in putting a stop to the 'Shinners'.[104] Anderson replied the following day, diplomatically pointing out that the introduction of flogging was a matter for the Chief Secretary and was considered undesirable.[105]

In early 1921, with the new threat of the Igoe's unit to contend with, Collins turned to an experienced IRA Volunteer from Castlegar, County Galway, to assist GHQ intelligence. This Volunteer was a member of the IRB and a 1916 veteran who had served with Commandant Liam Mellows.[106] He was Lieutenant Thomas Sweeney Newell.[107] Arriving in Dublin at Broadstone Station, Sweeney Newell was greeted by Captain Tommy Kilcoyne, B Company 2nd Battalion, and brought to his digs. He knew Head Constable Igoe by sight and was given the assignment of identifying him for the Squad. Each day Sweeney Newell would walk the streets of Dublin accompanied by one of the Dublin IOs. Tailing a ruthless unit such as Igoe's was an extremely dangerous mission. Máire Gleeson assisted IRA intelligence by giving them a description of Igoe's associates, as they had eaten in the West End Café a number of times. The Galway Volunteer managed to spot Igoe at Broadstone Station and near the Castle but the Squad were not in the vicinity on those occasions. Then, on 7 January 1921, Sweeney Newell spotted Igoe on Grafton Street. He immediately notified IO Charlie Dalton, who activated the Squad. Dalton and Sweeney Newell proceeded to Grafton Street with the Squad following behind. As soon as the two men reached Grafton Street they were surrounded by Igoe's men and taken to Dame Street where they were

Lieutenant Thomas Sweeney Newell, IRA Intelligence Officer. (Courtesy Terry & Éamon Newell)

separated. Dalton was put against a wall and questioned briefly before being told to walk on. With his intimate knowledge of the Dublin side streets and alleyways Dalton managed to give the detectives the slip. Sweeney Newell was taken across the Liffey to the Bridewell police station. After further intense questioning he was instructed to run into the street. Knowing what awaited him, Sweeney Newell refused, whereupon he was pushed into the street. Igoe's dectectives opened fire on the Castlegar Volunteer, hitting him in the stomach, hip and leg. He was also kicked and beaten and had some of his teeth knocked out with blows from the butts of revolvers. Sweeney Newell was eventually taken to the King George V Military Hospital but was not operated on to remove the bullets for a number of weeks. The metal plate that was put into his hip came loose a few days after the operation. He was operated on for a second time and would spend all of 1921 in the military hospital.[108]

In 1921 British intelligence began to recover from the losses experienced on Bloody Sunday. Captain Rymer-Jones raided numerous addresses in search of Michael Collins and Liam Tobin. During a raid on one house Rymer-Jones found a locked door and demanded it to be opened without delay. Upon entering the room, he found a cigarette still burning but the man he sought was gone. In another raid, Tobin left his gun behind. The woman of the house threw the gun into a kettle boiling on the stove. She stood there anxiously for the duration of the raid, terrified the ammunition might explode.

Very reliable information began to reach the British. All Michael Collins' old 'secret' addresses were no longer safe and were raided repeatedly. On one such occasion Collins was hanging from a windowsill while Captain Rymer-Jones and his men searched the house from top to bottom.[109] Acting on information from an informant, F Company and the 2nd Battalion Welsh Regiment organised a sting operation to capture Liam Tobin, 'the man with the scar'. The informant told his handlers that Tobin was known to frequent an Italian ice-cream parlour on the corner of Great Britain Street and Sackville Street. Two lorries of British troops, Auxiliaries and plain-clothes officers swooped on the ice-cream shop but Tobin did not show up.[110]

As well as trying to eliminate the IRA and Dublin Brigade command structure, the British also went after the communications network in the form of IRA couriers and field post offices (or 'postes restantes' as they are called in British military documents). The postes restantes were the homes and businesses of Sinn Féin and IRA supporters. One of them was coincidentally M. Collins, a hairdresser's at 110 North King Street.[111] Having learned from their own experience in using railway workers as couriers in occupied territory during the First World War, General Brind planned a major operation to arrest ten railway workers who had been identified as IRA railway couriers. In spite of the IRA's attempt to eliminate it on Bloody Sunday, British intelligence was still effective.

Dublin Brigade's reaction to the once-again increasing British pressure was to go after the informants and spies supplying the information to the British and execute them. Captain Frank Daly was O/C of B Company 1st Battalion and the brother of Paddy O'Daly, O/C of the Squad. Captain Frank Daly led a number of operations on the streets of Dublin. Over a period of months, his company carried out attacks on the British army and RIC. His unit also captured British soldiers and stripped them of their uniforms and equipment, and showed none of the usual IRA reluctance to engage armoured cars. At Blacquiere Bridge in Phibsborough, he led his men in an ambush on a car escorted by two armoured vehicles.[112] They also attacked British lorries at Ryder's Row and Blessington Street. At Mountjoy Street Daly's men captured two dispatch riders.

Lieutenant Thomas Bryan, Dublin Brigade Active Service Unit. He was executed by hanging on 14 March 1921 along with five other Irish Volunteers of No. 1 Section Dublin Brigade ASU, including Bernard Ryan, Patrick Doyle, Francis Flood, for their part in the Drumcondra ambush on 21 January 1921. Captain Patrick Moran and Thomas Whelan were executed for their part in Bloody Sunday on 14 March 1921. (Keogh Collection, Courtesy National Library of Ireland)

As the War of Independence entered the final few months the level of bitterness increased. Individual Auxiliaries and British troops set traps for IRA men desperate enough for weapons and ammunition to approach members of the British Crown forces looking to do a deal. Captain Joseph O'Connor of A Company 3rd Battalion received an offer of revolver ammunition, £1 per 100 rounds, in Nolan's pub on Lower Mount Street. O'Connor took delivery of the ammunition but ordered his QM to conduct a test firing with the revolver in a vice and using a string to pull the trigger. During the test firing the revolver was blown to pieces. The QM opened some of the rounds and removed the gunpowder. He found the rounds had been doctored by the addition of TNT. Any IRA Volunteer using this ammunition would have been killed or seriously injured. The casings of the rounds were marked with a 'Z'. Not wanting the supply to go to waste, O'Connor ordered the QM to collect the TNT and use it for explosives. He also refilled the casings with gunpowder and used them as normal.[113]

On Monday 14 March 1921, six members of the Dublin Brigade were executed. By dawn, up to 2,000 people had gathered in prayer outside the prison. The Volunteers were hanged in pairs, beginning with Thomas Whelan and Paddy Moran at 6 a.m., Patrick Doyle and Thomas Bryan at 7 a.m. and Bernard Ryan and Frank Flood at 8 a.m., by which time the crowd had swelled to 10,000. The people had quietly dispersed by 11 a.m. Labour leaders had called for all work in the city to be suspended and few shops were opened.

That night, the Dublin Brigade set an ambush for the Auxiliaries at 144 Great Brunswick Street in revenge for the hangings. The Auxiliaries of F Company were ensnared to raid the building of a supposed IRA meeting. When the two lorries and an armoured car pulled up at the house, fire was opened on them from all directions. It was very dark as the Volunteers had extinguished all the street lighting in the vicinity. The Auxiliaries held their ground and fired where they saw the flashes of gunfire, killing three Volunteers of 3rd Battalion, Dublin Brigade. Three members of the Crown forces were also hit; two of them, Section Leader Beard and Con O'Farrell, died of their wounds the following day. During the exchange of fire some of the Auxiliaries gave chase and captured Thomas Traynor and Jack Donnelly. Traynor would be executed by hanging at Mountjoy Gaol on 25 April 1921.

On their way home that same evening, another Volunteer, Seán Dolan, who was with a detachment under Sean MacBride, attempted to throw a grenade through the window of Great Brunswick Street DMP station. The grenade rebounded and landed at Dolan's feet, blowing his leg off. He was treated by members of the Tara Street fire brigade, who then got him to Mercer's Hospital with the cover story that a tram had run over his leg.[114]

It had been another very dark day in Dublin and the mood in the city was sombre but resolute. There was to be no giving in, as Michael Collins would later confirm two weeks later in an interview with Carl Ackerman, a journalist with the Philadelphia newspaper *Public Ledger*. When in Dublin he interviewed both Collins and General Macready. The real surprise is the ease with which Ackerman managed to secure access to Collins while the British Crown forces found the IRA senior officer impossible to locate. During the course of an interview with Ackerman, Collins declared: 'It is only a question of time until we shall have Ireland cleared of Crown Forces ... We are going on until we win.'[115]

As if to prove Collins' point through deed, the 2nd Battalion Dublin Brigade under Commandant Tom Ennis launched an attack on Q Company ADRIC HQ at the London and North Western Hotel on the North Wall on 11 April 1921. This Auxiliary Company were considered to be 'a great menace' as they continuously disrupted the rail and marine communications.[116] Grenades and bottles of paraffin were thrown through the windows of the building. Many of the grenades failed to explode. A furious exchange of gunfire followed in which seventeen-year-old Peter

Freyne, E Company 2nd Battalion, was killed. The Auxiliaries came off the best of the exchange with just one man wounded.

On Friday 20 May 1921, Captain Frank Daly's men from B Company 1st Battalion were given orders to arrest a suspected informer, John 'Hoppy' Byrne, and to take him to the Dublin ASU HQ at 17 Strand Street for questioning. Byrne was a shoemaker who walked with a limp. He lived at 44 North Brunswick Street. After the interrogation, Daly's men, along with some of the Dublin ASU, shot him. Byrne, however, was not killed and was taken to Jervis Street Hospital in a seriously wounded condition.[117] Byrne now knew his assailants and the location of the Dublin ASU HQ. The Dublin Brigade believed John Byrne was intent on making a statement to the British army. Paddy Flanagan, O/C of the ASU, issued an order to his men that John Byrne was to be 'liquidated'. Two men from the Dublin ASU entered Jervis Street Hospital at 2.15 p.m. on Saturday. They wore no disguise. They found John Byrne, placed him on a stretcher and carried him outside into the street where they shot him through the head a number of times, the coup de grâce being a bullet through the forehead. Byrne's skin was scorched by the gunfire, so close were the barrels of the revolvers when fired.[118]

The hospital authorities in Dublin were outraged, as was IRA GHQ. Pádraig Ó Conchubhair and Paddy Rigney, both members of the Dublin ASU, referred to the killing as a 'crude performance'. Those who looked after hidden IRA wounded in Dublin hospitals demanded the withdrawal of all the IRA's injured personnel within twenty-four hours. It was only the intervention of Michael Collins that calmed the medical authorities, ensuring them that this kind of brutal killing would not happen again.[119] The shooting of Byrne was followed the next day, Sunday 22 May, by the killing of 24-year-old ex-British army serviceman Leslie Fraser. He was taken from Walsh's pub in Stoneybatter and shot a number of times and mortally wounded. Three men were seen cycling away from the scene at North Brunswick Street.[120]

Captain Paddy Flanagan was beginning to show signs of strain and was taken off the ASU for a rest. When Captain Paddy O'Daly was released from Ballykinlar on 21 March 1921,[121] Michael Collins sent word that they needed the former Squad commander back in Dublin. O'Daly resumed command of the Squad after a big confrontation with Tom Kehoe, under whose command, in O'Daly's absence, the Squad had begun drinking heavily. Kehoe had to return to the ranks.[122]

In the general election of 24 May 1921, Sinn Féin swept the boards, with twenty-two candidates returned unopposed in six Dublin constituencies. Only one, Trinity College, voted for independent or Unionist candidates, who refused to recognise the Dáil. Of the Dublin Sinn Féin TDs, eight would become anti-Treaty.

One of the most dangerous operations in the whole war was given to the Dublin Brigade: they were ordered to occupy the Custom House, the centre of British customs and excise in Ireland, and burn it to the ground. The operation, planned for 25 May 1921, was a major undertaking and involved all battalions of the Dublin Brigade, the Squad and the ASU. The operation was to take place the day after the general election of 24 May and was to reinforce the message to the British that their days of rule in Ireland were at an end. The plans for the Custom House 'job' originated at a Dáil cabinet meeting in May. The possible targets decided upon were either Beggars Bush Barracks (HQ of the ADRIC) or the James Gandon-designed neoclassical masterpiece. Both suggestions came from President de Valera.[123] Beggars Bush was considered to be a suicide mission. However, the Custom House was little better as the flat, open thoroughfare of Beresford Place surrounding the building offered clear fields of fire for British machine-gunners. The Dublin Brigade estimated the operation could cost the liberty of 130 of their most experienced Volunteers. De Valera argued the sacrifice would be well justified as the financial cost to the British of the loss of the Custom House and its revenue-gathering apparatus would be £2 million. The Custom House was selected and approval of the Cabinet given.

Commandant Tom Ennis, O/C 2nd Battalion, known to his men as 'The Manager', was given command of the operation. Ennis requested the assistance of the Squad and the ASU. Plans for the building were obtained from the National Library of Ireland. Some 280 gallons of paraffin oil and petrol was 'obtained' and divided into 140 two-gallon petrol tins. Transport for the materials was arranged. Each Volunteer was issued with a revolver and six rounds. They were also told to arm themselves with hatchets. Once the British came into action, the Volunteer's six rounds would not last long against Vickers and Lewis machine guns and Lee-Enfield rifles. The officers and men of the Dublin Brigade must have thought this operation was madness. The tactics employed by them up to now were working. Ambush and assassination had allowed them the advantage of surprise. The Custom House 'job' would bring them into the open. And once in the open there would be nowhere to go.

The Volunteers arrived at 1 p.m. Companies of the Battalion were ordered to occupy a specific floor of the building. Each room was to be saturated with petrol or paraffin oil and, on a signal from Tom Ennis, set alight, beginning with the top floor. The 1st, 3rd and 4th Battalions were to provide cover on the wide expanses on Beresford Place. They were armed with some grenades and revolvers. The ASU were to lend fire support from the buildings adjacent and the railway bridge over the River Liffey.

At 1.10 p.m., the British authorities at Dublin Castle received word from the DMP that the IRA had taken over the Custom House. An armoured car was dispatched and arrived at 1.25 p.m. to cover the southern side of the building facing the quay. F Company ADRIC arrived shortly afterwards and covered the northern side. The final sealing of the building occurred within minutes as Q Company ADRIC arrived from the London and North Western Hotel to cover the eastern side.[124] Inside the building, as with most military operations, the Volunteers faced the unexpected. At first the staff thought the raid a joke, but the brandishing of revolvers and some robust direction from the Volunteers quickly dispelled that notion. The caretaker, Francis Davis, who lived on site with his wife and family, ran to telephone the British authorities at the Castle and was shot in the chest by Jimmy Conroy, a member of the Squad.[125] His wife, who witnessed the shooting, was in great distress. Davis' only thoughts, as he lay on the ground bleeding profusely, were what would become of his sons. He died later in hospital.

As the fires were ignited, civilians in the building began to panic. The Dublin Brigade cover guard outside threw their grenades and opened fire on the arriving British troops and Auxiliaries and then withdrew. In response, the British armoured cars opened up with machine guns, spraying the entire concourse with fire. Rounds smacked off the walls of the Custom House and some went through the windows, wounding the civilians gathered in the main hall. Once the IRA cover guard had expended their limited grenades and ammunition they began to withdraw, watching the fire taking hold and the smoke billowing from the eastern end of the Custom House.

Tom Ennis and his men were now trapped in a burning building with a petrified staff. They threw away their revolvers and mingled with the staff to try and avoid being shot. Humphrey Murphy, senior official at the Custom House, picked out his staff from among those leaving the building. The rest, especially those with a distinct scent of 'eau de petrol', were taken prisoner, a total of eighty-six men. Jimmy Conroy was among those captured although he was soon released. Vinny Byrne managed to bluff his way out as a carpenter on a repair job. Tom Ennis, Seán Doyle and Jimmy Slattery made a break for it. A machine-gunner saw them running and opened fire, hitting Ennis twice, in the hip and leg. Seán Doyle, whose brother had already been executed, was shot through the chest, receiving a mortal lung wound. Slattery lost a hand. Captain Sean Ward was also wounded but captured. The 'shawlies', Dublin trading women, crowded around the men in a laneway across from the Custom House and secured a car and a jarvey to bring them to hospital. When the surgeon at the Mater Hospital saw Ennis's shattered hip in the operating theatre he threw up his hands, but 'The Manager' made a remarkable recovery.[126]

The Dublin Brigade listed five either killed in action or who died of their wounds in hospital: Captain Paddy Reilly, Lieutenant Stephen Reilly, Eddie Dorrins, Seán Doyle and Dan Head, who was shot dead after he threw a grenade into an oncoming Auxiliary tender.[127] James Cahill of the Dublin ASU had the difficult task of visiting families to tell them their sons had been killed in action at the Custom House.[128] A number of civilians were also killed, among them Mahon Patrick Lawless, a clerk and nephew of Sinn Féin TD Frank Lawless.[129] The military action was over relatively quickly but the Custom House continued to burn. Various units of the Dublin fire brigade either sympathised with the action or were prevented from leaving their stations until it was too late to stop the blaze. Mr Murphy, the senior official at the Custom House, looked on: 'I watched the fire from various points, until about 5 pm, and had the misery of seeing it gradually envelop the whole building, fanned by a slight easterly wind which carried it to the western end, occupied mainly by the Ireland Revenue and Local Government Board.'[130]

In the days that followed Murphy made repeated inspection tours of the remains of the building, accompanied by a young British army officer. An unexpected event that occurred after the fire filled him with disgust: 'It was a fresh mortification to find looting, robbery and destruction committed by the very men, military or firemen or both, sent to guard the property. Safes burgled with sledgehammers and pickaxes.'[131]

Despite the losses incurred by the IRA, their city operations continued. One of the British units posted to guard the ruined Custom House was the East Surrey Regiment. On 1 June 1921, a light lorry with Major Gurdon, Sergeant T. Crowley, Lance-Corporal H. Goddard and Private G. Buckner was returning to barracks after a stint of guard duty when it was ambushed by the IRA. A grenade was thrown into the lorry, seriously wounding the driver, Private Lineker, in the legs and face but he kept going to return the detachment safely to Marlborough Hall. His wounds necessitated the amputation of one of his legs. Private Goddard was also caught by shrapnel and later died of his wounds. He was only twenty years old and had recently married. Private Lineker was awarded the MBE 'for his pluck and devotion to duty'.[132]

After the Custom House operation there were two major developments in the Dublin Brigade's campaign. The Squad and the Dublin ASU were brought under one command, with Paddy O'Daly appointed as O/C and Lieutenants Joe Leonard and Pádraig O'Connor as his junior officers. The city battalions were now severely depleted, especially the fighting 2nd Battalion, which was the linchpin behind most of the Dublin Brigade's major operations. The outlying areas of the city now became much more active and began sniping, patrolling, establishing roadblocks, attacking RIC barracks, assassinating policemen and executing spies. In the month before the Custom House operation, No. 4 Section of the Dublin ASU in the 4th Battalion area became very active, as did Andy McDonnell's 6th Battalion in south County Dublin. This activity was crucial at this point in the war as it relieved pressure on the inner-city battalions and their companies.

Life for Volunteers at this stage in the War of Independence was precarious. James Cahill was set up to be 'shot while trying to escape' after his capture. British soldiers got out of the lorry he was in and appeared to walk away, leaving him unattended with a Lee-Enfield rifle on the floor of the lorry. Cahill did not take the bait.[133] Sometimes, Irish Volunteers were just asked to stand up while in the lorry, as had happened to two men from Rathfarnham. On the night of 1–2 April Christopher Reynolds and Bernard Nolan of E Company 4th Battalion were arrested and taken via Rathfarnham RIC Barracks to the city. When they reached Rathmines, the two men were ordered to stand up in the back of the lorry in which they were travelling. Both of them were shot. Reynolds was seemingly killed but Nolan was still alive, though unconscious. When he came to, he found himself on the footpath lying beside his dead comrade. The Auxiliaries brought the two men they thought to be corpses to the King

George V Military Hospital, reporting the men had been 'shot while attempting to escape'. When the Auxiliaries departed Reynolds revived but it was clear he was dying. He asked for a priest who duly arrived and gave him the last rites. The Auxiliaries returned and attempted to take the wounded men but were prevented by the British army medical orderlies who grabbed their rifles from the rack and threatened the policemen if they persisted. In 1953 Nolan wrote, 'Only for those Tommies I certainly would not be alive to-day, and Reynolds would not have lived to receive the Rites of the Church.'[134]

The Dublin Brigade operations continued. No. 4 Section of the ASU carried out quite a number of varied operations. Based in Inchicore and Crumlin, they covered the Lucan road from Galway and the west, and the Naas road from Cork and the south-west, which included traffic from the RAF base at Baldonnel. In one ambush on 30 March 1921 at Ballyfermot, they lured an RIC cycle patrol out from Lucan to investigate some lorries that had been burned out. No. 4 Section ASU lay in wait and opened fire on the patrol when it arrived. Head Constable Edward Mulrooney, from County Limerick, died at the scene. Sergeant Hallissy, a Kerry man, died of his wounds later.[135] The junction at Blackhorse Bridge in Inchicore was a favourite target for sniping on British transports. No. 4 Section also set up a sniper's nest in the raised roof section of a guard van in the Inchicore railway yard. They set up a second nest just under the Norman tower house at Drimnagh Castle. The weapon used was a long-barrelled Parabellum with a shoulder-stock attachment. The pistol grip had twelve nicks in it, indicating the number of hits. Pádraig Ó Conchubhair trained some of the Fianna boys as snipers, one of whom, Paddy Farrell, proved to be particularly accurate at long range. On one occasion, after firing a few shots at a British convoy across the Lansdowne valley from Drimnagh Castle, Ó Conchubhair was satisfied he had completed his duty when British troops in an extended line came over the hill from Blackhorse intent on flushing out the sniper. He took off, tearing through hedges and fields, eventually only just escaping encirclement by making it through to the other side of Crumlin village.

No. 4 Section carried out a number of ambushes on the Long Mile Road. The most dangerous was in early May when they attacked an RAF lorry using one of the 'pineapple' grenades manufactured by Michael Lynch's munitions unit. By the time No. 4 Section were using this grenade, it was known as the 'Number 9'. They carefully installed themselves undercover along the wall at Drimnagh Castle Lodge, while Micky Sweeney and Jimmy McGuinness concealed themselves in the outdoor lavatory at Conway's Half Way House. McGuinness's grenade was on target and exploded in the lorry but Sweeney's rebounded and exploded at his feet, injuring him severely. McGuinness helped him escape towards Walkinstown where some Blessington Steamtram workers were relieved of their bicycles and No. 4 Section made good their escape. At 2 a.m. on 6 May, a unit of RAF personnel from Baldonnel Aerodrome, heavily armed and with faces blackened, arrived at the Half Way House and burned it to the ground.[136] Ó Conchubhair also went sniping on an Auxiliary barracks at Lissonfield House, from the roof of Rathmines Catholic church. Ó Conchubhair then began shooting British army mules and donkeys. He quickly received orders to cease the practice.[137] One of the most ruthless attacks carried out by No. 4 Section of the Dublin ASU was the attack on the Mayflower Hotel in Baggot Street where two Auxiliaries used to meet their families for afternoon tea. Ó Conchubhair assembled his men and, led by IO Paddy Drury, who was in touch with one of the maids there, they entered the dining room. In a scene from hell itself, No. 4 Section shot the two Auxiliaries in front of their families. Section Leader William Hunt was killed outright and Section Leader White was badly wounded. The families were inconsolable.[138]

Commandant Andy McDonnell O/C 6th Battalion was a very active IRA officer and was constantly out on duty. The mother of one of his comrades, Ma Chadwick, worried about them being gone for days on end. As they left her home, she used to bless them with a splash of holy water. One evening after departing, his comrade Mick Chadwick said, 'I smell like chips!' Sniffing their clothes they realised that, in her haste, Ma Chadwick had 'blessed' them with vinegar instead of holy water.[139] McDonnell spent a great deal of time in south County Dublin rooting out spies and executing them. Andrew Knight, a United Tramway inspector, was taken to Sandycove and executed on 8 July 1921. Peter Graham was executed at Killiney Golf Course on 15 May 1921. Arthur Barden, a Guinness employee, was shot and killed at Featherstonhaugh, Rathfarnham. He was shot six times.[140] A British officer, a Lieutenant Breeze, was out for a Sunday drive when he was captured at an IRA roadblock. He was armed but there is dispute over whether he was executed or 'shot while trying to escape'.[141] The 6th Battalion also repeatedly attacked Dundrum, Cabinteely and Bray RIC barracks.

The 6th Battalion suffered casualties during this time too. Volunteer Tommy Murphy was shot dead in his home in Foxrock on 30 May 1921.[142] Lieutenant Jim McIntosh, O/C D Company 6th Battalion, was killed on 19 June in an attack on the Royal Marine Hotel in Kingstown. He was shot through the arm, chest and abdomen.[143] The attack, described as 'a wild west show' by Andy McDonnell, saw guns drawn and shots fired as people dived for cover.[144] Lieutenant McIntosh was a former sergeant-major in the Royal Dublin Fusiliers and had served in the First World War. The 6th Battalion were also one of the few battalions to employ explosives: they used them to destroy part of Glasson's railway bridge at Milltown. They also made repeated attempts to destroy the Milltown and Sandyford bridges.

Dave Neligan, one of Michael Collins' men in the Castle, joined the British secret service and was posted to the Kingstown area during the last very active period. Given how easily Inspector McFeely of the DMP was dismissed, one has to wonder what 'scalps' Neligan had to present to his secret service senior officers in order to convince them he was in earnest.[145]

British army reinforcements continued to arrive to support the Dublin District. On 16 June the 2nd Battalion Queen's Own Royal West Kent Regiment arrived at Kingstown after a long journey from Upper Silesia in Germany. The battalion had left Germany without their machine-gunners and half their baggage. Their introduction to Dublin was an IRA ambush while their train waited in a siding near Drumcondra. A grenade thrown into the train exploded, showering the soldiers with metal fragments and wounding a Private William Saunders and two sergeants. Saunders died of a laceration to the brain later that day.[146] Like many of the British army casualties in Dublin, he was only twenty years old. The battalion were assigned to guarding prisoners en route to the Bridewell at the rear of the Four Courts. They were also on stop-and-search patrols in the Dublin streets and guarding the Magazine Fort and the British army GHQ at Parkgate.[147] The attack on the train was an indication that the Dublin Brigade was stepping up its attacks and seeking new targets. One of the last attacks carried out by the Dublin ASU was an attack on a train carrying British troops at Ballyfermot using grenades and a Thompson machine gun. A grenade went through the window of the train and exploded. A civilian on the train, John Rossiter, had his leg blown off and died in hospital. This IRA unit followed up the attack on the train with a first attack on Lucan RIC Barracks.[148]

The military action and the inevitable casualties continued into June and July as opportunities for peace arose. On Monday 2 July Michael Rock was unarmed and cycling from The Naul to his flying column camp at Mooretown near Oldtown. At Curragh West he encountered two lorries of Black and Tans who immediately opened fire on him. Rock was hit in the hip, the bullet smashing the socket joint, and in the arm. Rock was captured and taken to Balbriggan Coastguard Station where he received medical attention from the local doctor, a man called Fulham. The local women brought him some whiskey. Rock was taken to Dublin in a military convoy escorted by two armoured cars. He ended up in King George V Military Hospital. Another four IRA prisoners were being treated in the hospital at the same time. One of them was Sweeney Newell, who had been shot by Head Constable Igoe's men. During his stay in hospital, Rock was interrogated a number of times by British intelligence officers about the shootings carried out by the IRA in Balbriggan. Rock was certain if the truce had not been declared he would have been hanged.[149]

A truce was eventually declared, much to the surprise of most Volunteers. The Assistant Secretary at Dublin Castle, Andy Cope, had continued to keep channels of communication open with Dáil and IRA contacts. In the preceding months, Michael Collins had ordered that Cope was not to be touched.[150] On 30 April 1921 Field Marshall French said goodbye to Ireland and was replaced as Viceroy by Lord Fitzalan, the first Catholic Viceroy. The Government of Ireland Act, confirmed with King George V's opening of the Northern Ireland parliament on 22 June 1921, officially partitioned Ireland into two distinct political jurisdictions. This political reality would have profound consequences. The king's speech was conciliatory in tone and opened up an opportunity for another round of exploratory communication between de Valera and Lloyd George and they did not waste it. A truce came into effect at noon 11 July 1921. In Dublin, an essay competition was held in the primary schools with 'The Truce' as the topic. On the second day of the truce, the winning essay was that submitted by a girl of twelve, who wrote: 'The war which started 700 years ago was ended yesterday.'

'Was there', remarked Andy Cope, 'anything more cryptic and informal than that?'[151]

7

'Dark Deeds to be Done'

The Civil War 1922–1923

The declaration of the truce on 11 July 1921 gave the IRA vital breathing space. It enabled men and women who had been constantly on the move to return home and rest. Michael Collins appointed Emmet Dalton as Senior Liaison Officer for the IRA on top of his post as Director of Training at GHQ. Dalton based himself at the Gresham Hotel in Sackville Street. He worked mainly with Sir John Anderson, Andy Cope and General Nevil Macready representing the British, regarding breaches in the Truce and later over the withdrawal of British Crown forces from Ireland. Issues included the kidnapping and execution of British officers, IRA raids on RIC barracks and theft of British army stores and equipment, which made it a difficult posting for Dalton, but one which he managed well due to his former British military training and his pragmatic approach.[1] For the Dublin Brigade the truce allowed them time to recruit, to reorganise their battalions and to open training camps in different parts of County Dublin. In July, the RIC report for County Dublin summed up the situation:

> Since the truce a decided improvement has taken place and the people generally are sanguine that a settlement will be arrived at and hope that peace will be continued ... The truce is being well observed with the following exception, information has been received by the Police that a party of men took possession of a shooting lodge at Castlekelly, at the foot of the Dublin mountains. They are said to keep armed guards on the place and drill in the evenings.[2]

The RIC barracks in Rathfarnham village was occupied by E Company 4th Battalion Dublin Brigade IRA during the truce, from 1921–22. (Courtesy Kilmainham Gaol, OPW)

The Dublin Brigade had established a training camp at Cobb's Lodge in Glenasmole, south County Dublin. Senior Dublin Brigade officers attended the training camp first, followed by their companies. The syllabus included lectures on command and tactics, signalling, first aid and weapons training on both Thompson and Lewis machine guns and revolvers.[3] Ironically, just over the mountain, the soldiers of the British 3rd Battalion Rifle Brigade were using the truce for their annual proficiency test in musketry at Kilbride Camp. The officers took the opportunity to pursue grouse across the hills. The grouse proved more elusive than the IRA![4]

On 25 July, the Dublin ASU also presented for a five-day training course but the experience proved difficult for the officer in charge. At this stage, the ASU had renamed themselves the 'HQ Guard Company'. They were not easy to handle. Captain O'Brien, the camp O/C, submitted a report to Director of Training Emmet Dalton, in which he addressed the behaviour of 'The Guard' as follows:

The conduct of some of those men was most unsatisfactory from the start ... On the day after their arrival they chalked on the walls remarks such as, 'The guard will not be trained' 'The guard are the best trained men in the Dublin Bde.,' 'We won the war, [what] was it for?' 'The guard must get mass or break camp'

On Saturday after they had gone a Silver watch the property of Mr Wisdom Hely was missed from its usual place in the Recreation Room. This watch had been in the room ever since the arrival of my men in the camp and had never been interfered with.'[5]

Captain O'Brien did not keep notes on the behaviour of individual soldiers but provided a roll of the thirty-seven members of the Dublin ASU who attended the camp. O/C Commandant Paddy O'Daly was not among them but instead Lieutenant Joe Leonard as acting O/C, Pádraig Ó Conchubhair (now under the name Paddy O'Connor) as 1st Lieutenant and Mick Reilly, former Squad member, as 2nd Lieutenant. Paddy Griffin (Adjutant) and Tom McGrath (QM) were also senior officers. Captain O'Brien's collective impression of the 'HQ Guard' was one of an elite force found in most armies. The 'Guard' were battle-hardened and would have found it difficult to accept training on tactics, weapons and drill from men who had not served in the war in the same capacity as themselves. In many armies, elite forces are looked upon with great respect by their comrades, in recognition of their professionalism, experience and endurance on active service. The 'Guard', soon to become known as 'The Dublin Guards', also saw themselves as an elite and were looked upon as such by IRA GHQ. But they were a divisive influence and enjoyed their feared reputation. Fear had been one of the key tactics employed by IRA intelligence and the Squad during the War of Independence. The strategy had developed from operations implemented on the orders of Michael Collins. The Dublin Guards and other arms of the Free State would continue to use fear as a tactic during the Civil War. In doing so, they would have the complete support of the GHQ of the new National Army and also the Free State government.

The truce between the IRA and the British army was made permanent by the signing of the Anglo-Irish Treaty on 6 December 1921. Arthur Griffith and Michael Collins were the most influential of the signatories. The vote on the Treaty by Dáil Éireann was held after the Christmas holiday on 6 January 1922 with sixty-four in favour and fifty-seven against.

Michael Collins in uniform. During the War of Independence he displayed inspirational qualities of leadership: charisma, vision, initiative, great powers of command and organisational skills, driven by a tireless energy. (Courtesy the Military Archives)

The debate was bitter in the extreme and led to a polarisation of those who supported and those who opposed the Treaty. Conflict centred on the talking of an oath of allegiance to the king (Article 4) and partition of the country (Article 12). Michael Collins argued strongly that the Treaty was a stepping stone and that it was the best arrangement that could be obtained from the British at that time.

After the Dáil accepted the Treaty, the British withdrawal of troops began in earnest. The RIC, which included the Black and Tans and the Auxiliaries, were demobilised. From now on, it was up to the Irish people through their respective governments to establish law, order and defence for the country. In first two years of the Irish Free State the National Army held complete power.

General Michael Collins' National Army was small and owed a great deal to the loyalty of individual commanders who remained totally committed to their commander-in-chief. After the signing of the Treaty, Collins had secured the release of men and women who had fought and

The Dublin Guards, IRA, 4 February 1922, at Beggars Bush Barracks. (Courtesy Trophy and Carter Families Collection, South Dublin County Council)

worked to achieve an independent Ireland. At Christmas 1921, hundreds made their way home from camps and prisons in Ireland and Britain. Eileen McGrane was released from prison in Liverpool. Seán MacEoin and Michael Hogan were both released and, together with Michael Brennan of the 1st Western Division, Dan Hogan of the Monaghan Brigade and Paddy O'Daly of the Dublin Guards, they would form the backbone of the Free State National Army. Their experience in the War of Independence would be implemented with greater resolve and, unfortunately, great cruelty. Their lack of experience in structuring and maintaining a standing army would be addressed by the inclusion of former British army officers and NCOs. Their vast experience would be pivotal in establishing effective operatational structures, military procedures and the development of the various corps and services required by an army of the time. That it was accomplished remains a major achievement of the Irish Free State. The split in the Dáil over the Treaty was replicated in the IRA. While every attempt was made to prevent a division in the IRA it was inevitable as Michael Collins, Arthur Griffith and the pro-Treaty side took the measures required to enact the Treaty. The pro-Treaty faction within the IRA became the National Army and their inclusion of former British soldiers demonstrates the resolve and determination of the emerging Irish Free State to win the looming civil war. It would, however, be achieved at a terrible cost.

The Dublin Guard were officially formed in February 1922 when they paraded as a company on the square of Beggars Bush Barracks. In March, they took on enough additional men to form a battalion. In May 1922 the Dublin Guards became a brigade and O'Daly was promoted to the rank of brigadier. Of the original men of the Dublin ASU who joined the Dublin Guards in February 1922, only seven would leave to join the republican (anti-treaty) forces during the ensuing civil war. Paddy O'Connor was promoted to colonel and would become second in command of Waterford Command. Two others joined him: Captain Harper as assistant QM and Seán O'Connor as assistant adjutant.[6] After the election of 24 June 1922 the Free State Constitution was approved by the majority of Irish people. The Provisional government was returned with fifty-eight pro-Treaty TDs,[7] and was led by the president of the Executive Council, Arthur Griffith, and Michael Collins as commander-in-chief of the newly emerging pro-Treaty National Army. The GHQ of the National Army was initially at Beggars Bush but then moved to Portobello Barracks where Michael Collins had his personal accommodation in 'The Red House' (now the Army School of Music). The Irish Free State did not come into official existence until the Bills creating it passed through the Westminster parliament and received royal assent, which was granted on 5 December 1922.[8] The Provisional government then became the Free State government.

The republicans who opposed the Treaty retained their military organisation and the name of the IRA. Politically, the IRA was linked to de Valera's anti-Treaty wing of Sinn Féin, though its leadership took little heed of any advice or decisions offered by Sinn Féin. The republicans would be referred to as 'Irregulars' both by the Free State government and the national newspapers. They were, on occasion, also referred to as 'Bolshies', a reference to the Russian Bolshevik revolution and the influence of its ideas in spreading worldwide revolution. This fear of Bolshevism was also very much a part of the Catholic Church's opposition to republicanism.[9] With the Treaty signed, the British army began its withdrawal from the Irish Free State. The withdrawal was gradual due to the escalating tensions between pro- and anti-Treaty republicans. The different military factions occupied British army barracks as their troops pulled out. There were a number of flashpoints as the IRA and pro-Treaty troops came head to head over certain barracks. During this period there were also reputations to be won. Vinnie Byrne, initially Company Quartermaster Sergeant of the pro-Treaty Dublin Guards, was promoted to first lieutenant and assigned as guard commander at the Bank of Ireland on College Green. One afternoon, Oscar Traynor, now O/C Eastern Division of the IRA, tried to get the Guard to come over to the anti-Treaty republican side and permit them to occupy the bank. Lieutenant Byrne managed to seal the entrances and call for reinforcements. For his prompt action in saving the Bank of Ireland he was promoted to captain and his men in the ranks promoted to NCOs.[10]

On 13 April, the Dublin Brigade of the IRA seized as their HQ the Four Courts, the imposing legal complex of buildings centred on James Gandon's dome on Inns Quay. The IRA Executive had appointed an army council, which included Rory O'Connor, Joe McKelvey, Liam Mellows and Ernie O'Malley. During April and May, Collins and de Valera toured the country, addressing political rallies in support of their respective positions on the Treaty. Collins in particular sought to prepare an Irish Free State Constitution that would be acceptable to both sides. On 20 May an electoral pact between Collins and de Valera was declared. The aim was to avoid further division on the Treaty by focusing on the election of an Irish government by the people. The British cabinet were angry over the pact, which they believed compromised the Treaty. Churchill explained the situation to Collins and Arthur Griffith at a very tense meeting in London during the last week of May. Republicans could not become members of the Irish Free State government before first signing Article 17 of the Treaty, which bound the signatory to acceptance of the Treaty.[11] The draft constitution for the Irish Free State was presented to the British cabinet on 6 June 1922 by Griffith, Kevin O'Higgins and Hugh Kennedy

The Irish Free State government, c.1924. (L–r): Minister for Justice Kevin O'Higgins, Ceann Comhairle Michael Hayes, President of the Executive Council William T. Cosgrave, Attorney General Hugh Kennedy, Minister for External Affairs Desmond Fitzgerald and Minister for Finance Ernest Blythe. (Keogh Collection, Courtesy National Library of Ireland)

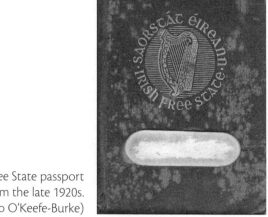

An Irish Free State passport dating from the late 1920s. (Courtesy Celio O'Keefe-Burke)

KC (legal adviser to the Provisional Government). Lloyd George rejected it outright. On 14 June Collins addressed an election rally in Cork. He encouraged the people to vote for whoever they thought would do best in the future they desired. This appeal to the people of Cork was interpreted as a repudiation of his pact with de Valera, causing a constitutional crisis for Collins and his pro-Treaty colleagues. The outbreak of a civil war, while not inevitable at this stage, was drawing ever closer.

During the occupation of the Four Courts, the republicans stored significant quantities of ammunition and explosives in the basement of the newly opened Public Record Office (PRO). The PRO was in the process of transferring official state and Church of Ireland records to the archives when the republicans seized the complex. The buildings were barricaded with sandbags and legal volumes and defended by experienced IRA Volunteers of the Dublin Brigade and their new young recruits. These recruits, sometimes known as 'Trucileers' because they joined during the truce, were shortly to face a baptism of fire. The anti-Treaty IRA Executive in the Four Courts appointed the following command structure:

IRA Executive Forces – Four Courts 30 June 1922[12]		IRA Field GHQ as on 1st July 1922[13]	
Chief of Staff	Joe McElvey	Chief of Staff	Liam Lynch
Dep. C/S & Dir. Organisation	Ernie O'Malley	Deputy C/S	Seán Moylan
Adj.-General	unknown	Adj.-General	Con Moloney
QM	Liam Mellows	QM	Joe O'Connor
Asst QM	Dick Barrett	Dir. Organisation	Ernie O'Malley
Dir. Engineering	Rory O'Connor	Dir. Intelligence	Seán Hyde
Dir. Intelligence	Joe Griffin	Dir. Engineering	'Daddy' Coughlan
Dir. Transport	Andy Doyle	Dir. Communications	Jim Moloney
Dir. Chemicals	Seumas O'Donovan	Dir. Medical Services	Dr Con Lucey
Dir. Munitions	Seán Russell	Dir. Publicity	Seán McCarthy

All through May and June, tensions had remained high between those who voted for and those who voted against the Treaty. The assassination of Sir Henry Wilson, former Chief of the Imperial General Staff of the British army outside his house in London on 22 June had brought matters to a head. Churchill blamed the republicans in the Four Courts and demanded that Collins deal with them once and for all. Joe Dolan, IRA intelligence, was sent to London to draw up plans around a possible rescue attempt of the two men who had shot Wilson, Commandant Reggie Dunne, O/C London IRA Battalion and Joe O'Sullivan, London Battalion IO. A rescue was never implemented and both men were hanged at Wandsworth Prison on 10 August 1922. Joe Dolan always firmly believed that Collins had ordered the killing of Wilson because of his role as military and police adviser to the new Northern Ireland government, which was leading to violent attacks on Catholics, and Protestant mobs attacking Catholic areas.[14]

Commandant Tom Ennis was promoted to major-general and appointed O/C of Dublin Command for the National Army prior to the attack on the Four Courts. At 3.40 a.m. on Wednesday 28 June 1922, General Ennis issued an ultimatum to the IRA Executive at the Four Courts to surrender. They ignored it.[15] Ennis then ordered the water supply to the republican strongholds in the city centre to be cut off and an artillery bombardment of the Four Courts to begin. This marked the opening of the Irish Civil War.

Major-General Emmet Dalton, who had sided with Michael Collins' pro-Treaty forces, was appointed Director of Operations.[16] Dalton had turned to former British army Lieutenant Colonel W. R. E. Murphy, a veteran of the First World War, for advice. When Murphy heard that Dalton only had 18-pounder guns he told him to go back to the British and get a loan of 4½-inch heavy howitzers, with gas shells.[17] Dalton made do with the 18-pounders although Collins afterwards admitted to Murphy that 'We could not follow your advice but you were undoubtedly right'.[18] The 18-pounders had a range of 7,000 yards (6.4 km) and fired an 18 lb shell (8.16 kg) at a rate of eight rounds per minute. The heavy howitzer had a similar range but fired a 35 lb shell (15.87 kg) at a rate of four rounds per minute.[19] At 4.20 a.m. Dalton ordered his guns to open up on the Four Courts. One was positioned on Bridge Street and the other at Winetavern Street.[20] Dalton later received two more 18-pounders which he positioned north of the Liffey.[21]

The IRA, in spite of their superior numbers, withdrew into specific buildings to defend themselves. As far back as the conscription crisis in 1918, the Dublin Brigade developed what was then known as the 'block system'. A block consisted of a series of buildings or houses in a street or streets that formed an isolated square. Each block was intended as 'a separate fort of resistance'.[22] It was a repeat of the Irish Volunteer strategy in 1916 when they had seized key buildings around Dublin such as Jacob's biscuit factory, the South Dublin Union, Four Courts, Boland's Mill and Clanwilliam House. They had made the GPO their HQ. Once they had seized the buildings, the Irish Volunteers simply waited to be attacked by the superior British forces. Some Irish Volunteer commanders established very effective outposts, which had some notable success, namely at Clanwilliam House, 25 Northumberland Road and North King Street. In general, the Irish Volunteer strategy of 1916 was passive. In 1922, the republican forces in Dublin handed the initiative to National Army as they sealed themselves into major buildings in O'Connell Street and awaited attack by their opponents. The bombardment of the Four Courts was terrifying for the defenders.

In the Four Courts, Fr Albert, a Capuchin priest who had ministered to the republicans during the conflict of the period, noted the developments:

3.40 a.m.	Ultimatum delivered.
4.20	War opened.
5.15	First Irish Republican soldier wounded.
5.15	Daly sent message: 'When will you come out with your hands up?'
	Reply from O/C: 'When you come for me.'
	Daly: 'Any chance of negotiations?'
	Reply: 'When your men retire.'
5.40	Second man wounded.
7.40	Third man wounded ...
12.30 p.m.	The fire was so heavy and so deafening that it was almost impossible for the priest who was hearing confessions to carry out his duties. The firing was carried on for 7½ hours. We have been heartened by the girls of Cumann na mBan and nurses and doctors who are here unselfishly giving their services to the wounded ...[23]

Major-General Paddy O'Daly was ordered to lead an infantry assault on the Four Courts when the bombardment came to a halt. On Thursday 29 June he directed Commandants Joe McGuinness and Patrick O'Connor to lead their Dublin Guards into the PRO on the north side of the Four Courts, capturing a number of the IRA garrison. Commandant Joe

Leonard led another detachment of Dublin Guards in an attack on the south side of the building. Raked with IRA machine-gun fire, Leonard was wounded, along with fourteen of his men. The bombardment of the Four Courts had begun on Wednesday and on Friday the building began to burn.[24] Around 12.30 p.m. there was a massive explosion, which completely demolished the PRO. Men and women were thrown off their feet while large blocks of masonry and a thousand years of Irish history rained down around them. Astonishingly, no one was killed. Ernie O'Malley led the Republican Dublin Brigade garrison of the Four Courts onto the street to surrender. The explosion in the ammunition dump in the PRO caused great anger among the National Army who believed a mine had been set to kill as many of their troops as possible. Their suspicions may have been right as mines had been laid. However, whether they were detonated by the IRA or by shellfire from Dalton's guns is unclear.[25] From this point on, members of the National Army who were veterans of the Dublin Brigade believed nearly every IRA mine was a trap mine. Both Ernie O'Malley and Joe Griffin escaped after the surrender at midday. Griffin escaped at about 3 p.m. and went straight to the city centre where the fighting continued.[26]

As the fighting at the Four Courts and in O'Connell Street intensified, snipers on both sides became active, making the surrounding streets extremely dangerous for combatants and any civilians who might venture out. Supplies of bread and milk for civilians were cut as no deliveries could be made. Oscar Traynor, Dublin Brigade O/C of the republican forces, was holding an area in O'Connell Street that became known as 'The Block'. Cathal Brugha was among the garrison defending the Hamman Hotel. He personally operated a machine-gun post from the rear of the hotel. The National Army took up positions surrounding 'The Block', placing troops at Cathedral Street and two machine guns at Cahill's Corner of Talbot Street and Marlborough Street. The National Army used the cover of armour-plated lorries and armoured cars to maintain sustained fire on the republican defenders.[27]

St John's Ambulance operative J. F. Homan went home and donned his civilian clothes. At the behest of Fr Albert, he went out to make contact with Michael Collins and Éamon de Valera to try and establish some terms for a truce. Homan saw Collins at Portobello Barracks first. Collins, though still quite angry about the explosion of what he believed to be a mine at the Four Courts, greeted him warmly and listened for a half an hour. At the end of the discussion Collins agreed to permit the 'insurgents' or republicans to leave their positions throughout the city and go home unharmed without facing imprisonment, on condition that they deposit their weapons in the national armoury.[28] Homan left Collins and tried to make contact with some of the republican leadership holding out in the increasingly ruined O'Connell Street area. Homan first met Robert Barton who, though he appreciated Collins' friendship and gracious offer, was very bitter. He doubted the sincerity of the surrender of arms and the offer to return to their homes unharmed. For Barton, a former British officer and one of the signatories of the Treaty, the message sent back was clear: 'We want no terms other than victory or death.'[29] Homan argued in great earnest for peace but to no avail. Later he met with de Valera, who listened and took the offer seriously. For de Valera, however, to agree to a truce, the republicans would have to be permitted to depart from their strongholds with their arms. It was a term the Free State government could not grant. Homan did not get to see Collins until the following morning, when he was ushered into the commander-in-chief's private room at Portobello Barracks. For the first time, Collins explained to Homan his views on the developing civil war and in particular:

> ... the uselessness of trying to reason with the insurgents, the crimes that so many of them had committed, the anarchy they had set out to achieve, the feeling on part of the law-abiding population of Ireland as well as the conviction of the friends of Ireland throughout the world that if the Government failed to assert itself now it could never be trusted to do so, the danger of strengthening that feeling resulting in (a) the complete loss of world opinion, (b) the destruction of all hope of bringing in Ulster, and (c) the return of the British. And all for what? To satisfy the alleged sentimental desire of a few desperadoes to retain in their hands the weapons which would enable them to hold up the Government of the country any time they liked ...'[30]

While the fighting raged throughout the centre of Dublin, Liam Lynch, O/C of the 1st Southern Division of the IRA and staunchly anti-Treaty, managed to slip through the hands of the National Army troops as they believed him to be neutral. Lynch's steadfast republican outlook and loyalty to the Irish Republic would lead to a prolonged civil war. When perhaps others would have surrendered, Lynch kept the IRA in the field for a lot longer than most of the leadership wished.

By Wednesday 5 July 1922, the republican 'Block' in O'Connell Street was ablaze. The St John's Ambulance operative J. F. Homan made one last effort to reach de Valera. Thinking the republican political leader was in the Hamman Hotel, Homan braved rifle and machine-gun fire and approached the burning building. He did not find de Valera there but instead spoke briefly with Cathal Brugha who said he would open fire on anyone coming towards the building. Homan left and continued his search, leaving Brugha amid the debris and the flames.[31] Oscar Traynor had led de Valera to a house in Mount Street.[32] On Wednesday evening, Brugha sent his small garrison out to National Army lines to surrender. He himself remained and refused to answer orders to surrender from Traynor. Brugha then loaded his revolvers and stepped out to face his foes. The soldiers of the National Army called on him to surrender but a revolver shot was the only reply. They had no option but to shoot him down. Cathal Brugha, a veteran and hero of the 1916 Rising, lay in the demolished street, bleeding heavily. He was taken to hospital and a nurse in the ambulance held his severed artery in her fingers to staunch the blood flow. Brugha died two days later.[33]

General Macready's assessment of the National Army's performance was communicated to the British cabinet in London:

> It is believed, that fear of mines and casualties caused the Government's forces to rely on the burning of buildings to bring about the rebels surrender rather than resort to direct assault. This is borne out by the cinema (Pathé Gazette). From an official source the P.G. casualties in the Dublin fighting up to the evening of July 9th have been 19 killed and 111 wounded. The wounded include 30 cases of 'shell shock'![34]

Traynor escaped Dublin with other republicans as they attempted to link up with their comrades at Blessington and Baltinglass. The National Army pursued them as they drove south out of the city but they managed to evade encirclement and capture. The capital was now lost to them. However, Traynor, as O/C IRA Dublin Brigade, felt it was his duty to return to the city to organise some form of resistance to the National Army and the Irish Free State. He was captured by the National Army in August 1922 and remained in prison until 1924.[35] The republican Dublin Brigade was destroyed by the fighting in Dublin. Most were captured at the surrender and in the weeks that followed. They ended up in Mountjoy Gaol or the internment camps in the Curragh, which were known as Tintown 1 and 2. Those still free were now hunted men. For the duration of the Civil War, the actions of the Dublin Brigade IRA were down to small isolated units.

The 2nd Battalion of the old Dublin Brigade, the ASU, the Intelligence Department and the Squad formed the backbone of the National Army at this point. They took the initiative and pursued the republican forces south to Munster. After Generals Tom Ennis and Emmet Dalton carried out a seaborne landing in Cork, Major-General Dan Hogan was appointed General Officer Commanding (GOC) Dublin Command. From Ninemilehouse in Tipperary, he was the brother of Michael Hogan, who had been shot dead on the field of play at Croke Park on 21 November 1920. Dan Hogan spent the War of Independence in Monaghan where he was assistant stationmaster at Clones for the Great Northern Railway Company. Hogan teamed up with Éoin O'Duffy and established a formidable Irish Volunteer organisation in the county. Their brigade flying column was one of the first to attack an RIC barracks in Ireland. Hogan also did his time in prison, being incarcerated in quite a number of jails, including Crumlin Road Gaol in Belfast.[36] After his appointment as GOC Dublin Command, Hogan was nearly killed as he drove through the city streets with Eoin O'Duffy on 23 September 1922, when their car was attacked by an IRA unit. Both men escaped unhurt.[37]

The lessons learned by Michael Collins' intelligence department in the War of Independence now came to the fore in the National Army's response to IRA activity. Each National Army command had their own intelligence department, as did battalions and companies. All intelligence gathered was filtered at company and battalion level and sent to the intelligence GHQ at Wellington Barracks (now Griffith Barracks) in Dublin. Intelligence operations were one of the major factors in gaining a constant advantage over the republican forces. National Army intelligence was initially commanded by Liam Tobin and Frank Thornton but they were reassigned to Cork. Lieutenant Colonel Charlie Dalton took over, with Frank Bolster and James Murray among the senior command staff.[38] The intelligence service was assisted by a number of corps, which cooperated but also worked independently. The Criminal Investigation Department (CID) was based at Oriel House, initially under the control of the National

Army intelligence department and later under the Department of Home Affairs. They would play a major role in defeating the republicans. Major-General Joe McGrath TD was director general with Captain Paddy Moynihan as operational commander. Captain Moynihan was Michael Collins' chief intelligence agent in the GPO under the code number 118. This force started out small in number but by February 1923, their operational strength was approximately thirty detective officers and forty-five members of staff who served on transport, administration, patrolling and guard duties.[39] A full breakdown of the allocation of members of the forces under jurisdiction of the CID is as follows:[40]

Efficient detective officers:	30
House & Personal Guards, Transport & Clerical:	175
Street patrols:	60
Observers or 'touts':	40
Women observers:	8
Part-time Volunteers:	50

The CID eventually amassed 2,200 files recording details on the activities of republicans or suspected republicans. The CID was in constant communication with Dublin Command HQ and National Army intelligence to ensure there was no overlap and that every lead was investigated. A summary of the daily reports and developments were issued to the commander-in-chief of the National Army and the adjutant of Dublin Command.

The most successful method employed for the capture of wanted republican men and women was the 'mousetrap' strategy. The location for the raid was chosen, say a known haunt of a republican. The suspect would enter and would be captured but held on the premises quietly. All callers to the location over the next number of hours or day would also be detained. All were then brought to Oriel House for interrogation. The interrogation methods, as described by the CID themselves, were 'at least as humane as that form at present [1923] extensively used in America and known as the Third Degree'.[41] The CID acted with almost complete immunity from prosecution as the following case shows:

Inspector Mooney CID was arrested by two DMP Constables caught in Camden Street, in the act of brutally ill-treating a girl who is to become the mother of his child. When placed under arrest he threatened to shoot the two D.M.P. The case was brought before the Courts the other day, but hushed up and he was let off with a fine of 40/-. Now, Horan the C.I.D. man, has stated that he will deal with the two D.M.P. men for interfering with any of his men and will make an example of them.[42]

Captain Moynihan was also in charge of the Protective Officers Corps, which was formed in November 1922. The corps' primary duty was to protect individual ministers and politicians. The corps also guarded the homes and offices of ministers, TDs and senators. Among those receiving protection were Ministers Fionán Lynch, Joe McGrath and Kevin O'Higgins. Attorney General of the Free State, Hugh Kennedy, also received protection from the corps. It numbered approximately twenty former members of the intelligence department and IRA who served from 1916 to 1921. Its eventual strength was 175 men but by 1923 this was reduced to fifty-eight. The best-known member of the Protective Corps was President William T. Cosgrave's bodyguard, Charlie Byrne, a former member of Collins' intelligence department, known by the nickname 'The Count'.[43]

An ex-British army officer was in charge of another secret organisation called the Citizens' Defence Force. This force was charged with guarding and patrolling the CID HQ at Oriel House and then at the CID's subsequent HQ at 88 Merrion Square. They also kept certain districts of Dublin under surveillance. All of these 'detective' forces were eventually disbanded after the Civil War. Most of the men and women were given a small pension or payment. A select few were transferred into the detective branch of the DMP formed with the dissolution of the old G Division. This new detective branch was intended to run on lines similar to the UK's Scotland Yard.[44]

Very soon into the Civil War concerns were raised about the treatment of prisoners at the hands of the National Army's intelligence services. Lawyer Dermot Crowley filed a writ of habeas corpus for the release of Count George Plunkett and other republican prisoners. He was arrested and brought to Mountjoy. He wrote to Cahir Davitt, son of Michael Davitt and legal officer in the National Army, describing the 'coarseness and savagery' of the 'Intelligence Officers', the filth and overcrowding of the cells and the food, which was the leavings of the soldiers' meals and which the prisoners had to eat without a knife or fork.[45] Crowley described how a prisoner in the cell with him was, on three separate occasions in one night, 'dragged out and savagely beaten because he could not or would not give information about other people'.[46] The prisoner then faced a mock firing squad although he believed it was real. Crowley said: 'My soul sickened at the thought that I belonged to a country where such abominations were committed and paid for by the people.'

Crowley placed responsibility for this situation squarely on the shoulders of Richard Mulcahy, Chief of Staff of the National Army.[47] The issues of the treatment of prisoners came before President Cosgrave in the Dáil on 4 October 1922. His response was evasive; he chose his words carefully, saying prisoners came into custody with 'old wounds' and while 'no one [is] suffering at present, investigation and disciplinary action will be taken if any charge is proved'.[48]

The brutality Crowley witnessed was no isolated case. Interrogations and torture were standard operating procedures for members of the Free State Army intelligence department based at Wellington Barracks. These procedures were also practised by members of the CID at Oriel House. Both departments were led by former members of IRA GHQ intelligence department and the Squad. It is most unlikely that torture as a method of interrogation suddenly appeared as a practice in the National Army. The men who carried it out had a long apprenticeship preceding and during the War of Independence. It was not long before the interrogations were accompanied by murder. Three republicans in Dublin were abducted, tortured and shot on 26 August. The bodies of Alfred Colley, Vice O/C Dublin Brigade IRA, and Seán Cole, Commandant Dublin Brigade, were found in Yellow Lanes, Drumcondra. Captain Bernard Daly's body was discovered in a ditch on the Malahide Road. Linked with these murders and a number of others was Captain James Murray of National Army intelligence and the CID. Michael Staines, TD and Chief Commissioner of the new Garda Síochána, had a row with Chief of Staff General Richard Mulcahy over the murders of Cole and Colley. It led to the resignation of Staines and the appointment of Éoin O'Duffy as new head of the police force.[49]

Charlie Dalton was another IO associated with the murder of three republicans, Edwin Hughes (seventeen years of age), Brendan Holohan (sixteen) and Joseph Rogers (also sixteen). Two bodies were found on Monastery Road in Clondalkin and the other at the bottom of a nearby quarry; all three men had been arrested by Dalton.[50] At the inquest, witnesses claimed they saw Dalton with the three young men in his car. A National Army officer, Nicholas Tobin, brother of Liam Tobin, confirmed this. He was shot dead by the 'accidental discharge' of Seán 'Flash' Bolger's weapon during a raid the following week. Bolger was also a National Army officer.[51] In a story that put Major King's defence in the Clonturk Park murder case in the shade, Dalton argued that he had released the three men alive and had then arrested another three men again on Clonliffe Road in Drumcondra later that night! Dalton claimed that someone else must have killed the unfortunate men. The popular IRA officer Commandant Bob Bonfield, 4th Battalion, suffered a similar fate to the three young men the following March. Bonfield had been captured at an IRA dump in the city in early March but had escaped from Portobello Barracks. Bonfield was arrested by the CID on 29 March 1923. His body was found on Monastery Road the following morning.[52] Dalton never stood trial for any offence.

So concerned were republicans about the brutal treatment of prisoners that Maud Gonne MacBride, Honorary Secretary of the Women's Prisoners' Defence League, and Charlotte Dupard, the league's president, went on record in a letter revealing the methods and locations of the sites of interrogation and the methods employed:

> Fully realising the responsibility we are taking and the risks we are incurring, for the sake of Ireland, as a public duty we make the following charges:
>
> Untried prisoners are being tortured to extract information. Officers of the forces of the Provisional Government now the forces of the Free State Government direct, and, in most cases, actually participate in the infliction of the torture:
>
> The Chambers where the tortures are carried out are called 'Interrogation Offices' or, in the more familiar language of the soldiers 'the knock out rooms', or 'the Slaughter House':
>
> Some of the forms of torture reported in letters of prisoners which, in spite of all sequestration precautions, have got outside the prisons, are: –
>
> Twisting the flesh with pliers:

Pulling out the hairs of the moustache with pincers: –

Blackening the eyes: –

Twisting the arms: –

Shooting round the head: –

Beating with the butt of revolvers and rifles, and scabbards of bayonets: –

Breaking teeth: –

Repeated punching of stomach: –

Repeated electric shocks: –

Driving forks into legs: –

When the patient faints under the torture he is revived to be tortured again: –

Some prisoners have been taken out to the interrogation room and tortured several times at intervals. Many have had to be removed to hospital for treatment after torture. From Wellington, Portobello, Oriel House and many different parts of the country complaints have come.

I charge General Mulcahy and the members of the Provisional Government with a guilty knowledge of this ill-treatment of prisoners and of taking measures to conceal it, but not to stop it. The provisional Government refused an inquiry into the matter. They refuse admission to the prisoners to visiting justices and sanitary officers: –

They have forbidden all visits of families of prisoners even when condemned to death: –

They have refused admission of solicitors to see prisoners: –

In some prisons all letters in or out are forbidden: –

They have censored the press; the editors of the three Dublin daily papers declare that they are not allowed by military censor to publish any letters referring to the ill-treatment of prisoners: –

Released prisoners have been threatened with 'plugging' if they reveal what they have heard and seen in the prisons. Since our work in connection with the Women's Prisoners' Defence League skulls and cross-bones were painted on the bed-room walls by General Mulcahy's soldiers during their raid of the house of one of the signatories of this letter. Young girls have been beaten by these soldiers for posting up notices of the meetings ...[53]

The issue of brutality to prisoners would continue beyond the Civil War.

The weeks following the surrender of the republican forces in Dublin were grim. Both republican and Free State sides were soon in deep mourning for the loss of their hallowed leaders. Harry Boland was mortally wounded on the night of 30–31 July 1922 while being arrested by National Army intelligence officers in the Grand Hotel, Skerries. Boland died at St Vincent's Hospital on 2 August. Just ten days later, on 12 August, Arthur Griffith, President of the Provisional Government of the Irish Free State, died. The country was still reeling from Griffith's death when, in the small hours of 23 August, came the catastrophic news that Michael Collins had been killed in an IRA ambush at Beal na Bláth in west Cork the previous evening. Collins had departed that morning for a tour of the county. The IRA became aware of Collins' presence in the area and Brigade Commandant Tom Hales set an ambush. The firefight in which Collins was killed took place in the fading light of the day. Most of the IRA column had departed. The firing lasted only twenty minutes and at the end of it Michael Collins had been shot through the head and killed.

The sense of loss for the men in Collins' convoy must have been overwhelming and yet they still had to withdraw from IRA territory. It was a long journey in the darkness, filled with uncertainty and anguish. It was after midnight when the convoy made it to Cork city. Dalton informed GHQ in Dublin that the commander-in-chief, the Big Fella, had been killed. Michael Collins' body was returned to Dublin where his remains lay in repose at City Hall. He was laid to rest at Glasnevin Cemetery after a requiem Mass in the Pro-Cathedral on 28 August 1922. Thousands of citizens joined with his fiancée, Kitty Kiernan, his family and his closest comrades from the Dublin Brigade as they said goodbye to their dear friend and comrade. During the truce Michael Collins had met with a journalist and Harley Street nerve specialist. It was not a medical appointment, just a meeting and a chat after lunch at the Gresham Hotel. The specialist observed Collins for a while and then was then introduced.[54] He offered this observation of Michael Collins: 'There is a characteristic native recklessness in his manner which scorns the idea of cost; but it is allied to a granite determination ever watchful, ever on guard to see that the cost shall nevertheless be justified.'[55] As the men prepared to take their leave of each other, the specialist remarked to Collins that it must be embarrassing to be at the centre of so much popularity in Ireland. The journalist noted Collins' reply: '"Faith, and you're right doctor," he said. "I find myself in far more danger since the peace came than ever I did in the war."' The journalist commented: 'It was a characteristically humorous Irish view, but that square jaw gave a grimness to the joke.'[56]

On 8 August, Generals Emmet Dalton and Tom Ennis ('The Manager') and the Dublin troops had sailed to Cork. It took them until 11 August to take the city and expel the IRA, who withdrew to west Cork. General Ennis was up against the Cork brigades of the 1st Southern Division IRA. With him were Colonel Tom Kehoe, Pat McCrea and some of the Squad. In September, as Ennis's men pushed westwards towards the Kerry border, the IRA set a mine at Carrigaphooca Bridge near Macroom. When the National Army arrived at the bridge, Colonel Tom Kehoe set about defusing the mine. The device was a trap mine and the resulting explosion mortally wounded Kehoe and killed the six men standing around him at the time: Captain Dan O'Brien, Sergeant William Murphy, Volunteers Thomas Manning, John O'Riordan, Patrick O'Rourke and Ralph Conway. Kehoe's badly torn body was taken to Cork Hospital where he died in the presence of former comrades and Mary Collins-Powell, the sister of Michael Collins. Mary cut a lock of his hair and enclosed it in a heartbreaking letter to Kehoe's mother, Julia, at Rathmoregrew, Hacketstown in County Carlow.

For the Squad, it was more grief than they could bear. They returned to Mallow, took a republican prisoner, forty-year-old James Buckley, from the cells and shot him in the head. They dumped his body into the crater the mine explosion had left in the bridge at Carrigaphooca. The former members of the Dublin Brigade were continuing with the methods of killing they had learned in the War of Independence. The local garrison of National Army troops in Macroom told their O/C Colonel-Commandant Peter Conlon that they refused to go into the mountains and track down the IRA. Conlon wrote to General Dalton, GOC Cork Command, telling him to rein in the Dublin officers or 'they would corrupt the army'. Conlon said the situation was critical and that the civilian population knew what happened also.[57] Dalton wrote to General Mulcahy and said that while he approved of the action taken by the Squad, it would be better to keep them out of his area. He and Ennis continued to take the fight to the republicans in Cork. The focus of attention now shifted to Kerry. What happened here at the hands of General O'Daly, former O/C of the Squad, would define the Irish Civil War.

Major-General Paddy O'Daly's Dublin Guards were re-equipped after the battle for Dublin and on 2 August his troops made a seaborne landing at Fenit, County Kerry, and set out on the road to Tralee. First Western Division troops under Major-General Michael Hogan landed at Tarbert from Kilkee in County Clare and joined up with O'Daly.[58] General W. R. E. Murphy established Kerry Command HQ at Ballymullen Barracks. Murphy had pushed south from Limerick and broken the republican defence line at Bruff, Bruree and Kilmallock in County Limerick.[59] The republicans had set Ballymullen Barracks on fire as they withdrew from Tralee but the National Army troops saved most of it and reconditioned the facilities. O'Daly was sent to Killarney and established the Great Southern Hotel as the HQ of the Dublin Guards.

The republican forces arrayed against the National Army in Kerry were divided into three command areas: Kerry No. 1 Brigade IRA occupying north Kerry, the Dingle Peninsula and part of the Iveragh Peninsula around Killorglin and west of the MacGillycuddy's Reeks. Tralee lay at its centre.[60] Kerry No. 2 Brigade Area took in the territory north of Castleisland to Knocknagoshel and to the south beyond Kenmare, taking in part of the Iveragh and Beara Peninsulas, with Killarney at the centre.[61] Humphrey Murphy was O/C, with John Joe Rice as his second in command. Kerry No. 3 Brigade Area occupied the Iveragh Peninsula south-west of a line from Mountain Station near Glenbeigh to Sneem via Bealach Óisín (Ballaghisheen).[62] General Murphy estimated the republican strength at the end of September 1922 as follows:[63]

Currahean Area	100 with Cahill
Kenmare and Killorglin	500 with [J. J.] Rice
Headley Bridge	100
Scartaglin	200
Robber's Den & Loo Bridge Area	200
Dingle	50
Waterville and Cahersiveen	200

The IRA in Kerry were well armed with SMLEs, Thompson and Lewis machine guns, revolvers, grenades and enough explosives for mines. They

Tom O'Connor
Scarteen,
murdered by
republicans
in Kenmare,
County Kerry
1922. (Courtesy
Patrick
O'Connor-
Scarteen)

had a plentiful supply of ammunition and they used it to devastating effect. On 4 September a National Army patrol ran into a forty-man IRA ambush at Ohermong Bridge just outside Cahersiveen on the Waterville road. Lieutenant Clement Cooper was shot dead, Sergeant John O'Donoghue died of his wounds and a number of other men were also wounded.[64] The situation soon became even worse for the National Army in Kerry. On 9 September, while Kenmare was still in slumber, the IRA moved in to occupy buildings in the centre of the town. An IRA column of men from Loo Bridge and Kilgarvan (3rd & 5th Battalion areas) and a detachment of rifle grenadiers from Ballyvourney in Cork were determined to take the town. Some of the column slipped into the back of Tom and John O'Connor-Scarteen's home. The ground floor was a bakery. Tom was brigadier of the National Army garrison in Kenmare. His brother John was a captain. The testimony of Nora O'Sullivan, a girl of twelve, and Kathleen Moriarty, a maid aged nineteen, described a Squad-like assassination of the two men. John was shot twice as he descended the stairs to investigate the disturbance in the house. Tom was pulled out of bed, put standing against the bedroom wall and shot twice in the head. The republicans claimed that Con Looney and 'Sailor Dan' Healy went to arrest the two men but that they resisted and went for their guns. Looney and Healy claimed self-defence to explain their actions.[65] In the subsequent investigation carried out by the Garda Síochána they received a report from General W. R. E. Murphy. He concluded that the IRA forced entry to the house at 6.30 a.m. and Tom O'Connor-Scarteen resisted capture. He was then shot dead by his would-be captors. Tom's brother, John, was killed in the same bedroom or on the landing. Of the brigadier and his family he wrote: 'Commandant O'Connor was a plucky young officer and a good one. His father suffered very much at the hands of the Irregulars afterwards and finally had to fly to Tralee where the Army supported him.'[66]

Another document further stated: 'The murder of their [Mr & Mrs O'Connor's] sons – under, even for that time, exceptional circumstances, caused very strong feeling throughout Kerry.'[67] The deaths of the O'Connor-Scarteen brothers and the loss of Kenmare was a major setback for General Murphy. Murphy's key National Army unit in Kerry were also short of men, machine guns, equipment and uniforms. General Murphy did not panic. He requested more troops and some 'Oriel House' men. Kenmare was only retaken on 6 December by a force of Dublin Guards and 1st Western Division.

On 27 September 1922, came the turning point of the campaign. A combined IRA column under John Joe Rice, O/C Kerry No. 2 Brigade, and David L. Robinson, a former British army officer and cousin of Erskine Childers,[68] attacked the four National Army posts at Killorglin, which were held by eighty men of the 1st Western Division. A massive explosion had demolished the building next to the barracks and breached the wall. In addition to their usual rifles, the IRA brought the fire of five Thompson guns and two Lewis guns to bear. The National Army lost Captain Lehane, who, though already wounded, threw himself back into the fight only to be killed. His defiance inspired his men to continue fighting. The republicans eventually withdrew, leaving the bodies of six of their dead behind.

After the battle of Killorglin, ten republican prisoners, Jack Galvin among them, were being brought to Tralee. A Galway man, Colonel Michael Hogan of the 1st Western Division, was one of the officers in charge of the prisoners. Hogan had lost a close friend on 22 August when Captain James Burke was shot and killed as he led a column through Castlemaine. Burke's father only learned of his son's death while reading the *Irish Independent* a few days later.[69] Colonel Hogan believed Galvin was responsible for the shooting of his friend. As the prisoners were approaching Tralee they came upon a series of trees felled by the IRA. Some of the prisoners were taken to clear the obstruction. When they returned, Jack Galvin was no longer present. He had been left in the custody of Colonel Hogan and some other officers. Galvin's body was discovered a short time later behind a hedge near the Church of Ireland church at Ballyseedy.[70] National Army officer Éamon Horan, formerly of Kerry No. 1 Brigade, resigned his commission in protest at the failure of General Murphy to hold an investigation into the death of Galvin while a prisoner.[71]

IRA flying column attacks on National Army posts continued into the autumn at Fenit and Rathmore. Acting on information received, General Murphy ordered sweeping searches around Killorglin, Ballyheigue, Barleymount, Aghadoe and Greenagh near Killarney, capturing many 'Irregulars' and large quantities of arms, ammunition and equipment. Included in the ammunition dump discovered at Barleymount were 200 rounds of .303 and 20 rounds of .45. All of the rounds were flat-nosed or dumdum. In his report for the week ending 30 September, General Murphy listed the following captures:[72]

Prisoners	40
Lewis gun	1
Rifles	26
Revolvers	5
Rounds flat-nosed .303 ammunition	200
Rounds flat-nosed .45 ammunition	20
Grenades	17
Tins of petrol	4
Electric fitting for mines	1
Four-ton lorry	1
Ford (motorcar)	1
Bicycles	8

Boxes Osram lamp bulbs	2
Telephone and wireless apparatus parts	1
Telephone and telegraph instruments	
Quantity of explosives	

At night, National Army commanding officers sent out patrols using the same methods the Squad had used in Dublin: patrols walked in pairs at a distance of 10 yards and on both sides of the street at the same time. Usually five to six men went on town patrol during the day. The National Army also established a network of scouts or watchers, eight in National Army towns and two in republican towns.

Despite these serious setbacks, with barely 1,000 men Murphy had achieved a great deal. As the autumn wore on, the Free State government introduced the Emergency Powers Bill to Dáil Éireann, on 26 September, and debated it the following day. The measures in the Bill allowed for military courts to try any republicans captured for a range of offences. For the charge of being captured with arms or ammunition the sentence was death. Thomas Johnson, leader of the Labour Party, was very disturbed by this development and said the Bill basically established a dictatorship by vote of the Dáil.[73] In part of what was a prophetic address, Johnson foretold the events to come:

> I predict with very great sorrow, that if this order is passed, we will learn of very many more cases of Colleys and Nevilles, and the other men who have lost their lives, for which no explanation has been given in the Courts or to the public ... You have not got within your Army to-day that perfect discipline and control which would prevent a fearful disaster coming upon the good name of this country ... you are going to make it possible for many dark deeds to be done by an Army which is not in the public eye, which has not command over all its units, and in which the discipline is not satisfactory, and no one will claim that it is.[74]

In response, Ministers Ernest Blythe and Kevin O'Higgins, and Richard Mulcahy TD argued that the country was experiencing anarchy at the hands of armed gangs. The measures contained in the Emergency Powers Bill would restore order and bring the conflict to a conclusion in a relatively short period of time. The Bill was passed by forty-eight votes to eighteen.[75] There followed a rapid sequence of events. The Free State government offered republicans a general amnesty on 3 October 1922. The Catholic bishops then issued a pastoral letter, 'To be read in all Churches and public oratories at principal Masses, on Sunday, October 22, 1922'.[76] The bishops did not hold back, declaring the activities of the 'Irregulars' to be 'without moral sanction'. The killing of National soldiers was declared to be murder, the breaking of public roads, bridges and railways defined as 'criminal destruction', and 'the invasion of homes and the molestation of citizens a grievous crime'. This letter was used by many priests to deny the sacraments of the Catholic Church to republicans in general. For members of the IRA who were Catholic, this denial placed their very souls in danger as they would face death perhaps without the sacraments and would thus die without the grace of God. There were priests who continued to minister to the republicans. They were identified by the Free State military authorities and subsequently 'transferred' from Ireland by their priors or diocesan bishops, mostly to the USA. A number of priests who ministered to the republicans were denied access to prisoners by the government of the Free State.

The general amnesty expired on 14 October 1922. The full measures of the Emergency Powers Act were introduced on 15 October 1922. The death penalty would be implemented officially seventy-seven times. The first to be executed were four young republicans with an average age of just nineteen; John Gaffney, Peter Cassidy, James Fischer and Richard Twohig were executed at Kilmainham Gaol on 17 November 1922. Erskine Childers followed them just a week later. Joe Spooner, Patrick Farrelly and John Murphy were captured after an attempt to blow up Oriel House. They faced a firing squad at dawn on 30 November 1922.[77] The IRA threatened the Free State government that if it did not cease the executions, then any of the forty-eight members of the Dáil who had voted for the Emergency Powers Act would be open to 'drastic measures'.[78] On 7 December Seán Hales, a National Army officer and TD for Cork Mid and West, was shot dead by the IRA in Dublin. Pádraic Ó'Máille, TD for Galway West, was wounded in the attack. The next morning, four republican prisoners, who had been captured after the surrender at the Four Courts, were taken out of their cells in Mountjoy Gaol and executed at dawn. They were chosen because they were republican leaders and each represented a province of Ireland: Liam Mellows (Connacht), Rory O'Connor (Leinster), Joe McKelvey (Ulster) and Dick Barrett (Munster).[79] The Civil War had entered its most bloody and vindictive stage.

For commanders of districts like Kerry, the possible execution of prisoners presented a terrible dilemma, one which General W. R. E. Murphy faced on 23 November 1922 when he presided at the trial of four men: Jeremiah O'Connor, Matty Maloney, Tom Devane and Con Casey. They had been captured at Farmers' Bridge on 1 November in a search for an IRA sniper. All four were taken with arms and ammunition. The men were found guilty and sentenced to death. The sentence was temporarily suspended.[80] The National Army Council stated to General Murphy that if the situation remained peaceful, then clemency would be granted. The indications from Murphy's reports are that the situation was looking very positive for the National Army at this point. Murphy, writing from his GHQ at Tralee, sent details of republican morale to Chief of Staff General Mulcahy:

> The ceaseless harrying that has been carried on has borne fruit. In North Kerry 13 armed Irregulars have carried out no operations for three weeks. M (Mossy) Nolan, second in command, is handing in his arms and signing the form of undertaking and giving guarantees ... In Mid Kerry – T[om] McEllistrum is now residing at home and states he is finished with the Irregulars. Another Irregular – Byrne (Creamery Manager) has approached us through his Parish Priest to be allowed to give up ... In Cahill's column – Tadg Brosnan (a very good chap in B. & T. war) has signified his intention of handing in his arms; In Dingle a prominent Irregular has approached the O.C. as regards handing over his arms. In H[umphrey] Murphy's column – there is discord. I heard that several of his men fired shots about Humphrey's hiding place – possibly to draw troops to it ... Rice we nearly had last week, and now that we have Kenmare his nest is broken up ...[81]

The temperance on the part of the National Army was not all due to General Murphy's effective campaigning. Humphrey Murphy, O/C Kerry No. 2 Brigade, let it be known that if the IRA prisoners were executed, then eight prominent Free State supporters would be shot in reprisal.[82] During the Christmas period a number of National Army troops were killed and injured. General Murphy called the condemned prisoners before him: 'they looked pale and I am sure they only expected the date of their death ... I told them that I was perhaps going to exceed my authority and was going to reprieve them. At first they did not seem to understand, but shortly did and seemed to appreciate what I had done.'[83]

General Murphy was 'ticked off by GHQ' for his action. He handed over Kerry Command to Major-General Paddy O'Daly in early January 1923 and assumed command as Director of Organisation and Training. Perhaps the most experienced senior commander of the National Army, he was 'put out to grass' writing manuals before being rescued by Kevin O'Higgins and appointed Commissioner of the DMP. Kerry Command now consisted of a garrison of 2,282 men located at twenty-one different barracks and outposts. O'Daly issued orders for the execution of James Daly, John Clifford, Michael Brosnan and James Hanlon on 20 January 1923.[84] They were the first of seven to be executed officially in Kerry in the last few months of the Civil War.

With the appointment of O'Daly as GOC Kerry Command, the National Army took a new direction in operations. Formal executions were now introduced. It had been something General Murphy had resisted. Extrajudicial killings by National Army officers increased and republican prisoners were now even more brutally treated. Colonel Dave Neligan, Michael Collins' former agent in the British secret service, directed interrogations. Volunteer Bill Bailey said of Neligan: 'He never put a thing on paper or never took part, that's how he always functioned ... possibly he never actually killed a man but no man killed without his sanction or without his approval.'[85] To say the interrogations were rigorous is putting it mildly. Men went insane from the beatings and being repeatedly clubbed unconscious with hammers and rifle butts. The methods employed in Dublin at Wellington Barracks and Oriel House by National Army intelligence and the CID respectively were also used in Kerry. Major-General O'Daly knew this went on as his office was above the interrogation room. Bill Bailey described the interrogations in his interview with Ernie O'Malley: 'Decent men never appeared live in Intelligence, would be sent out when this was going on. The bad eggs had been blooded through murder. Daly's office was on top and roars could be heard all over the barracks and that got everyone's goat, the roars. This went on for 5–6 months. November–February anyway.'[86]

Away from the interrogation centre in Tralee, the IRA proved difficult to overcome. On 5 March 1923, the National Army closed in on Kerry No. 3 flying column of thirty-six men at Gurrane, a high ridge with a pass to the Inny Valley. The scouts had not been vigilant and the National Army approached from four directions. A fierce firefight began and continued for most of the day. The house Commandant Dinny Daly was billeted in was completely surrounded and he was forced to surrender. The O'Connor family home nearby came under ferocious fire from the National Army as republican troops defended the position. The family put the mattresses up against the windows to keep out the firing. The children hid under the beds. In 2007, Paddy O'Connor related the story to his daughter Noreen O'Connor-O'Sullivan:

> The thatched roof kept out the bullets but the iron roof of the cow shed did not – a bullock and a donkey were killed in the cow shed.
>
> Dan Clifford was killed on the I.R.A. side and Tom & Kate O'Connor looked after his body and laid him out, for which his family were very grateful. Six IRA men were captured. The Free State had losses too – those killed included Thady Shea and [William] Healy from Valentia. Afterwards the Connor children used to find bullets up the hillside hidden under rocks – they would put them into a saucepan and put the saucepan over the fire and the bullets would explode one by one.[87]

A few days after the battle at Gurrane, the Dublin Guards arrived at Mountain Stage to bring in the captured prisoners to Killarney. Dinny Daly stood among the prisoners and later described how a Dublin Guards officer, Captain 'Tiny' Lyons, approached IRA officer Frank Grady: 'Lyons came up to him, "Frank is that you?" he said and shot him through the head twice with his Parabellum. His brains were scattered on my arm. They didn't know each other, but Lyons had heard of Grady. Magennis put a couple of bullets into him as he was wriggling on the ground.'[88]

On 6 March the IRA set a trap mine for an IO garrisoned at Castle-island National Army Barracks. Liam O'Doherty, 5th Battalion Engineers, Dublin Brigade, explained how a trap mine was constructed in his submission to the Bureau of Military History on 20 June 1952: the Dublin engineers used a standard landmine constructed by the munitions unit. The casing of the mine was ½-inch-thick cast steel with measurements of 8 inches in diameter by 16 inches in height with cast ends and a centre bolt. The explosive used by O'Doherty was called 'Cheddar' and contained DNT, potassium chlorate and castor oil. The primer was gelignite. The IRA Volunteers would then set the mine in a particular location, say on a road, covered with dirt and brushed to remove traces of the men who set it. The mine could then be detonated in a number of ways. One of the most common was using a command wire encased in lead-covered cable leading to an exploder or plunger. A large object like a boulder would be placed to cause the driver of a vehicle to move around it and into the path of the mine. Once the vehicle was over the mine it was detonated. The trap mine is used frequently by guerrilla armies fighting an army of greater force. In modern warfare it is referred to an improvised explosive device (IED). O'Doherty explained how the trap mine was set: 'For use as a trap mine it is inverted and Ring withdrawn weight of mine keeps lever in place, unless the mine is lifted or turned over.'[89]

The O'Connor family had fallen foul of the IRA. Old Pats O'Connor, the father, initially had a row with an IRA ASU who were in occupation of his field. O'Connor wished to bring in the hay but the IRA refused to move. Shortly afterwards the field was raided by National Army troops. The IRA suspected Old Pats O'Connor had tipped off the National Army about their presence in the field.[90] Old Pats was then kidnapped by them and threatened with death. His cattle were seized and £50 extorted from him as a fine. They also raided his home on 17 December 1922 and took two overcoats, a pony and trap, a pair of leather leggings, a bicycle, a substantial quantity of bacon and £36 10s in cash.[91] The old man's son, Paddy 'Pats' O'Connor, joined the National Army as an IO. He quickly organised the capture of local IRA officers. In retaliation, Humphrey Murphy, of Kerry No. 2 Brigade, ordered the killing of O'Connor. This was achieved by placing a trap mine in an IRA dugout at Knocknagoshel. When the National Army search party led by Paddy 'Pats' O'Connor arrived they went straight to the dugout and lifted the entrance. The trap mine detonated. The resulting explosion blew the men to pieces, killing Captains Michael Dunne and Edward Stapleton, Lieutenant Paddy 'Pats' O'Connor and Privates Laurence O'Connor and Michael Gallivan. Private Joseph O'Brien survived but was so severely wounded his legs had to be amputated below the knees.

The National Army could not accept the use of these weapons against their troops. But it was the losses incurred among these National Army officers, veterans of the War of Independence, which initiated a calculated response. After the devastating explosion causing the deaths and injuries at Knocknagoshel, Major-General O'Daly ordered that in future all obstacles, such as stone barricades and dumps, would be lifted by prisoners. This was to be the cover for three horrific episodes about to occur in Kerry. The senior officers of the Dublin Guards at Ballymullen Barracks set out to send a violent and bloody message to each of the IRA Kerry Brigade areas. They set out to kill, in a most calculated manner, prisoners already in their custody after they had already been savagely beaten and tortured.

Mines were prepared at Ballymullen Barracks in Tralee by Captains Eddie Flood and Captain Jim Clarke under the supervision of GOC Kerry Command, Major-General Paddy O'Daly. The actions were implemented by officers of the Kerry Command staff. The first atrocity was carried out at Ballyseedy, where nine republican prisoners of Kerry No. 1 Brigade, selected by Colonel Dave Neligan, were brought to Ballyseedy under the guise of clearing a barricade supposedly established by a republican flying column. Bill Bailey, a soldier in Ballymullen Barracks, recalled that the condemned men 'were given cigs going out and told they might as well have them for these were the last they were ever going to have'.[92]

The atrocity was carried out by Captain Ed Breslin and Lieutenant Joseph Murtagh. The men were tied together and then tied to the 'barricade', which was then detonated. Some of the prisoners were blown to pieces, others, though severely injured, were still alive. The National Army troops killed the survivors with machine guns and grenades. The prisoners' remains were collected and put into condemned men's coffins and returned to the relatives at 4 p.m. that afternoon. The Kerry Command Band played ragtime jazz as the remains were passed out through the main gate of Ballymullen Barracks. The relatives of the dead, distraught with grief and enraged at the disrespect shown to them, took the remains of their loved ones out of the wooden boxes supplied by Major-General Paddy O'Daly and placed them respectfully in their own caskets. They then smashed the National Army boxes to pieces.[93] Because the bodies of the dead had been so dismembered, the National Army officers did not notice that one man had been blown clear of the blast and had indeed survived.

Lieutenant Stephen Fuller, only two feet from the mine, was blown into the air. He landed in a nearby stream, covered in blood and minus most of his clothing, which he lost in the blast. Fuller crawled out of the stream and into a wood. When he reached Curran's farm, Mrs Curran took him in and did her best to treat his wounds. Kitty, her daughter, gave Fuller a cup of tea. He was given a sack of hay to lie down on in the corner. Word was then sent to John Joe Sheehy, O/C Kerry No. 1 Brigade. He organised for medical treatment to be given to Fuller. Major-General O'Daly, meanwhile, heard the stories circulating that Fuller had escaped the explosion. In an attempt to discredit the prisoner, O'Daly declared Stephen Fuller to be insane.[94]

A second atrocity soon followed in Killarney. In the early hours of 7 March, five Republican prisoners were taken from the cells at the National Army barracks at the Great Southern Hotel Killarney. The prisoners were already in a bad way and some of them, like Tadhg Coffey, had been merciless kicked, punched and beaten with a poker when captured.[95] The five prisoners were brought to Countess Bridge just outside the town and ordered to remove a small barricade of stones across the road. The men saw the soldiers back away and draw back the bolts of their rifles. Thinking they were about to be shot, the men jumped over the barricade to take cover. The mine was detonated by National Army officers and the prisoners were blown up. Grenades were thrown and rifle fire opened on those still alive. IRA Volunteers Jeremiah O'Donoghue and Tadhg Coffey attempted to crawl away. They had only gone a short way when O'Donoghue was hit and killed, leaving Coffey to make a break for freedom. This he achieved, after getting off the road and into a wood. Coffey eventually made it to a safe house, that of Jack Moynihan. He was soon under the protection of his comrades.[96]

On 12 March 1923 Commandant James J. Delaney and Lieutenant George Kavanagh arrived at Bahaghs, a large house operating as a National Army barracks and detention centre for republican prisoners. Lieutenant Kavanagh was an IO who worked closely with Colonel Dave Neligan. Formally, Kerry Command referred to these men as the 'Inspection Staff'. The republicans knew them as the 'Visiting Committee'. On arrival at Bahaghs, Commandant Delaney selected five republican prisoners and asked if they would like to go for a drive. The prisoners were then bundled into a tender with seven soldiers. They were taken a short distance down the road towards Cahersiveen and told to get out and clear an obstruction on the road left by an IRA flying column. The pattern was identical to the previous events at Ballyseedy and Countess Bridge, only this time they would make sure no one would escape alive. The prisoners were first shot in the legs and then blown up by the mine. There were no survivors.

Thus, over the course of six days, Paddy O'Daly had ordered three atrocities, each carried out in the three independent IRA Kerry Brigade areas. The message was savage, as was the manner in which the prisoners were treated before, during and after their deaths. These terrible few days in Kerry had resulted in the deaths of twenty-two men. The families, comrades and communities were grief-stricken. It was not over, either. On 23 March, Dan Murphy, the blacksmith in whose forge the IRA had constructed the casing for the Knocknagoshel trap mine, was taken from his home by Commandants Maurice Culhane, William McCauliffe and Lieutenant George Gaffney and shot dead at the same mine crater where Lieutenant Patrick O'Connor had been killed.[97] The officers put twenty-one rounds into his body.[98]

The Chief of Staff of the National Army and Minister for Defence, General Richard Mulcahy, was now under pressure to give a proper explanation of events in Kerry. A court of inquiry was instituted, of which the members were General Eamon Price, GHQ Portobello Barracks, Major-General Paddy O'Daly as President, and Colonel J. McGuinness, Staff Officer Kerry Command. The inquiry began on 7 April and found that the barricades had been planted as trap mines by the IRA. The attempted removal of barricades by 'civilians' had triggered the mines and caused their deaths and some injuries to members of the National Army. On 17 April Mulcahy addressed the Dáil with the findings. He also read of the mine explosions at Bahaghs and at Knocknagoshel along with the order issued by O'Daly on the removal of barricades.[99] In Kerry, Cumann na mBan were busy printing the stories circulating in the district about what really happened at Ballyseedy, Countess Bridge and Bahaghs. The republican accounts appeared in their paper, *The Invincible*. Walls in Tralee were painted with slogans which read 'Don't join Daly's murder gang.' The women were arrested and the National Army reports officers wrote: 'These ladies were prominent in the circulation of mean, and debased propaganda, and were just given enough rope to hang themselves. Their arrest came as a great surprise to them.'[100]

In April, Commandant Dave Neligan was reappointed to duties in Dublin. He was given a fine send-off from Killarney. 'Long Dave', as he was called in the Dublin Guards, was very popular. At a dinner given in his honour, he was given formal recognition for all he had done to 'enforce the will of the people' in Kerry. Paddy O'Daly presented him with a gold watch and chain on behalf of the officers.[101] The celebrations did not prevent O'Daly from obtaining sanction from General Mulcahy to carry out three more official executions by the Dublin Guards in Kerry. On Monday 23 April 1923, Richard Hatheway, James McEnery and Edward Greaney were shot at dawn by firing squad. They had fought at the battle of Clashmealcon Caves with republican column Commander Tim 'Aero' Lyons and Volunteer James McGrath on 16 April. In the battle, which lasted for three days, Lyons and his men were trapped in

Jessie MacCarthy courageously went to her sister's aid when she was assaulted by three Free State officers on the night of 1–2 June 1923 in Kenmare, County Kerry. (Courtesy Patricia Healy)

Florence MacCarthy's wedding in 1924. In the front row are Jessie MacCarthy (far left) and Florence (centre). (Courtesy Patricia Healy)

caves at the bottom of a cliff. Lyons eventually agreed to surrender. As he climbed a rope lowered by the National Army above, it was cut and he fell. As he lay dying below, he was used as target practice by the Dublin Guards.[102] Volunteers Tommy McGrath and Patrick O'Shea drowned attempting to find an escape route. Their bodies were never recovered. Hatheway, McEnery, Greaney and James McGrath were taken prisoner and 'savagely beaten' both en route to and at Ballymullen Barracks.[103] The National Army lost one officer (Lieutenant Henry Pearson) and a soldier (Volunteer James O'Neill).[104] Both were killed instantly as they attempted to clear the caves.[105] James McGrath was held prisoner for a number of weeks and released after the execution of the others.

The Civil War came to an end with the death of the IRA chief of staff, Liam Lynch, on 11 April 1923. He was shot and mortally wounded by National Army troops in the Knockmealdown Mountains, County Tipperary. His replacement, Frank Aiken, issued an order for the IRA to cease operations on 27 April 1923. The republicans simply buried their weapons in the hills and walked away. The survivors of the battle of the Clashmealcon Caves had been executed after Aiken's order. The Dublin Guards, the men of the Dublin ASU, were determined to extract every last ounce of blood from their enemy. The National Army continued their round-ups, raids and shootings beyond the end of the Civil War and numbers of people lost their lives needlessly. Paddy O'Daly had escaped without any official sanction for those murdered in the triple mine explosions in Kerry. At least eight and possibly ten officers of the National Army's Kerry Command are linked with, if not the actual perpetrators of, extrajudicial killings during the Civil War. Almost all of these killings took place under O'Daly's command. In this he was completely supported by General Richard Mulcahy, who had ignored the concerns of his own cabinet ministers and other politicians in the Dáil. O'Daly must have thought he was invincible. He had survived 1916, the War of Independence and the Civil War. Events, however, have a strange way of turning out. A Captain Niall Harrington had written to Minister Kevin O'Higgins informing him of what had happened in Kerry. Even though O'Daly was cleared, his desire to take revenge on a junior officer led to a shocking assault on two women and a scandal that rocked the Irish Free State.

Captain Harrington and his friend Lieutenant Michael Higgins had begun to call on sisters Florence and Jessie MacCarthy, daughters of Dr

Randal MacCarthy, at their home in Kenmare. The ladies were then invited by Major-General O'Daly to the Kerry Command dance. They declined the invitation with the remark, 'We will not have anything to do with murderers'.[106] Harrington and his friend were then forbidden from calling on the sisters on the strict orders of O'Daly. On the night of 2 June 1923, three officers of the National Army appeared at the MacCarthy home. One of the men wore goggles and the other two had their faces covered with scarves. Florence was dragged out of the front door screaming. Her sister Jessie, hearing her sister in distress, ran to her rescue. Jessie was then dragged down the garden by two of the officers and both women were assaulted. The officers then rubbed heavy axle grease into the womens' hair, which would cause their hair to fall out in clumps. Ella MacCarthy, Florence and Jessie's mother, grabbed a police whistle in the house and blew it repeatedly. This startled the assailants and they hurriedly departed the scene. The officers were later identified as Captain Edward Flood, 2 I/C 27th Infantry Battalion and Captain James Clarke, A Company 27th Infantry Battalion. The GOC of Kerry Command, Paddy O'Daly, was also identified, due to a witness statement given by a Volunteer on duty at the barrack gate who saw him leave with the other two officers shortly before the attack on the MacCarthy home.

Under pressure to explain the stories circulating in Kerry, Dublin and as far as London, the Free State government had to be seen to take some form of action. The way in which the Dublin Guards and National Army GHQ dealt with the Kenmare scandal followed the same procedural cover-up used in the aftermath of the Ballyseedy atrocity. A court of inquiry was held in which the National Army packed the board with their own carefully selected officers who could be relied upon to come up with the 'correct' findings. This suited the Minister of Defence Richard Mulcahy at the time. He quoted liberally from the whitewashed findings when addressing the Dáil. Eventually, reports of the atrocities would end up on the desk of the President of the Executive Council of the Irish Free State, William T. Cosgrave. In one such report, the transcript of the court of the inquiry into the mine atrocity at Bahaghs was attached with the inconsistencies in the statements of Commandant James J. Delaney and other National Army witnesses pointed out. The report was part of claims submitted by the relatives of those murdered in the mine explosions. While the relatives of the National Army troops killed in the Knocknagoshel received compensation under the 1924 Military Pensions Act, the relatives of the prisoners murdered in the three mine explosions received nothing. The reply of W. T. Cosgrave, Kevin O'Higgins and indeed the collective response of the Free State Executive Council was that, as the men were deemed to have taken up arms against the state, the relatives were thus entitled to no compensation.[107] The evidence upon which the Executive Council based its decision was the court of inquiry with Paddy O'Daly as president. The relatives of the victims of the atrocities would have to wait until de Valera and Fianna Fáil introduced the 1934 Military Pensions Act to receive compensation due to them.

At the time of the mine explosions, Richard Mulcahy stated from the court of inquiry report into Ballyseedy that there was no ill treatment of prisoners and that such allegations contained in 'Irregular' propaganda were untrue. He added that 'undue attention should not be paid to charges against the Army, based on statements contained in such propaganda'. In 1923 and 1924, republican and self-professed fanatic Dorothy Macardle[108] carried out research on the ground in Kerry. She spoke to local people and in particular to eyewitnesses of the horrors that occurred. Her home in Dublin was raided while she was writing the results of her work. Tadhg Coffey, the sole survivor of the explosion at Countess Bridge, who was sheltering there, had to be got out of the country fast. Countess Markievicz had information that the CID would kill him if they caught him. Republicans managed to get Coffey to Canada for a while until things calmed down.[109] While such accounts of events in Kerry were declared to be 'Irregular Propaganda' in 1923 and 1924, they are consistent with the accounts of two National Army personnel in Kerry at the time, William Bailey and Niall Harrington. Their accounts were written down and kept secret until revealed in the past twenty years.

These accounts are confirmed as accurate by a third one, written to the Chief of Staff Peadar McMahon on 7 August 1923 by Director of Intelligence, National Army, Major-General James Hogan. The date on this account is one month before McMahon visited Kerry Command to review the Dublin Guards. Hogan was worried about discontent within the National Army but went on to discuss the situation in Kerry Command. Hogan described the situation in Kerry Command as a 'regular inferno seething with suspicion and unrest'.[110] Hogan cautioned McMahon, saying this issue was a test for the new nation. While Hogan recognised the individuals in the Kenmare case had served the State with signal honours, he called for a full investigation without concealment or extenuating circumstances.[111] If the state did not act against those currently encouraging insubordination within the National Army a crisis would be forthcoming.

Meanwhile, Joe Leonard travelled to Dublin to canvass GHQ officers on Paddy O'Daly's behalf. It must have paid off, as Cahir Davitt was about to discover when he met with General Richard Mulcahy to discuss the scandal. Gearóid Ó'Sullivan, adjutant general of the National Army, received a Garda Síochána report about the assault on the MacCarthy sisters in June 1923. The witness statement given by Davitt to the Bureau of Military History on 9 January 1959 has had the name of Paddy O'Daly removed, but it is clear from the other sources listed here to whom Davitt is referring in detail. Mulcahy was concerned about Paddy O'Daly's 'distinguished and honourable military and national record' and said that it would be deplorable if he were put to the necessity of defending himself on such a charge before a court martial. Mulcahy had spoken with O'Daly: 'straight as man to man whether he had been concerned in the assault on the Misses McCarthy; and that [name blanked] had assured him, on his word of honour, that he had not.'[112]

Davitt suggested the matter be sent to Attorney General Hugh Kennedy for advice. A lengthy reply came back to the cabinet from Kennedy, in which he sought to assassinate the character of the MacCarthy women by first addressing their social standing as 'the type of Catholic bourgeoisie which existed in Irish country towns and villages under the British regime'.[113] Kennedy went on to explore bias and 'intense antagonism' on the part of the MacCarthys towards O'Daly and others who spoke with a Dublin accent. He said: 'Officers of the National Army have been in many cases the butt for the people of this kind and especially the broad Boric of Dublin has seemed a vulgarity after the accents of the British Military and Auxiliaries.'[114] Kennedy also questioned the veracity of the story, the injuries and apparent lack of a medical examination, stating that the claims were based on 'flimsy evidence'. One wonders was Hugh Kennedy aware or had he conveniently forgotten that Randal MacCarthy, the women's father, was a doctor. It appears from the document submitted by Kennedy that he was providing a defence of Major-General O'Daly and by default the Irish Free State.[115] Cahir Davitt later recalled that Kevin O'Higgins had some very bitter things to say about Hugh Kennedy and his opinion.[116] What is certain is that Hugh Kennedy had the benefit of the Protection Corps of the CID and was living in Dublin and not,

Kerry Command, National Army, photographed on Fenit pier. (L–r): Col. Michael Bishop, Capt. Kelly, Col. John Dunne, Senator William O'Sullivan, Major-General Paddy O'Daly (GOC Kerry Command), Col. Dave Neligan, General Seán McMahon (chief of staff), Major-General Seán Quinn, Major-General Peadar McMahon (GOC Curragh Command), Col. Pádraic O'Connor, Col. Joseph Maginnis. Featured in *An t-Óglach*, 6 October 1923. (Courtesy the Military Archives)

as were the MacCarthy family, in a martial law area under the control of a senior National Army officer with a lengthy track record of killing and vengeance. The family were in peril for their lives. The sole member of the Free State government who tried to have someone brought to justice was Kevin O'Higgins. He was prevented by the legal advice offered to W. T. Cosgrave by the Attorney General. O'Higgins was also stonewalled by General Mulcahy, who ignored the legal advice of Cahir Davitt, who called for O'Daly to be court-martialled.

A second court of inquiry into the case found that Captain Flood, Captain Clarke and General O'Daly were the perpetrators. The president of the court also found that Commandant Hancock, O/C 27th Infantry Battalion, knew of and connived in the raid on the MacCarthys. He also noted that Superintendent Hannigan, the Civic Guard (police force) refused to attend, as did the State Solicitor for Kerry, Mr Liston. No charge was ever brought against O'Daly for his involvement.

The ultimate question regarding the conduct of the National Army in Kerry during the Civil War is: did it have to be this way? The answer has to be a resounding no. General W. R. E. Murphy, GOC Kerry Command August–December 1922, demonstrated a different way of approaching the difficulties of fighting a war against IRA guerrilla units. Yes, there were extrajudicial killings carried out by officers under his command but nothing in comparison to the campaign of terror unleashed from January 1923. On 23 September 1923, 1,000 troops of the National Army's Kerry Command paraded before the Chief of Staff General Peadar McMahon. The troops on parade were under the command of Colonels Bishop, Brophy and Leonard. For the Chief of Staff the occasion marked the end of the Civil War in Kerry and was a demonstration of support for Paddy O'Daly, former commander of Michael Collins' Squad. Addressing the troops, General McMahon said, 'the spirit of the Army to-day was the same spirit that brought them through the fight for freedom, and it made it possible to stamp out one of the most treacherous mutinies that ever threatened the Army or life of the nation'.[117] The top brass of Kerry Command accompanied McMahon to Fenit for a group photograph to commemorate a year since the National Army landings in Kerry. Some old friends also turned up to commemorate the event, including Colonel Dave Neligan, who travelled from Dublin to join his former comrades. Tyranny is a relative term and it depends on which side of a divide you stand. What occurred in Kerry was unparalleled during the Civil War. The formal executions under the Emergency Powers Act, the individual extrajudicial killings, the mine atrocities at Ballyseedy, Countess Bridge and Bahaghs were an appalling record for the National Army. This does not take into account the savage interrogations and the assault on two young women in Kenmare with the involvement of the GOC of Kerry Command. As the senior officers of Kerry Command stood with the Chief of Staff on Fenit pier in September 1923 it was intended as a celebration of victory. With the passage of time, it has become a photograph of those responsible for grave misconduct, torture and murder.

What the Kenmare case in particular highlights is the influence of senior officers of the Dublin Guards and their commander Paddy O'Daly. The case also demonstrates the fear of addressing the truth in a state founded upon the belief in its own propaganda. That one of its most highly respected officers, in charge of one of its most highly respected commands, would be disgraced was unthinkable for the cabinet and many of the GHQ officers. But Ireland as a Free State was changing as peace was slowly restored. The methods of intimidation and bloodshed surely had no place in a democratic society. Florence and Jessie MacCarthy were two very courageous women who stood up against men who had killed others in cold blood for revenge. It is to the shame of the Irish Free State Executive Council that it lacked the same courage as the MacCarthy women in confronting those guilty of assault, torture and murder. With the Civil War over, those who had engaged in terrible bloodshed would have to live with themselves and the memory of their deeds. For some it made no difference and they lived as before, but for others the years of the Irish Revolution cast a dark shadow from which there was little escape.

8

'On the One Road'

Living with the 'Peace'

The War of Independence and the Civil War were over, but battles continued to be fought in many different forms, both the political and the personal. In the political battles, the continuously shifting sands over the decades led to more splits, division and rancour. At the same time, however, the focus shifted to the needs of the Irish state and the needs of the people. Economic development concentrated on the modernisation of farming and industry, and the provision of social housing. The personal battles concerned the veterans themselves, their families and their friends, and the physical and psychological scars. Some injuries healed, others did not and the veterans somehow managed to live with them. But some injuries were just too great.

The last few months of 1923 saw the National Army preparing to stand down from its war footing. Thousands of soldiers would be 'demobbed' as the Free State government began to address rebuilding the country after years of war. The Free State had much of its budget invested in financing the National Army's victory in the Civil War and was anxious to reallocate such valuable finances. President Cosgrave still feared the republican forces would return to military action and so refused to release an approximate 11,316 republican prisoners, 250 of whom were women, held in gaols and camps throughout the Free State.[1] A new Public Safety Act introduced on 16 January 1924 had given the Free State government the power to imprison people without trial.[2] After a republican hunger strike and protests from the public supported by the Catholic Church, the prisoners were gradually released. De Valera, who had been arrested in Ennis on 15 August 1923, was the last prisoner released from Kilmainham Gaol on 16 July 1924. As republicans returned home from the prisons the future for them was uncertain. Thousands would emigrate, never to return. Those who remained would look to de Valera to give them some form of hope and a place in the new Irish Free State.

In early 1924 President Cosgrave pressed ahead with the demobilisation of the army. This process also required a considerable reorganisation of the National Army, which in turn created considerable dissatisfaction among veterans who had served in 1916 and in the War of Independence. These veterans included Liam Tobin, Charlie Dalton and Tom Cullen, who had served with Michael Collins, Dick McKee and Peadar Clancy. Tobin formed an organisation called the IRA Organisation. Through this organisation Tobin and his comrades aimed at putting pressure on the National Army Command and the Free State government to pursue the aims of Michael Collins to secure 'completion of the national work',[3] a united Ireland as a republic.

The issue of the republic and the direction the Free State was taking had also been addressed by Thomas Markham as early as 1922. Markham, an agent installed by Michael Collins in Dublin Castle during the truce, had already found the informers' files in the Castle. He described his findings as 'sensational' and reported them to Collins. The commander-in-chief agreed with Markham 'that the utmost care and confidence should be exercised with respect to these documents – otherwise guns might continue to click for many a year'.[4] After Collins' death, Markham wrote to Archbishop Byrne of Dublin on 10 October 1922, concerned at the placement of Freemasons at the heart of the new Free State civil service. These appointments were being made by a senior civil servant newly arrived from London who was closely connected with the British government. He had formerly been private secretary to Sir Hamar Greenwood and was in contact with the British Minister for War, Sir Winston Churchill. It was Markham's view, after conversations with Andy Cope, that the British government was 'manoeuvring to the end of continuing the fratricidal strife until Ireland becomes absolutely dependent financially on Britain; and, at the same time is aiming at the development of Irish governmental systems along Freemason lines ... Both sides [Free State and republican] are being supplied with war material from Britain.'[5] It is interesting to note that in 1928 the Dublin archdiocese estimated the number of Freemason lodges in the Dublin area, including the Grand Master's Lodge, to be seventy-eight, the highest in the country.[6] As Markham was working alone and simply communicating his views to the Catholic Archbishop of

Dublin, there was little he could do to influence the direction taken by the civil service of the new Irish Free State. Liam Tobin and his comrades in the IRA Organisation presented a much more serious threat to the Irish Free State as they were senior officers of the National Army.

Liam Tobin had known Michael Collins even better than his own family. As deputy of IRA intelligence directly under Collins, Tobin knew the intentions of his commander-in-chief and the justification he offered for the assassinations and military actions carried out in the War of Independence and early Civil War. He knew Collins' political and military mind, a man who had, more than any other person, influenced the direction the Irish republic had taken since 1916. Of this Tobin wrote:

> By the Treaty which he [Collins] wrung from the British he won for Ireland the right and the power to achieve full freedom. With him, we accepted the Treaty on that basis, and we accepted the responsibility laid upon us to use it for that purpose ... But after the death of our Commander-in-Chief, we soon became painfully aware that those who succeeded him had not his outlook. We saw a state of things initiated and developed which we believed would prejudice and make impossible the ideal he had at heart, an ideal which we, his comrades, who are left, consider ourselves pledged to fulfill.[7]

Tobin believed that the unity of Ireland and full independence was yet to be accomplished. This was not his only concern. A considerable concern of his and his IRA comrades was the restructuring of the National Army. The Civil War National Army stood at 60,000 men. This could not continue to be financed in a state which had suffered millions of pounds of damage through personal injury claims and infrastructural destruction during the previous five years. The National Army was to be reorganised on a much smaller but more professional scale. Thousands of men were demobilised, among them soldiers who had fought the War of Independence. In their place the army retained ex-British officers and men who had fought against them in the War of Independence and with them in the Civil War. Tobin even claimed that former British secret service agents, whom he knew only too well, were recruited by the National Army.[8] He claimed bitterly that, based on the criteria currently employed for recruitment in the National Army, Michael Collins himself would not have secured a place.[9] When former IRA officers at the Curragh were presented with their National

Army demobilisation papers, they refused to accept them. The officers were court-martialled and discharged but reinstated on a technicality.[10] The Curragh, it would appear, had a particular penchant for mutiny, having witnessed a British, Civic Guard[11] and National Army revolt. However accurate Tobin's claims and those of the IRA Organisation may have been, there was little appetite in the country for further war and killing. The Free State government, allied with those in the National Army who secretly had by now had more than enough of the actions of the CID, National Army intelligence and units like the Dublin Guards, decided it was time to remove them from the army and from the offices of government.

As president of the IRA Organisation, Tobin issued an ultimatum to the Free State government on 6 March demanding that Cosgrave 'secure and maintain a Republican form of government'.[12] Cosgrave spoke in the Dáil on 11 March declaring Tobin's ultimatum to be 'a challenge which no Government could ignore without violating the trust conferred upon it'.[13] Arrests and resignations of IRA Organisation members followed and by the end of March the 'mutiny' was over. The majority of the officers were dismissed, although officially permitted to 'resign' in order to secure a military service pension. A subsequent committee of inquiry, established by President Cosgrave, found that senior National Army officers had reconvened the IRB with the intention of taking control of Liam Tobin's organisation. This move had actually caused the IRA Organisation to mutiny.[14] The inquiry also referred to the Kenmare case. General Richard Mulcahy accepted full responsibility for the decision to drop the Kenmare case.[15] The committee also found that the mutinous officers had been a problem to Michael Collins even before the Civil War.[16]

The final end to any hope of the realisation of an all-Ireland republic ended with the failure of the Boundary Commission to deliver even one inch of Northern Ireland to the Irish Free State. The Boundary Commission was established under the terms of Article 12 of the Anglo-Irish Treaty of 1921. Its aim was to examine the border areas of Northern Ireland and the Irish Free State with a possibility of changes taking into account the wishes of local inhabitants as well as economic and geographic conditions.[17] The findings of the Commission were 'leaked' in *The Morning Post* of 7 November 1924. The leaked findings suggested no territory from Northern Ireland, save for small strips in Fermanagh and Armagh, would be ceded to the Free State. On the contrary, it was thought land in east Donegal would be transferred to Northern Ireland. Éoin MacNeill, the Free State representative on the

Boundary Commission, resigned on 21 November. Three days later he resigned as Minister for Education in the Irish Free State.[18] In 1924–25, the failure of the Boundary Commission copper-fastened partition. Historian Robert Key wrote of the Anglo-Irish Treaty of 1921 that 'Englishmen had let themselves think that they had solved the Irish question ... but it had solved the problem for England, not for Ireland.'[19]

As President Cosgrave managed to hold the Irish Free State together in a period of great uncertainty, so too the National Army received a newly appointed chief of staff, General Seán McMahon, who calmed the crisis for men-at-arms. The National Army, over time, became known as 'The Army' and was highly respected as such by the Irish people. The Army, learning the lessons of the Civil War, concentrated on developing various corps required for an effective force. Artillery, signals, transport, medical, engineers, music, equitation corps and schools were all developed. They were supported by an educational army college. There was special emphasis on sport and competition in every possible field of endeavour. As chief of staff, General Seán McMahon directed the Army through this unsettled period with great skill. He also established the presence of the Irish Army on the international stage, taking a delegation of officers and men to honour the Tomb of the Unknown Soldier at the Arc de Triomphe in Paris. The inscription on the wreath read:

AU SOLDAT INCONNU:
L'ARMÉE IRLANDAISE,
30 JUILLET, 1923.[20]

The delegation also visited a number of French military colleges with particular interest shown by the visitors 'into the larger questions of Army Organisation and General Staff work.'[21] The Army were back in Paris the following year as their boxers attended the summer Olympic Games. There was controversy in the semi-finals when Sergeant Dwyer from Tipperary was the victim of some dirty tactics on the part of the Argentinian boxer Mendez whose use of the head gave the Irishman a split brow. Sergeant Dwyer fought on despite his injury, much to the admiration of the spectators. The official from the American team said: 'Dwyer has been adjudged the loser, whilst everyone knows that he is the virtual champion. Ill luck was certainly his portion. The Argentinian should have been disqualified'.[22]

Thomas Sweeney Newell in 1959
when he was sixty-five years
of age, a year before he died.
(Courtesy Terry & Éamon Newell)

With the Army now demobilising thousands of men, the question of pensions arose. An important reality for veterans, their families and the families of those killed during the 1916–24 period was the introduction by the Free State Government of a military pension under the terms of the Army Pensions Acts 1923 and 1927. De Valera's Fianna Fáil government introduced a further Army Pensions Act in 1932. Subsequent Acts, to provide pensions for disabled veterans, those incapable of self-support, dependent members of family and widows were introduced in Pensions Acts of 1941, 1943, 1946 and 1953.[23] The Military Service Pensions Collection, a great deal of which is available on the Military Archives website, is 'the single most important archival collection relating to Ireland's revolutionary period'.[24] Within the pension application files are accounts of great heroism and dedication to the cause of Ireland's independence. Also in the files are harrowing accounts of action in the War of Independence and Civil War. The accounts present the experiences of men, women and their families as they sought to live their lives in an independent Ireland. Obtaining a pension was not always easy. Medical examinations were frequently required to assess claims. James Dempsey, E Company 2nd Battalion and Dublin Guards, was one such case. He was shot in the left wrist in 1916 (bullet extracted), was blown up and

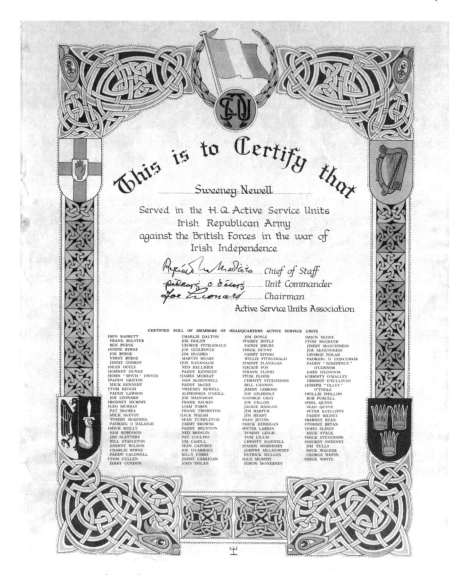

The service certificate for Thomas Sweeney Newell, IRA GHQ Active Service Unit, Dublin. Signed by former Chief of Staff Richard Mulcahy, former Squad Commander Paddy O'Daly and Chairman of Active Service Units Association Joe Leonard. (Courtesy Terry & Éamon Newell)

suffered 'shell shock' in the Four Courts explosion in 1922, lost an eye (bullet extracted) and was captured in action against the IRA in Kerry in 1922. The military doctor examining Dempsey for his pension application noted: 'General condition Good. Is obviously a hypochondriac.'[25]

Support for some veterans began just after the War of Independence. At the end of 1921 Lily Mernin was dismissed by the British from her

post as a shorthand typist at Dublin Castle. Soon afterwards she suffered a
nervous breakdown, due to the perpetual strain caused by the risks she had
taken in obtaining intelligence and getting it to the IRA. Michael Collins
acted promptly and gave Lily the money for a holiday out of Ireland.[26]
She returned in June 1922 and immediately began work as a typist for
the CID at Oriel House and also at Eastern Command National Army
intelligence HQ. Her sister, May, also worked as a typist at the CID. With
the closure of the CID at the end of the Civil War, Lily was employed at
National Army GHQ at Parkgate, Dublin. In the early years she was only
employed on a part-time basis. By special order of the Executive Council
of the Irish Free State she received permanent employment status in view
of her previous national service.[27] Frank Saurin, who had become her IRA
intelligence contact in 1920, wrote in support of her pension application:
'The undersigned was in personal touch with Miss Mernin for most of the
years mentioned, and cannot speak too highly of her efficiency in carrying
out this invaluable work.'[28]

Saurin, who in the Civil War was promoted to Colonel Commandant
Director of Intelligence Eastern Command in 1924, became director of
employment in the Irish Hospital Sweeps in October 1936.

As the War of Independence concluded, there were numbers of IRA
personnel, broken in body and mind, in hospital and also in asylums in
Britain. Michael Collins, with great attention to their needs, sought
them out. Those in the asylums he had moved to Ireland so that family
members could be close to them. Those in hospital were also cared for.
Thomas Sweeney Newell, who had been shot a number of times by Igoe's
unit, languished with insufficient medical care at King George V Hospital.
Michael Collins had Newell moved to the Mater Hospital, to undergo
a series of operations to restore him to good health. Sweeney Newell
underwent eleven operations over the years as a result of his injuries (his
hip was damaged when he was shot by the Igoe Gang). He eventually left
hospital in May 1922 and returned to Castlegar, County Galway, only to
find his house had been burned down by the Black and Tans and his family
were now living in a barn.

Sweeney Newell did some intelligence work for Commandant Duggan
in Galway but his health began to deteriorate, necessitating a return to
the Mater Hospital in Dublin. After more medical treatment he found
convalescent rest in Marlborough Hall, an army convalescent home in
Dublin, until 1924.[29] He was fitted with a special shoe to enable him to

walk. On his return to Galway he took up his old trade as a blacksmith and metalworker. He worked at Renmore Barracks for the Army and later for Galway County Council. Perhaps demonstrating fortitude and belief in a brighter future, he married Winifred Grogan in 1933. Together they raised a family and put their four children through college. He never spoke about his experiences in the War of Independence to his children. To them he was always just 'Dad'.[30]

Michael Collins maintained a personal interest in all the veterans who were invalided out of the conflict. He maintained this contact up to the time of his death. Mick McDonnell, the O/C of the first Dublin Brigade Service Unit in 1920, wrote very openly of how the war had affected him when he applied for his pension: 'during my active service I was under very heavy strain, terrible excitement, and had a great deal of worry'. He attributed his present state of health to the strain he had been under during the War of Independence.

McDonnell was eventually certified as having tuberculosis but the symptoms described appear to be associated with what is now called post-traumatic stress disorder. Paddy O'Daly wrote of McDonnell, 'The applicant carried out more jobs in Dublin during the Black and Tans regime than any man living. His health was completely broken down in 1920 owing to [being] constantly out day and night on Volunteer work.'[31] In support of McDonnell's application, Gearóid O'Sullivan TD wrote:

> I consider the case of Michael McDonnell unique in that he insisted on remaining an active service even when his health had begun to fail. The number of suitable persons available for duties of the nature he carried out was naturally small at the time, with the result that McDonnell's health became more and more impaired as time went on. I have no hesitation in stating that his is a case, the type for which the army pensions act 23-27 was passed.[32]

In early 1921, Collins sent McDonnell, or 'Mick Mac' as the Dublin Brigade called him, out of Ireland to recover his health. Collins knew he would not recover. Mick McDonnell left for England with Eileen O'Loughlin. The pair were married on 18 February 1921 at St Edward's Church at Rusholme, Manchester. Afterwards they travelled to California in the USA where their first child, Eileen Brigid, was born on 4 October 1921. In 1922, Michael Collins wrote to 'Mick

Mac' in California with great consideration and support for his former operational commander:

RIALTAS SEALADACH NA HÉIREANN
(Irish Provisional Government)
BAILE ÁTHA CLIATH
12 Bealthaine [*sic*], 1922.

Mr. Michael McDonnell,
212 Johnson Avenue,
Los Gatos,
Santa Clara Co.
CALIFORNIA.

Dear Mick,
I was very glad to get your letter of 26th April and to know your address, and that you are getting on fair enough. I wire you to-day as follows:–

"INSTEAD OF WRITING TO WARD AT FOUR HUNDRED AND ELEVEN FIFTH AVENUE WRITE TO HEALY SAME ADDRESS. "EXPLAIN CASE AND SAY I AM WRITING ADVICE."

This will make matters all right with for present. Our chief man in charge of financial matters in U.S.A. is Professor Smiddy. Healy, who used be in O'Brien Hishon's office in O'Connell Street here has taken Ward's place. There was no necessity for Ward to write you as he did, he could merely have passed on the letter to his successor, and the thing would have been all right so far as you were concerned. There is no necessity for any arrangement in Philadelphia.

Dan Breen is back. I have seen him several times lately. He is in quite good form and pretty much the same as he was before the various wounds.

Tom Keogh, Ennis and all the old bunch are in good form. I believe Slattery is going to be made a T.D. for Clare, and it is likely that Tom Ennis may be one for Dublin City. The thing that would surprise you most now is all the fellows who were looking for a fight. I wish you were here to see some of them and to hear their professions about dying in the last ditch. You can imagine the expressions made to some of them by the Old Guard.

Don't worry about the work part of it. Keep on at the fruit and the sun until you are all right.

> With every best wishes
> As always,
> (Signed) Miceal[33]

A second child, a boy, was born to Michael and Eileen on 20 December 1922 whom they named Michael Collins McDonnell in honour of his father and of the 'Big Fella'. The marriage did not last and ended in divorce.[34] McDonnell lived on at Los Gatos in California, returning to Ireland occasionally. In 1948 he returned to Ireland for the last time on the occasion of a reunion of his old comrades. Present were: Vinnie Byrne, Piaras Béaslaí, Frank Thornton, Jim Slattery, Frank Bolster, Ben Byrne, Frank Saurin, Joe Guilfoyle, Pat McCrea, Barney McMahon, Charlie Dalton, Joe Leonard, Seán Ó'Tuama and Jimmy Shiels.[35] McDonnell signed and dated his contribution to the Bureau of Military History on 29 March 1949.[36] Considering the importance of his involvement, the statement is short, just seven pages. But considering the nature of the actions he carried out it is likely he could not write more. The task of writing on events the Squad had long tried to forget must have brought a lot of incidents back into his mind. On 12 October 1950, Charlie Dalton signed off on his witness statement to the Bureau. He included a few pages relating to events concerning 'Mick Mac' and the operations of the Squad. McDonnell had passed away on 15 July and Dalton was anxious to include incidents and events that could no longer be told by the former IRA operations unit commander.[37]

Michael McDonnell was lucky. In spite of ill health, he lived a good thirty years after the events that defined his generation. Others did not fare so well and Paddy Flanagan, O/C of the Dublin Brigade ASU and leader of the attack at 28 Upper Pembroke Street, was one of them. He lived at 'Sunnyside', Oakley Road, Ranelagh with his wife, Evelyn (née O'Brien), and their five children. Evelyn was a member of Cumann na mBan and served with the Inghinidhe Branch attached to the 3rd Battalion Dublin Brigade. She had carried arms for the 3rd Battalion and a list of descriptions of eight British secret service officers who were to be assassinated on

Bloody Sunday. Her husband died of a cerebral haemorrhage on 10 February 1935 at Farnham House Asylum, Finglas. A carpenter by trade, he was only thirty-nine years old.

His wife and family were left in very difficult financial circumstances, receiving only £2/5- per week from the White Cross fund. Evelyn wrote to de Valera, who had been Paddy's O/C in Boland's Mill in 1916, saying that her husband had 'devoted himself so strenuously to the struggle for independence that the hardships he endured were, according to medical opinion, the direct cause of his early death'. His children at the time of his death ranged from eighteen months to twelve years of age. In the letter to de Valera, Evelyn wrote about her two young children, one of whom was sent to Peamount, a sanitorium for those suffering from TB. She was appealing for a widow's pension, which had not yet been enacted in 1937. Her application for a widow's pension states that the executions at Pembroke Street on Bloody Sunday, the execution of a wounded man taken out of Jervis Street Hospital and the constant active service as a commanding officer 'undermined his [Paddy's] nervous system'.[38]

Flanagan was first treated at St Patrick's Hospital. He was then moved to Farnham in Finglas in August 1934, where he died seventh months later. Paddy Flanagan was undoubtedly suffering from post-traumatic stress disorder. His wife reported that the Civil War seemed to affect him most of all. He had been captured by the National Army and imprisoned at Maryboro (Portlaoise) Prison. On his return home in 1923, he 'showed signs of abnormality'. He began talking to himself about past activities and his condition gradually worsened until he went into hospital. Dr O'Grady reported that Flanagan suffered from 'bronchitis and dermatitis' which could have been brought on by exposure and imprisonment. Dr Dunne, Resident Medical Superintendent at Farnham, wrote just a month before Flanagan died: 'In my opinion he is suffering from a form of dementia with delusions and hallucinations, with very little probability of recovery; rendering him totally unfit for work or responsibility of any kind. This is in my opinion almost entirely due to the continuous extreme mental and nervous strain of his experience in Oglaigh na h-Eireann during the Anglo-Irish War.'[39]

On 21 January, the anniversary of the first Dáil, Evelyn Flanagan received a reply to her application for a widow's pension from the Department of Defence. Her application was turned down. Evelyn received support from a number of parties, including Margaret Pearse, mother of Patrick Pearse, and Oscar Traynor, who intervened to have the case reopened. The case was reopened but due to Paddy Flanagan suffering from syphilis, the symptoms of which are similar to post-traumatic stress, Evelyn was denied a pension. She received a pension for her membership and active service in Cumann na mBan but it was insufficient for raising a family of five. John O'Flanagan MD, New York, wrote a declaration in support of Evelyn's claim to the Pensions Board in September 1937:

> There is no doubt that Patrick Flanagan was considered an outstanding and invaluable Officer of the Dublin Brigade ... he carefully nurtured the Military and Patriotic spirit of his men ... His worth as an Officer was recognised by Brigade Command. This is best proved by the fact that when Brigade headquarters decided to form an Active Service Unit, Patrick Flanagan was the man selected to organize and command it ... I as Medical Officer of the Unit can testify to the untiring zeal with which Patrick Flanagan endeavoured to make it as hot as possible for the enemy forces ... I was in constant daily contact with him, and so was in a position to note the strain of his great responsibility. His self-control in times of stress was never lacking. At the completion of an especially hazardous undertaking, he was wont however to give vent to emotional outbursts of a hysterical type. These outbursts did not last long and apparently acted for him as a safety valve. He quickly recovered his normal grim poise and resumed the planning of new exploits.
>
> That later on, this evidence of nervous instability became more obvious was due in my opinion, to the mental havoc which his War experiences wrought. Apart from the fact that he may have been suffering from an organic disease, I believe that the mental strain that his duties entailed was sufficiently nerve-wracking to bring about mental deterioration in his later years.
>
> To deny him a pension is in my opinion, a most flagrant injustice from the Medical point of view, exceeded only by the injustice of a Country which has so quickly forgotten its debt to him.[40]

A widow's pension was denied to Evelyn in the 1930s on the grounds that her husband's death 'was due to disease not attributable to service', which must have been an awful blow. She made a further appeal and was eventually awarded a widow's pension in 1962.

Paddy Flanagan was not the only member of the IRA involved in the attack on 28 Upper Pembroke Street who displayed psychological problems in the years that followed. So, too, did Charlie Dalton. After the Civil War, Dalton was briefly assigned to the Air Corps at Baldonnel. After resigning from the National Army, he wrote a book entitled *With the Dublin Brigade*. Published in 1929 it outlined the fight for independence in Dublin. In the years that followed, Dalton began to show signs of strain. By November 1938, Dalton, like Paddy Flanagan before him, was attending Saint Patrick's Mental Hospital. According to his wife, Teresa, her husband's illness was due solely to the strain of his activities during the War of Independence and his delusions were also connected with that period.[41] The emphasis on the War of Independence may be partly the fear that a disability pension would be denied by a Fianna Fáil government due to Charlie Dalton's record against republicans during the Civil War. Later that year he suffered a complete psychological collapse and was made a ward of court. His illness was attributed to his active service during the War of Independence and Civil War. A letter supporting his claim came from Seán Lemass, Minister for Supplies in the Fianna Fáil government at the time.[42] This is surprising because Lemass's older brother, Noel, was abducted and murdered by the CID after the Civil War. His body was dumped in the Dublin Mountains at an isolated spot now commemorated by a granite monument on the Military Road.

Charlie Dalton was admitted to Grangegorman Mental Hospital on 9 May 1941. His wife, Teresa, and their four children were totally dependent on him. On 7 November the same year, Charlie was 'declared to be a person of unsound mind and incapable of managing his person or property'.[43] After a time of recovery in hospital, he was discharged as a ward of court on 20 December 1943. His doctors diagnosed him as suffering from:

> severe strain and Nervous shock sustained at a very important period of his life ... all his impressions and hallucinations were referred back to those early years ... He is suffering from a mixed [psychosis], which has totally and probably permanently incapacitated him ... Investigation of his condition revealed, that since his active service as a very young man he has been subject to alternative moods of Depression and Excitement. The content of his Delusional state had been throughout associated with the period of Mental Strain during his active service.

Charlie Dalton suffered extreme mental anguish. The doctors described how he lived in fear of being shot and that he believed he was wanted for various crimes. Most haunting of all, he was pursued by voices who accused him of murder. It was his doctor's professional opinion that 'The outlook in his case is very grave'.[44] Seán Lemass knew Charlie Dalton and they had shared lodgings during the War of Independence. At the time, Lemass knew the strain was beginning to take its toll on the young Dalton, in particular the events on Bloody Sunday. That night Lemass and another IRA comrade took Dalton out for a walk to calm his nerves, but it had no effect and he became hysterical. His condition was made worse by a tap that made a gurgling sound, which, Dalton claimed, was similar to the noise made by the men who had been shot.[45] Charlie Dalton was only fourteen years old when he joined the Irish Volunteers in 1917. In 1920, when he joined IRA intelligence and went on active operations with Michael McDonnell, he was seventeen. In support of his comrade, Frank Saurin wrote: 'Charles Dalton served his country well. The application on his behalf, I respectfully submit, deserves the best consideration and sympathy of the State.'[46]

General Emmet Dalton, older brother of Charlie, also found life difficult after the fighting ceased. In particular, his presence at Beal na Bláth on the day Michael Collins was shot dead drew much comment and the suspicion that he had killed Collins. Despite the numbers who defended him, the accusations must have had an effect on him. His record in the British army in the Middle East and on the Western Front would have been enough to make its mark on any man, but he then experienced the rapid pace and endless 'looking over the shoulder' life with the IRA. The Civil War followed and then arguments with National Army GHQ over men and resources, the death of Michael Collins and the expected executions of republicans caught in possession of arms. It became too much. Dalton resigned from the National Army in December 1922. He served as clerk of the Irish Free State Senate, which caused a storm as W. T. Cosgrave went head to head with the Senate over whose prerogative it was to make such an appointment.[47] Dalton resigned in 1925. There followed bleak years with a good deal of alcohol for support but he eventually managed to regain some focus and direction in his life. He established Ardmore Studios, the Irish film production centre, in 1958 with the support of Seán Lemass, Minister for Industry and Commerce.[48] Emmet Dalton died on 4 March 1978 at eighty years of age.

As members of the IRA, Cumann na mBan, Na Fianna and their families tried to establish a civilian life after years of conflict, the political battles continued. In 1924, the Free State government had finally released the republican prisoners. Michael O'Hanlon, C Company 3rd Battalion Dublin Brigade, who took part in Bloody Sunday, was considering running for TD but was dissuaded by his IRA commanders, who told him his work was far too important. It was evident that the IRA were still operating. O'Hanlon, more concerned about the years of education he had missed, finished his medical training and qualified as a doctor. He worked in Shrewsbury in England until returning to Ireland and joining the Irish Army as a medical officer in 1932.[49]

Republicans faced difficult years in the wilderness. Denied pensions for their 1916 and 1919–21 military service, denied jobs, or advancement in the jobs they had, because of their political views increased the hardship they endured after the ordeals of the Irish revolutionary period. Éamon de Valera changed all of that and managed to bring most of the IRA back in from the cold. He did this by causing yet another split in Sinn Féin and establishing a new political party in 1926. That party chose as its name Fianna Fáil, from the letters FF on the Irish Volunteers' cap badge (meaning 'soldiers of destiny', referring to the mystical Celtic legendary warrior élite Na Fianna). The party has been known ever since as Fianna Fáil, the Soldiers of Destiny. A series of developments, one of them the tragic murder of Kevin O'Higgins, Minister for External Affairs, on 10 July 1927, led to President W. T. Cosgrave implementing an Electoral Amendment Act. This obliged elected TDs to swear to take the oath of allegiance to the British monarch before taking their seats in the Dáil.[50] It was a masterstroke by Cosgrave, ensuring that de Valera and Fianna Fáil henceforth became fully engaged in the electoral process.

Making full use of the Statute of Westminster negotiated at the Commonwealth Conference in 1931 with the help of the Cumann na nGaedheal government, which gave the Irish Free State and Commonwealth countries the legal ability to pass laws without referring them for sanction at Westminster, de Valera demolished the 1921 Treaty with the introduction of the new constitution of 1937. The oath was removed and the Irish Free State disestablished. In its place, Éire appeared, an Irish republic in all but name. The withdrawal of British troops and the Royal Navy from the 'Treaty Ports' of Lough Swilly, Berehaven and Cobh secured political independence. De Valera gave the vast majority of Irish republicans a focus through politics rather than through ammunition and explosives. The establishment of *The Irish Press* in 1931 enabled de Valera to bypass the filter of the *Irish Independent* and *The Irish Times*.

With Kevin O'Higgins dead, W. T. Cosgrave, Eoin O'Duffy and Richard Mulcahy united the Army Comrades Association with the now-exhausted Cumann na nGaedheal political party to form a new political movement in 1933. The new party was called Fine Gael. Mulcahy became its leader in 1944 after the retirement of W. T. Cosgrave. In 1949, the first Inter-Party Government, led by John A. Costello and including Clann na Poblachta, the Irish Labour Party, Fine Gael and Clann na Talmhan, declared Ireland a republic and left the Commonwealth. These political organisations provided a sense of belonging, identity and purpose for thousands of Irish people who had a passionate interest in politics.

During the 1920s and 1930s a number of successful attempts were made to improve the lives of Irish people. Commissioner of the DMP, former General W. R. E. Murphy supported Frank Duff of the Legion of Mary in his efforts to close the infamous red-light district 'Monto' in the mid-1920s. Commissioner Murphy later said one of his proudest moments was closing down 'Monto'. Murphy was also with the Army and helped organise the first Irish Olympic Team in 1924. The National Stadium on the South Circular Road was built by funds raised by a drive organised by W. R. E. Murphy and his wife, Mamie. During 'The Emergency', as the Second World War was called in Ireland, Murphy organised an auxiliary police service called the Local Security Force. He died on 5 March 1975.[51]

The Emergency also led to the establishment of the Local Defence Force or LDF. One of the battalions, the 26th Infantry, was composed of IRA veterans. The 26th Battalion members collected memories of 1916 in typed manuscripts and put together a broadcast for RTÉ for the 1946 commemoration of the Easter Rising. This recording helped to inspire the establishment of the Bureau of Military History in 1947. For the next ten years, the Bureau collected 1,773 witness statements, 34 sets of original historical documents, 42 sets of photographs and 13 voice recordings of primary source material dating from 1913 to 1921.[52] The Bureau did not record the history of the Civil War period, although some witness statements refer to it. Fortunately, Ernie O'Malley began to apply himself to this monumental task.

O'Malley was appointed Acting Assistant Chief of Staff and O/C of the Northern and Eastern Division of the IRA during the Civil War. He was traced by National Army intelligence to 36 Ailesbury Road, the home of Sheila Humphries, a sister of The O'Rahilly. The house was raided and O'Malley was captured in a ferocious gun battle, which saw a soldier killed and a number wounded. O'Malley himself was seriously wounded and was not expected to survive. His inner strength prevailed, however; he pulled through and was released from the Curragh Camp in July 1924.[53] O'Malley left Ireland and sought solace for a time in the Pyrenees on the Spanish and French border. He moved to the US and there met Helen Hooker. They married in 1935 and settled near Newport, County Mayo. O'Malley wrote *On Another Man's Wound*, published in 1936. In Mayo O'Malley spent his time farming, painting, taking photographs and writing articles. His soul was in the arts and it brought him great peace.[54] During this period he began interviewing IRA veterans and writing up accounts of their experiences. The result was 450 interviews contained in notebooks, which are now kept at UCD Archives. The notebooks are of great historical importance as they describe events in the Civil War, albeit from a republican perspective.[55] Ernie O'Malley passed away in March 1957 at sixty years of age. He had been wounded a total of fourteen times from grenade fragments but mainly gunshots.[56] Five bullets remained in his body and were never extracted.[57] He suffered from cardiac disease and neurasthenia, both attributable to his experiences in the Irish revolutionary period.

As veterans recorded their experiences behind the scenes through Military Service Pension documents, the Bureau of Military History and Ernie O'Malley's interviews, the country commemorated 1916. The fiftieth commemoration was a momentous occasion for the veterans and for their families. Given their experiences and deprivation for the cause of an Irish republic, the acknowledgement for the veterans was very important. Parading in public as Volunteers, members of Cumann na mBan and Na Fianna Éireann brought them together once again. There is, however, always a common thread when family members speak of their parents' involvement in the Irish revolution: 'They never talked about it.' This is very understandable. How do you speak to people who did not go through what you experienced? Veterans spoke to their former comrades, however. While others had no wish to relive the trauma of the past and focused on the present and the future, some families hosted a monthly get-together for veterans to meet, talk and relive old times. Veterans often talked late into the night; younger family members who showed little interest later regretted not having listened a little more.

President of the Executive Council/Taoiseach Éamon de Valera (*right*), with Commandant Oscar Traynor, former O/C Dublin Brigade, inspects Dublin Brigade IRA veterans at 1916 Commemorations *c.*1930s. (Author's collection)

This pattern had developed even during the War of Independence. Éamon Broy wrote that sometimes Michael Collins, Liam Tobin, Jim McNamara and himself met up, with no specific reason other than to talk.[58] This comradeship remained with them. During one of these gatherings in the years that followed, Frank Thornton was present. He broke down and said the National Army troops who were at Beal na Bláth often wondered if it was one of their own who had shot Collins by accident. Thornton thought it was possible he had put his head up and been hit by one of their own men.[59] Thornton was lucky to survive the shocking wounds he received in an ambush outside Clonmel in 1922. He served in the Army and worked as a director of the New Ireland Assurance Company. He gave many lectures on the IRA intelligence network during the War of Independence. He died on 23 September 1965 aged seventy-four. Liam Tobin, his O/C in IRA intelligence, went into the car-hire business, running Gresham Motor Hire at Upper O'Connell Street after his resignation from the National Army. He became an organiser for the Irish Hospital Sweepstakes run by Joe McGrath. In 1940 he was appointed as superintendent of Leinster House, retiring in 1959. Tobin passed away on 30 April 1963 at sixty-eight years of age.[60]

For those who were broken in body or in mind, it was the family who offered support. One such case is that of Mollie O'Shea, a veteran of the Kilflynn branch of Cumann na mBan during both the War of Independence and Civil War in Kerry. Very soon after the mine explosion and the murder of the republicans at Ballyseedy, Mollie had a nervous breakdown. Her brother, Captain George O'Shea, was one of those killed at Ballyseedy. She was admitted to Killarney Hospital in 1928. When the time came for the members of Cumann na mBan to apply for their pensions, Mollie was unable to lodge an application. Her brother Daniel made the application on her behalf. The women of Cumann na mBan in Kerry did not forget her and in 1941 at a special meeting of Cumann na mBan veterans, Julia Hassett signed a submission on their behalf giving details of Mollie's service. Their account tells of a totally dedicated and selfless woman who longed for an Irish republic and placed her own life in repeated danger to support the IRA.

Mollie had worked in an intelligence role, watching RIC movements, and, in conjunction with a Mrs Wilmot, a housekeeper at Abbeydorney RIC Barracks, obtained hand grenades and .303 ammunition. Mollie transported additional arms and ammunition from Ned Slattery at Tralee Railway Station to Kilflynn. She kept two revolvers and ammunition in her home for the local IRA unit. She worked tirelessly carrying dispatches and distributing propaganda and was present with an IRA column on active service. Her brother Georgie was O/C Kilflynn Company. Other members of the company included Stephen Fuller and Tim 'Aero' Lyons. On the day of the truce, the Black and Tans raided Mollie's family home, which was the Kilflynn Company HQ. They ill treated her, smashed up the house and stole a gold watch and chain. Julia Hassett wrote that Mollie was very ill after this raid but recovered and carried out much work in support of the training camps at Ballyheigue and Ardfert.[61]

Once the Civil War began Mollie was in charge of looking after an IRA dugout at Glenballyma Wood. Mollie fed and clothed them and obtained a few small comforts to make their existence more bearable. She also scouted for them and personally came under fire many times. Her Cumann na mBan comrades said she covered great distances carrying dispatches, which took her through lonely, bleak places. Tim Toumey died with her brother Georgie at Ballyseedy, while 'Aero' Lyons was killed at the battle of Clashmealcon Caves. Of all the men she cared for in the dugout, only Lieutenant Stephen Fuller and Jack Shanahan survived. Mollie was distraught and mentally broken because of what she had endured. After a stay in Killarney Hospital, she was brought home to live with her mother Anne, brother Daniel and sister Ellen. She was granted her pension and continued to live with her younger sister Ellen in Ashe Steet, Tralee. Mollie O'Shea died on 29 July 1949, aged fifty-two.

In Dublin, veterans were well known. Tom Ennis had joined the Irish Volunteers in 1914, rising through the ranks to become a major-general. On active service all through the revolutionary period, he took part in many key engagements. He resigned from the National Army in 1924 and became Chief Ranger with the Phoenix Park OPW. He lost his daughter Úna in horrific circumstances in April 1942 when her boyfriend, John Prendergast, shot her through the heart and then took his own life.[62] Ennis was a resident at Farnham House Asylum in Finglas when he died of a duodenal haemorrhage on 10 March 1945.[63] The death of his daughter may have been too much for a man who had been at the heart of IRA and National Army operations during the revolutionary period. He was a strict commander, refusing to permit his men to drink, yet was held in great affection by them. During the Civil War he had refused to execute any republicans in his command area and had also made great attempts to reach a peace.

Ennis shared his work space at the Phoenix Park with another well-known veteran, Tom Cullen. The Wicklow man lived at the Under-Secretary's Residence, serving as aide-de-camp to the king's representative to Ireland, Governor General Tim Healy. Cullen had to be evicted from the residence by order of the High Court in 1925.[64] Cullen was defended in court by the one-time legal representative of the IRA, Michael Noyk. On 20 June 1926, Cullen went boating on Lough Dan, County Wicklow, with brothers Joseph and Michael Fitzgerald and Frederick Boland. They rowed across to the east shore where Tom, Joseph and Frederick went swimming. Michael remained in the boat as he had a disability. While returning to the boat, Tom suddenly disappeared from sight. Joseph made a number of attempts to rescue his friend but was forced to save himself or risk being drowned by the panicked Cullen. Tom Cullen's body was later recovered by the Garda Síochána. His funeral took place in Wicklow town on Tuesday 26 June 1926. President of the Dublin Brigade Association, Francis X. Coghlan (E Company 4th Battalion), seconded by George

Lyons (B Company 3rd Battalion), passed a resolution expressing deep sorrow at the tragic death of their former treasurer.

Seán Russell, O/C of 2nd Battalion and one of the main organisers of Bloody Sunday, could not accept the Treaty of 1921 nor the ceasefire order at the conclusion of the Civil War. He became chief of staff of the IRA and, in 1939, he ordered a bombing campaign in Britain. During the Second World War, Russell went to Germany to seek aid from Hitler with the aim of ending the British presence in Ireland. Russell was brought to watch the elite Brandenburg Commandos in training. One of them, Clissmann, said: 'Russell made an excellent impression in Berlin; he was a munitions man and he knew what he was about. We thought then that the IRA was a fairly coherent organization and we had no inkling that anything was wrong with it.'[65] Seán Russell was returning to Ireland on board German submarine U-65 in August 1940 when he was taken seriously ill with internal cramps and vomiting. He died on 14 August and was buried at sea. Two doctors later concluded that the cause of death was a perforated duodenal ulcer, although there were rumours he had been poisoned by his travelling companion and fellow IRA man, Frank Ryan.[66]

Of those who followed Michael Collins there is none more controversial than Paddy O'Daly, O/C of the Squad and GOC of Kerry Command. O'Daly was dismissed from the National Army in 1924. He became an overseer at the Governor General's residence in the Phoenix Park in 1928 and lived at one of the artisan cottages in the park. His wife Brigid died in their home on 2 March 1930 from complications giving birth to their stillborn child. Paddy O'Daly was with her as she died.[67] He continued to work at the Phoenix Park until 1935 when he resigned from the Office of Public Works. He re-enlisted in the Army during the Second World War, with the rank of captain. His brother Frank also enlisted, also with the rank of captain. Paddy spent a lot of time with his brother and they got on well in latter years. Frank had taken the republican side in the Civil War. Paddy and Frank got to know their nieces and nephews. The children loved Paddy and found him generous. Frank's wife, Maisey, could not bring herself to speak to him for a long time over what had happened in Kerry. In the 1940s Paddy arrived one day and Maisey asked him why he had allowed the unfortunate men in Kerry to be blown up. His reply was that it had been a long time ago and he had had no control over his men. There was no acceptance of responsibility from the former major-general. O'Daly died of cancer of the bone at the age of sixty-six on 16

January 1957, having been ill for eighteen months.[68] He passed away in his family home on the Naas Road, attended by his daughter Philomena. Joe Leonard was named executor of his will. The two had soldiered together for some forty-one years. Leonard, former member of the Squad and commandant of the Dublin Guards, died four years later on 14 October 1961, aged sixty-five.[69] Captain Frank Daly, Paddy's brother, passed away on 1 January 1976, aged eighty-nine.

The introduction of the Military Service Pension Acts under de Valera's administration in the 1930s and '40s brought to light the membership rolls of the IRA in the War of Independence and in the Civil War. Proving membership of the IRA was generally accepted but proving 'active service' was more difficult as the Pensions Committee seemed to favour people who had 'pulled triggers' and tended to discriminate against less-well-known IRA and Cumann na mBan members who undertook dangerous intelligence work. By its very nature intelligence work is secretive and difficult to prove after the event. Leo Duffy, a company commander, remarked when interviewed: 'You cannot pin down Active Service to firing a few shots.'[70] The role of women in Cumann na mBan and as civilian sympathisers was revealed but it was still difficult for them to achieve the recognition they deserved. When the different Dublin Brigade battalions drew up their membership rolls, only one drew up a list of the women of Cumann na mBan on active service who had supported them and in many cases ensured their survival during the War of Independence. Captain Seamus Kavanagh, O/C C Company 3rd Battalion, became commanding officer when Captain James Doyle was captured after the attack on the Custom House. It was Kavanagh who submitted the list of the Cumann na mBan women to the Military Service Pensions committee for his company. The women were:

Members of Cumann na mBan[71] University, Ringsend & Inghinidhe Branches (on active service with C Company 3rd Battalion)	
Miss [unclear] Butler	Mrs Carroll
Miss N. Fagan	Mrs Fitzroy
Miss Lilly Harris	Miss May Harris (both Harrises Eamon Ceannt Branch)
Mrs Henley	Mrs McNamara
Mrs Bridie Murphy	Josephine Tucker
Mrs York	

Women faced a difficult time in post-revolutionary Ireland. The hopes for equality enshrined in the 1916 Proclamation faded as soon as the Irish Free State was established. Women were seen in the traditional role of wife and mother – as enshrined in Article 41.2 of the constitution. Mollie Gleeson, who ran the West End Café at Parkgate, set up a new hotel-restaurant called An Stád at 30 North Frederick Street. She had served in the War of Independence as an IRA intelligence agent and courier. Former IRA men on a visit to Dublin for GAA matches or on political business would stay at An Stad. Mollie Gleeson died of breast cancer in Harold's Cross Hospice on 10 February 1949. Were it not for her former friend and comrade Eílis Uí Chonaill (née Ní Riain) who wrote a special tribute to her, Mollie's sacrifices for the freedom of her country would have gone unrecorded.[72]

During Mollie's life, An Stad attracted all sorts of unusual visitors. Even a former Black and Tan called Rogers, a patron of Mollie's restaurant in 1920/21, came on leave from Palestine to visit.[73] Like many Black and Tans and Auxiliaries, he joined the British Palestinian Police after the war in Ireland. Captain Rymer-Jones, the British army officer assigned to Richmond Barracks in Inchicore, was Inspector-General of the Palestinian Police from 1943 to 1946. Rymer-Jones could possibly have met another officer who served in Ireland, Major William Lorraine King. After the war in Ireland King became a travelling salesman. His marriage to Helen Sophie Gilbert did not work out and she initiated divorce proceedings in June 1926.[74] There are curious postage stamps on the back of the couple's marriage certificate at the National Archives at Kew, which are identified as the Selangor River Rubber Estates Malaya, dated 10 March 1921, and Interoceanic Railway Acapulco to Vera Cruz, 7 May 1921.[75] One can only assume the couple took a world cruise after King was found not guilty at the military court trying the Clonturk Park murders case. Major King was only at home in the army. During the Second World War he found himself in Palestine. He died in Gaza on 14 November 1942, aged fifty-seven, and is buried in the Commonwealth War Cemetery there.[76] His friend, Captain Jocelyn Lee Hardy, became a successful novelist. His most successful book, *I Escape*, published in 1927, contained an introduction written by Sir Arthur Conan Doyle and told the story of his break for freedom from a German prisoner-of-war camp during the First World War.[77] His 1936 novel, *Never in Vain,* although supposedly a work of fiction, was in effect based on his experiences in Dublin during the War of Independence.[78] Hardy died in England in 1958, just short of his sixty-fourth birthday.

Volunteers who adapted to the uncertainty of the future took on many unusual jobs. Thomas McGrath, who was on active service with the Dublin Brigade ASU, had many different jobs. Before joining the IRA he was a shipyard worker; afterwards he was a dance promotor, a minerals salesman and he also worked in a parcels office.[79] One of the most unusual jobs was that taken up by one of Paddy O'Daly's senior officers, Waterford-born Michael Joseph Bishop. Bishop was awarded his pension after retiring from the Army in 1927. Leaving all his affairs in the hands of his wife, Patricia, the former colonel travelled to British-occupied Sudan where he worked at Wady Oyo for the Kassala Gold Mine Ltd. Bishop worked and lived in the Sudan for the rest of his life. Occasionally his wife visited him there for a holiday or he returned to Ireland for a brief period. He died in the Sudan on 2 December 1953, aged fifty-five.[80] Others also went abroad: General Dan Hogan, brother of Michael, who was killed at Croke Park on Bloody Sunday, and O/C Dublin Command during the Civil War, left for the US rather than serve under de Valera. Hogan walked out the door of his family home, leaving his wife, Betty (née O'Flynn), and daughter on his way to work. He disappeared and was never seen again.[81]

After the fiftieth commemoration of the Easter Rising in 1966, veterans were aware that they were becoming older. Some of them sought to encourage others to pass on their stories, even after the Bureau of Military History had concluded collecting witness accounts and contemporary documents. In 1968, Jimmy Slattery, a former member of the Squad and a close comrade of Mick McDonnell, put pen to paper: 'I have seen hundreds of men die in the past decade who helped to shape this country's history. I think they died without realising how important their story was. I beg of the survivors, active or inactive, to record on tape or paper, their memories for safe keeping.'[82]

Some of the veterans took Slattery's exhortation on board. Some wrote accounts which were discovered after they died and were then deposited in the Military Archives or National Library of Ireland. These accounts have been of great historical significance due to certain papers, even today, being restricted. Other relatives kept the accounts of their veteran relative secret, believing their stories to be too controversial even nearly a century later.

In 1968 conflict erupted in the north of Ireland. Partition enacted in the Government of Ireland Act 1920 and confirmed by the Anglo-

Irish Treaty of 1921 had left Catholics isolated and marginalised. The civil rights movements in the United States and in Europe in the 1960s encouraged those denied the right to housing, education and jobs to agitate for equality and justice. The agitation escalated and resulted in a British army presence in Northern Ireland. The conflict lasted for thirty years and caused a fracturing of how the republican ideals of the 1916 leaders and the sacrifices of the 1913–23 period were viewed. A small minority of veterans supported the renewed conflict against Britain, seeing it as inevitable and as 'unfinished business'. Others deplored it and sought to make a strong distinction between the 'Old' IRA and the Provisional IRA. The history of 1916–23 was seen either as an embarrassment or as a powerful tool to inspire young people to engage in renewed violence.

As the violence in Northern Ireland continued, the veterans faded from the public eye. In old age, some faced the challenge of finding themselves isolated. Veterans had always relied on each other for support and understanding but as their numbers dwindled, some found themselves completely alone. William James Stapleton, or Bill Stapleton as he was known to the Squad, was dismissed in 1925 as part of the clear-out of veterans associated with the army mutiny. Stapleton held the rank of colonel at the time of his dismissal. Unlike the other leading officers in the army mutiny, Stapleton was initially denied a pension and faced serious financial difficulties. Stapleton wrote to President Cosgrave to make his case: 'Since 1916, I have been in close association with the late Major-General Tobin and his followers. I have fought and bled with those men, but never have I in any shape or form been a party to an action subversive of the State or the present Government.'[83]

Stapleton was eventually given the recognition he deserved. After working as a taxi driver he was appointed camp superintendent, overseeing the workers building the Ardnacrusha hydroelectric dam. However, at the age of eighty, he suffered a complete nervous breakdown and was in hospital a number of times. On his doctor's advice he sold his home in Rathgar and moved to a nursing home at Nazareth House on the Malahide Road in Dublin. The Mother Superior felt that, despite his illness, Stapleton was able to look after himself. In 1977 a deterioration saw Stapleton go into St John of God's in Stillorgan for psychiatric care. He remained there for just over a year. No one knew where he was. Finally, a nephew found him and brought him to his family home at Millmount Terrace in Drumcondra. Ironically, it was just around the corner from

Veteran medals (*l–r*): the Service (1917–1921) Medal with *comhrach* ('combat') bar and the 1916 medal of Thomas Sweeney Newell, 1st Battalion Galway No. 1 Brigade and IO ASU, Dublin Brigade. (Courtesy Terry & Éamon Newell)

where Mick McDonnell's unit had carried out their first assassination attempt on Detective Sergeant Smyth on Millmount Avenue in 1919.[84]

As the veterans became fewer in number, they began to make their peace in their own way. Dan Breen was interviewed a number of times for films and documentaries. In one clip he showed the respect he had for the leaders of the Irish revolution, saying: 'When I was a boy we were serfs, slave minded. Anyone who came along and lifted us out of that belittling I looked on them as gods.'[85]

Breen had no regrets about the active service he had engaged in. For Dan, his country was occupied and military action was necessary to change that situation. Before he died, he called for his friend Paddy Dwyer of the 3rd Tipperary Brigade to come and see him. They had been at Soloheadbeg on 21 January 1919, together with Seán Treacy, where war had been renewed after the Rising of 1916. Dwyer and Breen talked in private for hours. When Dwyer returned home that evening he was asked what Dan had spoken about. Dwyer said not a word. It was the last time they would meet.[86] Dan Breen died in December 1969, aged seventy-five, and was buried at Donohill in County Tipperary. His wife, Brigid, a veteran of the Ard Craobh Dublin branch of Cumann na mBan and sister of Áine Malone, died in 1984.

The oldest surviving member of the Squad was Vinny Byrne. He was interviewed a number of times and described the events of Bloody Sunday in *Ireland – a Television History* by Robert Key.[87] He was also in 'Get Collins – The Intelligence War in Dublin', a *Hidden History* programme for RTÉ. In 1986 Byrne drew up his last will and testament. Among the details were donations of £100 each to the local St Vincent de Paul, the parish priest at Knock Shrine in County Mayo and the St Camillian Fathers at Killucan, County Westmeath, for the repose of his soul. He died at ninety-two years of age on 13 December 1992.

On 12 October 1950, Charlie Dalton signed off on his witness statement to the Bureau of Military History:

> It might not be inapt to add in conclusion that throughout the whole period of active service in which I was associated with members of the squad and Intelligence and Volunteers in the city, I found that the morale was always very high and that everyone was anxious to do his part without any consideration as to personal danger or inconvenience and that a very strong spirit of comradeship resulted which, I am glad to say, survived in the years that followed.[88]

The reunion of former Squad and IRA intelligence comrades held in Mick McDonnell's honour in 1949 may have helped give Dalton support and encouragement as well as easing his troubled mind.

Seán Lemass never spoke about the past and even his pension application was sparse on detail. When the future Taoiseach of Ireland was called before the Military Pensions Committee he would not elaborate on

Bloody Sunday. Lemass had shot dead his one-year-old brother, Herbert, in a terrible accident as he sat at the table in his home cleaning his pistol in January 1916.[89] The committee were left approaching other veterans to see if they could supply information in his case.[90] In a number of cases, veterans of Bloody Sunday stated they were instructed not to give information about what had happened or who was involved. A number also stated that they could not give information about other Volunteers present that day. The Pensions Committee was trying to assemble a list of those who participated in order to determine who was entitled to a pension. The revolutionary period was a time Seán Lemass did not wish to return to. For him, it was enough to state that he was there. Lemass's compassion for Dalton speaks volumes about his character. The manner in which he embraced the opportunity to establish the first real cordial ties with Northern Ireland is a real indication of where the priorities of this veteran and leader really lay.

Lemass was one of a number of like-minded men who sought peace and aimed to influence the future in a positive way. Another such was Stephen Fuller of Kilflynn, who survived the Ballyseedy mine explosion, and who suffered from neurasthenia and TB. X-rays revealed 'several fine bodies embedded in the musculature of his back', fragments from the mine explosion.[91] Fuller was elected as a TD for Fianna Fáil in the 1937 and 1938 general elections. He never used the story of Ballyseedy as part of his campaign to get elected. His son Paudie said his father 'held no bitterness against those who tried to blow him up; in fact, he was full of forgiveness ... My father once said to me that the Civil War divisions should not be passed on to the next generation.'[92] Like Seán Lemass, Stephen Fuller also signed a statement to help a veteran who had suffered in the Irish revolution wars. He signed a joint statement with Julia Hassett, secretary of the Cumann na mBan veterans of Kilflynn in support of Mollie O'Shea. Stephen Fuller passed away on 23 February 1984, at the age of eighty-four.

In the aftermath of the Civil War some veterans made it their mission to reach out to former comrades and heal them spiritually. Maurice Walsh, a Volunteer from F Company 2nd Battalion, was originally from Cahersiveen in County Kerry. He was born on Christmas Day 1896. He joined both the IRB and the Irish Volunteers in 1917. He fought in the War of Independence and remained with the republican forces who opposed the Treaty in the Civil War. Walsh fought with Cathal Brugha in O'Connell Street in 1922 and spent the rest of the war in Mountjoy Gaol. He went on hunger strike before being released at Christmas 1923. He continued his IRA activities, taking part in a jailbreak at Mountjoy in 1925. Then life took a completely unexpected turn: he joined the Dominican Order in Tallaght in 1929. He spent a few years at the monastery of San Clemente in Rome and was ordained in 1935. Returning to Ireland he set himself the task of healing the wounds that were beyond medical aid. Because of the Irish bishops' pastoral letter excluding republicans in 1922, many had been alienated from the Church and the sacraments. Fr Walsh began a ministry of reconciliation which he followed until the end of his days. He attended commemorations and met veterans individually. He brought peace to lives that had been shattered and to those who were now worried at facing their own end. He was named Preacher General by the Dominican Order in 1961. Fr Maurice Walsh died on 16 August 1987 and is buried in Glasnevin Cemetery, Dublin.[93]

The former Under-Secretary at Dublin Castle, Sir Alfred Cope (Andy Cope, as he had been known in Dublin), became the focus of considerable ire from imperialists. On 5 March 1924, in a debate in the House of Lords on 'Claims of Irish Loyalists', Cope was accused of communicating information to Sinn Féin that he gathered at joint meetings of the Chief of Police, General Sir Hugh Tudor, GOC British army General Sir Nevil Macready and Assistant Secretary to Ireland, Sir John Anderson, which, as Under-Secretary, he had attended. As a result of the information supposedly passed on by Cope, it was alleged, policemen and soldiers lost their lives.[94] Lord Muskerry was accusing Cope of treason and said the guilty party should have been taken out and shot. Lord Fitzalan Derwent, the last Lord Lieutenant of Ireland, who had actually been shot and captured by Peadar Clancy in 1916, responded on 19 March 1924, describing the Cope he knew as 'a man of great capacity, perfect integrity and great courage'.[95] Fitzalan acknowledged the work carried out by Cope to facilitate meetings and negotiations in resolving the war in Ireland. However, Sir Alfred Cope's reputation was ruined and he could not defend himself against the privilege of the House of Lords. In the years that followed Cope underwent a religious experience that completely changed his life. On 1 March 1927 he was invited to the Tabernacle chapel at Cwmgorse in Wales to enlighten people to the benefits of coming face to face to solve political and industrial difficulties. Cope was sought after due to his experience in Ireland. He spoke about the lust for blood: Bloody Sunday, the burning of an Irish village and the story of Commandant Seán

MacÉoin. Cope addressed the conflict in Ireland and chose to focus on the hand of friendship, encouraging people not to be suspicious but to grasp opportunites. The peacemaker is the person 'who will count in the end'.[96] In 1950 Cope was asked to contribute to the Bureau of Military History. He replied with regret that he preferred to 'let sleeping dogs lie'. He believed it was not possible for the history project embarked upon by the Bureau to be truthful.[97]

For most veterans of the Irish revolutionary period, it was the simple things in life which finally brought some measure of peace. Gearóid Ua hUallacháin (Garry Holohan) was in a bad way after the Civil War. He later wrote that his spirit and heart were broken. Then one day in 1924 or 1925, he met an old friend, Harry Heelan, who was on his way home from a St Vincent de Paul meeting. Gearóid and Harry had been friends in Na Fianna Éireann before 1916 but Harry had dropped out. Harry invited his old friend out to his home at Bullock Harbour near Dalkey to meet his wife, a Belgian woman, and their three children. It was just the tonic for Ua hUallacháin. They welcomed him into their lives. Harry brought him sailing on weekends. As they set out from Bullock Harbour they would pass Dalkey Island and head back past Dún Laoghaire Harbour and on into Dublin Bay. Spread out before him were the Dublin Mountains across to the Hill of Howth. In the centre the Liffey flowed out from the heart of Dublin. The sailing may have reminded Ua hUallacháin of happier days as a child and the fun he had with Na Fianna, marching in the hills above St Enda's in Rathfarnham, camping for weekends at Belcamp and sailing in the bay. 'I can never count what I owe to Mr and Mrs Heelan for the pleasure I got from those happy days.'[98]

Drong Átha Cliath or the Dublin Brigade was established in November 1913 with the founding of the Irish Volunteers. The men in this brigade, together with the women of the assigned branches of Cumann na mBan, came from every county in Ireland. The events of 1916 taught them valuable lessons in terms of tactics and deployment of troops. The men and women who fought in Dublin knew they were part of something momentous but they kept the true nature both of what they had done and what they had endured from later generations. A mythology developed around the violence and a certain dark humour surrounded stories of assassinations and ambushes. With the passing of time a clearer picture of what happened has emerged and it has been told with the assistance of the veterans themselves and from eyewitness accounts and medical reports.

The War of Independence as conducted by the Dublin Brigade under Dick McKee and Michael Collins' intelligence department and Squad was brutal. War is little else. What numbers of them learned in Dublin as to how to conduct their type of war was applied with a vengeance during the Civil War. The members of the Dublin IRA, Cumann na mBan and Na Fianna Éireann embraced revolution. They took it on in the culture of their time with total commitment to the cause of an Irish republic. It was a reality that had eluded every preceding generation. By international standards casualties were relatively light. But Ireland is a small island and memories are long. The experience left the generation who lived through it changed for the rest of their lives. This generation set the country on a different course. They opted to separate themselves from a powerful empire and, to a large degree, accomplished that. It was truly an astonishing achievement. The Civil War soured the dream as it fractured the country and damaged its financial potential for decades. The Civil War left people bitter, suspicious and untrusting of those who took an alternative stance. It also left the prospect of a unified island further away than ever. And still people cherished their country as independent and free, standing among the nations of this world. It was a freedom that came with a heavy cost and it is well to remember it.

APPENDIX A

Organisational structure of the Dublin Metropolitan Police 1920–21

Dublin Metropolitan Police 1920–21[1]
HQ, Lower Castle Yard, Dublin Castle.
Commanding Officers
Chief Commissioner Lt-Col Walter Edgeworth Johnson (1920 & 1921)
Asst Commissioner Fergus Quinn (1920)
Asst Commissioner Denis Barrett (1921)
Chief Superintendent Lawrence W. Murphy (1920 & 1921)

Division	Senior Officers	Other Ranks	Division HQ	District Area
A Division	**Superintendent**	28 sergeants	**Kevin Street Upper**	Dublin city south-west
	Michael Freeman	131 constables		
	(1920)	(1919)		Stations:
				Kevin Street Upper
	Superintendent			Chancery Lane
	Denis Carey (1921)			Newmarket
				Kilmainham
				Harbour
	Inspectors			
	Denis Carey			
	John Kelleher			
	Andrew Lawler			
	Jeremiah Murphy			
	Robert J. Parkes			
	David White			

Division	Senior Officers	Other Ranks	Division HQ	District Area
B Division	**1920** **Superintendent** George Willoughby (1920) **Superintendent** James Campbell (1921) **Inspectors** Daniel Barrett William Griffin Gerald J. Herbert Bernard McGarry Robert Pursley (Storekeeper) John Winters	21 sergeants 150 constables (1919)	**Dublin Castle** **Lower Yard**	Dublin city south-east Stations: Great Brunswick Street Dublin Castle Lad Lane Clarendon

A & B Divisions occupied the section of the city South of the Liffey from the estuary of the Dodder at Ringsend to the Chapelizod Bridge on the Liffey, from there in a direct line to Blackhorse Bridge on the Grand Canal and then by the Grand Canal to the Grand Canal Basin at the Estuary of the Dodder, Ringsend. These Divisions were separated by a line running from Portobello Bridge through Richmond Street, Camden Street, Wexford Street, Redmond's Hill, Peter's Row, Whitefriar Street, Great Ship Street, Castle Steps, Castle Street and Fishamble Street to the Liffey.

Division	Senior Officers	Other Ranks	Division HQ	District Area
C Division	**Superintendent** James Campbell (1920) **Superintendent** Michael Freeman (1921) **Inspectors** Thomas Crosbie Thomas Haugh Henry Dixon Jeremiah Murphy John J Purcell	29 sergeants 168 constables (1919)	**Store Street**	Dublin city north-east Stations: Store Street Fitzgibbon Street Clontarf

Division	Senior Officers	Other Ranks	Division HQ	District Area
D Division	**Superintendent** Hugh Travers (1920) **Superintendent** George Willoughby (1921) **Inspectors** Thomas F. Byrne Michael Lowry Jeremiah J. O'Neill John Quinn Michael Walsh	31 sergeants 121 constables (1919)	**Green Street**	Dublin city north-west Stations: Green Street Bridewell Mountjoy Chapelizod Parkgate Street Bessboro

C & D Divisions occupied the section of the District lying north of the Liffey between the Nanikin River, Dollymount and the ferryboat station on the Liffey at the foot of the Knockmaroon Hill. They were separated by a line from Grattan Bridge through Capel Street, Bolton Street, Dorset Street and Drumcondra Road to Whitehall and Upper Drumcondra Road.

E Division	**Superintendent** Cornelius Kiernan (1920) **Superintendent** Cornelius Kiernan (1921) **Inspectors** Jeremiah Herlihy Michael Kelly Alexander McCaig Alexander O'Keefe Michael Walsh	27 sergeants 102 constables (1919)	**Rathmines**	Dublin city suburbs south of Grand Canal Stations: Irishtown Rathmines, Donnybrook Crumlin Terenure

E Division occupied the section of the district south of the Grand Canal and the Liffey, between the Blackhorse Bridge on the Grand Canal and the Railway Gates at Merrion Strand. It embraced the urban districts of Rathmines and Pembroke.

Division	Senior Officers	Other Ranks	Division HQ	District Area
F Division	**Superintendent** James Doran (1920)	27 sergeants 99 constables	Kingstown Upr George's St	Dublin city south-east urban districts
	Superintendent James Doran (1921)			Stations: Dalkey Kingstown Blackrock
	Inspectors Robert Bell Richard H. Boyle Matthew Kirwan			Booterstown Kill of the Grange

F Division occupied the section of the district between the railway gates at Merrion along the sea coast to a point two furlongs south of the southern wall of Mount Malpas, Killiney. It took in the urban districts of Blackrock, Kingstown, Dalkey and part of Killiney and Ballybrack.

G Division (Detective Branch)	**Superintendent** Owen Brien MBE (1920)	18 sergeants 5 constables	**Great Brunswick Street**	Detective Branch Dublin District
	Inspectors Patrick Murphy (Chief) George Love Samuel J. Stedmond Neil McFeely Andrew Lonergan Maurice Ahern			
	Superintendent John J. Purcell (1921)			
	Inspectors John Bruton (Chief) Robert Forrest Edward Hally Owen Kerr Alexander McCabe Michael Mannion			

APPENDIX B

British Army organisation of the Dublin District

Includes regiments along with their respective commanding officers and barracks where garrisoned.

British Army – Dublin District (March 1920 – July 1921) HQ Dublin Castle GOC Major General Sir Gerald Farrell Boyd CB, CMG, DSO, DCM (1877–1930)		
Battalion	**Officer Commanding**	**Location**
24th (Provisional) Infantry Brigade (North of the River Liffey)	Maj-General Richard Deare Furley Oldman DSO (1877–1943)[2]	Dublin District
1st Bn East Surrey Regiment (relieved by 2nd Bn Duke of Wellington Regiment)	Lt-Col R. H. Baldwin	Collinstown North Dublin
1st Bn Lancashire Fusiliers	–	North Dublin Union Grangegorman
1st Bn Wiltshire Regiment	Lt-Col B. T. Buckley	Royal Barracks Arbour Hill
2nd Bn Worcestershire Regiment (Transferred to 25th Infantry Brigade April 1921)	Lt-Col H. A. Carr	Portobello Barracks Rathmines
1st Bn South Wales Borderers	Lt-Col A. J. Reddie	County Meath (June 1920)
2nd Bn East Surrey Regiment	Lt.-Col. R. H. Baldwin DSO	Marlborough Hall Glasnevin (January 1921)
2nd Bn Royal West Kent Regiment	Lt.-Col. C. E. Kitson DSO	Phoenix Park, North Dublin Union (June 1921)

Battalion	Officer Commanding	Location
25th (Provisional) Infantry Brigade [South of the River Liffey]	Brigadier General Cranley Charlton Onslow, CMG, CBE, DSO (1869–1940)[3]	Dublin District
1st Bn King's Own Royal Lancaster Regiment	Lt-Col B. D. L. G. Anley	Richmond Barracks Inchicore
2nd Bn Prince of Wales' Volunteers (South Lancashire Regiment) (relieved by 2nd Bn Welch Regiment June 1920)	Lt-Col H. C. Herbert 2nd Welch O/C Lt-Col H. J. B. Span DSO	Richmond Barracks Inchicore
1st Bn Prince of Wales' Volunteers (South Lancashire Regiment)	Lt-Col D'O. B. Dawson	Wellington Barracks South Circular Road
2nd Bn Royal Berkshire Regiment	Lt-Col W. B. Thornton	Portobello Barracks Rathmines
1st Bn Cheshire Regiment	Lt-Col B. A. Chetwynd Stapylton	County Wicklow Bray & Enniskerry
3rd Bn Rifle Brigade (Transferred to 24th Infantry Brigade April 1921)	Lt.-Col Reginald Alexander	Ballsbridge
1st Bn Loyal (North Lancashire) Regiment	Lt.-Col Woodcock	Portobello Barracks Rathmines (July 1921)

The Order of Battle for the British army in the Dublin District listed here is composed of information from the official British army's account: Dublin District Historical Record from Volume IV Record of the Rebellion. The information supplied with kind permission of Kautt, W.H. *Ground Truths*, Irish Academic Press, Sallins, 2014, pp. 26–30, 72. Also from information collated from research in the files at Kew and Regimental Archives of Queen's Own West Kent Regiment, 2nd Bn East Surrey Regiment, 3rd Rifle Brigade and The Royal Welsh.

Appendix C

Organisation and Structure of the Auxiliary Division RIC[4]

HQ Command Structure, Auxiliary Division, Beggars Bush Barracks	Officer Commanding: Brigadier-General Frank Crozier
	Second-in-Command: General Edward Wood
	Adjutant: Major McVeigh (became Second-in-Command)
	Adjutant: Captain Martins
Auxiliary Company Command Structure	Company Commander: 1 District Inspector (1st Class)
	Second-in-Command: 1 District Inspector (2nd Class)
	Section Commanders: 4 District Inspectors (3rd Class)
	Section Leaders: 12
Auxiliary Company Structure	Auxiliary Company: 144 Cadets
	Platoons: 4 (in each Company)
	Sections: 4 (in each Platoon)
National Structure	19 Field Companies named A to R appointed to particular trouble spots throughout Ireland. All Companies under a unified HQ Command situated at Beggars Bush with the exception of F Company who came under exclusive Command of Chief of Police Dublin Castle. Q Company were a specialist Naval Company appointed to the London North Western Railway Hotel, North Wall, Dublin. Mostly former Royal Navy but some Royal Engineers. K Company was disbanded after the burning of Cork in 1920.
Tactical Handling	3 Companies confined to Barracks at all times with 2 on duty, 1 one reserve and 1 on leave. This arrangement was rotated every day.

Recruitment Profile	All ex-British Army & Empire Officers some with very distinguished War records. Nationalities included English, 25% from the north of Ireland and Scotland.
Recruitment Centres	Bristol, Glasgow, Liverpool, London & Newcastle.
Total Strength	1,600
Character	Some very good types. About 10% bad eggs.
F Company ADRIC, Profile	HQ Exchange Court, Dublin Castle.
	Picked men and under Command of Chief of Police Dublin Castle.
	Nationalities included British, 3–4 Canadians, 3 Australian [1 South African].
Individual Armament & Ammunition	Lee-Enfield rifle, bayonet, revolver
	50 rounds .303 and 40 rounds revolver ammunition. Rifle ammunition carried in a distinctive 1903 pattern five-pocket bandolier worn across the chest.
Company Armament & Ammunition	16 Winchester Repeating Shotguns
	Buckshot Shotguns (20 rounds per man)
	4 Lewis Guns (5 pans of ammunition per gun)
	Verey Light Pistol
Transport	7 Crossley Tenders per Company (2 of F Coys had 'caged' tops)
	2 five-seater Ford Touring Cars
Transport Extra Reserve	Beggars Bush Barracks or Gormanstown
Pay	£7. 16s per week
Uniform	British Officer's tunic, usually their own from Corp of former service.
	Glengarry or Balmoral Cap in khaki or navy

APPENDIX D

British army, ADRIC & RIC Raids in Dublin District 2, 3, 4 December 1920

Response to IRA operations on Bloody Sunday, 21 November 1920[5]

Military/police Unit	Raids 2 Dec. 1920	Raids 3 Dec. 1920	Raids 4. Dec. 1920	Military/police Total Raids
24th (Provisional) Infantry Brigade [North of the River Liffey]				Dublin District North
2nd Bn Duke of Wellington Regiment	5	9	–	14
1st Bn South Lancashire Fusiliers	5	6	–	11
1st Bn Wiltshire Regiment	4	5	2	11
2nd Bn Worcestershire Regiment	1	–	–	1
1st Bn South Wales Borderers	9	2	2	13
5th Brigade Royal Garrison Artillery	1	–	–	1

Military/police Unit	Raids 2 Dec. 1920	Raids 3 Dec. 1920	Raids 4. Dec. 1920	Military/police Total Raids
25th (Provisional) Infantry Brigade [South of the River Liffey]				Dublin District South
1st Bn King's Own Royal Lancaster Regiment	4	2	4	10
2nd Bn Welch Regiment	2	8	–	10
1st Bn Prince of Wales' Volunteers (South Lancashire Regiment)	16	11	–	27
2nd Bn Royal Berkshire Regiment	14	1	3	18
1st Bn Cheshire Regiment	3	–	–	3
1st Bn Loyal (North Lancashire) Regiment	1	–	–	1
Police				
F Coy ADRIC	7	4	2	13
RIC	–	3	–	3
Dublin District Total Raids				136

Appendix E

The men of the ASU, Dublin Brigade

Dublin Brigade Active Service Unit (ASU) December 1920[6]
(ASU 1st Phase: Jan–May 1921)
HQ 17 Eustace Street
Capt. Paddy Flanagan O/C
1st Lt. Frank Flood 2nd Lt. Johnny Dunne
Adj Christie O'Malley/Jim Gibbons, QM Michael White/Tommy Bryan
IO William Doyle, MO Seamus Flanagan
(ASU 2nd Phase)
HQ Morelands, Abbey Street
Capt. Paddy O'Daly O/C (appointed June 1921)
1st Lt. Joe Leonard 2nd Lt. Pádraig O'Connor
QM Vinny Byrne IO Paddy Drury

Dublin Brigade Active Service Unit (ASU)	O/C	Volunteers	Company & Battalion of Origin
No. 1 Section 1st Bn Area north side HQ: Morelands, Abbey Street	O/C Lt. Frank Flood succeeded by Lt. Tom Flood Section Cmdr Mick Dunne O/C Lt. Joe Leonard (June 1921)	Joe O'Carroll	1st Bn
		Tommy Bryan	C Coy 3rd Bn
		Paddy Doyle	1st Bn
		Mick White	F Coy 4th Bn
		Patrick Morrissey	A Coy 4th Bn
		Eugene Carton	F Coy 1st Bn
		Seán Burke	1st Bn
		Jack Foy	1st Bn
		Paddy 'Ninepence' O'Connor	C Coy 1st Bn
		Dermot O'Sullivan	C Coy 1st Bn
		Seán Quinn	C Coy 1st Bn
		Tom Flood	D Coy 1st Bn
		Peter O'Connor	Unknown
		Jackie Foy	A Coy 3rd Bn
		Johnny Sliney	1st Bn
		Ned Breslin	1st Bn
		Christy Maxwell	Unknown
		Peter Ratcliffe	C Coy 1st Bn
		Jimmy Carrigan	1st Bn
		Barney Ryan	1st Bn
		Mick McGee	1st Bn

Dublin Brigade Active Service Unit (ASU)	O/C	Volunteers	Company & Battalion of Origin
No. 2 Section 2nd Bn Area north side HQ: Morelands, Abbey Street	O/C Lt. Frank Flood succeeded by Lt. Tom Flood	Seán Anthony Caffrey	D Coy 2nd Bn
	Section Cmdr. & Armourer Tom McGrath	George Gray	2nd Bn
	C Coy 2nd Bn	James Heery	C Coy 2nd Bn
	O/C Lt. Joe Leonard	Joe Gilhooly	C Coy 2nd Bn
	(June 1921)	Paddy Evers	2nd Bn
		Jim Cahill	2nd Bn
		John Muldowney	D Coy 2nd Bn
		Christy Fitzsimons	2nd Bn
		Bob Purcell	2nd Bn
		Joe Gillon	2nd Bn
		Paddy Drury	F Coy 1st Bn & IO GHQ intelligence
		Bill Gannon	C Coy 1st Bn
No. 3 Section 3rd Bn Area south side	O/C Lt. Johnny Dunne	Jimmie Grace	C Coy 3rd Bn
		QM George White	C Coy 3rd Bn
	Section Cmdr. Willie Corrie	George White	C Coy 3rd Bn
		Mick White	Unknown
	O/C Lt. Pádraig O'Connor (June 1921)	Jimmy Browne	E Coy 1st Bn formerly C Coy 3rd Bn
		Phil Quinn	3rd Bn
		John Dolan	3rd Bn
		Jackie Hanlon	Unknown
		Paddy Brunton	Unknown
		Jim 'The Shelmalier' Doyle	C Coy 3rd Bn
		Dan Jevins	Unknown
		Joe Carroll	Unknown
		Mick Stephenson	3rd Bn
		Willie Philips	Unknown
		Peter Larkin	Unknown
		Willie Fitzgerald	B Coy 3rd Bn
		Mick Kerrigan	Unknown

Dublin Brigade Active Service Unit (ASU)	O/C	Volunteers	Company & Battalion of Origin
No. 4 Section 4th Bn Area south side HQ: Brickworks Drimnagh & Kavanagh's Hills, Crumlin Road Dump: Alderman Flanagan's near Rialto Bridge, Mrs Coyle's, Meath St & Jimmy O'Neill's (The Sweep's) Francis St	Section Cmdr. Gus Murphy killed in action & succeeded by Micky Sweeney O/C Lt. Pádraig O'Connor (June 1921)	Patrick Morrissey (Reassigned to organise Leitrim Brigade early 1921) Jim McGuinness Joe McGuinness Paddy Rigney Jim Tully Tom Lillis Patrick Mullen George Nolan Pat Collins Jim Harpur M. Walshe Tommy Leigh Mick Stack Simon McInerney	A Coy 4th Bn F Coy 1st Bn C Coy 4th Bn C Coy 4th Bn Unknown Unknown C Coy 4th Bn A Coy 4th Bn Unknown F Coy 4th Bn Unknown Unknown Unknown G Coy 1st Bn

Total numbers include replacements brought in due to arrests, capture and deaths in action.

Irish Volunteers executed in Mountjoy Gaol, Dublin, during the War of Independence 1919–21[7]

Name	Age	County of origin	Unit	Charge	Date of execution
Kevin Barry	18	Dublin	C Coy 1st Bn Dublin Brigade	Murder of a British soldier at North King Street	1 Nov 1920 6 a.m.
Thomas Whelan	22	Clifden, Co. Galway	C Coy 3rd Bn Dublin Brigade	Murder of Capt. Bagalley Baggot St.	14 Mar 1921 6 a.m.
Paddy Moran	33	Crossna, Co. Roscommon	D Coy 2nd Bn Dublin Brigade	Murder of Lt. Ames Mount St.	14 Mar 1921 6 a.m.
Patrick Doyle	29	Dublin	No. 1 Section Dublin ASU	Drumcondra Ambush	14 Mar 1921 7 a.m.
Bernard Ryan	20	Dublin	No. 1 Section Dublin ASU	Drumcondra Ambush	14 Mar 1921 7 a.m.
Frank Flood	19	Dublin	No. 1 Section Dublin ASU	Drumcondra Ambush	14 Mar 1921 8 a.m.
Tommy Bryan	22	Dublin	No. 1 Section Dublin ASU	Drumcondra Ambush	14 Mar 1921 8 a.m.
Thomas Traynor	39	Tullow, Co. Carlow	B Coy 3rd Bn Dublin Brigade	Great Brunswick St. Ambush	25 April 1921
Edmond Foley	24	Galbally, Co. Limerick	Galbally Coy, East Limerick Brigade	Murder of RIC Sgt. Wallace and Con. Enright at Knocklong Railway Station	7 June 1921 7 a.m.
Patrick Maher	32	Knocklong, Co. Limerick	Cush Coy, East Limerick Brigade	Murder of RIC Sgt. Wallace and Con. Enright at Knocklong Railway Station	7 June 1921 7 a.m.

Criminal Investigations Department Staff[8]

Director CID: Major-General Joe McGrath TD
Asst. Captain H. Murray
Operational Commander: Captain Paddy Moynihan

Name	Details
Comdt. W. J. Whitmore Brennan	–
Hubert Byrne	Intelligence Agent. Infiltrated IRA
M. J. Byrne	–
Harry J. Clancy	–
David Crowley	–
Richard Duffy	–
Patrick Egan	CID 33
Paddy Ennis	–
Thomas Fitzgerald	Killed on active service 19 Oct. 1923
Michael Fleming	–
Martin Hore	CID 4
John Keogh	Killed on active service 17 Dec. 1922
Capt. Michael Kilkelly	–
Lt. N. Leonard	–
James McNamara	Key agent of Michael Collins in G Division DMP. Injured in motor accident Grafton St 13 Sept. 1922, died 15 Sept. 1922
Thomas J. McCarthy	–
Bernard McGinley	–
Ross Mahon	–
John F. Mooney	–
Capt. Henry S. Murray	–
John J. Murray	–

Name	Details
James O'Connor	–
Joseph O'Carroll	–
William O'Grady	–
Patrick O'Kelly	–
Denis O'Leary	–
Richard O'Leary	18 months' imprisonment for manslaughter of Richard Aylward 9 Mar. 1924
Loughlin Rourke	–
Capt. J. Stafford	–
John Treacy	–
Lt. S. Ua Dálaigh (J. O'Daly)	–
John Young	Mortally injured on active service 3 Oct. 1923, died 13 Oct. 1923

Protective Corps

Operational Commander: Captain Paddy Moynihan

Name	Details
Charlie Byrne	Former member of the Squad, nicknamed 'The Count'
H. Hall	–
Daniel Horan	–
George Nolan	–

Endnotes

1. 'A Few Hundred Rounds under God's Blue Sky'

1   Lynch, Michael. Witness Statement (hereafter WS) 511, pp. 9–10. Bureau of Military History. Military Archives, Cathal Brugha Barracks, Dublin (hereafter BMH).
2   The number of Cumann na mBan totalled approximately 150. O'Mahony, Seán. *Frongoch. University of Revolution*. FDR Teoranta, Dublin, 1987, p. 17.
3   O'Mahony, *op. cit.*, p. 18.
4   O'Malley, Ernie. *On Another Man's Wound*. Anvil Books, Dublin, 2002, p. 46.
5   Nunan, Seán. WS 1744, p. 4. BMH.
6   *Hidden History*. 'The Man Who Lost Ireland.' A Mint-Flame Co Production for RTÉ 2006.
7   O'Malley, *op. cit.*, p. 46.
8   Barton, Brian. *The Secret Court Martial Records of the Easter Rising*. The History Press, United Kingdom, 2010, p. 210.
9   Lynch, Michael. WS 511, pp. 9–10. BMH.
10 Barton, *op. cit.*, p. 219.
11 *The Irish Times,* 6 May 1916. National Library of Ireland, Dublin.
12 *Irish Independent*, 26–29 April 1916, 1–4 May 1916 (1 issue). National Library of Ireland, Dublin.
13 *Irish Independent*, 6 May 1916. National Library of Ireland, Dublin.
14 *Hidden History*. 'The Man Who Lost Ireland.' A Mint-Flame Co Production for RTÉ 2006.
15 http://hansard.millbanksystems.com/commons/1916/may/11/continuance-of-martial-law# S5CV0082P0_19160511_HOC_338
16 O'Mahony, *op. cit.*, pp. 18–19.
17 *Ibid.*, p. 21.
18 *Ibid.*, p. 23.
19 Peppard, Thomas. WS 4399, p. 6. BMH.
20 Coogan, Tim Pat. *De Valera. Long Fellow, Long Shadow*. Hutchinson, London, 1993, p. ix.
21 *Ibid.*, p. 94.
22 *Irish Independent*, 12 July 1917. National Library of Ireland, Dublin.
23 *Ibid.*
24 *Ibid.*
25 *Ibid.*
26 White, G. and O'Shea, B. Illustrated by Younghusband, B. *Irish Volunteer Soldier 1913–23*. Osprey Publishing, Oxford, 2003, p. 41.

27 Macardle, Dorothy. *The Irish Republic*. Irish Press Ltd., Dublin, p. 233.

28 Ferriter, Diarmaid. *Judging Dev*. Royal Irish Academy. Dublin, 2007, p. 31.

29 Walsh, Richard. WS 400, p. 33. BMH.

30 Macardle, *op. cit.*, p. 235.

31 Coogan, Tim Pat. *op. cit.*, p. 101.

32 RIC reports on the tour of West Clare by Éamon De Valera and Peter [Peadar] Clancy 2–6 October 1917. CO 904/105 (p. 57 of original file).

33 Ernie O'Malley Notebooks. Interview with Pat McCrea, p. 115. EOM P17b/109.

34 Henderson, Ruaidhrí. WS 1686. Easter Week Rising: A Tabulated Summary of Events in Dublin, 24–29 April 1916. BMH.

35 Dunphy, Mark. Lecture on Peadar Clancy: Clare's Easter Rising Hero. *The Clare Herald*, 4 May 2016.

36 *Ibid.*

37 RIC reports on the tour of West Clare by Éamon De Valera and Peter [Peadar] Clancy 2–6 October 1917. CO 904/105 (pp. 47–104 of original file).

38 *Ibid.* (p. 47 of original file).

39 *Ibid.* De Valera at Ennistymon (p. 53 of original file).

40 *Ibid.* Report of RIC District Inspector T. O'Brien, Ennistymon (p. 74 of original file).

41 *Ibid.* Report of RIC Sergeant P. Connell 55789 at Corofin (pp. 91–92 of original file).

42 *Ibid.* Peadar Clancy at Ennistymon (p. 58 of original file). On 11 July 1917 Irish Volunteers in Ballybunion held a victory parade to celebrate de Valera's victory in the East Clare by-election. The Volunteers did not carry arms that evening. As the parade passed the RIC barracks a bystander threw a stone at the building, smashing one of the windows. Later that night, as the parade returned through the town and was passing the barracks a second time, RIC Constable Lyons opened fire, hitting Volunteer Dan Scanlon in the back. He died five hours later. The coroner recommended that both Constable Lyons and Sergeant Mulcahy, who was in charge of the barracks, be charged with murder. The case was dismissed at the Cork Assizes despite evidence of a witness, Mary Mason. In August, six local men were charged with offences relating to incidents that night in Ballybunion. The members of the RIC were not among those charged.

43 Woodham-Smith, Cecil. *The Great Hunger. Ireland 1845–1849*. Penguin Books, London, 1991, pp. 301–302 quoting Mr G. Woodhouse report 9 August, 1847, T 64/369 C.

44 RIC Inspector General's reports and Various County Inspectors' reports throughout 1918, National Archives of Ireland, Microfilm MFA/54/65.

45 Stapleton, William James. WS 822, p. 21. BMH.

46 Dalton, Charles. *With the Dublin Brigade. Espionage and Assassination with Michael Collins' Intelligence Unit*. Mercier Press, Cork, 2014, p. 62.

47 Stapleton, *op. cit.*, p. 22.

48 Thornton, Frank. WS 615, p. 1. BMH.

49 Noyk, Michael. WS 707, pp. 27–28. BMH.

50 Ua h-Uallacháin, Gearóid. WS 336, p. 2. BMH.

51 Superintendent George Love writing about Michael Collins 29 May 1917 (p. 214 of original file). Colonial Office file on Michael Collins CO 904/196/65 The National

Archives, Kew, UK. Featured in Sinn Féin and Republican Suspects 1899–1921. Dublin Castle Special Branch Files CO 904 (193–216). Eneclann, Trinity College, Dublin.

52 26 September 1917 (p. 228 of original file). Colonial Office file on Michael Collins CO 904/196/65 The National Archives, Kew, UK. Featured in Sinn Féin and Republican Suspects 1899–1921. Dublin Castle Special Branch Files CO 904 (193–216). Eneclann, Trinity College, Dublin.

53 *Ibid.* (p. 197 of original file). The description of Collins was printed in the RIC's gazette *Hue and Cry* on 4 April 1919. Because the charges against him were dropped by the Attorney General, a request was made to remove the description from future editions.

54 Constable Hugh Maguire 59496 notes on speech of Michael Collins at Legga, County Longford 3 March 1918 (p. 159 of original file). Colonial Office file on Michael Collins CO 904/196/65 The National Archives, Kew, UK. Featured in Sinn Féin and Republican Suspects 1899–1921. Dublin Castle Special Branch Files CO 904 (193–216). Eneclann, Trinity College, Dublin.

55 *Ibid.*

56 District Inspector Charles Collins' report on speech and drilling carried out by Michael Collins at Legga, County Longford 3 March 1918 (p. 178 of original file).

57 *An t-Óglach*, 15 November 1918. Military Archives, Cathal Brugha Barracks, Dublin (hereafter MA).

58 Coogan, *op. cit.*, p. 85.

59 Colonial Office File on Michael Collins CO 904/196/65, National Archives, Kew, UK. Featured in *Sinn Féin and Republican Suspects 1899–1921*. Dublin Castle Special Branch Files CO 904 (193–216). Eneclann, Trinity College, Dublin (p. 180 of original file).

60 Arrest and Trial of Michael Collins. Cutting from *The Roscommon Herald,* 6 April 1918. Bureau of Military History, CD1 /8/2, Group 8 II from Seán Collins. MA.

61 Sligo Gaol Register. Sligo Library Local Studies Collection.

62 Coogan, *op. cit.*, p. 89.

63 Message to the Chief Secretary of Ireland at Dublin Castle from the Governor at Lincoln Prison dated 4 February 1919. Colonial Office file on Éamon De Valera CO 904/199 (pp. 19–21 of original file). The National Archives, Kew, UK. Featured in Sinn Féin and Republican Suspects 1899–1921. Dublin Castle Special Branch Files CO 904 (193–216). Eneclann, Trinity College, Dublin.

64 Everett, Susanne. *World War One*. Tiger Books International Ltd. Bison Books. London, 1980, p. 200.

65 Sheffield, Gary. In Association With Imperial War Museums. *The First World War Remembered*. Index Books. André Deutsch Limited. London, 2014, p. 103.

66 *Ibid.* pp. 110–111.

67 Boff, Jonathan. *World War One. Military Structures and Ranks*. British Library. https://www.bl.uk/world-war-one/articles/military-structures-and-ranks   and Chappell, Mike. *The British Army in World War I* (1) The Western Front 1914–16. Osprey Publishing, Oxford, 2008, p. 35.

68 Basic Fighting Unit of the American Expeditionary Force. The Square Division. Doughboy Center. http://www.worldwar1.com/dbc/squarediv.htm

69 Macardle, *op. cit.*, p. 249.

70   Lloyd George on Conscription in Ireland. HC Deb 09 April 1918 vol. 104 cc1357–62.

71   *Ibid.*

72   Liddell Hart, B. H. *History of the First World War.* Pan Books, London, 1972, p. 205.

73   William O'Brien MP. HC Deb 09 April 1918 vol. 104 cc1357–62.

74   Macardle, *op. cit.*, p. 249.

75   *Ibid.,* p. 250.

76   *Ibid.*

77   Ferriter, *op. cit.*, p. 32.

78   Macardle, *op. cit.*, p. 251.

79   *Ibid.*, p. 252.

80   U-boat: *Unterseeboot*: German word for submarine.

81   Macardle, *op. cit.*, p. 252.

82   *Ibid.* Also, *An t-Óglach*, 14 October 1918. MA.

83   Ibid.

84   *An t-Óglach*, 1 February 1919. MA.

85   *Ibid.*

86   *An t-Óglach*: Companies 14 October 1918, Battalions 30 November 1918 and 16 December 1918, railway demolition 14 and 29 October 1918, railway demolition without explosives 1 February 1919, scouting and tracking 30 November 1918. MA.

87   Military Service Pensions Collection. File No. W24SP12702 Application of Jeremiah Joseph 'Ginger' O'Connell. MA.

88   *An t-Óglach*, 1 February 1920. MA. http://antoglach.militaryarchives.ie/PDF/1920_02_Vol_11_No_5_An_t-Oglac.pdf

89   Military Service Pensions Collection. File Number: WMSP 34REF20034. Joseph Michael Stanley. MA.

90   *Ibid.* 24 June 1922.

91   *Ibid.*

92   *An t-Óglach*, 21 October 1922. MA.

93   Bridie O'Reilly, WS 454, p. 8. BMH.

94   Cabinet Papers. 16 December 1918. CAB/24/72. The National Archives, Kew, UK.

95   *Ibid.*

96   Cabinet Papers. 15 May 1919. CAB/24/79. The National Archives, Kew, UK.

97   O'Connor, Joseph. WS 157, p. 3. BMH.

98   *Ibid.*

99   *Ibid.*, p. 3–4.

100 Mulcahy, Mary Josephine née Min Ryan. WS 399, p. 1. BMH.

101 *Ibid.*

102 Little, Patrick J. WS 1769, p. 6. BMH.

103 Century Ireland 1913–1923. RTÉ & Boston College. 'New Lord Lieutenant Makes First Public Appearance in Ireland.' http://www.rte.ie/centuryireland/index.php/articles/new-lord-lieutenant-makes-first-public-appearance-in-ireland

104 Little, Patrick J. WS 1769, p. 39. BMH. Little could not recall the exact time or date but estimated it to be around September 1919.

105 Parliament and Ireland. Living Heritage. http://www.parliament.uk/about/living-heritage/evolutionofparliament/legislativescrutiny/parliamentandireland/overview/two-home-rule-bills/

106 Walsh, Oonagh. *Ireland's Independence 1880–1923*. Routledge, London, 2002, p. 38

107 An eyewitness account of the Voyage of 'The Fanny' 1914. MS 46,806. National Library of Ireland, Dublin.

108 Jocelyn, Viscount. CO 904/204 File on Provocative Drilling by the UVF in County Down, August 1914.

109 RIC Inspector General's report, September 1918. National Archives of Ireland, microfilm, MFA/54/65.

110 RIC Inspector General's report, October 1918. National Archives of Ireland, microfilm, MFA/54/65.

111 Townshend, Charles. *The Republic. The Fight for Irish Independence*. Allen Lane. Penguin Books. London, 2013, p. 60.

112 RIC Inspector-General J. Byrne's report. Cabinet Papers. 16 December 1918. CAB/24/72. The National Archives, Kew, UK.

113 *Ibid.*

114 DMP Superintendent Owen Brien's report. Cabinet Papers. 16 December 1918. CAB/24/72. The National Archives, Kew, UK.

115 *Ibid.*

116 Lieutenant-General Frederick Shaw's report. Cabinet Papers. 16 December 1918. CAB/24/72. The National Archives, Kew, UK.

117 Little, Patrick J. WS 1769, p. 39. BMH.

118 Irish Volunteers of the South Tipperary Brigade who carried out the ambush at Soloheadbeg on 21 January 1919: Seumas Robinson, Dan Breen, Seán Treacy, Seán Hogan, Michael Ryan, Patrick McCormack, Tadgh Crowe and Patrick Dwyer. Listed in Patrick Dwyer's WS 1432. MA.

119 Abbott, Richard. *Police Casualties in Ireland 1919–1922*. Mercier Press, Cork, 2000, pp. 30–33.

120 Breen, Daniel. WS 1739, p. 21. BMH.

121 *An t-Óglach*, February 1919. MA.

122 *Ibid.*

123 Breen, Daniel. WS 1739, p. 23. BMH.

124 *An t-Óglach*, 14 September 1918. MA.

2. 'DUBLIN: THE HEART OF THE WHOLE CONSPIRACY'

1   Sheehan, William. *Fighting for Dublin. The British Battle for Dublin*. The Collins Press, Cork, 2007, p. 79.

2   Hart, Peter (ed.). *Narratives. British Intelligence in Ireland 1920–21. The Final Reports*. Cork University Press, Cork, 2002, p. 31.

3   'The Construction of Dun Laoghaire Harbour.' Dun Laoghaire Harbour Company, Crofton Lodge, Harbour Road, Dun Laoghaire. http://dlharbour.ie/historical/

4   F Company, 6th Battalion, Dublin Brigade, IRA. MA-MSPC-RO-7. Military Service Pension Collection. MA. Kautt, W.H. *Ground Truths. British Army Operations in the Irish War of Independence*. Irish Academic Press, Sallins, County Kildare, 2014 (Various IRA operations listed throughout this publication). A more comprehensive list is provided by F Company 6th Battalion, Dublin Brigade, IRA in the Military Service Pensions Collection under IRA Organisations and Membership.

5   Henderson, Frank. WS 821, pp. 37–38. BMH.

6   *Ibid.*

7   IRA Nominal Rolls. RO/1–9 and RO/20–25. Military Service Pensions Collection. MA.

8   Military Service Pensions Collection. File Number: MSP34REF9462. Application of Michael Joseph Lynch. MA.

9   Sheehan, *op. cit.*, p. 127.

10   Military Service Pensions Collection. 4th Battalion Roll, Dublin Brigade. MA-MSPC-RO-5. MA.

11   Joye, Lar. 'The Mauser Model 71 Rifle.' *History Ireland*, Volume 19, Issue I, January–February 2011.

12   Pegler, Martin. Illustrated by Chappell, Mike. *British Tommy 1914–18*. Warrior. Osprey Publishing, 2008, Oxford, United Kingdom, p. 16.

13   Laffan, Nicholas. WS 703, p. 3. BMH.

14   *Ibid.*, pp. 6–7.

15   Pegler, *op. cit.*, p. 17.

16   *Ibid.*

17   Lynch, Michael. WS 511, p. 43. BMH.

18   O'Donovan, James [Seumas] L. WS 1713, p. 8. BMH.

19   McHugh, Patrick. WS 664, p. 25. BMH.

20   Lynch, Michael. WS 511, pp. 57–59. BMH.

21   O'Donovan, James [Seumas] L. WS 1713, p. 9. BMH.

22   Lynch, Michael. WS 511,p. 41–62. BMH.

23   Hogan, Rev. Fr William, 1895–1964. Spent over 32 years on the teaching staff of St Aloysius College. Buried at the Jesuit Plot at Gore Hill with Rev. Fr Tom Hehir. From County Kerry, Fr Bill Hogan went to secondary school at the Cistercian College Roscrea, County Tipperary. He then went to the Jesuits at Rathfarnham to study for his Juniorate. His biography states that his superiors may have felt he was becoming too active among the revolutionaries and moved him to Limerick and then to Jersey in the Channel Islands. Rev. Fr Bill Hogan was ordained in 1926 and was sent to Sydney, Australia where he began teaching at St Aloysius. It is recorded that he had a special devotion to the Holy Souls and prayed every day for them. From *Irish Province News*, October 1964. Irish Jesuit Archives, Dublin.

24   O'Donovan, James [Seumas] L. WS 1713, p. 4. BMH

25   O'Donoghue, Michael V., WS 1741, p. 190. BMH.

26   O'Donovan, James [Seumas]. *An t-Óglach*, 1 March 1920. MA.

27   *Ibid.*, pp. 3–4.

28   *Ibid.*

29   McDonnell, Andrew. WS 1768, p. 68. BMH.

30   Brennan, Patrick J. WS 1773, p. 10. BMH.

31   *An t-Óglach*, 15 March 1920. MA.

32   McDonnell, Andrew. WS 1768, pp. 32–33. BMH.

33   Fitzgerald, George. WS 684, p. 17. BMH.

34   McDonnell, Daniel. WS 486, p. 6. BMH.

35   'The Tragic Fire of 1920. Rathmines Parish Church Fire 1920.' http://rathminesparish.ie/about-us/parish-history

36   Lynch, Michael. WS 511, pp. 108–109. BMH.

37 *Ibid.*, pp. 110–111.

38 Article on Spanish-Cuban War 1895–98 quoting reports and observations of Lt Barnes (eyewitness) and Major Calwell, English Military Writer. *An t-Óglach*, March 1920. MA. http://www.winstonchurchill.org/the-life-of-churchill/young-soldier/380-lt-churchill-4th-queens-own-hussars

39 *An t-Óglach*, 1 March 1920. MA.

40 *An t-Óglach*, 5 April and 1 May 1920. MA.

41 Kautt, W. H. *Ground Truths. British Army Operations in the Irish War of Independence.* Irish Academic Press, County Kildare, 2014, pp. 94–95.

42 List of Sinn Fein [Irish Volunteers] Arklow District: Grade A, B and C Types. WO35/86B Part 2. Raids and Searches F Coy ADRIC, Intelligence and Military Reports. Also Report on prominent IRA member who carries a gun: 15 February 1921. And 2 July 1921 on J. Conroy. WO35/87/1 Operations Requested by D Branch, Chief of Police. The National Archives, Kew, UK.

43 Mac Caisin, Seumas. WS 8, pp. 5–6. BMH.

44 Ua h-Uallachain, Gearoid [Holohan, Garry]. WS 328, p. 3. BMH.

45 Mac Caisin, Seumas. WS 8, p. 8. BMH.

46 Ua h-Uallachain, Gearoid. WS 328, p. 5. BMH.

47 *Ibid.*, p. 3.

48 Price, John Patrick. Memoirs of Na Fianna written in 1956. Family collection of historical documents.

49 Ua h-Uallachain, Gearoid. WS 328, p. 12. BMH.

50 *Ibid.*, p. 42.

51 *Ibid.*, p. 4.

52 Na Fianna members were photographed armed with pickaxe handles transporting arms away from Howth after the successful gunrunning mission by Erskine Childers on board the Yacht *Asgard*. Gillis, Liz. *Revolution in Dublin. A Photographic History 1913–1923.* Mercier Press, Cork, 2013, p. 17. Also a photograph of Irish Volunteers parading on the quayside at Howth during the gunrunning July 1914, some of whom are armed with pickaxe handles as well as rifles. Coogan, Tim Pat. *1916: The Easter Rising.* Weidenfeld & Nicolson, United Kingdom, 2010, pp. 54–55.

53 Ua h-Uallachain, Gearoid. WS 328, pp 55–62. BMH. Also O'Daly, Patrick. WS 220. Bureau of Military History. MA, pp. 3–9.

54 Ua h-Uallachain, Gearoid. WS 328, p. 4. BMH. Also *Irish Independent*, 12 and 13 June 1917. National Library of Ireland, Dublin.

55 Ua h-Uallachain, Gearoid. WS 328, p. 7. BMH.

56 *Ibid.*

57 *An t-Óglach*, 21 October 1922. MA.

58 Ernie O'Malley Notebooks, P17b/110. Interview with Pat McCrea. UCD Archives, Dublin, pp. 114–115.

59 *Ibid.*

60 *Memoirs of Miles Byrne, edited by his widow.* A new edition with an introduction by Stephen Gwynn. Vol II. Dublin: Maunsell & Co., London: A.H. Bullen, 1907.

61 Von Spohn, Colonel. *The Art of Command.* Trans. by General Staff, War Office [British] from the 'Jahrbücher für die deutsche Armee und Marine, October, 1907, by permission of the publisher, Herr A. Bath, Berlin, pp. 1, 7 and 16.

62 *Ibid*, p. 10.

63 Military Service Pensions Collection. File No. DP23324. Application of Maire McKee, sister of Richard McKee, Brigadier Dublin Brigade. MA. Also Henderson, Frank. WS 821, pp. 34–35. BMH.

64 Ernie O'Malley Notebooks, P17b/103. Interview with Maire McKee. UCD Archives, Dublin, p. 169.

65 Lynch, Michael. WS 511, p. 35. BMH.

66 *Ibid.*, pp. 35–38.

67 Hunter, Tom. Military Service Pensions Collection. File Number: DP4587. MA.

68 Dalton, Charles. *With the Dublin Brigade. Espionage and Assassination with Michael Collins Intelligence Unit.* Mercier Press, Cork, 2014, pp. 67–68.

69 Laffan, Nicholas. WS 703, p. 5. BMH.

70 Constabulary of Ireland Act, House of Commons debate 18 February 1836 Vol 31 CC 532–51.

71 *Thom's Official Directory 1920.* Entries on the Dublin Metropolitan Police. Alex Thom and Co. Ltd., Dublin, 1920, pp. 755–756 and 1433. Also *Thom's Official Directory 1921.* Alex Thom and Co. Ltd., Dublin, 1921, pp. 1432–1433. An Garda Síochána. 'Divisions and Boundaries of the Dublin Metropolitan Police District.' Chapter 29, 4 July 1836. http://www.garda.ie/Documents/User/Divisons%20and%20Boundaries%20of%20the%20DMP.pdf

72 Brewer, J. D. *The RIC: An Oral History.* Institute of Irish Studies, Queen's University Belfast, 1990, p. 6.

73 Cabinet Papers Cab/24/72. Superintendent Owen Brien, DMP Report, 4 December 1918.

74 *Ibid.*

75 Malcolm, Elizabeth. *The Irish Policeman 1822–1922: a life.* Four Courts Press, Dublin, p. 124.

76 Brewer, *op. cit.,* p. 5.

77 *Ibid.*

78 Royal Irish Constabulary List and Directory January 1920, His Majesty's Stationery Office (HMSO). The Archive CD Books Project, Eneclann, Trinity College, Dublin, p. 200.

79 Ernie O'Malley Notebooks. P17b/110. Interview with Tom Carney. UCD Archives, Dublin, p. 29.

80 Royal Irish Constabulary List and Directory January 1920, HMSO. The Archive CD Books Project, Eneclann, Trinity College, Dublin, p. 199.

81 James, Garry. 'The Royal Irish Constabulary Carbine.' *Guns & Ammo*, 15 August 2016.

82 Ernie O'Malley Notebooks, P17b/109. Interview with Tom Carney. UCD Archives, Dublin, p. 29.

83 *Ibid.*, pp. 29–30.

84 Brewer, *op. cit.,* p. 6.

85 Broy, Eamon. WS 1280, p. 38. BMH.

86 Statistics gathered and reproduced with the kind permission of Abbott, Richard. *Police Casualties in Ireland 1919–1922.* Mercier Press, Cork, 2000.

87 Mulkeen, Eddie. *A Night of Burnings – of RIC Stations.* Foxrock Local History Club, Publication No 42. October 1996.

88 *Ibid.*

89 Kautt, W. H. *Ground Truths. British Army Operations in the Irish War of Independence.* Irish Academic Press, County Kildare, Ireland, p. 2.

90 Cabinet Papers. CAB/24/72. Lieutenant-General Frederick Shaw, Report from the General Officer Commanding-in-Chief in Ireland. 7 December 1918.

91 *Ibid.*

92 *Thom's Official Directory 1918.* Entries on the Military Establishment. Alex Thom and Co. Ltd., Dublin, 1918, pp. 770ff.

93 Cabinet Papers. CAB/24/79. Lieutenant-General Frederick Shaw, General Officer Commanding-in-Chief, Ireland, 10 May 1919.

94 *Ibid.*

3. Collinstown, Assassinations & Ashtown

1   Historical Dáil Debates. Tuesday 21 January 1919.

2   O'Hegarty, Diarmuid. *Dictionary of Irish Biography Online.* Cambridge University Press and Royal Irish Academy, 2016.

3   RIC Dublin, County Inspector's Report for February 1919. National Archives of Ireland. Microfilm of PRO File: CO 904/108.

4   RIC Dublin, County Inspector's Report for January 1919. National Archives of Ireland. Microfilm of PRO File: CO 904/108.

5   *Ibid.*

6   *Ibid.*

7   Lynch, Michael. Raid on Collinstown Aerodrome. Collins Papers. Item A/0800/VIII. MA.

8   *Ibid.*

9   Holohan, Paddy. A statement in Michael Lynch's account of the Collinstown Raid. Collins Papers. Item A/0800/VIII. MA.

10 McDonnell, Dan. WS 486, p. 3. BMH.

11 Report of the RIC Inspector General contained in RIC Dublin, County Inspector's Report for March 1919. National Archives of Ireland. Microfilm of PRO File: CO 904/108.

12 Ernie O'Malley Notebooks. P17b/110. Interview with Pat McCrea. UCD Archives, p. 5.

13 Lawless, Joseph V. WS 1043, p. 258. BMH.

14 RIC Dublin, County Inspector's Report for March 1919. National Archives of Ireland. Microfilm of PRO File: CO 904/108.

15 Broy, Eamon. WS 1280, pp. 69–73. BMH.

16 *Ibid.*, p. 76.

17 *Ibid.*, p. 78.

18 *Ibid.*

19 *Ibid.*, p. 79.

20 Macardle, Dorothy. *The Irish Republic.* Irish Press Ltd., Dublin, pp. 306–307.

21 Colley, Harry. WS 1687, p. 40. BMH.

22 Broy, Eamon. WS 1280, p. 80. BMH.

23 Ernie O'Malley Notebooks. P17b/110. Interview with Pat McCrea, UCD Archives, Dublin, p. 29.

24 Nunan, Seán. WS 1744, pp. 9–10. BMH.

25 Broy, Eamon. WS 1280, p. 105. BMH.

26 Macardle, *op. cit.*, p. 300.

27 Rev. Fr John Hagan was made a Monsignor on 6 December 1921. http://www.irishcollege.org/wp-content/uploads/2011/02/Hagan-Catalogue-Part-1-Intro-+-1904-1919.pdf

28 Military Service Pensions Collection. Trades listed by members of the Squad prior to their military service. MA.

29 Byrne, Vincent. WS 423, p. 21. BMH. Also Leonard, Joseph. WS 547, p. 2. BMH.

30 Ernie O'Malley Notebooks. P17b/110. Interview with Pat McCrea, UCD Archives, Dublin, p. 30.

31 *Ibid.*, pp. 31–32.

32 Abbott, Richard. *Police Casualties in Ireland 1919–1922,* Mercier Press, Cork, 2000, pp. 40–43. Also Ryle Dwyer, T. *The Squad and the Intelligence Operations of Michael Collins.* Mercier Press, Cork, 2005, pp. 46–48. Also Ernie O'Malley Notebooks. P17b/109. Interview with Jim Slattery, UCD Archives, Dublin, pp. 102–103.

33 Ernie O'Malley Notebooks. P17b/109. Interview with Jim Slattery, UCD Archives, Dublin, p. 103.

34 Abbott, *op. cit.*, p. 45.

35 1911 Census for the Family of James Daly, father of Patrick O'Daly. National Archives of Ireland 1911 Census.

36 O'Daly, Patrick. WS 220, p. 36. BMH.

37 1911 Census for the Family of Archibald Gillies, brother-in-law of Paddy O'Daly. National Archives of Ireland 1911. Also https://civilrecords.irishgenealogy marriage of Patrick Daly and Margaret Gillies on 16 May 1910 at St Columba's Roman Catholic Church Drumcondra.

38 List of The Squad as stated by: Vincent Byrne. WS 423, p. 33. BMH. Also Ernie O'Malley Notebooks. P17b/110. Interview with Pat McCrea, UCD Archives, Dublin, p. 5. (The list given by Pat McCrea is the one given by him to Piaras Beaslaí when he wrote *Michael Collins and the Making of a New Ireland*, Phoenix, Dublin, 1926.)

39 Military Service Pensions Collection. File No. 3D197. Application of Mary Keogh, widow of Captain Michael Keogh. Proceedings of Court of Enquiry, Mallow, 28 June 1923. MA.

40 O'Daly, Patrick. WS 220, p. 36. BMH.

41 *Ibid.*, p. 4. Also Béaslaí, Piaras. *IRA Jailbreaks 1918–1921* (Foreword by Florence O'Donoghue) Mercier Press, Cork, 2010, p. 147.

42 O'Daly, Patrick. WS 387, pp. 4–5. BMH. There is a slight adjustment in the details of aspects of Paddy O'Daly's account of his imprisonment and the escape in March 1919. See corrections list provided at the beginning of the WS on p. 2.

43 Leonard, Joseph. WS 547, p. 2. BMH.

44 Dáil Éireann Debate Vol. F No. 13. 20 August 1919.

45 Oireachtas History: http://www.oireachtas.ie/parliament/about/history/parliament inireland/

46 Lawless, Sr. Eithne (E. Lawless). WS 414, pp. 1–10. BMH.

47 Hurley, J. CO 904/204 File on the Court Martial of James Hurley for intent to wound Detective Officer Wharton on 10 November 1919. The National Archives, Kew, UK.

48 O'Daly, Patrick. WS 220, p. 12. BMH.

49 Colonial Office File on Captain Kearns Batchelor CO 904/193/9. The National Archives, Kew, UK. Featured in Sinn Féin and Republican Suspects 1899–1921. Dublin Castle Special Branch Files CO 904 (193–216). Eneclann, Trinity College, Dublin.

50 *Ibid.*

51 O'Daly, Patrick. WS 220, p. 13. BMH.

52 The Tipperary 'Big Four' of Seumas Robinson, Seán Treacy, Dan Breen and Seán Hogan were the leading members of the Tipperary Brigade who organised the attack at Soloheadbeg on 21 January 1919. Seán Hogan was later captured leading to one of the most dramatic rescues ever attempted in Ireland. The successful rescue was organised by Robinson, Treacy and Breen aided by the Galbally Coy and a Volunteer from Cashel.

53 Abbott, Richard, *op. cit.,* pp. 46–47.

54 Yeates, Padraig. "'Oh God, what did I do to deserve this?" The Life and Death of Detective Sergeant John Barton', *History Ireland*, Vol. 24, No. 5, Edited by Tommy Graham, September/October 2016, pp. 36–39.

55 Leonard, Joseph. WS 547, p. 2. BMH.

56 1901 and 1911 Censuses The National Archives of Ireland. http://www.census.nationalarchives.ie/reels/nai000079837/ and http://www.census.nationalarchives.ie/reels/nai001232033/

57 HO 317/46 Miscellaneous police and intelligence reports. Various letters to and from London Cabinet Office and the branch of the Chief of Police Dublin Castle. Material relates to relations between General Hugh Tudor, Colonel Winter concerning some of their subordinate officers who did not have their trust. Appeals were made to Sir John Anderson, Assistant Under-Secretary, Dublin Castle. Letters dated August to December 1921.

58 Military Service Pensions Collection. File No. MSPC34REF4945. Application of Lily Mernin, MA.

59 *Ibid.*

60 Military Service Pensions Collection. File No. W24SP10942 Application of Thomas Markham, MA.

61 O'Duffy, Seán M. WS 618, p. 19. BMH.

62 Broy, Eamon. WS 1280, p. 84. BMH.

63 *Ibid.*

64 McDonnell, Daniel. WS 486, p. 15. BMH.

65 *Ibid.*, p. 20.

66 *Ibid.*, p. 22.

67 The Piaras Béaslaí Papers. Ms 33,913 (14). List of IRA intelligence officers' code numbers with their respective contacts in different locations in Dublin. While dated November 1921 the likelihood is that these venues and people listed were *in situ* throughout the latter part of the War of independence. National Library of Ireland, Dublin.

68 Kennedy, Patrick. WS 499, p. 2. BMH.

69 Hughes, James F. WS 535, pp. 5–6. BMH.

70 *Ibid.*

71 *Ibid.*, p. 9.

72 Ernie O'Malley Notebooks. P17b/110. Interview with Pat McCrea, UCD Archives, Dublin, pp. 7, 11, 13 and 16.

73 Byrne, Vincent. WS 822, p. 35. BMH.

74 *Ibid.*, p. 36.

75 Stapleton, William James. WS 822, p. 37. BMH.

76 Ernie O'Malley Notebooks. P17b/109. Interview with Jim Slattery, UCD Archives, Dublin, p. 102.

77 List of IRA men present at the Ashtown Ambush as given by Michael McDonnell: Michael McDonnell, Paddy O'Daly, Martin Savage, Tom Kehoe, Jim Slattery, Vinny Byrne, Joe Leonard, Ben Barrett, Seán Hogan, Seán Treacy, Seumas Robinson and Dan Breen. Paddy O'Daly mentions that Seán Doyle and Ben Barrett were also there. WS 225, p.5. BMH.

78 Accounts of the ambush are taken from the participants Paddy O'Daly WS 387, Mick McDonnell WS 225 and Dan Breen WS 1739, BMH. Also Breen, Dan. *My Fight for Irish Freedom*, Anvil, Tralee, Kerry, 1964, pp. 83–96. Also contributing to the account of the event are the WSs given by eyewitnesses from Kelly's Pub, British soldiers, DMP policemen and civilians to Alan Bell RM and DMP detectives during the course of the subsequent investigation: CO 904/188(1) Black Ledger. Private Papers of Sir John Anderson. The National Archives, Kew, UK.

79 Paddy O'Daly wrote that it was he who gave Breen a lift on his bicycle and it was the both of them who held up Michael Donohoe. But Michael Dohonoe's description of the two men who held him up according to CO 904/188(1) was as follows: '... appeared to be between 20 & 25, fairly tall and clean shaven. They wore fawn coats and soft hats.' This is not the usual description given when describing Dan Breen who was 5' 7" [1.70 m] and described thus: 'big round face and of heavy build' (CO 904/188(1)). The account fits with Dan Breen's description of the incident in *My Fight for Irish Freedom*, pp. 92–93.

80 Breen, *My Fight for Irish Freedom*, p. 93.

81 RIC Dublin, County Inspector's Report for December 1919. National Archives of Ireland. Microfilm of PRO File: CO 904/110.

82 Lynch, Michael. WS 511, pp. 79–87. BMH.

83 CO 904/188(1) Black Ledger. Private Papers of Sir John Anderson, containing details of the investigation into the assassination attempt on Lord French. The National Archives, Kew, UK.

84 *Ibid.*

85 International Committee of the Red Cross: https://ihl-databases.icrc.org/customary-ihl/eng/docs/v2_rul_rule77

86 McDonnell, Michael. WS 225, p. 6. BMH.

87 Henderson, Frank. WS 225, p. 71. BMH.

88 Lynch, Michael. WS 511, p. 82. BMH.

89 Byrne, Vincent. WS 225, p. 20. BMH.

90 *Ibid.*

91 Breen, *My Fight for Irish Freedom*, p. 95. Also Ua hUallacháin, Gearóid. WS 336, p. 11. BMH.

92 Ua hUallacháin, Gearóid. WS 336, p. 12. BMH.

93 Lynch, Michael. WS 511, p. 87. BMH.

94 *An t-Óglach*, Vol. I, No. 9, 31 January 1918. MA.

95 www.firstworldwar.com/bio/northcliffe.htm

96 Liddell Hart, B. H. *History of the First World War*. Pan Books, London, 1972, p. 31.

97 The Central Powers of the First World War: Germany, Austria-Hungary and Turkey.

98 Liddell *op. cit.*, p. 378.

99 No. 36 NAI DE 2/10 Dáil Éireann Report on the Propaganda Department (Copy) Dublin (Undated), June 1920. http://www.difp.ie/docs/1920/Propaganda-Department/36.htm

100 Right Rev. Monsignor M. Curran PP, WS 687, p. 394. BMH. After the 1918 general election *The Freeman's Journal*, the Irish Parliamentary Party's unofficial newspaper, went bankrupt. It was bought by Mayo man Martin Fitzgerald and an Englishman, Hamilton Edwards. These two men, together with the editor P. J. Hooper, were supportive of the Dáil's assertion of independent Irish sovereignty and steered *The Freeman's Journal* through the War of Independence and Civil War.

4. 'INDOMITABLE SPIRIT'

1   RIC Dublin, County Inspector's Report for February 1919. National Archives of Ireland. Microfilm of PRO File: CO 904/108.

2   RIC Dublin County Inspector's Report, February 1920. National Archives of Ireland. Microfilm of PRO File: CO 904/111.

3   Abbott, Richard. *Police Casualties in Ireland 1919–1922*. Mercier Press, Cork, 2000, p. 67.

4   House of Commons, UK Parliament. Lloyd George speech introducing the Better Government of Ireland Bill 22 December 1919.

5   Spoor, Benjamin. Labour MP for Bishop Auckland, County Durham in Northern England. Response to Winston Churchill MP in the House of Commons 23 February 1920, Vol. 125 CC1339–455.

6   Churchill, Winston S. Minister for War Speech on the Army Estimates for 1920–21. 23 February 1920, Vol. 125 cc1339–455.

7   Question from Lt.-Commander Kenworthy to the Secretary of State for War on the cost of the British army in Ireland per month. House of Commons Debate 5 August 1919 Vol. 119 C157

8   *Evening Telegraph*, 19 and 20 January 1920, also *Irish Independent*, 17, 19 and 20 January 1920. National Library of Ireland, Dublin.

9   Macardle, Dorothy. *The Irish Republic*. Irish Press Ltd., Dublin, 1951, pp. 325–327.

10 *Ibid.*, p. 328.

11 Abbott, *op. cit.*, p. 170.

12 *Ibid.*, p. 54.

13 Dolan, Joseph. WS 663, p. 1. BMH.

14 *Ibid.*, p. 2. Also https://civilrecords.irishgenealogy.ie/churchrecords/images/deaths_returns/deaths_1920/05131/4412979.pdf

15 CAB 24/97. Report to cabinet on visit to Ireland, January 1920. The National Archives, Kew, UK.

16 Macardle, *op. cit.*, p. 300.

17 CAB 24/97. Report to cabinet on visit to Ireland, January 1920. The National Archives, Kew, UK.

18 *Ibid.*

19 *Ibid.*

20 *Ibid.*

21 McFeely, Neil. CO 904/209/203 File on Inspector McFeely's forced retirement from G Division DMP February 1920. The National Archives, Kew, UK.

22 'Get Collins. The Intelligence War in Dublin.' *Hidden History.* A Mint Production for RTÉ, 2007.

23 Thornton, Frank. WS 615, p. 42. BMH.

24 O'Daly, Patrick. WS 387, p. 25. BMH.

25 Leonard, Joseph. WS 547, p. 25. BMH.

26 *Irish Independent*, 3 March 1920. National Library of Ireland, Dublin.

27 Caldwell, Paddy. WS 638, p. 22. BMH.

28 There is some confusion in the witness statements concerning the assassination of Molloy. Jimmy Slattery claims when interviewed by Ernie O'Malley that both himself and Mick McDonnell carried out the shooting while Vinny Byrne and Tom Kehoe covered them: Ernie O'Malley Notebooks. Interview with Jimmy Slattery. UCD Archives, P17b/109, p. 104. Paddy Caldwell claims that he and Joe Guilfoyle acted as cover: Caldwell, Patrick. WS 638, p. 22. BMH. This operation was carried out by Mick McDonnell's Special Duties Unit and it is likely both McDonnell and Jimmy Slattery carried out the assassination.

29 O'Donoghue, Daithí. WS 548, pp. 16–17. BMH.

30 *Ibid.*

31 *Ibid.*, p. 20.

32 Noyk, Michael. WS 707, pp. 27–28. BMH.

33 Dolan, Joseph. WS 663, p. 6. BMH.

34 O'Daly, Patrick. WS 644, pp. 27–28. BMH.

35 Dolan, Joseph. WS 663, pp. 6–7. BMH.

36 Ernie O'Malley Notebooks. Interview with Jimmy Slattery. P17b/109. UCD Archives, p. 104.

37 Bell, A. CO 904/193/10 Investigation into the murder of Alan Bell RM. The National Archives, Kew, UK.

38 *Ibid.*

39 Macardle, *op. cit.*, p. 343 quoting *A Soldier in Ireland*, published by the Peace with Ireland Council.

40 Irish Civil Records. Registration of marriage of Michael McDonnell and Ellen O'Toole, 9 October 1912.

41 Richard Mulcahy Conversation with Vinny Byrne 7 January 1964. P7/D/104. Mulcahy Papers, UCD Archives, Dublin.

42 Military Service Pensions Collection. File No. W24SP4528. Application of Colonel Michael McDonnell. MA. Also Richard Mulcahy Conversation with Vinny Byrne 7 January 1964. P7/D/104. Mulcahy Papers, UCD Archives, Dublin.

43 Byrne, Vincent. WS 423, p. 44. BMH.

44 *Ibid.*, pp. 44–45.

45 Stapleton, William James. WS 822, p. 35. BMH.

46 *Ibid.*

47 Breen, Daniel. WS 1739, p. 30. BMH.

48 Ernie O'Malley Notebooks. P17b/109. Interview with Jim Slattery. UCD Archives, Dublin, p. 111.

49 *Ibid.*, p. 102.

50 Byrne, Vincent. WS 423, pp. 44–45. BMH.

51 Slattery, Jim. From a newspaper cutting dated 28 January 1968. P7/D/69, The Mulcahy Papers. UCD Archives, Dublin.

52 Lieutenant Commander Joseph Kenworthy, MP for Central Hull, revealed in the House of Commons the truly shocking details of the beating and flogging received by Hales and Harte. The MP mentioned the 'pliers' but not wishing 'to harrow the House' he did not give further details. House of Commons Debate 20 October 1920. Vol. 133 CC 925–1039; also Broy, Eamon. WS 1280, p. 85. BMH.

53 O'Daly, Patrick. WS 387, pp. 32–33. BMH.

54 *Ibid.*, p. 34.

55 The killing of Thomas Dwyer at The Ragg was thought to be revenge for the killing of Constable John Heanue (69188) and the wounding of Constable Flaherty in Larry Fanning's Pub in The Ragg County Tipperary on 4 March, 1922 (Abbott, *op. cit.*, p. 62). Also Leahy, James. WS 1454, pp. 27–28. BMH. Retired RIC Sergeant Anthony Foody was shot dead on 7 July 1921 at Carralavin, County Mayo and a placard placed around his neck 'Revenge for Dwyer and The Ragg'.

56 Balfe, Edward. WS 1373, pp. 8–9. BMH. Also Hyland, Joseph. WS 644, pp. 7–8. BMH.

57 Kautt, W. H. *Ground Truths. British Army Operations in the Irish War of Independence.* Irish Academic Press, Sallins, County Kildare, 2014, p. 26.

58 *Ibid.*, p. 32.

59 Macardle, *op. cit.*, p. 330.

60 *Ibid.*, p. 328.

61 Barton, Robert C. WS 979, p. 21. BMH.

62 *Ibid.,* p. 37.

63 Sheehan, William. *Fighting for Dublin. The British Battle for Dublin 1919–1921.* The Collins Press, Cork, 2007, p. 11.

64 Rymer-Jones, John Murray (Oral History – Audio Interview). British Officer serving in Dublin 1920–1921. Reel 12. Catalogue number: 10699. Recorded by Peter Hart. Imperial War Museums, UK, 1989.

65 This is a reference to the British intelligence raid on Professor Carolan's house at 'Fernside' in Drumcondra on night of 11/12 October 1920. There was no priest present in the house that night.

66 Rymer-Jones, *op. cit.* Reel 13. Catalogue number: 10699.

67 McMahon, Paul. *British Spies and Irish Rebels.* The Boydell Press, Woodenbridge, Suffolk, UK, 2008, p. 37.

68 Memorandum by the Secretary of State for War, W.S. Churchill containing a Memorandum on the Military Situation in Ireland from General C.F.N. Macready, Parkgate, Dublin, dated 26 July 1920. Appendix B, referencing CAB 24/110/263 (CP 1750), Kautt, *op. cit.*, pp. 222–225.

69 *Ibid.*

70 Kautt, *op. cit.*, pp. xx, 12.

71 Bourne, Dr John. 'The British Generals: Biographies. Major-General (Gerry) Farrell Boyd CB CMG DSO DCM, Confidential Report 1918.' www.western frontassociation.com

72 Sheehan, *op. cit.* pp. 11–15.

73 *Ibid.*

74 Cabinet Papers CAB/23/21 cabinet meeting 7 June 1920. The National Archives, Kew, UK.

75 Seedorf, Martin F. Greenwood, Hamar, first Viscount Greenwood (1870–1948), politician and businessman. The National Archives of Ireland, online Anglo-Irish Treaty Exhibition, Dublin, 2011. http://treaty.nationalarchives.ie

76 Bridges, Lord & Dale, Henry. 'John Anderson. Viscount Waverley. 1882–1958.' *Biographical Memoirs of Fellows of the Royal Society*, Vol. 4, Royal Society, November 1958, pp. 307–310.

77 During the course of research at The National Archives, Kew, the author sought to view Sir John Anderson's files: HO 317/59/1 'Intelligence Reports, correspondence and secret service accounts, Sir John Anderson's Office'. Access was denied as the files had been withheld by the British Home Office. The files were to be released in 2004 but have been resealed until 2018. An appeal was lodged under FOI to view the papers but it was rejected on security grounds. Author's reference of appeal: Case 35676.

78 Duggan, George Chester. WS 1099, pp. 29–30, 39–40. BMH.

79 Cabinet Papers CAB/23/21 cabinet Meeting Monday 7 June 1920. The National Archives, Kew, UK.

80 Abbott, *op. cit.*, pp. 277–278.

81 26 September 1917 [p. 228 of original file] Colonial Office File on Michael Collins CO 904/196/65 The National Archives, Kew, UK.

82 McMahon, Paul. *British Spies & Irish Rebels. British Intelligence and Ireland 1916–1945*. The Boydell Press, UK, 2011, p. 32.

83 'Get Collins. The Intelligence War in Dublin.' *Hidden History*. A Mint Production for RTÉ, 2007.

84 McMahon, *op. cit.*, p. 34.

85 *Ibid.*

86 Thornton, Frank. WS 615, p. 22. BMH.

87 McMahon, *op. cit.*, pp. 37–38.

88 *Ibid.*, p. 34.

89 Macardle, *op. cit.*, pp. 330–331.

90 McGrane, Eileen. WS 1,434, p. 2. BMH.

91 McCarthy, Cal. *Cumann na mBan and the Irish Revolution*. The Collins Press, Cork, 2014, p. 15.

92 *Ibid.*, p. 73.

93 Military Service Pensions Collection. Cumann na mBan Nominal Rolls. Cumann na mBan GHQ MA-MSPC-CMB-163. Dublin City District Council. File Number: MA-MSPC-CMB-126. MA.

94 Military Service Pensions Collection. Cumann na mBan Nominal Rolls. Dublin City District Council. File Number: MA-MSPC-CMB-126. 0. Statement made before the Advisory Committee by Lily Brennan on 29 March 1933 on the structure and organisation of Cumann na mBan.

95 Mrs McCarville (Eileen McGrane) WS 1752, p. 6. BMH.

96 MA-MSPC-CMB-124/125/126/163 Cumann na mBan Nominal Rolls, GHQ, Dublin City and County – Dublin and Fingal Brigade Areas. MA.

97 Uí Chonnaill, Éilis. (née Ní Riain, Áine) WS 568, Appendix A to WS titled 'Tribute to the Late Máire Gleeson'. BMH.

98   *Ibid.*

99   *Ibid.*

100 Military Service Pensions Collection. File Number: MSP34REF22326. Application of Ellen Sarah Bushell. MA.

101 *Ibid.*

102 *Ibid.*

103 Pádraig Ó Conchubair [Patrick O'Connor]. WS 813, p. 11. BMH.

104 Dwyer, George. WS 678, pp. 12–14. BMH.

105 Monkstown was the G Company area.

106 Military Service Pensions Collection. File Number: 1D273. Application of Mrs Bridget Meaney, mother of Patrick Meaney. MA.

107 Mulkeen, Eddie. *A Night of Burnings – of RIC Stations.* Foxrock Local History Club, Publication No 42. October 1996. Mulkeen's account of the burning of Kill of the Grange and Ballybrack Barracks contains some evidence from *The Freeman's Journal* 13 and 14 May 1920.

108 Tully, James. WS 628, p. 4. BMH.

109 Raheny RIC Barracks was burned out by the 2nd Bn. Dublin Brigade during the first week of April 1920 – Lawless, Joseph V. WS 1043, pp. 309–310. BMH.

110 Abbott, *op. cit.*, p. 170.

111 *Ibid.*, p. 66.

112 *Ibid.*

113 'A Bullet for the General.' Chris Brookes. Broadcast 14 January 2012 on RTÉ Radio 1: *Documentary on One*; Also Quinlan, Ailin. 'The English General Behind the Black and Tans.' *Irish Independent*, 15 January 2012.

114 Mee, Jeremiah. WS 379, p. 3. BMH.

115 During the First World War Smyth had served with the Royal Engineers and the King's Own Scottish Borderers. He had been wounded twice, losing an arm in a German artillery barrage and shot through the neck. He was also blown through a window during a grenade instruction class when a Mills bomb exploded prematurely, killing a number of NCOs.

116 *Ibid.*, pp. 2–12.

117 *Ibid.*, pp. 11–12.

118 Abbott, *op. cit.*, pp. 96–103. Italics are my own emphasis.

119 Leeson, D. M. *The Black and Tans.* Oxford University Press, Oxford, UK, 2011 quoting British cabinet papers, 23 July 1920, CAB 24/109, CP 1693, ff. 448–51. The National Archives, Kew, UK.

120 Culhane, Seán. WS 746, pp. 5–7. BMH.

121 Macardle, *op. cit.*, pp. 356–357 quoting *Belfast Newsletter* of 16 July 1920.

122 Chief Secretary for Ireland Sir Hamar Greenwood during a Vote of Censure proposed by Arthur Henderson MP, Labour Party MP for Constituency of Widnes, Cheshire, England. House of Commons Debate 20 October 1920 Vol 133 CC 925–1039.

123 Lt.-Commander Kenworthy, MP for Central Hull, during a Vote of Censure proposed by Arthur Henderson MP, Labour Party MP for Constituency of Widnes, Cheshire, England. House of Commons Debate 20 October 1920 Vol 133 CC 925–1039.

124 American Commission Conditions in Ireland. Interim Report, 1921. Chapter IV p.19. Archive CD Books Ireland, 2008. Eneclann, Trinity College, Dublin. Ref. IE0038.

125 O'Malley, Ernie. (Ed. O'Malley, Cormac K.H. and Ó'Comhraí, Cormac) *The Men Will Talk to Me. Galway Interviews*. Mercier Press, Cork, 2013, p. 108.

126 Joyce's body remained undiscovered for seventy-eight years, being unearthed only in 1998. 'A sad story from 1920 unearthed in a Galway bog.' *The Irish Times*, 13 July 1998.

127 The American Commission was formed from the Committee of One Hundred called together by the New York weekly paper *Nation*. The Commission received submissions, reports, eyewitness testimony, official documents and photographs concerning events in Ireland during 1920 and 1921. Hearings before the Commission were held in Washington DC over twelve days in December 1920 and January 1921.

128 American Commission on Conditions in Ireland. Interim Report, 1921. Chapter IV, pp. 35–37. Archive CD Books, Ireland, 2008. Eneclann, Trinity College, Dublin. Ref. IE0038.

129 Crozier, Brigadier-General F. P. *Ireland For Ever*. Cedric Chivers Ltd, Bath, UK, 1971, p. 75.

130 Gaynor, John. WS 1447, pp. 15–16. BMH.

131 Abbott, *op. cit.*, pp. 69–70.

132 Gaynor, John. WS 1447, pp. 17–18. BMH.

133 Abbott, *op. cit.*, pp. 122–123. Also: Rock, Michael. WS 1398, p. 12. BMH.; Gaynor, John. WS 1447, pp. 19–20. BMH.

134 Witness testimony of John Derham, Urban Councillor of Balbriggan, given to the American Commission on Conditions in Ireland. Interim Report, 1921. Chapter IV, p. 96. Archive CD Books, Ireland, 2008. Eneclann, Trinity College, Dublin. Ref. IE0038.

135 *Ibid.*

136 Lawless, Joseph V. WS 1043, pp. 319–321. BMH.

137 Gaynor, John. WS 1447, pp. 19–22. BMH.

138 RIC Dublin, County Inspector's Report for October 1920. National Archives of Ireland. Microfilm of PRO File: CO 904/113.

139 American Commission on Conditions in Ireland. Interim Report, 1921. hapter V, p. 63.

140 *Ibid.* Chapter IV, p. 47.

141 Correspondence between the War Office at Whitehall London and British Army GHQ Parkgate Dublin regarding Recognition of Services of British Army Officers in Ireland 1920–21. WO 141/42. The National Archives, Kew, UK.

142 Recognition of Services of British Army Officers in Ireland 1920–21. WO 141/42. The National Archives, Kew, UK.

143 Letter dated 30 July 1920 re awarding of medals for services of gallantry in Ireland in file named 'Recognition of Services of British Army Officers in Ireland 1920–21'. WO 141/42. The National Archives, Kew, UK.

144 American Commission, *op. cit.*, Chapter IV, p. 96.

145 Vote of Censure proposed by Arthur Henderson MP, Labour Party MP for Constituency of Widnes, Cheshire, England. House of Commons Debate 20 October 1920 Vol 133 CC 925–1039.

146 *Ibid.*

147 Abbott, *op. cit.*, pp. 128–129.

148 Address of Sir Hamar Greenwood during a Vote of Censure proposed by Arthur Henderson MP, Labour Party MP for Constituency of Widnes, Cheshire, England. House of Commons Debate 20 October 1920 Vol 133 CC 925-1039.

149 *Ibid.*

150 Address of Lt.-Commander Kenworthy during a Vote of Censure proposed by Arthur Henderson MP, Labour Party MP for Constituency of Widnes, Cheshire, England. House of Commons Debate 20 October 1920 Vol 133 CC 925–1039.

151 *Ibid.*

152 Michael Fitzgerald was one of three hunger strikers who died during an IRA hunger strike that began on 11 August 1920. Volunteer Joseph Murphy died after a 76-day fast and Lord Mayor of Cork Terence McSwiney died after a 73-day fast.

153 Address of Lt.-Commander Kenworthy during a Vote of Censure proposed by Mr Arthur Henderson MP, Labour Party MP for Constituency of Widnes, Cheshire, England. House of Commons Debate 20 October 1920. Vol. 133 CC 925–1039.

154 Vote on a Motion of Censure proposed by Arthur Henderson MP 20 October 1920, Labour Party MP for Constituency of Widnes, Cheshire, England. House of Commons Debate 20 October 1920 Vol 133 CC 925–1039.

155 Letter 26 November 1920 to Archbishop of Dublin William J. Walsh from Rev. Fr. James B. Curry, Church of the Holy Name, Rectory, 207W 96th Street, New York, USA. 380/2. Archbishop Walsh Papers 1920. Dublin Diocesan Archives, Clonliffe College, Dublin.

156 Letter 26 November 1920 to Archbishop of Dublin William J. Walsh from Rev. Fr. M. J. Foley, President and Editor *Western Catholic*, Quincy, Illinois, USA. Archbishop Walsh Papers 1920. Dublin Diocesan Archives, Clonliffe College, Dublin.

5. Bloody Sunday

1   Sheehan, William. *Fighting for Dublin. The British Battle for Dublin 1919–1921.* The Collins Press, Cork, 2007, p. 19.

2   Dolan, Joseph. WS 663, p. 8. BMH.

3   Bauer, Lt.-Col. Eddy. *World War II.* Vol. 2, Part 15. Orbis Publishing Ltd., London, 1978.

4   Rock, Michael. WS 1398, p. 13. BMH.

5   *Ibid.*, p. 14.

6   Barry, Tom. *Guerilla Days in Ireland.* Anvil Books Ltd. 1981, reprinted by Mercier Press, Cork, 2010, p. 39.

7   O'Neill, Sean. WS 1154, p. 6. BMH.

8   *Ibid.*

9   Luger P08 semi-automatic pistol.

10 O'Neill, Sean. WS 1154, p. 7. BMH. Also McGrane, Lieutenant Thomas. Extract from Report on Monk's Bakery attack and capture of Kevin Barry. Submitted to the Military Archives by P.H. Holohan. Collins Papers, IRA Operations 1920, A/0408 XVIII. IE/MA/CP/136. MA.

11 O'Neill, Sean. WS 1154, p. 10. BMH.

12 Irish Civil Records. Registration of death of Private Marshall Whitehead, 2nd Bn Duke of Wellington Regiment 20 September 1920.

13 Sheehan, *op. cit.*, p. 19. Also, O'Neill, Sean. WS 1154, p. 11. BMH.

14 *Dublin Brigade Review 1939*. National Association of the Old IRA, 1939. Kevin Gerard Kevin Barry. Declaration by Virtue of Statutory Declarations Act 1835, made before Myles Keogh, Justice of the Peace for County Dublin, 28 October, 1920. CD 6/51/14, pp. 72–73. BMH.

15 Kautt, W. H. *Ground Truths. British Army Operations in the Irish War of Independence.* Irish Academic Press, County Kildare, p. 91.

16 Traynor, Oscar. Audio Recording S 1412.

17 O'Malley, Ernie. *On Another Man's Wound.* Anvil Books, Dublin, 2002, p. 267–268.

18 House of Commons Question on Gallantry of the members of the Auxiliary Division's service in the First World War. 11 April 1921 Vol 140 CC 722-3. Hansard.

19 Kautt, W. H., *op. cit.*, p. 90.

20 Healy, Patrick. *Rathfarnham Roads.* Local Studies Section, South Dublin Libraries, 2005, p. 49.

21 Operations Requested by D Branch Chief of Police. WO 35/87/1. The National Archives, Kew, UK.

22 Piaras Béaslaí Papers. Ms 33, 913 (13) British Army captured IRA membership rolls with comments on various IRA and Cumann na mBan figures known to them. National Library of Ireland, Dublin.

23 *Ibid.*

24 *Ibid.*

25 Thornton, Frank. WS 615, p. 27. BMH.

26 O'Sheil, Kevin R. WS 1770, p. 1024. BMH.

27 Neligan, David. WS 380, p. 206. BMH.

28 *Ibid.*, pp. 6–7.

29 Irish Civil Records. Registration of death of Detective Joseph Kavanagh DMP, 21 October 1920.

30 Broy, Eamon. WS 1280, p. 101. BMH.

31 O'Rourke, Peter. 'Michael Fitzgerald, Joseph Murphy and Terence MacSwiney.' *An Phoblact/Republican News*, 25 October 1990. Published online 24 October 2015.

32 *The Mayoman*, 30 October 1920. Microfilm. Mayo County Library, Castlebar, County Mayo.

33 Breen, Daniel. WS 1739, p. 8. BMH.

34 Ambrose, Joe. *Sean Treacy and the Tan War.* Mercier Press, Cork, 2007, pp. 73–74.

35 Breen, Daniel. WS 1739, pp. 1–3. BMH.

36 *Ibid.*, pp. 4-7.

37 Breen, Daniel. *My Fight for Irish Freedom.* Anvil Books, Tralee, 1964, pp. 131–133.

38 Breen, Daniel. WS 1739, pp. 24–25. BMH.

39 Irish Civil Records. Registration of death of John Carolan, Drumcondra, 27 October 1920.

40 Sworn Statement of Professor John Carolan submitted to the Labour Party Commission to Ireland and published in its Report: Appendix III (2) Shooting by Cold Blood, Caladonian Press, London, pp. 81–82. DA 962 L25 1921, The Library of The University of Toronto, Canada.

41 Lawless, Joseph V. WS 1043, p. 339. BMH.

42 McHugh, Patrick. WS 664, pp. 14–16. BMH.

43 Irish Civil Records. Registration of death of Matthew Furlong, 14 October 1920.

44 Ambrose, Joe. *Sean Treacy and the Tan War*. Mercier Press, Cork, 2007, p. 150.

45 Thornton, Frank. WS 615, p. 32. BMH.

46 'Report On The Death of V. Com. Seán Treacy, Tipp. No. 3', handwritten eyewitness account of the death of Seán Treacy attributed to Commandant Dick McKee, O/C Dublin Brigade. Confirmed as McKee's handwriting by his sister Maura McKee. IE/MA/CP, A/0436/I (i), IRA Casualties 1920. Item A/0473/VIII. On 16 February 1948, Lt.-Col. McCarthy obtained confirmation from Maire McKee that the eyewitness report on the death of Seán Treacy was written by her brother, the late Dick McKee. MA.

47 Sheehan, *op. cit.*, p. 27.

48 Ambrose, *op. cit.*, pp. 152–155.

49 Abbott, Richard. *Police Casualties in Ireland 1919–1922*. Mercier Press, Cork, 2000., p. 134.

50 Neligan, Dave. *The Spy in the Castle*. MacGibbon & McKee, Worcester and London, 1968, pp. 130–131. David Neligan disguises the name of Sergeant Daniel Roche in this account referring to him as Comerford.

51 Neligan, David. WS 380, pp. 10–11. BMH.Also, Dolan, Joseph. WS 663, pp. 2–3. BMH.

52 Dolan, Joseph. WS 663, pp. 2–3. BMH.

53 Memorandum from George Cockerill MP, house of Commons 29 October 1920 to Sir Hamar Greenwood. Macready and Sir John Anderson correspondence regarding Sinn Féin approaches with proposals for Peace, 2 November 1920. CO 904/188/(1).

54 Steele-Moylett Negotiations, March 1920 – January 1921. DE/2/251. The National Archives of Ireland, Dublin.

55 Thornton, Frank. WS 615, p. 11–12. BMH.

56 Military Service Pensions Collection. File No. MSPC34REF4945. Application of Lily Mernin, MA.

57 McDonnell, Daniel. P. WS 486, p. 10. BMH.

58 Thornton, Frank. Collins Papers. Item 4. A/0800/IV. Account of I.R.A. Intelligence during the Anglo-Irish War, pp. 13–14. MA.

59 Ernie O'Malley Notebooks. P17b/122. Interview with Charlie Dalton, UCD Archives, Dublin, pp. 20–22.

60 Ernie O'Malley Notebooks. P17b/094. Interview with Liam Tobin, pp. 96–100.

61 Thornton, Frank. WS 615, p. 25. BMH.

62 Broy, Eamon. WS 1280, p. 94. BMH.

63 Byrne, Vincent. WS 423, p. 54. BMH.

64 Saurin, Frank. WS 715, p. 7. BMH.

65 *Ibid.*, p. 8.

66 British army accounts of the assassinations of British Secret Service agents in the various locations on Bloody Sunday 21 November, 1920. HO 317/46. Miscellaneous Police and Intelligence Reports. The National Archives, Kew, UK.

67 Dolan, Anne. 'Killing and Bloody Sunday, November 1920.' Trinity College Dublin, *The Historical Journal*, 49, 3 (2006), Cambridge University Press, UK, 2006, p. 792, quoting *An Officer's Wife in Ireland* (anonymous), London and Dublin, 1994, p. 71.

68 Sworn statement of British dispatch rider in Baggot Street on Bloody Sunday, 21 November 1920. Case against Thomas Whelan and James Boyce. MS 36, 223/1/2/3. Noyk Papers. National Library of Ireland, Dublin. Also Lawless, Michael Joseph. WS 727, p. 3. BMH.

69 Handwritten notes of Michael Noyk, legal adviser to the IRA, referring to the sworn statement of the British Medical Officer who examined the injuries sustained by Lieutenants Ames and Bennett. Noyk Papers. Case against Paddy Moran and James Rochford. Ms 36, 224. National Library of Ireland, Dublin.

70 Byrne, Vincent. WS 423, p. 55. BMH.

71 Cahill, James. WS 503, p. 7. BMH.

72 Sir Hamar Greenwood. House of Commons Statement 'Murder of Officers, Dublin. Monday 22 November 1920, Vol. 135 CC 34–38.

73 Kennedy, Paddy. WS 499, p. 5. BMH.

74 Noyk Papers. Case against Frank Teeling, William Conway & Daniel Healy. Ms 36, 222. National Library of Ireland, Dublin.

75 Ibid.

76 Military Service Pensions Collection. File No. MSP34REF1746. Application of James Francis Cullen, MA. The 3rd Bn had been under the command of Commandant Éamon de Valera in 1916 and Northumberland Road and Mount Street Bridge had been the scene of a serious battle during the Rising. For details on Mount Street Bridge Street in 1916 see An Foras Feasa, NUI Maynooth website: http://mountstreet1916.ie

77 Dolan, op. cit., pp. 789–810.

78 Abbott, op. cit., pp. 152–153.

79 Handwritten notes listing the names of the people living in the house at 28 Upper Pembroke Street in the Sworn Statement of Witness 2 for the Prosecution (Col Woodcock) in the Case against James Green. MS 36, 221. The Noyk Papers, National Library of Ireland, Dublin.

80 Dalton, Charles. *With the Dublin Brigade. Espionage and Assassination with Michael Collins' Intelligence Unit*. Mercier, Cork, 2014, p. 118.

81 Irish Civil Records. Registration of death of Lt.-Col. Hugh Montgomery, 10 December 1920.

82 British Army accounts of the assassinations of British Secret Service agents in the various locations on Bloody Sunday 21 November, 1920. HO 317/46. Miscellaneous Police and Intelligence Reports. The National Archives, Kew, UK.

83 Ibid.

84 Nugent, Larry. WS 907, p. 210. BMH.

85 Dolan, Joseph. WS 663, p. 805. BMH.

86 Lawless, Michael Joseph. WS 727, p. 4. BMH.

87 Ernie O'Malley Notebooks. P17b/122. Interview with Charlie Dalton, UCD Archives, Dublin, p. 23.

88 Ernie O'Malley Notebooks. P17b/110. Interview with Pat McCrea, UCD Archives, Dublin, p. 14.

89 O'Daly, Patrick. WS 387, p. 43–44. BMH.

90 Ernie O'Malley Notebooks. P17b/110. Interview with Pat McCrea, UCD Archives, Dublin, p. 15.

91 Rymer-Jones, John Murray (Oral History – Audio Interview). British Officer serving in Dublin 1920–1921. Reel 13. Catalogue number: 10699. Recorded by Peter Hart. Imperial War Museums, UK, 1989.

92 *Ibid.*

93 Captain R. D. Jeune's account of activities on Bloody Sunday. Sheehan, William. *British Voices.* The Collins Press, Cork, pp. 88–89.

94 British Army accounts of the assassinations of British secret service agents in the various locations on Bloody Sunday, 21 November, 1920. HO 317/46. Miscellaneous police and intelligence reports. The National Archives, Kew, UK.

95 The names, locations and operations listed are all that could be identified from the following sources: Military Archives Military Service Pensions Collection (individual pensions and Dublin Brigade Membership Rolls), Bureau of Military History Witness Statements, Ernie O'Malley Notebook Interviews with IRA veterans, Anne Dolan TCD 'Killing and Bloody Sunday, November 1920, and the British Army Charge Sheets & Witness Statements to the events of Bloody Sunday from the Noyk Papers at NLI. The numbers involved were far greater than identified but reluctance of those who engaged on Active Service on Bloody Sunday to reveal names and in some cases even units makes a full listing a challenge.

96 Foley, Michael. *The Bloodied Field.* The O'Brien Press, Dublin, 2014, pp. 169, 171–172.

97 *Ibid.,* pp. 170–171.

98 *Ibid.,* pp. 177–178.

99 Ryan, Tom. WS 783, pp. 34–35. BMH.

100 *Ibid.,* pp. 35–38.

101 Labour Party (Great Britain). *Labour Commission to Ireland. Report of the Labour Commission to Ireland.* Caledonian Press Ltd., London, 1921. DA 962 L25 1921. The Library of the University of Toronto, Canada, pp. 41–43.

102 Foley, *op. cit.,* pp. 267–270. Also Irish Civil Records. Registration of deaths of some of the victims at Croke Park November 1920, 10 December 1920.

103 Sir Hamar Greenwood. House of Commons Statement 'Croke Park, Dublin'. Hansard 1803–2005. Tuesday 23 November 1920. Vol. 135 CC 199–202.

104 Labour Party (Great Britain). *op. cit.,* pp. 41–43.

105 *Ibid.*

106 *Ibid.*

107 Ernie O'Malley Notebooks. P17b/103. Interview with Maire McKee, UCD Archives, Dublin, p. 169.

108 Irish Civil Records, Death Certificates of Volunteer Conor Clune, Vice-Commandant Peadar Clancy and Commandant Richard McKee as received from Military Court of Inquiry held at King George V Hospital City of Dublin.

109 Ernie O'Malley Notebooks. P17b/103. Interview with Maire McKee, UCD Archives, Dublin, p. 170.

110 Ernie O'Malley Notebooks. P17b/110. Interview with Pat McCrea, UCD Archives, Dublin, pp. 15–16.

111 Ernie O'Malley Notebooks. P17b/103. Interview with Maire McKee, UCD Archives, Dublin, p. 169.

112 Neligan, David. *The Spy in the Castle.* MacGibbon & Kee Ltd., London, UK, 1968, p. 125. Also Ryle Dwyer, T. *The Squad and the Intelligence Operations of Michael Collins,* Mercier, Cork, pp. 194–196.

113 Ryle Dwyer, T. *op. cit.*, p. 196.
114 Barry, *op. cit.*, pp. 42–46.

6. 'Knee-Deep in Gelignite'

1   Sir John Anderson to Chief Secretary Hamar Greenwood, 21 November 1920. (Black Ledger) CO 904/188(1). The National Archives, Kew, UK.
2   Chief Secretary Hamar Greenwood to Sir John Anderson, 21 November, 1920. (Black Ledger) CO 904/188(1). The National Archives, Kew, UK.
3   Collections/Sound/Oral History/Rymer-Jones, John Murray. Reel 13. Catalogue number: 10699. Recorded by Peter Hart. Imperial War Museums, UK, 1989.
4   Lawless, Joseph V. WS 1043, p. 355. BMH.
5   McHugh, Patrick. WS 664, p. 23. BMH.
6   O'Daly, Patrick. WS 387, pp. 48–49. BMH.
7   *Ibid.*, pp. 50–54.
8   *Ibid.*, pp. 54–56. Also Kautt, W. H. *Ground Truths*. Irish Academic Press, County Kildare, 2014, p. 192.
9   Brigadier-General J. Brind. 'The Military Situation in Ireland at the end of September, 1921' in Appendix I, Kautt, *op. cit.*, p. 200.
10 Documents listing details of raids carried out by British army, ADRIC and RIC Units in the Dublin District November and December 1920. WO 35/75. The National Archives, Kew, UK.
11 Collins, Stephen. 'On the Run and In Disguise: why W. T. Cosgrave dressed up as a "Br Doyle" and dyed his hair blazing red.' *The Irish Times*, 18 October 2014 from Laffan, Michael. *Judging W. T. Cosgrave*. Royal Irish Academy, Dublin, 2014.
12 Boyne, Sean. *Emmet Dalton: Somme Soldier, Irish General, Film Pioneer*. Merrion Press, County Kildare, p. 51.
13 *Ibid.*, pp. 52–53.
14 *Ibid.*, p. 46.
15 Traynor, Oscar. WS 340, pp. 80–83. BMH.
16 Sheehan, William. *Fighting for Dublin*. The Collins Press, Cork, pp. 41–42.
17 McMahon, Paul. *British Spies and Irish Rebels*. The Boydell Press, Suffolk, UK, 2008, p. 42.
18 From DVD written and presented by Peter Barton. Produced and directed by Alastair Laurence. Programme 2 of 3: 'Defence in Depth. The Somme 1916.' *From Both Sides of the Wire*. Dazzler Media, BBC, 2016.
19 O'Laoghaire, Michael. WS 797, p. 44. BMH.
20 Ua h-Uallacháin, Gearóid (Holohan, Garry) WS 336, pp. 19–26. BMH.
21 Search Report 9 December 1920 of Raid and capture of 'Bernard Stewart' aka Ernie O'Malley at Cappagh, Inistioge, County Kilkenny signed by Lt. J. Wainwright Royal Navy, District Inspector & intelligence officer A Coy ADRIC. Full Report attached written by Captain Charles V. Webb O/C A Coy ADRIC. WO35/75. The National Archives, Kew, UK.
22 O'Malley, Ernie. *On Another Man's Wound*. Anvil Books, Dublin, 2002, p. 271–272.
23 *Ibid.*, pp. 273–284.
24 *Ibid.*, pp. 280–281.
25 *Ibid.*, pp. 282–285.

26 Doorley, Michael. '"The Judge" versus "the Chief" – Daniel Cohalan and the 1920 split within Irish America.' *History Ireland*, Issue 2 (March/April 2015), Volume 23.

27 Coogan, Tim Pat. *De Valera*. Hutchinson, London, 1993, pp. 158–159.

28 *Ibid.*, p. 148.

29 Ferriter, Diarmaid. *Judging Dev*. Royal Irish Academy, Dublin, 2007, p. 36.

30 Bryan, Cyril. Journalist. 'Irish letter---Archbishop Clune "Held Up!"', *The Western Australia Record*, 27 November 1920. Archives of the Roman Catholic Archdiocese of Perth, Highgate, Western Australia.

31 *Ibid.*

32 Macardle, Dorothy. *The Irish Republic*. Irish Press Ltd., Dublin, 1951, pp. 413–414.

33 Prime Minister's Announcement. House of Commons 10 December 1920 Vol 135 CC 2601–16. Hansard.

34 Macardle, *op. cit.*, pp. 413–414 quoting Healy, T. M. *Letters and Leaders of My Day*. Frederick A. Stokes, New York, 1929, p. 625.

35 Prime Minister's Announcement, *op. cit.*

36 Summary of Evidence taken by the Commission in regard to Fires in Cork. Appendix II (2) Labour Party (Great Britain). Labour Commission to Ireland. Report of the Labour Commission to Ireland. Caledonian Press Ltd., London, 1921. DA 962 L25 1921. The Library of the University of Toronto, Canada, p. 74–75.

37 Telegram dated 15 December 1920 from Bishop of Cork to Archbishop Walsh of Dublin thanking him for his sympathy and for the assistance of the Dublin fire brigade in Cork. Archbishop Walsh Papers, 1920. Correspondence from Bishops 380/1, Dublin Diocesan Archives, Clonliffe College, Dublin.

38 Labour Party (Great Britain). Labour Commission to Ireland. Report of the Labour Commission to Ireland. Caledonian Press Ltd., London, 1921. DA 962 L25 1921. The Library of the University of Toronto, Canada, p. 33.

39 'Dr Clune was Diplomat During the Black and Tan Regime.' *The Western Australia Catholic Record*, 10 April 1946. Archives of the Roman Catholic Archdiocese of Perth, Highgate, Western Australia.

40 Rymer-Jones, John Murray (Oral History – Audio Interview). British officer serving in Dublin 1920–1921. Reel 13. Catalogue number: 10699. Recorded by Peter Hart. Imperial War Museums, UK, 1989.

41 O'Daly, Patrick. WS 387, pp. 56–60. BMH.

42 Military Services Pensions Collection. File No. W24SP424 Application of Pádraig Ua Dálaigh (Patrick O'Daly), MA.

43 Mrs McCarville (Eileen McGrane) WS 1752. BMH.

44 McGrane, Eileen. Possession of Revolvers and Literature. CO 904/44/14. The National Archives, Kew, UK.

45 *Ibid.*

46 *Ibid.*

47 2nd Battalion East Surrey Regiment Digest of Service 1921. ESR/3/6/6. Surrey History Centre, Woking, UK.

48 Irish Genealogy. Civil Records. Registration of death of Private Stanley Manley, 20 January 1921.

49 3rd Battalion Ballsbridge, Dublin. Letters to the Editor. *The Rifle Brigade Chronicle*. Compiled and edited by Major H. G. Parkyn OBE. John Bale & Sons, London, 1922.

Royal Green Jackets (Rifles) Museum Archives, Hampshire Record Office, Peninsula Barracks, Winchester, UK, p. 61.

50 *Ibid.*, p. 63.

51 *Ibid.*, p. 62.

52 *Ibid.*, pp. 62–63.

53 *Ibid.*, p. 64.

54 *Ibid.*, p. 62. Colonel Moore joined the Irish Volunteers on their foundation, becoming Inspector General. He initially sided with John Redmond's National Volunteers at the time of the split in the Volunteer movement in 1914 but abandoned them to support Sinn Féin in an attempt to become a TD. He was never fully trusted by Sinn Féin but eventually became a senator in Seanad Éireann.

55 *The Mayo News,* Saturday 5 February 1921. Microfilm. Mayo County Library, Castlebar, County Mayo.

56 Sheehan, William. *Fighting for Dublin. The British Battle for Dublin.* The Collins Press, Cork, 2007, pp. 33–34.

57 Rock, Michael. WS 1398, pp. 21–22. BMH.

58 General Instructions on intelligence, IRA GHQ. Group 9, A/0604 Item II. Collins Papers. MA.

59 Active Service Unit, Dublin Brigade, 1921. A/0650 I. Collins Papers, MA.

60 *Ibid.*

61 IRA Membership Roll. Dublin Brigade Active Service Unit. Interview with Leo Duffy 17 June 1935. Military Service Pensions Collection. MA-MSPC-RO-9. MA. Also White, George. WS 956, p. 5. BMH.

62 Gilhooley, Joseph. WS 390, p. 4. BMH.

63 Ó Conchubhair, Pádraig and Rigney, Paddy. The Active Service Unit in Dublin Brigade Review. CD 6/51/14, p. 77. BMH.

64 Military Service Pensions Collection. Thomas McGrath File Nos. WDP3169 and MSP34REF21184. Bill Gannon File No. WMSP34REF25776. George Leo Nolan File No. WMSP34REF60676 and Simon McInverney File No. MSP34REF56841.

65 Gilhooley, Joseph. WS 390, pp. 4–5. BMH.

66 Military Service Pensions Collection. File No. WDP3169. Application of Thomas McGrath. MA.

67 *Ibid.* Interview before pension committee referring to Bachelors Walk.

68 Cahill, James. WS 503, p. 11. BMH.

69 Active Service Unit, Dublin Brigade, 1921. A/0650 I. Collins Papers, MA.

70 *The Freeman's Journal*, 16 May 1921. National Library of Ireland, Dublin.

71 *The Freeman's Journal*, 13 May 1921. National Library of Ireland, Dublin.

72 Traynor, Oscar. Account of the War of Independence on the streets of Dublin in 1921. Voice Recording: S1412. BMH.

73 Brennan, P. J. WS 1773, p. 15. BMH.

74 Noyk Papers. MS 36,226/1 MS 36, 226/2. Court Martial Papers of Frank Flood, Patrick Doyle, Dermot O'Sullivan, Thomas Bryan and Bernard Ryan. National Library of Ireland, Dublin.

75 Irish Genealogy. Civil Records. Registration of death of Michael Magee.

76 Colley, Harry. WS 1687, pp. 63–65. BMH.

77 Charge Sheet No – 1. Noyk Papers. MS 36,226/1 MS 36, 226/2. Court Martial Papers of Frank Flood, Patrick Doyle, Dermot O'Sullivan, Thomas Bryan and Bernard Ryan. National Library of Ireland, Dublin.

78 House of Commons questions on Outrages and Reprisals. Oswald Mosley MP. 24 February 1921. Vol. 138 CC 1152-4W. Hansard.

79 House of Commons debate on Decree of the Bishop of Cork in Reference to ambushes, kidnapping and murder. Joseph Devlin MP. 21 February 1921. Vol. 138 CC 624–723. Hansard.

80 British army GHQ Dublin District A List No. 75, 29 March 1921. Captain W. L. King (No. 1929) and Welsh, F. J. (1930), ADRIC, Arbour Hill. Charged with Murder. Collins Papers, A/0619/XLVII. MA.

81 *The Freeman's Journal*, 13 April 1921. National Library of Ireland, Dublin.

82 Leeson, D. M. *The Black & Tans. British Police and Auxiliaries in the Irish War of Independence, 1920–1921*. Oxford University Press, 2012, pp. 185–186.

83 *The Freeman's Journal*, 13, 14 and 15 April 1921. National Library of Ireland, Dublin.

84 *The Freeman's Journal*, 16 April 1921. National Library of Ireland, Dublin.

85 Broy, Eamon. WS 1280, pp. 113–114. BMH.

86 British army Military Service File of William Lorraine King the First World War. WO 0399/139377. The National Archives, Kew, UK. Also *The Freeman's Journal*, 13 April 1921. National Library of Ireland. Dublin.

87 Irish Genealogy. Civil Records. Death Certificate of Isabella King. No. 289. Home address listed as Sunnyside, Rush, County Dublin. Mrs King was thirty-eight years of age.

88 Marriage Certificate of William Lorraine King and Helen Sophie Gilbert. Divorce Papers of King, Helen Sophie v King, William Lorraine. Filed 18 June 1928. J77/2304. The National Archives, Kew, UK.

89 Broy, Eamon. WS 1280, p. 116. BMH.

90 Military Service Pensions Collection. File No. 24SP1153 (W24D15). Application of Charlie Dalton, MA.

91 Kelliher, Ned. WS 477, pp. 5–6. BMH.

92 Dolan, Joseph. WS 663, p. 4. BMH. There is a different description offered by William James Stapleton WS 822. BMH. Stapleton maintains Doran walked out of the hotel and down to Grafton Street. A signal was given by Charlie Dalton whereupon Peter Doran was 'eliminated', p. 36–37.

93 Abbott, Richard. *Police Casualties in Ireland*. Mercier Press, Cork, 2000, p. 202.

94 Dalton, Charles. WS 434, p. 26. BMH.

95 Cadet Wilford MC, Thomas Jocelyn. M Coy ADRIC & formerly Royal Field Artillery. Appendix D. The Clonfin Ambush 2 February 1921 featured in MacÉoin, Seán. WS 1716. MA.

96 Boyne, Sean. *Emmet Dalton. Somme Soldier, Irish General, Film Pioneer*. Merrion Press, Sallins, County Kildare, p. 61–63;

97 Leonard, Joseph. WS 547, p. 18. BMH.

98 Ernie O'Malley Notebooks. Interview with Pat McCrea. P17b/110. UCD Archives, Dublin, p. 24.

99 O' Conchubhair, Pádraig. WS 813, pp.17–19. BMH.

100 O'Malley, Ernie. *On Another Man's Wound*. Anvil Books, Dublin 2007, pp. 310–311.

101 Letter from General Macready to Sir John Anderson 15 February 1921. CO 904/188.

102 *The Freeman's Journal*, 10 October 1922. The National Library of Ireland, Dublin. Also Kennedy, Patrick. WS 499. BMH.

103 Ackerman, Carl W. Interview with General Macready. April 1921. CO 904/188 Miscellaneous Correspondence with General Macready. The National Archives, Kew, UK, p. 3.

104 Letter from General Macready to Sir John Anderson 30 May 1921. CO 904/188. The National Archives, Kew, UK.

105 Letter from Sir John Anderson to General Macready 31 May 1921. CO 904/188. The National Archives, Kew, UK.

106 Military Service Pensions Collection. File No. MSP34REF8996. Application of Thomas Newell. MA.

107 When Thomas Newell came to Dublin at the invitation of Michael Collins (to identify Igoe) he adopted the cover name of 'Sweeney'. The name stuck and he was known ever since as Thomas Sweeney Newell. Author conversation with Sweeney Newell's son, Terry (June 2017).

108 *Ibid*. Also Dalton, Charles. WS 434, pp. 21–27. BMH.

109 Rymer-Jones, John Murray (Oral History – Audio Interview). British officer serving in Dublin 1920–1921. Reel 13. Catalogue number: 10699. Recorded by Peter Hart. Imperial War Museums, UK, 1989.

110 F Company Auxiliary Division Operation to capture Liam Tobin, IRA GHQ intelligence. January 1921. WO 35/86B Part 2. Raids and Searches F Coy ADRIC. Intelligence and Military Reports. The National Archives, Kew, UK.

111 Operations Requested by D Branch Chief of Police. WO 35/87/1. The National Archives, Kew, UK.

112 Military Service Pensions Collection. File No. MSP34REF20270 Sworn Statement made by Frank Daly before the MSP Advisory Committee 12 April 1937. MA.

113 O'Connor, Joseph. WS 487, pp. 30–31. BMH.

114 Court Martial of Heron, Áine. WS 503, p. 10. BMH. Also Dorney, John. 'The Pearse Street Ambush March 14, 1921'. Published online 26 January 2015 on www.theirishstory.com ; Also *The Freeman's Journal*, 6 April 1921. National Library of Ireland, Dublin.

115 Michael Collins in an interview with Carl W. Ackerman. *Public Ledger Philadelphia*, 2 April 1921 and printed in *The Freeman's Journal*, 22 April 1921. National Library of Ireland, Dublin.

116 Foley, James. WS 774, p. 7. BMH.

117 *The Freeman's Journal*, 23 May 1921. National Library of Ireland, Dublin.

118 Ó Conchubhair, Pádraig and Rigney, Paddy. The Active Service Unit in Dublin Brigade Review. CD 6/51/14, p. 80. BMH. *The Freeman's Journal*, 23 May 1921. National Library of Ireland, Dublin.

119 Ó Conchubhair & Rigney, *op. cit.*, p. 80.

120 *The Freeman's Journal*, 23 May 1921. National Library of Ireland, Dublin.

121 There is a discrepancy between O'Daly's BMH WS 387 p. 64 (which says he was released on 20 February 1921) and MSPC 24SP424 p. 4 (which gives the release date in March 1921).

122 White, George. WS 956, pp. 9–10. BMH.

123 Commandant O'Kelly, M. Burning of the Dublin Custom House, 25 May 1921. Collins Papers. A/0618/IV. MA.

124 Sheehan, William. *The British Battle for Dublin*. The Collins Press, Cork, 2007, p. 52.

125 Beaslaí Papers MS 33914 (18). The National Library of Ireland, Dublin.

126 O'Donel, Geraldine. WS 861, p. 5. BMH.

127 Colley, Harry. WS 1687, p. 84. BMH.

128 Cahill, James. WS 503, p. 18. BMH.

129 *The Freeman's Journal*. 27 May 1921. National Library of Ireland, Dublin.

130 Custom House Report from Mr Murphy, senior official. CUST 49/532. Raid and Burning. The National Archives, Kew, UK.

131 *Ibid.*

132 2nd Battalion East Surrey Regiment Digest of Service 1921. ESR/3/6/6. Surrey History Centre, Woking, UK. Also Irish Civil Records. Registration of death of Private H. Goddard, 1 June 1921.

133 Cahill, James. WS 503. p. 11. BMH.

134 Nolan, Bernard. WS 844, pp. 6–10. BMH.

135 O'Conchubhair, Pádraig. WS 813, p.16. BMH.Also Abbott, Richard. *Police Casualties in Ireland* 1919–1922. Mercier Press, Cork, 2000, p. 216.

136 *The Freeman's Journal*, 7 May 1921. The National Library of Ireland.

137 Ó Conchubhair, *op. cit.*, pp. 21–26, 25.

138 *Ibid.*, p. 41. Also Abbott, Richard. *Police Casualties in Ireland 1919–1922*. Mercier Press, Cork, 2000, p. 259.

139 McDonnell, Andrew. WS 1768, pp. 38. BMH.

140 *The Freeman's Journal*, 21 May 1921. National Library of Ireland, Dublin.

141 Mannix, Patrick. WS 502, pp. 26–27. BMH.

142 Brennan, P. J. WS 1773, p. 23. BMH.

143 Military Service Pensions Collection. File No. 1D75. Application of Mary McIntosh, mother of Lt. James McIntosh. MA.

144 McDonnell, Andrew. WS 1768, pp. 57–58. BMH.

145 Neligan, David. WS 380, pp. 17–21. BMH.

146 The Queen's Own Royal West Kent Regiment. *The Aftermath of War 1920–1923. 2nd Battalion in Germany, Upper Silesia and Ireland,* p. 57. Maidstone Museum, Kent. Also Irish Genealogy. Civil Records. Registration of the death of Private William Saunders.

147 The Queen's Own Royal West Kent Regiment, *op. cit.*, p. 57.

148 RIC Dublin, County Inspector's Report for July 1921. National Archives of Ireland. Microfilm of PRO File: CO 904/116.

149 Rock, Michael. WS 1398, pp. 25–27. BMH.

150 O'Connor, Joseph. WS 487, p. 46. BMH.

151 'Sir Alfred Cope at Cwmgorse.' Talk given by Sir Alfred Cope at the Amman Valley Church, Cwmgorse on Monday 7 March 1927. Printed in the Amman Valley Chronicle on 10 March 1927. National Library of Wales, UK.

7. 'Dark Deeds to be Done'

1   Boyne, Sean, *Emmet Dalton*. Merrion Press, County Kildare, pp. 90–107.

2   RIC Dublin, County Inspector's Report for July 1920. National Archives of Ireland. Microfilm of PRO File: CO 904/116.

3   Report on the conduct of the Dublin ASU or 'HQ Guard' during a training camp at Cobb's Lodge, Glenasmole, County Dublin. Collins Papers A/0710/I–V. 9 August 1921. MA.

4   3rd Battalion Ballsbridge, Dublin. Letters to the Editor. *The Rifle Brigade Chronicle*. Compiled and edited by Major H. G. Parkyn OBE, John Bale & Sons, London, 1922. Royal Green Jackets (Rifles) Museum Archives, Hampshire Record Office, Peninsula Barracks, Winchester, UK, p. 69.

5   Report on the conduct of the Dublin ASU, *op. cit.*

6   'A Page from the Army's History. The Fortunes of the First Regular Unit.' *An t-Óglach*, 7 April 1923. MA.

7   Macardle, Dorothy. *The Irish Republic*. Irish Press Ltd, 1951, Dublin, p. 722.

8   *Ibid.*, pp. 818–820. The Bills creating the Irish Free State were: the Irish Free State Constitution Bill and the Irish Free State (Consequential Provisions) Bill.

9   The Catholic Church had experienced the erosion of the influence of religion in Europe since the French Revolution in 1789. The establishment of secular independent states in Europe had further undermined the Church. The hierarchy was determined it would not happen in Ireland.

10 Richard Mulcahy Conversation with Vincent Byrne, 7 January 1964. P7/D/104. Mulcahy Papers pp. 9–19.

11 Macardle, Dorothy. *op. cit.* pp. 711–716.

12 Military Service Pensions Collection. IRA Membership Rolls: MA-MSPC-RO-601. GHQ IRA. MA.

13 *Ibid.*

14 Dolan, Joseph. WS 900, p. 5. BMH.

15 Gillis, Liz. *The Fall of Dublin. Military History of the Irish Civil War*. Mercier Press, Cork, 2011, pp. 49–50.

16 Boyne, Sean, *op. cit.*, p. 139.

17 Murphy, Karl. 'General W. R. E. Murphy and the Irish Civil War.' MA Thesis 1994. NUI Maynooth Library, p. 4.

18 *Ibid.*

19 *Ibid.*

20 Gillis, *op. cit.*, pp. 48–49.

21 *Ibid.*, pp. 48–49 and 55–56.

22 Henderson, Frank. WS 821, p. 35. BMH.

23 Account from inside the Four Courts under bombardment 28 June 1922. Archbishop Byrne Papers. Box 466. Government and Politics. Dublin Diocesan Archives.

24 Gillis, *op. cit.*, pp. 48–49.

25 Boyne, *op. cit.*, pp. 152–153.

26 O'Malley, Ernie. Sworn Statement to the Advisory Committee Military Service Pensions Collection 6 January 1936. IRA Membership Rolls: MA-MSPC-RO-601. GHQ IRA. MA.

27 Homan, J. F. Memorandum of Ambulance Work (Saint John's Ambulance Brigade) and Efforts for Peace in Dublin 28 June–5 July 1922. Archbishop Byrne Papers. Box 466. Government and Politics. Dublin Diocesan Archives, p. 9.

28 *Ibid.*, pp. 1–2.

29 *Ibid.*, p.3.

30 *Ibid.*, p.6.

31 *Ibid.* p.9.

32 Ernie O'Malley Notebooks. P17b/096. Interview with Oscar Traynor. UCD Archives, Dublin, pp. 70–73.

33 Macardle, *op. cit.*, pp. 753–754.

34 Report by General Officer Commanding-in-Chief on the situation in Ireland for week ending 8 July 1922. CAB/24/138. Cabinet Papers. The National Archives, Kew, UK.

35 Military Service Pensions Collection. File No. MSP34REF236. Application of Oscar Traynor. MA.

36 'GOC Dublin Command.' *An t-Óglach* 5 May 1923. MA.

37 Report on the Situation in Ireland for the week ending 23 September 1922. General Macready. CAB/24/139. Cabinet Papers. The National Archives, Kew, UK.

38 Comdt. Mortell Collection. IE/MA/PRCN/0072/02 (6) and IRA Intelligence (National Army) Pay Book September–December 1922, Collins Papers A/0921. MA.

39 Letter to Major-General McGrath TD from Captain A. S. Muireadhaigh 12 October 1923 re operational structure of Criminal Investigation Department, Protective Officers Corps and Citizens Defence Force. TSCH/3/S3331 Home Affairs. Proposed Disbandment of the CID National Archives of Ireland, Dublin.

40 *Ibid.*

41 Psychological or physical pain inflicted during interrogation was banned in the USA after the Wickersham Commission 1931.

42 Attempted prosecution of Inspector Mooney CID. FIN1/2753, National Archives of Ireland, Dublin.

43 Gillis, Liz. *Revolution in Dublin. A Photographic History 1913–23.* Mercier Press, Cork, 2013.

44 Memorandum on the disbanding of the CID by Minister for Justice Kevin O'Higgins, 9 July 1923. TSCH/3/S3331 Home Affairs. Proposed Disbandment of the CID National Archives of Ireland, Dublin.

45 Ó Craudhlaoich, Diarmaid (Crowley, Dermot). Letter to Cahir Davitt in Davitt's WS 993, pp. 107–109. BMH.

46 *Ibid.*, p. 108.

47 *Ibid.*, pp. 107–109.

48 'The Treatment of Prisoners.' W. T. Cosgrave. Wednesday 4 October 1922. Dáil Éireann Debate Vol. 1 No. 17.

49 British Army Intelligence File on Richard Mulcahy. WO 35/207. The National Archives, Kew, UK.

50 O'Dwyer, Martin (Bob). *Death Before Dishonour.* Cashel Folk Village, Cashel, County Tipperary, 2010, pp. 89–97.

51 Boyne, *op. cit.*, pp. 268–69.

52 O'Dwyer, *op. cit.*, pp. 244–245.

53 Prisoner statement of torture by forces of the Free State government signed by Maud Gonne MacBride and Charlotte Dupard of the Women's Prisoners' Defence League. Dated: 'Copied 18/12/22'. CD 333/38. BMH.

54 'Michael Collins. The Sword of Sinn Fein.' *Daily Mail*, 19 August 1921, by a Harley Street nerve specialist. Seán Collins. CD1/8/3. BMH.

55 *Ibid.*

56 *Ibid.*

57 Communications re the murder of prisoner James Buckley, Cork, by former members of the Squad as a revenge killing for the death of Tom Kehoe in a mine explosion at Carrigaphooca, Cork, September 1922. P7/B/82. Mulcahy Papers. UCD Archives, Dublin.

58 'Our Front Page Portrait. Major-General Michael Hogan, GOC Claremorris Command.' *An t-Óglach*, 28 July 1923. MA.

59 O'Callaghan, John. *The Battle for Kilmallock. Military History of the Irish Civil War.* Mercier Press, Cork, 2011.

60 Military Service Pensions Collection. Kerry I Brigade. IRA Nominal Rolls. RO/88–101A. MA.

61 Military Service Pensions Collection. Kerry II Brigade. IRA Nominal Rolls. RO/102-110. MA.

62 Military Service Pensions Collection. Kerry III Brigade. IRA Nominal Rolls. RO/111-116. MA.

63 Kerry Command Weekly Reports. 'Irregular Positions and Strength in Area.' Report for week ending 17 September 1922. CW/OPS/08/01. MA.

64 Doyle, Tom. *The Summer Campaign in Kerry. Military History of the Irish Civil War.* Mercier Press, Cork, 2010, pp. 92–94.

65 *Ibid.*, pp. 97–107.

66 Military Service Pensions Collection. File No. 2D126. Application of Thomas O'Connor. MA.

67 *Ibid.*

68 O'Malley, Ernie. *The Men Will Talk to Me. Kerry Interviews.* Mercier Press, Cork, 2012, p. 280, 289. Interview with John Joe Rice.

69 Military Service Pensions Collection. File No. 2D21. Application of James Burke. MA.

70 O'Malley, *op. cit.*, p. 147. Interview with Tom O'Connor. Horgan, Tim. *Dying for the Cause. Kerry's Republican Dead.* Mercier Press, Cork, pp. 335–337.

71 Col.-Comdt. Éamon Horan letter to Commander-in-chief General Mulcahy 30 September 1922. CW/OPS/08/01 29 September – October 1922. MA.

72 Kerry Command Weekly Reports. Total captures for the week ending 30 September 1922. CW/OPS/08/01. MA.

73 Thomas Johnson, leader of the Labour Party, speaking in a debate on the Emergency Powers Bill, 27 September 1922. Precedence for Ministerial Business. Wednesday 27 September 1922. Dáil Éireann Debate Vol. 1 No. 13.

74 *Ibid.*

75 Vote on the Emergency Powers Bill, 27 September 1922. Precedence for Ministerial Business. Dáil Éireann Debate Vol. 1 No. 13.

76 Pastoral Letter of His Eminence Cardinal Logue, the Archbishops and Bishops of Ireland, to the Priests and the People of Ireland. Browne and Nolan Limited, Dublin, October 1922. Dublin Diocesan Archives.

77 Macardle, *op. cit.*, p. 816.

78 *Ibid.*, p. 822.

79 *Ibid.*, pp. 822–823.

80 Murphy, Karl, *op. cit.*, p. 44.

81 General W. R. E. Murphy, GOC Kerry Command. Report to Commander-in-Chief General Richard Mulcahy, GHQ, Portobello Barracks. 7 December 1922. P7/B/72. Mulcahy Papers. UCD Archives, Dublin.

82   Murphy, Karl, *op. cit.*, p. 44.

83   Murphy, General W. R. E., diary entry 28 December 1922. Murphy, Karl, *op. cit.*, pp. 45–46.

84   O'Dwyer, Martin (Bob). *Seventy-Seven of Mine Said Ireland.* Deshaoirse, Cashel, County Tipperary, 2006, pp. 207–214.

85   O'Malley, *op. cit.*, pp. 102, 107–108. Interview with Bill Bailey.

86   *Ibid.*, p. 104.

87   Written account of 'The Battle of Gurrane', Cahersiveen, County Kerry. O'Connor, Paddy. Father of Noreen O'Connor-O'Sullivan, Librarian, Cahersiveen Library, County Kerry.

88   O'Malley, *op. cit.*, pp. 102, 107–08. Interview with Dinny Daly.

89   O'Doherty, Liam. WS 689. BMH. Descriptions and drawings on various explosive devices and techniques used by the 5th Bn Engineers, Dublin Brigade, IRA.

90   *Ballyseedy*, produced and directed by Frank Hand. RTÉ, 1997.

91   Rev. Fr M. O'Connor CSSP, St Mary's College, Rathmines, Brother of Paddy O'Connor, Letter to General Gearóid O'Sullivan, 30 April 1923. Military Service Pensions Collection. File No. 3D58. Application of Patrick O'Connor. MA.

92   O'Malley, *op. cit.*, p. 101. Interview with Bill Bailey.

93   *Ibid.*, p. 105.

94   *Ballyseedy*, produced and directed by Frank Hand. RTÉ, 1997.

95   Military Service Pensions Collection. File No. MSP34REF23009 Application of Tadhg Coffey. MA. Also Horgan, *op. cit.*, pp. 285, 300, 302, 304, 305; Macardle, *The Tragedies of Kerry,* The Euston Press Ltd, Dublin, 1924, pp. 27–29.

96   Military Service Pensions Collection. File No. MSP34REF23009 Application of Tadhg Coffey. MA. Also Macardle, *Tragedies of Kerry, op. cit.*, pp 32–34.

97   *Ballyseedy*, produced and directed by Frank Hand. RTÉ, 1997. Also Irish Army Census 1922.

98   Horgan, *op. cit.*, pp. 210–212. *Ballyseedy*, RTÉ, 1997.

99   Mulcahy, General Richard. Chief of Staff National Army and Minister for Defence. Dáil Debates. Questions: Kerry Prisoners' Deaths. Tuesday 17 April, 1923.

100 Kerry Command Operational Reports. Casualty/Reports/Routine Orders. CW/OPS/08/10. Reports and Statistics. Submitted 26 March 1923. MA.

101 'Kerry Notes. Great Send-Off to Commandant Dave Neligan.' *An t-Óglach*, 21 April 1923. MA.

102 O'Dwyer, *Seventy-Seven of Mine, op. cit.*, pp. 354–372. Also, Horgan, *op. cit.,* pp. 105–106.

103 Military Service Pensions Collection. File No. MSP34REF9505. Application of James McGrath. MA.

104 Military Service Pensions Collection. File No. 3D233. Application of Jane O'Neill, mother of James O'Neill. MA.

105 'The Caves of Clashmealcon.' *An t-Óglach*, 16 June 1923. MA.

106 Interview with Mrs Patsy Healy, daughter of Jessie MacCarthy, Kenmare, County Kerry, 23 July, 2016.

107 Applications for Compensation Kerry Mine Explosions Cases. H 197/52. JUS/2008/152/27 National Archives of Ireland. Also Military Service Pensions Collection. File No. DP3816. The application on behalf of the family of Volunteer Eugene Dwyer. Note on the file stating 'Claim should not be considered as he was an Irregular.' MA.

108 Macardle, Dorothy. WS 457, p. 1. BMH.
109 Military Service Pensions Collection. File No. MSP34REF23009. Application of Tadhg Coffey. MA.
110 Hogan, James. Letter to Chief of Staff National Army Peadar McMahon and a Copy of the Court of Inquiry, Kenmare Case. MS 49, 612. National Library of Ireland, Dublin.
111 *Ibid.*
112 Davitt, Cahir. WS 1751, p. 94. BMH.
113 Hugh Kennedy Papers. Attorney General Irish Free State. P4/560 (1) Procedural and Advisory February 1922–May 1924. Jessie and Florence MacCarthy. UCD Archives, Dublin.
114 *Ibid.*
115 *Ibid.*
116 Davitt, Cahir. WS 1751, p. 95. BMH.
117 'Troops Reviewed at Tralee.' *An t-Óglach*. 6 October 1923. MA.

8. 'ON THE ONE ROAD'

1 Macardle, Dorothy. *The Irish Republic*. Irish Press Ltd., Dublin, 1951, p. 862.
2 *Ibid.*, p. 868
3 Tobin, Liam. *The Truth About the Army Crisis. The Irish Republican Army Organisation.* Dublin, 1924. Box 2660. Monsignor M. Curran Political Papers. Dublin Diocesan Archives, p. 3.
4 Thomas Markham re Dublin Castle structure and documents c. 1921–22. P7/B/104. Mulcahy Papers. UCD Archives, Belfield, Dublin.
5 Thomas Markham. Personal & Confidential letter to Archbishop Byrne of Dublin, 10 October 1922. Box 466. Archbishop Byrne Papers. Government and Politics. Dublin Diocesan Archives, Clonliffe College, Dublin.
6 List of Masonic Lodges in the Irish Free State 1928. Box 467. Government and Politics. Archbishop Byrne Papers. Dublin Diocesan Archives, Clonliffe College, Dublin.
7 Tobin, *op. cit.*, p. 3.
8 *Ibid.*, p. 4.
9 *Ibid.*, p. 11.
10 Report of the Army Inquiry Committee. Saorstát Éireann. The Stationery Office, Dublin, June 1924. Dáil Éireann Library and Research Service, paragraph 19.
11 The first detachment of Civic Guards (Garda Siochána) staged a mutiny while on parade at the Curragh in 1923. They refused to accept among their senior staff former members of the RIC.
12 Tobin, *op. cit.*, p. 12.
13 *Ibid.*, p. 13.
14 Report of the Army Inquiry Committee. Saorstát Éireann. The Stationery Office, Dublin, June 1924. Dáil Éireann Library and Research Service, paragraph 15.
15 *Ibid.*, paragraphs 26–27.
16 *Ibid.*, paragraph 6.
17 The Anglo-Irish Treaty. Article 12. CAB/24/131. The National Archives, Kew, London.
18 Macardle, *op. cit.*, pp. 884–85.

19 Kee, Robert. *The Most Distressful Country. The Green Flag. Volume I.* Quartet Books, London, 1983.

20 'Army Delegation Visit France' *An t-Óglach*, 11 August 1923. MA.

21 *Ibid.*

22 'Revelations From The Olympiad' *An t-Óglach*, 2 August 1924. MA.

23 Crowe, Catriona. Military Service Pensions Collection: Introduction. *Guide to the Military Service Pension (1916–1923).* Óglaigh na hÉireann, Military Archives & National Museum of Ireland, 2012, pp. 17–18.

24 Shatter, Alan, TD, Minister for Defence. *Guide to the Military Service Pension (1916–1923).* Óglaigh na hÉireann, Military Archives & National Museum of Ireland, 2012, p. 9.

25 Military Service Pensions Collection. File No. 24SP3908. Application of James Dempsey. MA.

26 Military Service Pensions Collection. File No. MSPC34REF4945. Application of Lily Mernin, MA.

27 *Ibid.*

28 *Ibid.*

29 Military Service Pensions Collection. File No. MSP34REF8996. Application of Thomas Newell. MA.

30 Author interviews with Terry Newell 2015–17.

31 *Ibid.*

32 *Ibid.*

33 *Ibid.*

34 *Ibid.*

35 'Presentation to Mick McDonnell, Officer Commanding Original H.Q. Squad of the Army of the Irish Republic in the fight for Independence 1916–1921.' BMH Photographic Collection, P-35-001.jpeg and P-35-002.jpeg.

36 McDonnell, Michael. WS 225, p. 7. BMH.

37 Dalton, Charles. WS 434, pp. 40–42. BMH.

38 Military Service Pensions Collection. File No. MSP34REF1515. Application of Evelyn Flanagan, MA.

39 *Ibid.*

40 *Ibid.*

41 Military Service Pensions Collection. File No. 24SP1153 (WDP4). Application of Charlie Dalton, MA.

42 *Ibid.*

43 *Ibid.*

44 *Ibid.*

45 *Ibid.*

46 *Ibid.*

47 Boyne, Seán. *Emmet Dalton. Somme Soldier, Irish General, Film Pioneer.* Merrion Press, County Kildare, 2016, pp. 284–285.

48 http://www.ardmore.ie/history

49 Author interview with Dr Rory O'Hanlon, 24 February 2014.

50 Vote on the Electoral Amendment Bill Thursday 4 August 1927. Dáil Éireann Debate Vol. 20, No. 19.

51 Murphy, Karl. 'General W. R. E. Murphy and the Irish Civil War.' MA Thesis 1994. NUI Maynooth Library, p. 64.

52 *An Introduction to the Bureau of Military History*, 2002, p. 1.

53 O'Malley, Cormac K. H. and Dolan, Anne. *'No Surrender Here!' The Civil War Papers of Ernie O'Malley 1922–1924*. The Lilliput Press, Dublin, 2007, pp. xxxviii–xli.

54 O'Malley, Cormac K. H. 'Ernie O'Malley (1897–1957) Life Beyond the Pale.' A talk in Mayo County Library, Castlebar, 16 January 2015.

55 Ernie O'Malley Papers. IE UCDA P17. UCD Archives, Dublin.

56 O'Malley & Dolan, *op. cit.* p. lvi.

57 O'Malley, Ernie. *The Singing Flame*. Mercier Press, Cork, 2012, p. 17.

58 Broy, Éamon. WS 1280, p. 87. BMH.

59 Author interview with Eithne Daly, daughter of Frank Daly and niece of Paddy O'Daly. 16 January 2016.

60 *Irish Independent*, 1 May 1963. National Library of Ireland, Dublin.

61 Military Service Pensions Collection. File No. MSP34REF57057. Application of Mollie O'Shea. MA.

62 Daniel Seery on RTÉ Arena speaking about his great-granduncle, 4 September 2015; also Irish Civil Records. Registration of death of Úna Ennis 12 April 1942 and registration of death of John Prendergast 12 April 1942.

63 Irish Civil Records. Registration of death of Thomas Ennis 10 March 1945.

64 'An Irish Eviction.' *Irish Independent*, 27 November 1925; *Morning Post*, 28 November 1925; *Sunday Independent*, 29 November 1925. Military Service Pensions Collection. File No. 24SP7328. MA.

65 Fisk, Robert. *In Time of War. Ireland, Ulster and the Price of Neutrality 1939–45*. Gill & Macmillan, Dublin, 1985, p. 342. Quoting Clissmann interview 14.4.79.

66 *Ibid.*, p. 343.

67 Irish Civil Records. Registration of death of Brigid O'Daly, 16 January 1941.

68 Irish Civil Records. Registration of death of Paddy O'Daly, 16 January 1941.

69 Irish Civil Records. Registration of death of Richard Joseph Leonard, 14 October 1961.

70 Military Service Pensions Collection. IRA Nominal Rolls. MA- MSPC-RO-9. MA.

71 Military Service Pensions Collection. Cumann na mBan on Active Service with C Company 3rd Battalion, Dublin Brigade. IRA Nominal Rolls MA-MSPC-RO-04. MA.

72 Tribute to Máire Gleeson as Appendix I in Bean Uí Chonaill, Eilís. WS 568. BMH. Also Irish Civil Records. Registration of death of Mary Gleeson, 10 February 1949.

73 Uí Chonnaill, Éilis (née Ní Riain) WS 568, pp. 15–16. BMH.

74 King v King. Divorce Papers. J77/2304. The National Archives, Kew, UK.

75 *Ibid.*

76 King, William Lorraine. Service No: 125401. Gaza War Cemetery. Commonwealth War Graves Commission. http://www.cwgc.org/find-war-dead/casualty/2897924/KING,%20WILLIAM%20LORRAINE

77 Bunbury, Turtle. 'Hardy: the great escaper.' *The Irish Times*, 30 June 2017.

78 http://www.cairogang.com/escaped/hardy/hardy.html

79 Military Service Pensions Collection. File No. WDP3169. Application of Thomas McGrath. MA.

80 Military Service Pensions Collection. File No. 24SP11719. Application of Michael Joseph Bishop, MA.

81 Military Service Pensions Collection. File No. 24SP3411. Application of Daniel Hogan MA.

82 Slattery, Jim. Newspaper article, 28 January 1968. Mulcahy Papers P7/D/69. UCD Archives, Dublin.

83 Military Service Pensions Collection. File No. 24SP6854. Application of William James Stapleton, MA.

84 *Ibid.*

85 Daniel Breen interview featured in *Hidden History*, 'Get Collins – The Intelligence War in Dublin.' Mint Production for RTÉ, 2007.

86 Pauline Price (née Shanahan), relative of Paddy Dwyer, County Tipperary.

87 A BBC Production in association with RTÉ, 1980.

88 Dalton, Charles. WS 434, p. 42. BMH.

89 O'Halpin, Eunan. 'Seán Lemass's silent anguish.' *The Irish Times*, 21 July 2013. Also death certificate of Herbert Lemass, 28 January 1916 (No: 241).

90 Military Service Pensions Collection. File No. MSP34REF2078. Application of Seán Lemass. MA.

91 Military Service Pensions Collection. File No. MSP34REF6759. Application of Stephen Fuller. MA.

92 O'Regan, Michael. 'Stories of the Irish Revolution: Ballyseedy and the Civil War's worst atrocity.' *The Irish Times*, Friday 11 December, 2015.

93 Acts of the Elective Chapter of the Province of Ireland, 1988, Part II (Obituaries). Dominican Archives, St Mary's Priory, Tallaght, Dublin.

94 Debate on 'Claims of Irish Loyalists' in the House of Lords Westminster. Statement of Lord Muskerry. House of Lords Debate 5 March 1924. Vol. 56 CC535-65.

95 *Ibid.*, statement of Lord Fitzalan.

96 'The Opening of a New Chapter. Sir Alfred Cope at Cwmgorse.' *Amman Valley Chronicle*, 10 March 1927. Llyfrgell Genedlaethol Cymru/The National Library of Wales.

97 Cope, Sir Alfred. WS 469. BMH.

98 Ua hUallacháin, Gearóid. (Garry Holohan). WS 328, p. 31. BMH.

APPENDICES

1 *Thom's Official Directory 1920*. Entries on the Dublin Metropolitan Police. Alex Thom and Co. Ltd., Dublin, 1920, pp. 755–756 and 1433. *Thom's Official Directory 1921*. Alex Thom and Co. Ltd., Dublin, 1921, pp. 1432–1433, National Library of Ireland. Royal Irish Constabulary List and Directory January 1920, His Majesty's Stationery Office. The Archive CD Books Project, Eneclann, Trinity College, Dublin.

2 Haileybury and Imperial Service College Register. https://www.haileybury.com/medals/dso%20h%20pre1912.htm

3 Fuller, Steve & Lutt, Nigel. 'The Bedfordshire Regiment in the Great War. Officers Photographs and Biographies from the 1st Battalion.' http://www.bedfordregiment.org.uk/1stbn/1stbtnphotos1.html

4   Interview with Mr Reynolds, a former member of the ADRIC. IE/MA/CP Item
    X, A/0416. Military Archives, Cathal Brugha Barracks, Dublin. Information
    supplemented from Leeson, D. M. *The Black & Tans. British Police and Auxiliaries in
    the Irish War of Independence.* Oxford University Press, UK, 2012, pp. 99–101.
5   Documents listing details of Raids carried out by British army, ADRIC and RIC
    Units in the Dublin District November and December 1920. WO 35/75. The
    National Archives, Kew, UK.
6   Sources for names in ASU: Military Service Pensions Collection. IRA Membership
    Roll. File No. MSPC MA-MSPC-RO-9 List from Joe Leonard 17 December 1939.
    Colonel J. V. Joyce. WS 1762 18 February 1959. James Doyle WS 127, pp. 11–12, 18
    May 1948. Bureau of Military History. Military Archives, Cathal Brugha Barracks,
    Dublin. Thomas Sweeney Newell ASU Certificate, Terry and Éamon Newell.
7   Military Service Pensions Collection. Files: Thomas Bryan 1D142, Francis Flood
    1D35, Edmond Foley 1D279, Patrick Maher 1D343, Patrick Moran DP7559,
    Bernard Ryan 1D131, Thomas Traynor 1D134, Thomas Whelan 1D125 (Kevin
    Barry File not available at time of writing). Also 'Profiles of 10 Volunteers Executed
    in 1921'. *The Irish Times*, 14 October 2001.
8   Lists of operatives were noted as research continued through the Department of
    Justice Files (Jus/14/177 (1076), Jus/14/293 (1320); Department of Finance Files
    (Fin/1/3544) and (Fin/1/3543) at the National Archives and in the Military Service
    Pensions Collection in which different files contained lists of CID men applying for
    pensions.

Bibliography

BOOKS

Abbott, Richard. *Police Casualties in Ireland 1919–1922*. Mercier Press, Cork, 2000.

Ambrose, Joe. *Dan Breen and the IRA*. Mercier Press, Cork, 2006.

Ambrose, Joe. *Seán Treacy and the Tan War*. Mercier Press, Cork, 2007.

American Commission. *Conditions in Ireland. Interim Report, 1921*. Archive CD Books, Ireland, 2008. Eneclann.

Barton, Brian. *The Secret Court Martial Records of the Easter Rising*. The History Press, UK, 2010.

Bennett, Richard. *The Black and Tans*. Edward Hulton, London, 1959.

Borgonovo, John. *The Battle for Cork. July – August 1922. Military History of the Irish Civil War*. Mercier Press, Cork, 2011.

Boyne, Sean. *Emmet Dalton. Somme Soldier, Irish General, Film Pioneer*. Merrion Press, Sallins, County Kildare, 2016.

Brewes, J. D. *The RIC: An Oral History*. Institute of Irish Studies. Queen's University, Belfast, 1990.

Bridges, Lord & Dale, Henry John Anderson. *Viscount Waverley. 1882–1958. Biographical Memoirs of Fellows of the Royal Society*, Volume 4, November 1958.

Byrne, Miles (edited by his widow). *Memoirs of Miles Byrne. A New Edition with an Introduction by Stephen Gwynn*. Vol. II. Dublin: Maunsell & Co., London: A.H. Bullen, 1907.

Chappell, Mike. *The British Army in World War I (1). The Western Front 1914–16*. Men-at-Arms Series. Osprey Publishing, Oxford, UK, 2008.

Coogan, Tim Pat. *Michael Collins. A Biography*. Hutchinson, London, 1990.

Coogan, Tim Pat. *De Valera. Long Fellow, Long Shadow*. Hutchinson, London, 1993.

Cottrell, Peter. *The Anglo-Irish War. The Troubles of 1913–1922*. Essential Histories Series. Osprey Publishing, Oxford, UK, 2006.

Cottrell, Peter. *The Irish Civil War 1922–23. Essential Histories Series*. Osprey Publishing, Oxford, UK, 2008.

Crowe, Catriona (ed.). *Guide To The Military Service (1916–1923)*. Pensions Collection, Óglaigh na hÉireann, Military Archives, 2012.

Crozier, Brigadier-General F. P. *Ireland For Ever*. Cedric Chivers Ltd., Bath, UK, 1971.

Dalton, Charles. *With The Dublin Brigade. Espionage and Assassination with Michael Collins' Intelligence Unit*. Mercier Press, Cork, 2014.

Doyle, Jennifer. Clarke Frances, Connaughton, Eibhlis, Somerville, Orna. *An Introduction to The Bureau of Military History 1913–1921*. Military Archives, Cathal Brugha Barracks, Dublin, 2002.

Doyle, Tom. *The Summer Campaign in Kerry. Military History of The Irish Civil War*. Mercier Press, Cork, 2010.

Ferriter, Diarmaid. *Judging Dev*. The Royal Irish Academy, Dublin, 2007.

Ferriter, Diarmaid. *A Nation And Not A Rabble. The Irish Revolution 1913–1923*. Profile Books, London, 2015.

Fisk, Robert. *In Time of War. Ireland, Ulster and the Price of Neutrality 1939–45*. Gill & Macmillan, Dublin, 1985.

Foley, Michael. *The Bloodied Field: Croke Park. Sunday 21 November 1920*. The O'Brien Press, Dublin, 2014.

Gillis, Liz. *The Fall of Dublin. Military History of The Irish Civil War*. Mercier Press, Cork, 2011.

Gillis, Liz. *Revolution in Dublin. A Photographic History 1913–23*. Mercier Press, Cork, 2013.

Gudmundsson, Bruce I. *The British Army on the Western Front 1916*. Battle Orders Series. Osprey Publishing, Oxford, UK, 2007.

Harrington, Michael. *The Munster Republic. The Civil War in North Cork*. Mercier Press, Cork, 2009.

Hart, Peter (ed.). *Irish Narratives. British Intelligence in Ireland, 1920–21. The Final Reports*. Cork University Press, 2002.

Hart, Peter Mick. *The Real Michael Collins*. Viking Penguin, New York, 2006.

Healy, T. M. *Letters and Leaders of My Day*. Frederick A. Stokes, New York, 1929.

Herlihy, Jim. *The Royal Irish Constabulary. A Short Geneaological Guide*. Four Courts Press, Dublin, 1999.

Horgan, Tim. *Dying for the Cause*. Mercier Press, Cork, 2015.

Kautt, W. H. *Ground Truths. British Army Operations in the Irish War of Independence*. Irish Academic Press, Sallins, County Kildare, 2014.

The Kerryman. *Dublin's Fighting Story 1916–21. Told By The Men Who Made It*. Introduction by Diarmaid Ferriter. Mercier Press, Cork, 2009.

Labour Party of Great Britain, *Labour Party Commission to Ireland*. Caledonian Press, London, 1921.

Leeson, D. M. *The Black and Tans. British Police and Auxiliaries in the Irish War of Independence, 1920–1921*. Oxford University Press, Oxford, UK, 2012.

Macardle, Dorothy. *The Irish Republic*. Irish Press Ltd., Dublin, 1951.

Macardle, Dorothy. *The Tragedies of Kerry*. The Emton Press Limited, Dublin, 1924.

MacCarron, Donal. *The Irish Defence Forces since 1922*. Men-at-Arms Series. Osprey Publishing, Oxford, UK, 2004.

McCarthy, Cal. *Cumann na mBan and The Irish Revolution*. The Collins Press, Cork, 2007.

McMahon, Paul. *British Spies & Irish Rebels. British Intelligence and Ireland 1916–1945*. The Boydell Press, Woodbridge, Suffolk, UK, 2011.

Military Archives. *An Introduction to the Bureau of Military History*. Military Archives, 2012, Dublin.

Monthly Army List: July 1919. His Majesty's Stationery Office, E. Ponsonby Limited, Grafton Street, Dublin, Ireland.

Neeson, Eoin. *The Civil War 1922–23*. Poolbeg Press, Dublin, 1989.

Neligan, Dave. *The Spy in the Castle*. MacGibbon & McKee, Worcester and London, 1968.

O'Callaghan, John. *The Battle for Kilmallock. Military History of The Irish Civil War*. Mercier Press, Cork, 2011.

O'Dwyer, Martin (Bob). *Seventy-Seven of Mine Said Ireland*. Deshaoirse (Cashel Folk Village), Cashel, County Tipperary, 2006.

O'Dwyer, Martin (Bob). *Death Before Dishonour*. Cashel Folk Village, Cashel, County Tipperary, 2010.

O'Mahony, Seán. *Frongoch. University of Revolution*. FDR Teoranta, Dublin, 1987.

O'Malley, Cormac K. H., Dolan, Anne (eds). *The Civil War Papers of Ernie O'Malley 1922–1924*. Lilliput Press, Dublin, 2007.

O'Malley, Ernie. *On Another Man's Wound*. Anvil, Dublin, 2002.

O'Malley, Ernie. *The Singing Flame*. Mercier Press, Cork, 2012.

O'Malley, Ernie. '*No Surrender Here': The Civil War Papers of Ernie O'Malley 1922–1924*. Lilliput Press, Dublin, 2007.

O'Malley, Ernie. *The Men Will Talk to Me. Kerry Interviews*. O'Malley, Cormac K. H. and Horgan, Tim (eds). Mercier Press, Cork, 2012.

O'Malley, Ernie. *The Men Will Talk To Me. West Cork Interviews*. Bielenberg, Andy, Borgonovo, John & Ó Ruairc, Pádraig Óg (eds). Mercier Press, Cork, 2015.

Pegler, Martin. *British Tommy 1914–18*. Warrior Series. Osprey Publishing, Oxford, 2008.

Riccio, Ralph A. *Irish Costal Landings 1922*. Green Series. MMP Books No 4117. Published by Stratus s.c. in Poland for Mushroom Model Publications, Hampshire, UK, 2015.

Royal Irish Constabulary List and Directory, 1 July 1920, His Majesty's Stationery Office, E. Ponsonby Ltd. Dublin. Archive CD Books, Ireland, 2010. Eneclann.

Ryan, Meda. *Liam Lynch: The Real Chief*. Mercier Press, Cork, 2005.

Ryle Dwyer, T. *The Squad and the intelligence operations of Michael Collins*. Mercier Press, Cork, 2005.

Ryle Dwyer, T. *Michael Collins and the Civil War*. Mercier Press, Cork, 2012.

Sheehan, William. *British Voices. From the Irish War of Independence 1918–1921. The Words of British Servicemen Who Were There*. The Collins Press, Cork, 2007.

Sheehan, William. *Fighting for Dublin. The British Battle for Dublin. 1919–1921*. The Collins Press, Cork, 2007.

Sheehan, William. *Hearts and Mines. The British 5th Division, Ireland, 1920–1922*. The Collins Press, Cork, 2009.

Townshend, Charles. *The Republic. The Fight for Irish Independence*. Penguin Books, London, 2013.

Von Spoen, Colonel. *The Art of Command*. Translated by the General Staff, War Office (British) from the 'Jahrbücher für die deutsche Armee und Marine, October, 1907', by permission of the publisher, Herr A. Bath, Berlin.

Walsh, Oonagh. *Ireland's Independence, 1880–1923*. Routledge, London and New York, 2002.

White, G. & O'Shea, B. *Irish Volunteer Soldier 1913–23*. Warrior Series. Illustrated by Younghusband, B. Osprey Publishing, Oxford, 2003.

Younger, Calton. *Ireland's Civil War*. Fontana/Collins, Glasgow, 1979.

ARCHIVES & MUSEUMS

Dominican Provincial Archives, St Mary's Priory, Tallaght, Dublin
Acts of the Elective Chapter of the Province of Ireland, 1988, Part II (Obituaries) Fr
   Maurice Walsh

Dublin Diocesan Archives
Archbishop Walsh Papers 1920
Letter 26 November 1920 Rev Fr James B. Curry New York to Archbishop Walsh. Priest,
   Diocesan and Other Dioceses.
Letter 26 November 1920 Rev M J Foley Illinois to Archbishop Walsh. Priests, Diocesan
   and Other Dioceses.
Telegram 15 December 1920 Bishop of Cork to Archbishop of Dublin expressing thanks
   for dispatch of Dublin Fire Brigade to Cork.
 Correspondence from Bishops 380/1.

Archbishop Byrne Papers 1922
Account from inside the Four Courts under bombardment 28th 1922. Government and
   Politics. Box 466.
Homan, J. Memorandum of St John's Ambulance work and Peace Effort in Dublin Civil
   War fighting 28 June – 5 July 1922. Government and Politics. Box 466.
Letter from Thomas Markham to Archbishop Byrne 10 October 1922. Government and
   Politics Box 466.
Logue, Cardinal Michael and the Bishops of Ireland. Pastoral Letter to the Priests and
   People of Ireland. October 1922. Box 466.
List of Masonic Lodges in the Irish Free State 1928. Government and Politics.
   Sympathetic [Republican] Priests. List. 1923. Government. Box 467.

Monsignor M. Curran Political Papers
Tobin, Liam. *The Truth About the Army Crisis*. The Irish Republican Army Organisation,
   Dublin, 1924. Box 2660.

Imperial War Museum, Lambeth
Oral History – Audio Interview. Rymer-Jones, John Murray. British Officer serving in
   Dublin 1920–21. Reel 12 & Reel 13, Catalogue No. 10699, 1989.

Irish Jesuit Archives
Obituary of Rev Fr William Hogan, previously Volunteer with Munitions Unit, Dublin
   Brigade IRA, Irish Province News, October 1964.

Military Archives
An t-Óglach Magazine Online Collection 1918–1924.

Bureau of Military History

Balfe, Edward WS 1373
Barton, Robert C. WS 979
Breen, Daniel WS 1739 & 1763
Brennan, Patrick J. WS 1773
Broy, Éamon WS 1280
Byrne, Vincent WS 423
Cahill, James WS 503
Caldwell, Patrick WS 638
Colley, Harry WS 1687
Cope, Sir Alfred WS 469
Culhane, Seán WS 746
Curran, Right Rev. M WS 687
Dalton, Charles WS 434
Davitt, Cahir WS 993 & WS 1751
Dolan, Joseph WS 663 & WS 900
Doyle, James WS 127
Duggan, George Chester WS 1099
Dwyer, George WS 678
Dwyer, Patrick WS 1432
Fitzgerald, George WS 684
Foley, James WS 774
Gaynor, John WS 1447
Gilhooley, Joseph WS 390
Henderson, Frank WS 821
Henderson, Ruaidhrí WS 1686
Heron, Áine WS 503
Hughes, James F WS 535
Hyland, Joseph WS 644
Joyce, J. V. WS 1762
Kelliher, Ned WS 477
Kennedy, Patrick WS 499
Laffan, Nicholas WS 703
Lawless, Sr Eithne WS414
Lawless, Joseph V. WS 1043
Lawless, Michael Joseph WS 727
Leahy, James WS 1454
Leonard, Joseph WS 547
Little, Patrick J. WS 1769
Lynch, Michael WS 511
Macardle, Dorothy WS 457
MacCaisin, Seumas WS 8
McCarville, Eileen (née McGrane, Eileen) WS 1752

McDonnell, Andrew WS 1768
McDonnell, Daniel P. WS 486
McDonnell, Michael WS 225
Mac Eoin, Seán WS 1716 (Appendix D)
McHugh, Patrick WS 664
Mannix, Patrick WS 502
Mee, Jeremiah WS 379
Mulcahy, Mary Josephine (née Ryan, Min) WS 399
Neligan, David WS 380
Nolan, Bernard WS 844
Noyk, Michael WS 707
Nugent, Larry WS 907
Nunan, Seán WS 1744
Ó Conchubhair, Pádraig (O'Connor, Patrick) WS 813
O'Connor, Joseph WS 157 & WS 487
O'Daly, Patrick WS 220 & WS 387
O'Doherty, Liam WS 689
O'Donoghue, Daithí WS 548
O'Donoghue, Michael V. WS 1741
O'Donovan, James L. (Seumas) WS 1713
O'Duffy, Sean M. WS 618
O'Laoghaire, Michael WS 797
O'Neill, Seán WS 1154
O'Reilly, Bridie WS 454
O'Sheil, Kevin WS 1770
Peppard, Thomas WS 4399
Rock, Michael WS 1398
Rooney, Catherine (née Byrne) WS648
Ryan, Thomas WS 387
Saurin, Frank WS 715
Stapleton, William James WS 822
Thornton, Frank WS 615
Traynor, Oscar WS 340 & Voice Recording SI412
Tully, James WS 628
Ua hUallacháin, Gearóid (Garry Holohan) WS 336
Uí Chonnaill, Éilis (née Ní Riain, Éilis) WS568
Walsh, Richard WS 400
White, George WS 956

Bureau of Military History Miscellaneous
Arrest and Trial of Michael Collins CD 1/8/2. Group 8 II.
British Government Publications – Restoration of Order in Ireland Act. CD6 Group 17.
Dublin Brigade Review. CD 6/51/14.
Michael Collins, The Sword of Sinn Féin. CD 1/8/3.
Photographic Collection. Squad Reunion. P-35-001 & P-35-002.
Torture of Prisoners. CD 333/38.

Civil War Papers
Civil War Operations Kerry Command CW/OPS/08. Kerry Command Weekly Reports
     1922–23. CW/OPS/08/01,02,03.
Kerry Command Operation Reports: Casualties, Reports and Routine Orders. Reports
     and Statistics 26 March 1923. CW/OPS/08/10.
Letter from Col. Comdt. Éamon Horan to General Richard Mulcahy, 30 September
     1922. CW/OPS/08/01.

Collins Papers
Active Service Unit, Dublin Brigade, 1921. A/0710 I–V.
British Army Prisoner 'A' List, No. 75, 29 March 1921, A/0619 XLVII.
Burning of the Customs House 25 May 1921, Comdt. M. O'Kelly. A/0618/IV.
Interview with Mr Reynolds a former member of F Company ADRIC at Dublin Castle,
     Item X, A/0416.
IRA Intelligence Department (National Army) Pay Books. A/0921.
IRA Intelligence Instructions. A/0604 II.
IRA Intelligence in the Anglo-Irish War by Frank Thornton. A/0800/IV.
IRA Operations 1920. A/0408/XVIII.
Raid on Collinstown Aerodrome by Michael Lynch. A/0800/VIII.
Report on the death of Seán Treacy, Tipp No. 3 thought to have been written by Comdt.
     Dick McKee. A/0436/I.
Report on the Dublin ASU or 'HQ Guard' 9 August 1921 A/0710 II.

Commandant M. Mortell Collection
National Army Intelligence Department Pay Lists. IE/MA/PRCN/0072/02(6).

Irish Army Census 1922

Military Service Pensions Collection (Individual Pensions)

Bishop, Michael Joseph 24SP11719
Bryan, Thomas 1D142
Buckley, Stephen DP878
Burke, James 2D21
Bushell, Ellen Sarah MSP34REF22326
Coffey, Tadhg MSP34REF23009
Courtney, Michael DP2261
Cullen, James Francis MSP34REF1746

Dalton, Charles 24SP1153, WDP4 &
     W24D15
Daly, Francis MSP34REF20270
Daly, John DP51
Dempsey, James 24SP3908
Dunne, Michael 3D164
Dwyer, Eugene DP3816
Flanagan, Evelyn MSP34REF1515

Flood, Francis 1D35
Foley, Edmund 1D279
Fuller, Stephen MSP34REF6759
Galvin, Michael 3D137
Gannon, Bill WMSP34REF25776
Hartnett, Patrick DP9533
Hogan, Daniel 24SP3411
Hunter, Tom DP4587
Lemass, Seán MSP34REF2078
Lynch, Michael Joseph MSP34REF9462
Maher, Patrick 1D343
Markham, Thomas W24SP10942
McDonnell, Michael W24SP4528
McGrath, James MSP34REF9509
McGrath, Thomas WDP3169 &
    MSP34REF21184
McIntosh, Mary (mother of Lt. James
    McIntosh) 1D75
McInverney, Simon MSP34REF56841
McKee, Maire (sister of Richard McKee)
    DP23324
Meaney, Bridget (mother of Patrick
    Meaney) 1D273
Mernin, Lily MSP34REF4945
Moran, Patrick DP7559
Murphy, Tim DP8168
Newell, Thomas MSP34REF8996
Nolan, George Leo WMSP34REF60676

O'Brien, Joseph 4P66
O'Connell, Jeremiah Joseph 'Ginger'
    W24SP12702
O'Connell, Michael DP6068
O'Connor, John DP4098
O'Connor, Laurence 3D57
O'Connor, Patrick 3D58
O'Connor, Thomas 2D126
O'Donel, Geraldine WS 861
O'Donoghue, Dan DP739
O'Neill, James 3D233
O'Shea, George DP6572
O'Shea, Mollie MSP34REF57057
Ryan, Bernard 1D131
Shea, Daniel DP2588
Stanley, Joseph Michael WMSP
    34REF20034
Stapleton, Edward 3D70
Stapleton, William James 24SP6854
Traynor, Oscar MSP34REF236
Traynor, Thomas 1D134
Twomey, Tim DP5819
Ua Dálaigh, Pádraig (O'Daly, Patrick)
    W24SP424
Walsh, James DP4728
Whelan, Thomas 1D125

IRA Membership Rolls
Active Service Unit (ASU) Dublin I Brigade MA-MSPC-RO-9; GHQ IRA MA-MSPC-RO-601; Cumann na mBan on active service with C Coy 3rd Bn. Dublin I Brigade; Dublin I Brigade RO/1-9 & Fingal Brigade RO/20-25; 4th Bn. Dublin I Brigade MA-MSPC-RO-5; 6th Bn. Dublin I Brigade MA-MSPC-RO-7; Kerry I Brigade RO/88-101A; Kerry II Brigade RO/102-110; Kerry III Brigade RO/111-116.

Cumann na mBan
GHQ MA-MSPC-CMB-163; Dublin City Council Branches MA-MSPC-CMB-124/125/126/163; North Dublin/Fingal District Council MA-MSPC-CMB-124 & MA-MSPC-CMB-125.

Na Fianna Éireann
Dublin & GHQ MA-MSPC-FE-1; Dublin Brigade MA-MSPC-FE-2.

National Archives of Ireland
Inspector Mooney CID. Attempted prosecution. Fin/1/3544
Captain Moynihan CID JUS8/2007/56/065
CID Related Files: Inspector Mooney FIN/1/2753; Absorbtion of CID into DMP memorandum from Home Affairs to Executive Council FIN/1/3543; CID establishment of protective force 1923–24 FIN/1/2745; CID payment to hospitals for injured officers FIN/1/2749; Moynihan director CID FIN/1/2752; CID disbandment October 1923 TSCH/3/S3331; CID Estimates 1923–24 FIN/1/1731.
Compensations Kerry Mine Cases H197/52 & JUS3/2008/152/27.
Disbanding of CID. Memorandum for Minister for Justice, Kevin O'Higgins 9 July 1923. TSCH/3/S3331.
Joseph Bergin Case JUS8/2007/56/015.
Letter from Capt. A.S. Muireadhaigh to Major-General McGrath TD re operational structure of CID, Protective Officers Corps and Citizens Defence Force, 12 October 1923. TSCH/3/S3331.

RIC Reports
RIC Inspector General's Reports for Ireland: September & October 1918 MFA/54/65.
RIC County Inspector's Monthly Report Dublin (NAI Ref: MFA 24/1-21) January CO 904/108 (Reel 69 Box 108); February 1919 CO 904/108 (Reel 69 Box 108); March 1919 CO 904/108 (Reel 69 Box 108); December 1919 CO 904/110 (Reel 71 Box 110); February 1920 CO 904/111 (Reel 72 Box 111); October 1920 CO 904/113 (Reel 72 Box 113); July 1921 CO 904/116 (Reel 76 Box 116).
Steele-Moylett Negotiations March 1920–January 1921 DE/2/251.

Perth Diocesan Archives, Highgate, Western Australia
Bryan, Cyril. The Western Australia Record, 27 November 1920.
Dr Clune. Diplomat during the Black and Tan Regime. The Western Australia Catholic Record, 10 April 1946.

Queen's Own Royal West Kent Regiment Archives, Maidstone Museum, Kent, UK
The Aftermath of War 1920–23. 2nd Battalion in Germany Upper Silesia and Ireland.

Royal Green Jackets (The Rifles) Museum, Hampshire Record Office, Winchester, UK
3rd Battalion Ballsbridge, Dublin. Letters to the Editor. *The Rifle Brigade Chronicle*. 1920 edition compiled and edited by Col. Willoughby Verner. Printed by John Bales & Sons, London, 1921.
3rd Battalion Ballsbridge, Dublin. Letters to the Editor. *The Rifle Brigade Chronicle*. 1921 edition compiled and edited by Major H.G. Parkyn OBE. Printed by John Bale & Sons, London, 1922.

Surrey History Centre, Woking, UK
2nd Battalion East Surrey Regiment Digest of Service 1921 ESR/3/6/6.

The National Archives, Kew, UK

Cabinet Papers: 16 December 1918 CAB/24/72; 15 May 1919 CAB/24/79; January 1920 CAB 24/97; 26 July 1920 CAB/24/110/263; 7 June 1920; CAB/23/21; 23 July 1920 CAB/24/109; 26 July 1920 CAB/24/110/263 (Appendix B); 8 July 1922 CAB/24/138; 23 September 1922 CAB/24/139.

Colonial Office

Attempted assassination of Lord French; General Nevil Macready & Sir John Anderson correspondence; Private Papers of Sir John Anderson (Black Ledger); CO 904/188(1).

Bachelor, Captain Kearns. Protection and reassignment after IRA death threat. CO 904/193/9.

Court of Inquiry ROIR Regulations/Inquest into execution of Patrick Doyle, Patrick Moran, Thomas Whelan, Thomas Bryan, Bernard Ryan, Frank Flood on 14 March 1921. CO 904/188.

Hurley, James. Court Martial for attempt to wound Detective Wharton. CO 904/204/198.

McGrane, Eileen. Possession of revolvers and literature. CO 904/44/14.

Miscellaneous correspondence of General Macready. CO 904/188.

Customs & Excise

Custom House report on the raid and burning by official Mr Humphrey Murphy. CUST 49/532.

Home Office

Miscellaneous Police and Intelligence Reports: Including IRA instructions on execution of spies; Accounts of the victims of Bloody Sunday; Mrs Lindsay Case. HO 317/46.

Justice

King, Helen Sophie v King, William Lorraine. Divorce Petition/Probate. Filed 18 June 1928 J77/2304.

War Office

British Army Intelligence Files: Mulcahy, Richard; Murphy, W. R. E.; O'Sullivan, Gerald [Gearóid]; Price, Eamon [Bob]; Traynor, Oscar; WO 35/207.

King, William Lorraine. Military Service File WWI WO 0399/139377.

Operations Requested by D Branch, Chief of Police. WO 35/87/1.

Raids and Searches F Company Auxiliary Division, Intelligence & Military Reports WO 35/86B Part 2.

Raids (British Army Raids November & December 1920). WO 35/75.

Recognition of Services of British Officers in Ireland 1920–21. WO 141/42.

War Diary General Staff HQ Dublin District. WO 35/92 Vols. 13, 16, 17.

Treasury

Copy of Memorandum on assassination of Irish civil servants. T192/44.

UCD Archives
Hugh Kennedy Papers
Procedural and Advisory Feb 1922–May 1924. Kenmare Case. P4/560 (1).

Richard Mulcahy Papers
Communications re death of Vol James Buckley in revenge for trap mine explosion
    death of Tom Kehoe and six National Army soldiers at Carrigapooka Bridge, Cork,
    September 1922. P7/B/82.
Letter from Thomas Markham (alias Tom Donovan) Structure of the RIC, Dublin
    Castle organisation 1921–22. P7/B/104.
Report from General W. R. E. Murphy, GOC Kerry Command to General Richard
    Mulcahy, Commander-in-Chief, 7 December 1922. P7/B/72.
Richard Mulcahy conversation with Vincent Byrne 7 January 1964. P7/D/104.
Slattery, Jim. Newspaper article 28 January 1968 & Thoughts on Michael Collins
    P7/D/69.

Ernie O'Malley Notebooks
Carney, Tom P17b/109; Dalton, Charlie P17b/122; McCrea, Pat P17b/110 &109;
    McKee, Marie P17b/103; O'Hanlon, Michael P17b/106; O'Reilly, Mick P17b/115;
    Slattery, Jim P17b/109 & 94; Thornton, Frank P17b/100; Tobin, Liam P17b/094;
    Traynor, Oscar P17b/096.

Maynooth University Library
Mulkeen, Eddie. Burning of RIC Barracks at Ballybrack & DMP Barracks at Kill-of-the-
    Grange. Foxrock Local History Club Journal No. 42 October 1996.
Murphy, Karl. 'General W.R.E. Murphy and the Irish Civil War.' MA Thesis 1994.

National Library of Ireland
Béaslaí Papers
Burning of the Customs House. Ms 33, 914 (18).
Captured IRA membership rolls with British Army remarks on various members. Ms
    33,913 (13).
D1 Pals File. List of IRA Intelligence agents, contacts and locations. Ms 33,913 (14).
Letter and documents on Court of Inquiry into the Kenmare Case from National Army
    Officer James Hogan to Chief of Staff McMahon. Ms 49, 612.
The Squad Activities compiled by Joseph Leonard, 9 March 1948. Ms 33, 914 (15).

Manuscripts: Voyage of 'The Fanny' 1914. UVF gun running to Larne. Ms 46,806.

Newspapers
The Evening Telegraph
The Freeman's Journal
The Irish Independent
The Irish Times
The Mayoman

Noyk Papers
Court Martial Papers of Frank Flood, Patrick Doyle, Dermot O'Sullivan, Thomas Bryan and Bernard Ryan Ms 36,226/1 Ms 36,226/2.
Court Martial Papers of James Green Ms 36,221.
Court Martial Papers of Paddy Moran & James Rochford Ms 36,224.
Court Martial Papers of Frank Teeling, William Conway & Daniel Healy Ms 36,222.
Court Martial Papers of Thomas Whelan & Thomas Boyce Ms 36,223/1 Ms 36,223/2, Ms 36,223/3.

National Library of Wales, UK
Amman Valley Chronicle, March 1928.

Sligo Library Local Studies Collection
Sligo Gaol Register.

South Dublin County Libraries
Digital Archive, Irish Revolutionary Period.

The British Library
The Illustrated London News, 28 November 1920; 4 December 1920. General Reference Collection: MIC. B51/110.

Documentaries
TV
Ballyseedy. Produced and Directed by Frank Hand. RTÉ, 1997.
Hidden History, 'The Man Who Lost Ireland'. Mint Flame Productions for RTÉ, 2006.
Hidden History, 'Get Collins. The Intelligence War in Dublin'. A Mint Production for RTÉ, 2007.
Ireland – A Television History by Robert Key. A BBC Production in association with RTÉ, 1980.

Radio
A Bullet for the General. Chris Brookes. Documentary on One , RTÉ Radio 1, 2012.

DVDs/CDs
BBC: *The Somme 1916. From Both Sides of the Wire*. Written and Presented by Peter Barton, UK, 2016.
Eneclann: *American Commission on Conditions in Ireland*. Interim Report, 1921. Archive CD Books, Ireland, 2008. IE0038.
Eneclann: *Royal Irish Constabulary List & Directory 1920*. IE0093.
Eneclann: *Sinn Féin and Republican Suspects 1899–1921*. Dublin Castle Special Branch Files CO 904 (193–216) Colonial Office Record Series Vol 1. Eneclann Ltd, Trinity College Enterprise Centre, Dublin in conjunction with The Public Record Office, The National Archives, Kew, UK, 2006.

Magazines, Historical Journals & Personal Documents

Dolan, Anne. 'Killing and Bloody Sunday, November 1920.' *The Historical Journal*, 49, 3, Cambridge University Press, UK, 2006.

Doorley, Michael. '"The Judge" versus "The Chief": – Daniel Cohalan and the 1920 split within Irish America.' *History Ireland*. Issue 2, Vol. 23, March–April 2015.

O'Connor, Paddy. 'The Battle of Gurrane.'

Yeates, Padraig. '"Oh God, what did I do to deserve this?" The Life and Death of Detective Sergeant John Barton.' *History Ireland,* Vol. 24 No. 5, Sept/Oct 2016.

Interviews with author

Terry Newell 2015–2017
Patricia Healy 23 July 2016
Ethne Daly 16 January 2016
Tim Horgan 31 July 2015
Michael Walsh 24 July 2015
Dr Rory O'Hanlon 24 February 2014

Websites

www.ardmore.ie
www.ark.co.uk
www.bedfordregiment.org.uk
www.census.nationalarchives.ie
www.civilrecords.irishgenealogy.ie
www.clareherald.com
www.cwgc.org
www.danielseery.com
www.dlhabour.ie
www.firstworldwar.com
www.garda.ie
www.gunsandammo.com
www.haileybury.com
www.hansardmillbanksystems.com

www.heritageireland.ie
www.historyireland.com
www.ihl-databases.icrc.org
www.irishcollege.org
www.irishindependent.ie
www.irishtimes.com
www.iwm.org.uk
www.militaryarchives.ie
www.oireachtasdebates.oireachtas.ie
www.parliament.uk
www.rte.ie
www.treaty-nationalarchives.ie
www.westernfrontassociation.com
www.winstonchurchill.org
www.worldwar1.com

Index

Illustrations are indicated by page numbers in **bold**. Individual locations are in Dublin unless otherwise specified.